# THE ANZAC ILLUSION

# THE
# ANZAC ILLUSION
## Anglo-Australian relations
## during World War I

### E. M. ANDREWS

*Department of History,*
*University of Newcastle*

CAMBRIDGE
UNIVERSITY PRESS

Published by the Press Syndicate of the University of Cambridge
The Pitt Building, Trumpington Street, Cambridge CB2 1RP, UK
40 West 20th Street, New York, NY 10011-4211, USA
10 Stamford Road, Oakleigh, Melbourne 3166, Australia

Printed in Australia by Brown Prior Anderson

*National Library of Australia cataloguing in publication data*
Andrews, E. M. (Eric Montgomery), 1933–
The Anzac illusion: Anglo-Australian relations during World War I
Bibliography
Includes index.
ISBN 0 521 41914 X.
ISBN 0 521 45989 3 (pbk.).
1. World War, 1914–1918 – Australia. 2. World War, 1914–1918 –
Australia – Public opinion. 3. Public opinion – Australia. 4. Public
opinion – Great Britain. 5. Australia – Relations – Great Britain.
6. Great Britain – Relations – Australia. 7. Australia – Foreign public
opinion, British. I. Title.
940.394

*Library of Congress cataloguing in publication data*
Andrews, E. M. (Eric Montgomery), 1933–
The Anzac illusion: Anglo-Australian relations during World War I
E. M. Andrews.
Includes bibliographical references and index.
ISBN 0-521-41914-X (hardback)
1. Great Britain. Army. Australian and New Zealand Army Corps –
History – World War, 1914–1918. 2. World War, 1914–1918 – Australia.
3. World War, 1914–1918 – Great Britain. 4. Australia – Military
relations – Great Britain. 5. Great Britain – Military relations –
Australia. 6. Australia – Foreign relations – Great Britain.
7. Great Britain – Foreign relations – Australia. I. Title.
D547.A8A53 1993
940.3'2241 – dc20                                                    93-1484
                                                                          CIP

*A catalogue record for this book is available from the British Library.*

ISBN 0 521 41914 X hardback

*To Shirley*

# Contents

# Illustrations

## MAPS

# Acknowledgements

This book could not have been written without the assistance and support of many people and institutions. My thanks are accordingly due to Michael McKernan of the Australian War Memorial, who provoked the idea in the first place; Richard Langhorne, of St John's College, Cambridge, who discussed the scheme in its early stages and provided very pleasant accommodation while I was working in the archives in that university; Professor Geoffrey Bolton, then head of the Australian Studies Centre in London; and Major Bede Jordan, of the Australian Army Reserve, for suggesting the two battles I have studied and educating me in battle analysis. I also owe an especial debt to my research assistant, Sue Armstrong, who read, checked and discussed the chapters, and without whose painstaking work I could never have ploughed through the vast body of secondary literature (537 books, 158 articles and 27 theses) on World War I and Australia's part in it.

Primary research in archival collections was supported by study leave from Newcastle University and grants from the Australian War Memorial and the Australian Research Council—to whom I extend my grateful thanks. They are also due to the staffs in the archives and libraries concerned: the Australian Archives in Canberra and Melbourne; the Australian War Memorial; the National Library of Australia, Canberra; Churchill College, Cambridge; the National Library of Scotland, Edinburgh; the Bodleian Library, Oxford; Richmond Borough Library; Wiltshire County Record Office; and the Liddell Hart Collection, King's College, London University; Imperial War Museum; the National Army Museum; the Old War Office Library; the British Library; the Public Record Office; the House of Lords Record Office; the India Office Library and Mr Julian Amery, MP, all in London.

Finally I owe a debt of gratitude to my wife, for her tolerance and encouragement while the MS was being created and then rewritten under pressure. The book is accordingly dedicated to her.

# A note on usages

1. The volumes of the official history written by C. E. W. Bean are referred to simply by his name followed by a roman numeral.

2. 'Anzac', as an adjective, and 'the Anzacs' as a description of Australian soldiers in the first AIF, are used extensively in this book. Australian readers will not need reminding that the letters formed the code name of the Australian and New Zealand Army Corps. (See Bean I: 124–5.)

3. The word 'British' in this book refers to all the nations now occupying the British Isles, i.e. English, Scots, Welsh and Irish. This usage is an anachronism, for in 1914 Australians *were* British. They were simply members of the British race in the antipodes, and entitled to carry British passports. Nevertheless, to distinguish the parties to the discussion, 'British' will be used in its modern—not its historic— connotation.

4. 'Empire' is given a capital letter if it refers to the British Empire, but a small one if it refers to 'empire' in general.

5. The name of the Australian Labor Party is so spelt. Since 1907 it has officially used American spelling for its title. The 'labour movement', however, is spelt according to normal English usage.

6. To keep the endnotes simple, since many books and articles are referred to—often in several chapters—all references in the notes, even on the first occasion they occur, are in shortened form, i.e. surname of author, short title, and page number. The endnote indicates if the work is from an archive, or a thesis or unpublished paper. All other references are to published articles or monographs, which can be found in alpha-betical order in the full bibliography at the end of the book.

## CURRENCY

In the currency used during the period dealt with in this book, there were 12 pennies (d) in one shilling (s), and 20 shillings in one pound (£).

The sum of 10 shillings and 6 pence could be written as 10s 6d or as 10/6. A guinea was £1 1s.

When Australia changed to decimal currency in 1966, $2 was equal to £1.

# Introduction

It is my duty to tell what is told. To believe it is no part of my duty.
                                                    HERODOTUS,
                                            *Histories*, Book VII

There have been many, some would say too many, books on World War I. A. G. S. Enser's bibliography lists approximately 5895 books in English alone.[1] There has been a tidal wave of material aimed at the 'general reader', since war studies seem to appeal to a wider audience than many other kinds of history. At the other extreme are ponderous, but not necessarily more accurate, official histories; and in between are memoirs, shorter unit histories, diaries, accounts written during the war and immediately after it, reminiscences, biographies and autobiographies. Australia has followed these trends, from the official histories by C. E. W. Bean, through scholarly works such as Bill Gammage's *The Broken Years*, to the more popularising books of Patsy Adam-Smith and John Laffin. Indeed, there has been a resurgence of 'the Anzac legend' and almost an 'Anzac industry' in the country.[2]

There are, however, many weaknesses in the extensive literature on the Great War, despite its scope. Serious gaps exist. British public opinion towards the Empire and Australians—indeed public opinion in both countries—remains largely unexplored. A comparative analysis of the press and the effect of censorship and propaganda is an urgent necessity.[3] In military history there is a need to continue the reassessment of tactics, strategy and grand strategy, despite the difficulty, since so much of the documentation has been culled.[4] It is only recently that modern scholars have begun to work on documents now being made available in the archives, so that fresh interpretations are at last being published.[5]

Till now, however, most books on World War I have trodden well-worn paths, so that there is considerable repetition in the literature, illustrating the dictum that 'History never repeats itself, but historians always repeat each other.'[6] Stories originally told at second hand are repeated as truth, rumours circulated, and assumptions and

1

misconceptions perpetuated. The same photographs, cartoons and maps constantly appear, although—with the development of technology—in more glossy format.

The official histories have not helped. In Britain they have too often protected reputations and aroused the derision and indignation of independent scholars. In Australia, where military history has till recently been neglected in the universities, Bean's volumes have become the basis for popular surveys, whose authors thereby save themselves the trouble of going back to the original documents and thinking for themselves. At the same time too many Australian social historians have accepted his military history and elaborated his views on the Anzacs and Australian society,[7] instead of re-examining them in the light of fresh evidence and the history of the last seventy-five years.

Bean himself noted the problems in writing military history, yet his own emotional propagandising made his task more difficult. In particular, his stress on the front-line soldier has swamped readers with a tidal wave of detail, and hidden or ignored matters like logistics, weapons and their use—especially the vital subject of artillery, which is probably the gravest weakness in his work—training, generalship and the strategy of the war.[8] Much of his writing therefore needs to be reconsidered and his pre-conceptions reassessed.

So often, however, Australian books for the general public simply retell the old story, which fits comfortably with accepted clichés and—so their publishers think—guarantees sales. A vivid example of this was provided in 1990 by the seventy-fifth anniversary of the landing on Gallipoli. Many old volumes were reprinted, such as Kevin Fewster's *Frontline Gallipoli* and Bean's *Gallipoli Mission*, while a number of glossy coffee-table productions appeared. There was also an international celebration on the Gallipoli peninsula, which turned into what looked suspiciously like a junket, with dignitaries from Britain, France, Canada, Turkey and Australia in attendance. This last was inevitable, given the significance Gallipoli has assumed in Australian folklore, but the presence of the Australian prime minister of the day, Bob Hawke—given his penchant for emotional public occasions—was always likely. Exaggeration and hype therefore became the order of the day, and the deeper implications of the Gallipoli affair were largely lost. Only the *Journal of the Australian War Memorial* produced an edition which—apart from the inevitable pieces celebrating the event—should have made discerning readers suspect that there were strong revisionist implications in the latest research.[9] Nevertheless, one wonders what the original Diggers, suffering from heat, dirt, sweat, flies and dysentery, as well as the smell of rotting corpses and the other horrors of trench warfare, compounded by the enclosed confines of the peninsula, would have said about it all. No doubt their remarks would have been unprintable.

To a jaundiced eye, the politicians wishing to bask in the reflected glory of their respective veterans and so gain public support were joined by most of the literature printed and reprinted in 1990. Its most serious weakness in Australia was probably its parochialism, preoccupied with heaping praise on Australian soldiers, and failing to compare them with those of the other nations present—apart from the usual disparaging comments about the British high command and the reputed poor physique of the British troops. It also virtually disregarded the New Zealand element in the Anzac story.

This corpus of nationalistic writing, which all too often either concentrates on Australians and their experiences, or looks exclusively inward to the impact of the war on Australia, has been adopted and used by the popular media. Several television series have repeated the old themes from the human-interest angle. *The Anzacs* had an Australian star cast, including Paul Hogan, then famous for his Crocodile Dundee films. Popular dramas, however, too often simply perpetuate the myths that surround the subject. For example, the film *Gallipoli* featured as its climax the fateful charge of the light-horsemen across the Nek, but gave the responsibility for the order to continue the pointless attacks to an actor with a refined English voice and monocle, thus hiding the fact that it was a regular *Australian* officer, Colonel J. M. Antill, who insisted on the third and fourth lines of men rushing to their deaths.[10]

Indeed, the importance of the Gallipoli campaign, and Australia's part in it, has been exaggerated, as a glance at the statistics will confirm. Australians comprised a minority of the force that landed, and had as comrades New Zealand, British and French troops. Their dead were fewer per head of population than either New Zealand or Britain—and in any case six times as many Australians died on the Western Front.[11] Moreover, the glorification of the Anzacs on Gallipoli hides their comparative inexperience there, and detracts from the very real improvement in discipline, training and effectiveness that occurred in France, especially under Monash in 1918. It is not unusual in that respect, however, for perhaps the strangest aspect the historiography of World War I is the seeming blank in the public mind where the events of 1918 are concerned. It is almost as if the soldiers were doomed, in a parody of the Flying Dutchman, to continue to fight their hopeless battles in the mud of Flanders for ever. Little as this author supports John Terraine's attempted rehabilitation of Haig, he agrees that the final triumph of 1918[12] has been lamentably overlooked—not least by the merchants of emotion. Some people seem to assume that to accept that the war ended successfully is to belittle the horror, destruction, suffering and loss of life caused by it.

Finally, too many books on World War I concentrate on one aspect to the exclusion of the general picture. For example, military historians often ignore other factors, as if the war was being fought in a political and social vacuum, while social historians often take the military events for granted, as if only the implications for society were important. Economic and diplomatic historians have equally operated within the confines of their disciplines. Arthur Marwick's stress on the role of total war has been attacked, and his critics have argued that most of the developments in Britain in the post-war years would have happened anyway.[13] It is as if the war were an irrelevancy, or at most a necessary—albeit regrettable—backdrop to other more 'long term', and therefore important, issues or trends in history.

This book both looks directly at the war and also attempts to put it in its social, international, diplomatic, economic, intellectual and political setting. It is therefore a work of synthesis, combining specialist research by other historians on the general picture of the war, which hopefully brings out its significance, and interspersing detailed research by the author. Its central theme is the Anzac legend which grew up during the war, compared with the realities of the Anglo-Australian relationship. The chapters on military events are therefore not intended to be a short military history of the war, but freely select those topics which throw light on Anglo-Australian relations, and ignore others. Moreover, the author's focus is upon the Western Front more than the Middle East[14]—since the former was more important both to the war and to Anglo-Australian relations.

A reassessment of Australia's relations with Britain in World War I leads inexorably to a reconsideration of 'the Anzac legend': why it was created in the first place; what truth there is in it; what role it fulfilled in later years; whether it has any relevance today, or whether it was a trap which has led Australian leaders into mistaking the significance of major developments in the twentieth century. 'Anzac Illusion' in the title therefore refers to two ideas: firstly that the Australian soldiers were basically different from, and better than, other soldiers in the British armies in World War I; and secondly that Australia enjoyed a special relationship with Britain, which served both countries' ends—a loyal Australia having her interests defended by a grateful Britain.

For Australian readers this is therefore not only military history but also a case study in Australian foreign policy, having important implications for the question whether we should rely on 'great and powerful friends' (to use Sir Robert Menzies' favourite phrase), or whether such alliances, instead of providing security, have simply dragged us into wars in which we might not have been involved if we did not have their 'protection'. Those who defend reliance on allies have often argued that Australia can adopt their policies, and then through consultation influence them to follow our interests. History would not seem to support that argument.

This study, however, should also be relevant to British readers and students. At a time when Europe is seeking financial integration, and the old independent Britain with its Empire a dream of the past, this book takes the British reader back to the age of imperialism, when a proud and independent Britain ruled an Empire on which the sun never set, and when British men and women all over the earth regarded themselves as members of one British 'race'—before Adolf Hitler made that word seem tawdry for ever.

All this raises the question whether the Empire itself—and its offshoot, the 'Commonwealth'—was a viable ideal, or little more than an illusion, giving the British people, and especially some of their politicians and newspaper-owners, delusions of grandeur that prevented them from facing the reality of their position in the world and taking practical steps to improve it. If so, it was an illusion cherished on all sides: the British dreamt of an Empire which would strengthen them on the world scene at a time when the great nations of Russia, Germany and America seemed to threaten their predominance: the Australians dreamt of an international brotherhood of free 'British' nations across the seas, who, led by Britain, would defend them against any threats, especially from Asia. These illusions prevented both countries from making a realistic assessment of the changing international situation in the twentieth century. It was the illusion of Anzac.

It was also, however, the illusion of the Empire—and later the Commonwealth—in general. This study should therefore be of interest to Canadian and New Zealand readers, whose countries will also be mentioned in due course, though regrettably only fleetingly.

In the chapters which follow, social and political events are interspersed with military, in more or less chronological order. Chapter 1 sets the scene. It is an attempt in time travel—to take the reader back into a world which is long dead, when Australia was an integral part of the British Empire. It considers the constitutional and economic links, the foreign and military policies, and finally the ties of emotion and race, public opinion and the educational system before the outbreak of war in 1914. This should explain why 412,953 Australians volunteered to cross the seas to fight in Britain's 'Great War'.[15] At the time it seemed to bring nearer the dream of the imperial federationalists, but looking back a number of questions demand answers. Prime among these are how important the Empire really was to Britain—as distinct from the rhetoric of politicians and the media; to what extent British politicians really cared for the Dominions, or considered their interests; whether Australian interests were really served by membership of the Empire; and if so, what obligations and opportunities that membership implied. Those questions should be kept in mind, as the reader is taken through the war to the peace at its end. They will be reconsidered in the Conclusions.

Two admissions need to be made. First, generalisations are notoriously difficult, for men's experiences in wartime vary widely.[16] Some have a pleasant war, particularly those in the bases, store depots or lines of communication, and look back on their time in the forces as one of the best in their lives. Others are killed, maimed or traumatised. Similarly, their relations with allied troops and civilians, and their reactions to them, are diverse. No one account can possibly be 'true' for all people at all times.

Secondly, any historian faces a distinct problem in assessing past 'public opinion' in an age long before opinion polls and modern sampling techniques. The present author therefore does not claim scientific validity for this work. Historians can in the last resort only base their judgement, honestly and to the best of their ability, on the scattered and incomplete evidence that is left to them. Certainty is rarely arrived at. As Pieter Geyl has said, 'History is indeed an argument without end.'[17]

Typical of this is the question of Australia's *need* to be involved in World War I. The question seems to have been tackled head-on by only one writer, who argued—with all the enthusiasm of youth—that objectively there was no necessity, and that despite Australia's sacrifices her contribution to the conflict was not decisive.[18] To the present author, the matter does not seem quite so simple. The 'guilt' for the outbreak of war in 1914 has been the subject of a major historiographical debate which is extremely complex. Moreover, as Chapter 1 will show, aspects of militarism were also apparent in Britain, although in a lower key. The public-school ethos, the rifle clubs, Scouts, the link between the Church Lads' Brigade and the Territorial Army, the Volunteers, the National Service League, together with the stress on nationalism and the growth of the British Empire, made British society, and by extension Australian, appear almost as militaristic—though nowhere near as bellicose—as Germany. Finally, it is difficult to avoid nagging doubts about the policy of the British Liberal government, which joined the anti-German *entente* of France and Tsarist Russia, and even eventually offered Constantinople to the Russians. The long-term implications of the latter seem debatable in the extreme.

Nevertheless, Correlli Barnett's argument, that Imperial Germany was not Nazi Germany and that 'Civilization' belonged to neither side exclusively, though true enough, is hardly relevant.[19] Britain may not have faced extinction—for even victorious German generals were unlikely to have considered occupying her or doing more than exacting heavy reparations—but Australia as a British colony would have suffered serious consequences if Britain had been defeated. At the very least she could expect that Britain, from whom she gained the bulk of her investment, would have been financially drained, and Germany would gain all of New Guinea and the British islands in the Pacific. At the worst she might have been obliged to accept German settlers and financial domination as well. For, as a New Zealand historian has noted,

> colonies had a nasty habit of changing hands as part of peace settlements. Racial disaffinity was no barrier to incorporation in another empire, as the French-speaking parts of Canada attested.

Another New Zealand historian has therefore recently concluded that a 'decisive victory of the Central Powers ... would have had disastrous consequences' for New Zealand, including 'economic collapse'.[20]

Indeed, as the war continued the government of the unstable Kaiser was displaced by ultra-nationalistic German generals, who dominated politics and ruthlessly used the propaganda machine to support their expansionist and racialist aims, which were all too clearly revealed by their peace of Brest-Litovsk with the Russians. John Robertson is probably right, therefore, when he argues that, *once the war had begun,* it was in Australia's own interests that Britain and her allies should win it—a point the newspapers made at the time.[21]

The debate, however, is irrelevant for our purposes, for legally Australia had no option. Internally, under the *Commonwealth Act* of 1901 she was a 'self-governing colonial federation', but externally she was part of the British Empire, and ruled by the King of England, George V. When her king was at war, under international law Australia was also at war—and legally part of the prize if British forces were defeated. She became an independent sovereign state, and therefore capable of choosing whether to go to war or remain at peace, only much later.[22]

Nevertheless, the *extent* to which the Australian government cooperated with the British, and the manner of that cooperation, was a matter for its decision,[23] as the very different attitudes and policies adopted by Canada reveal. But it was not until 1918, after grievous losses on the Western Front, that some Australians began to abandon their assumption that British leaders knew best, and to demand a share in military decision-making. This change, which was in itself most significant, came very late in the day, and will be considered in due course in the chapters which follow.

This study therefore should throw considerable light on World War I and Anglo-Australian relations in the twentieth century. It suggests that, to both Britain and Australia, stress on the bonds of Empire or the Anzac connection was an illusion. This should make author and reader ponder afresh the patterns in British and Australian foreign policy and the fate of the British Empire, on which the sun has now—finally—set.

# CHAPTER ONE

# *The British Empire and Australia*

Wider still and wider shall thy bounds be set;
God, who made thee mighty, make thee mightier yet.
A. C. BENSON,
*'Coronation Ode'*

## THE BRITISH AND THEIR EMPIRE

In the opening years of the twentieth century, Britain's was one of the great empires in world history. It covered nearly nine million square miles and 348 million people, in all the continents of the world; it produced a large proportion of Europe's foodstuffs and raw materials, and controlled just under one-half of the world's shipping and one-third of its trade. Its vast extent, its wealth and naval power, its financial and trading supremacy, based on Britain's early industrial revolution and population growth, impressed observers as diverse as the Germans and the Americans.[1]

Yet, behind the facade, weaknesses existed. The very extent of the Empire meant that it included totally diverse peoples, races, languages, religions—and, in the last resort, interests. The colonies of conquest, such as India or those in Africa, were inhabited by coloured races of a different religion to the British. They were policed, and in the last resort held down, by British arms. The white colonies of settlement were different. Their total population, added to that of Britain, was nearly 51 million, which looked impressive, for it was then greater than Germany's and nearly double that of France. Moreover, the peoples of those colonies often revealed the exaggerated patriotism which nostalgic emigrants usually adopt—in their case loyalty to Britain, their mother country. Meanwhile, in Britain itself there was much discussion of greater imperial unity in some circles: revealed by J. R. Seeley's *The Expansion of England* (1883) and C. W. Dilke's *Problems of Greater Britain* (1890).

Yet British class consciousness—so noticeable to outsiders—was also applied to 'the colonies'. Rich colonials visiting Britain were accepted, although with reservations; the idea of 'the black sheep of the family' being sent overseas was common in novels and plays. But more ordinary visitors, who so often had come from poor British backgrounds, were regarded as uncouth and 'pushy', especially if they spoke with an accent. Travelling Australians were often struck by the assumption of inborn superiority of many British people they met, a feeling which was reinforced by the British newspapers, then the overwhelmingly powerful source of information, and the primitive film industry in the fairs, music halls and the new speciality outlets, which stressed the more 'primitive' and exotic subjects of the distant parts of the Empire, who were regarded as 'loyal'.

There was little imaginative sympathy for the white colonists. For example the media was prone to criticise Australia for its immigration policy, protectionist tariffs, and large borrowing on the London money market—ignoring the need to develop a large and distant continent. The feeling of superiority was revealed, according to one commentator, as 'the slight movement of the shoulders, and the imperceptible lifting of the eyebrows, that, in certain exclusive circles, greets the mention of the word Australian'. Another remarked on the combination of ignorance of Australian affairs and a patronising attitude.[2]

In politics, despite imperial rhetoric, the good of the Empire as a whole, rather than that of Britain, did not usually move British politicians. During World War I the Prime Minister, H. H. Asquith, made Bonar Law, leader of the Unionist Party, Colonial Secretary, despite a low opinion of his capacity, in order to exclude him from both the Exchequer and the Ministry of Munitions and to win the loyalty of his followers.[3] In other words, in the midst of a life-and-death struggle to which the Dominions were heavily committed, British political expediency decided who was appointed to the office which was most important to them.

This attitude was mirrored by British bureaucrats—with a few notable exceptions, such as Maurice Hankey, the ubiquitous Cabinet Secretary, who had a South Australian mother and a father who had farmed there for a while and retained investments in the country. Usually, in both the Colonial Defence Committee and the Colonial Office, 'the tendency was to speak down, as if to intellectual inferiors.' One head of the Colonial Office commented when the social status of the British High Commissioner to Canada was criticised, 'I should have thought that he would have been considered quite suitable for Canadian conditions.' As for Australia, no one in that office had actually travelled there until C. P. Lucas in 1909. But travel was no cure either. Sir George Clarke, the British governor of Victoria, sneered at Australians' demand for their own navy as 'natural in a community which is much inclined to overrate its capabilities, and is profoundly ignorant of the function which the Royal Navy discharges'. In 1909 Atlee Hunt, the Secretary of the Australian Department of External Affairs, who had accompanied his prime minister to the 1907 Imperial Conference, wrote that

> the Colonial Office was simply Downing Street, and that meant a mixture of red tape, ignorance of and indifference to Australian conditions, disregard of Australian feelings and aspirations, and a certain lofty contempt for the

Australian politicians to whom it once or twice threw a few titular distinctions to be scrambled for.

'The Foreign Office as a rule, and the Admiralty sometimes, saw the colonists as damned nuisances inclined to impertinence', though some in the Colonial Office considered the economic value of the colonies. Even *The Times*, which prided itself on support for Empire, adopted a patronising tone. Open British admiration for 'colonials' was limited to their military exploits: 'picturesque brown horsemen . . . leathery . . . big, fit, sunburnt' was one description of them in the Boer War.[4]

This was an important qualification, however, for after the unification of Germany in Bismarck's wars interest in warfare had steadily increased. Military tattoos, royal tournaments and the drilling of the volunteers became immensely popular; and uniforms, medals, battle scenes and officers were featured on the ephemera produced by the new techniques of coloured printing, such as picture postcards, cigarette cards and juvenile journals.[5] A cult of personality developed around 'colonial heroes' and affected even the churches. Christian organisations such as the Salvation Army and the Church Army were set up on military lines—and 'many of the Churches were swept up into "the tidal wave of race patriotism"'.

These feelings were noted and fostered by the new wide-circulation newspapers, such as Alfred Harmsworth's mass circulation *Daily Mail*. War provided dramatic news items, and a 'dangerous interest in war as a romantic and patriotic exploit was fanned'.[6] Harmsworth, who became Lord Northcliffe in 1905, regarded Germany as the arch-enemy, and joined the demand of the National Service League for conscription in Britain to enable her to match Continental armies. In 1906, with help from Lord Roberts, the president of the National Service League, he commissioned the famous invasion serial, which was republished as a novel, *The Invasion of 1910*. Northcliffe followed this by fomenting, with the aid of the irascible and eccentric First Sea Lord, Admiral Sir John ('Jacky') Fisher, the dreadnought panic of 1909, when the British newspapers created a scare that Germany was outproducing Britain in this new type of swifter and immeasurably more powerful battleship.

The Empire was inextricably involved in the new British militarism. In education, teachers in the local primary schools regarded history as a basis for moral and civic training and used it to inculcate patriotism, stressing imperial military heroes, such as Drake, Wolfe and Nelson. The prestigious British 'public schools', reformed in the second half of the nineteenth century following Dr Arnold at Rugby, increasingly trained colonial administrators and the officer class to lead the country's army.

A tidal wave of juvenile literature followed the same trend, with heroes who represented middle-class, sporting, public-school ideals, and stress on the civilising mission of the white man. (All this was heavily male-orientated: women's role was to support the men and produce the children who would be the new citizens of the Empire.) Accordingly, juvenile magazines, such as the *Boy's Own Paper* (produced by the Religious Tract Society) reflected this, together with the link between militant Christianity and imperialism. They stressed heroism, adventure and 'the Empire', and paved the way for youth movements such as Baden Powell's Scouts and the Boys' Brigade. In this way,

> hero-worship moved from Europe to the Empire; colonial exploits were enthusiastically followed by the public; war became a remote adventure in which heroism was enhanced by both distance and exotic locales.

The result, predictably, was a series of emigration schemes from the 1870s onwards. These began from philanthropic motives, but soon adopted racial and patriotic language, with talk of fostering imperial unity and defence, and 'empire building'.[7]

## AUSTRALIA

Australia was inevitably affected by these developments: her press reprinted British articles, British books were imported and sold in the country, and British attitudes, theories, and modes of thinking were common. The incipient signs of independence and even republicanism in the colonies in the nineteenth century[8] had been reduced by improvements in technology. It had been easy to adopt an air of detachment when sailing ships took approximately ten weeks to reach Melbourne from Liverpool, and letters three months to be delivered. The affairs of Britain and Europe were far away in both time and place, and might almost have been on another planet. But by the late 1870s the average time for letters to travel from England to the colonies, using the improved steamships and the Suez canal, had been halved to forty-five days. Even more crucial, the overland telegraph, which reached Port Darwin in 1872, and the railways, much used by the popular press, meant that news then ran quickly to the small townships deep in the bush. The world had shrunk, and overseas events could no longer be regarded as distant and irrelevant.[9]

These technological developments affected Australian attitudes. The response to the Sudan War of 1885, the second Boer War in 1899 and the Boxer 'rebellion' in 1900 revealed how little support radical ideas really had in the colonies, and the speed with which jingoistic fervour could be roused. Thus when General Gordon was killed in Khartoum in 1885 there was a frenzy of British imperial patriotism, the colonies offered troops, and 'nationalist and republican movements collapsed'.[10]

The Australian settlers had, moreover, become increasingly British in origin by 1914. Interest in emigration had been encouraged by the 1911 Imperial Conference, and all Australian governments except South Australia and Tasmania had adopted extensive assistance and publicity programmes. Migration from the British Isles peaked between 1909 and 1913. In 1912, 146,602 British migrants entered the country, which by 1914 had a population of 4,733,359.[11] These migrants

> were British citizens, travelling on British ships to British territory where they spoke the old language, worshipped in the old churches, lived under a version

of the old law ... The colonists continued to think of themselves as British, and the home government in London continued to think of them as British.

Not only were most Australians of British descent, but nearly one in five of them had been born in the United Kingdom.

To most Australians in the early years of the twentieth century, therefore, Britain was 'home', and their affection for it was passed on to their children.[12] They corresponded with their relatives in the old country, read British material in their newspapers, periodicals and books, learnt of the goings-on in London and the British countryside, built houses on modified British lines and used British-style furniture, while the ladies aped British fashions. To both sexes, the highlight of a lifetime was the trip 'home' to England. One septuagenarian, describing his first trip in 1930 to the author, remarked that he experienced a thrill of recognition when his ship went up the English Channel, the fog suddenly lifted— and there before him were what *had* to be the white cliffs of Dover![13]

## ECONOMIC TIES

With the emotional bond went economic interest, for the Australian economy was intimately linked with that of Britain. The colonies had developed their urban, semi-industrialised societies based almost entirely on British capital, labour and markets. At one time in the later 1870s they were receiving half the United Kingdom's overseas investment, and throughout the 1880s they received a quarter. Nearly two-thirds of both their exports and their imports went to or came from Britain. In the early years of the century British coins and banknotes remained in circulation, and when Australia issued its first stamps in 1913, the royal head was the main emblem. There was almost no public criticism of British economic dominance in Australia, and the ideas of J. A. Hobson in Britain about economic imperialism roused no echo. Instead, the weight of Australian opinion favoured the closest economic ties with Britain, feeling that Australia's prosperity depended on her.[14]

Nevertheless, the Australian decision to adopt protectionist tariffs militated against the proposals for imperial political and military federation, or even the fall-back position, the apparently more innocuous 'trading bloc', of Joseph Chamberlain, the British Colonial Secretary from 1895 to 1903. At the 1907 Imperial Conference, the Australian prime minister, Alfred Deakin, softened the blow and argued for a system of 'imperial preference'—but British Liberal free-traders had come to office in the meantime. As long as they stayed in power, the idea was doomed. Moreover, it was easy to see what Australia had to gain from preferential access to the British market, but difficult to see the advantage to Britain. Australia was a small market for British manufacturers, while Australian food products were expensive in the United Kingdom.[15]

Each side was therefore following its own interests. When the British talked about an integrated imperial system, they naturally assumed that

Britain would remain the advanced industrial partner and the colonies would provide markets, foodstuffs and raw materials. On the other hand Australians were not willing to remain in that position, and Deakin's talk of preferences hid the fact that since all Australian tariffs had been raised, even lower ones on British goods still meant the British importer usually had to face a higher bill.[16] It was this underlying clash of interests—along with American hostility—which would ultimately foil all attempts at an imperial system, and decades later lead Britain to join the European Community and abandon the idea of the Commonwealth as an economic entity altogether.

Even in this period, economic ties between Britain and Australia were gradually weakening. Though the value of British exports to Australia rose between 1886 and 1914, their proportion of all Australian imports fell from 89.31 to 69.89 per cent. Australia was increasingly importing direct from other countries such as Germany and the United States instead of through London, while her shipping regulations, to protect her own workers and exclude other races, made life difficult for the British shipper. British trade with Australia, when taken as a proportion of her total overseas trade, therefore declined. This was paralleled by increasing financial independence. Australia ceased before 1914 to be a major borrower of British capital, and began to finance her own development. When war broke out, nearly one-third of the public debt was owed to Australian investors. All these were signs of increasing Australian economic maturity and a 'decline in the colonial character of the Australian economy'.[17]

## CONSTITUTIONAL BONDS

Constitutionally, however, Australia remained tightly bound to Britain. On 1 January 1901 the six Australian colonies coalesced into a federation, the Commonwealth of Australia. The celebrations of the event naturally stressed loyalty to the British monarchy and the 'motherland', and lavishly praised British parliamentary government as the basis of Australian freedom. Nevertheless, federation was granted by Britain through an Act of the British parliament which did not include 'independence'. Nor did it create a new 'nation'; for the official view was that 'the British nation' spread across the world, from the United Kingdom, through Canada and parts of Africa to the antipodes. So in 1901 the governor-general of the new Commonwealth was appointed by the Queen, on the advice of the British government, and was her representative in the Commonwealth— as the colonial governors in the separate colonies had been before him. Australian ministers had no direct access to her. The governor-general would normally act on the advice of Australian federal ministers, but was also responsible to the Colonial Office in London. Like the colonial governors he was the agent of Britain, appointed primarily to protect British interests, including commercial interests, not Australian. To

protect those interests the British government had insisted on retaining
the right of appeals from Australia to the Privy Council in London.
Finally, it was only through the governor-general and the Colonial Office
that the Australian prime minister could communicate with the British
government.[18]

Australian dependency was also seen in the lack of control over foreign
and defence policy. The first governor-general, the Earl of Hopetoun,
assumed as a matter of course that Australia would continue to supply
contingents to the Boer War and share the burden of imperial defence.
His successor, Baron Tennyson, was involved in a dispute with the prime
minister, Edmund Barton, over the use of a private secretary, through
whom he sent confidential matter to London that the Australian government did not see; and when in 1903 a memorandum by the Colonial
Defence Committee criticised the schemes of the commandant of the
Australian forces, Major-General Hutton, Tennyson withheld the document from the Australian government, until directly ordered by London
to pass it on. For he shared the Colonial Office belief that governors-
general 'should safeguard imperial [i.e. British] interests'. The third
governor-general, Lord Northcote, adopted the same attitude.[19] British
and Australian leaders therefore saw the role of the governor-general
differently. Australians wanted a constitutional monarch, sympathetic to
their aspirations, while

> The British government saw him more in the role of diplomat and intelligence
> officer, exercising 'the personal influence which he should have with his
> Government' in favour of the British government's policy.[20]

The belated opening of the Australian High Commission in Britain
in 1910 only reinforced the point. It had been assumed that the new High
Commissioner would act in a semi-diplomatic manner, representing the
Australian government in London. As such the position would strengthen
the bonds of Empire, and illustrated the dual loyalty of the members
of the Australian federal parliament. In fact the governor-general and
the Colonial Office insisted that *they* were the only channels of
communication, and the first High Commissioner, Sir George Reid, was
restricted to dealing with very minor matters with Whitehall officials. The
delay in opening the office was itself partly to blame, but the instability
of Australian politics and the reputation of Australian Labor Party MPs
for anti-British nationalism had fed British newspaper prejudices—
already roused by the White Australia policy and shipping regulations.
As a result, Australia received much adverse sensation-mongering attention
in the British press and Reid felt obliged to institute an expensive major
press and film publicity campaign, as well as using posters in trains,
buses, shops and libraries.[21]

The British had everything to gain from allowing Australia local
autonomy, but absolutely nothing from encouraging her and the other
Dominions to act more independently, which would only complicate
Britain's international problems. 'External affairs' were therefore probably

only mentioned in the constitution out of a British desire to give the federal government—rather than the States—the monopoly of implementing imperial treaties and negotiating with London. This simplified British administration, but the Australian government was granted no control over foreign affairs as such. It therefore did not seek to play a part in running the Boer War, nor a voice in the peace settlement.[22]

The situation has been expressed with brutal frankness by Hudson and Sharp:

> The colonies were at war when their sovereign, advised exclusively by United Kingdom ministers, was at war, and they were at peace when their sovereign, advised by United Kingdom ministers, was at peace.[23]

In 1901 they had formed a separate entity, a federation, established by the British government—nothing more. The Queen was still the sovereign; and the old rules applied.

Indeed, one section of British opinion wanted to go further, and formally bind the Dominions in 'imperial federation'. This roused the hostility of Canada and South Africa, but all planning broke down anyway over the extent of representation to be given to each component part of the Empire. Chamberlain was an avid supporter of the idea, and at the 1897 Colonial Conference had looked forward to a time when the colonies would share in the management of the Empire 'which we like to think is as much theirs as it is ours', but was unwise enough to add that that would involve responsibility and 'some form of contribution towards the expense' and talked of the interchangeability of British and colonial armies. Few remarks could have been more injudicious, especially as he also suggested that the white settlement colonies and Britain be given representation in proportion to their population—which meant that Britain would dominate the organisation. He flatly rejected an Australian proposal for equal representation for each part of the Empire—which would have given the various colonies the ability to outvote Britain.[24]

In Australia, there were fears that the country would be dragged into Britain's innumerable wars, which led even the *Sydney Morning Herald* in 1900, when Australia was supporting Britain in the Boer War, to oppose joining an imperial federation. The Australian *Defence Act* of 1903 therefore did not change colonial legislation, but—against the wishes of the British government which wanted Australian troops in imperial wars—allowed conscription only for the defence of Australia itself. Service overseas was only on the basis of specific volunteering. Even so, support for imperial federation by British and Australian conservatives still made the movement suspect in the eyes of Australian nationalists and the left wing.

Yet the idea dragged on. For a time the Imperial Federation League had some influence, especially under the presidency of Alfred Deakin, three times prime minister of Australia. Then in 1909 Lord Milner and members of his 'Kindergarten' in London formed the Round Table group, to organise influential citizens in Britain and the self-governing colonies to discuss the future of the Empire. Its journal, the *Round Table*, published anonymous reports and commentaries on matters of imperial importance. But even in this, the most imperialist of journals, the Australian commentators were keenly aware of Australia's special security needs; and ready to criticise Britain and the organisation itself if they were ignored. They also noted a reluctance on the part of their fellow Australians to accept any diminution in their powers of self-government. The Sydney *Daily Telegraph* spoke for them when it chided Tennyson, on the eve of his departure from Australia in 1904, for hoping for closer union with Britain, and described representation in an imperial parliament as 'a backward step on the road of British destiny'.

Among the Australian public there was a deep apathy towards the dull and intricate task of creating some form of imperial constitution. Most Australians assumed that they were in a flexible empire, where their needs would be met. There was no need to rush into formal—and dangerously novel—agreements. They might consider the idea eventually, but in the meantime they were happy with their measure of self-government, and did not want to lose it.[25]

## IMPERIAL DEFENCE

This desire for independence was reinforced by defence matters, in which Australia and Britain had divergent interests. British leaders' eyes were on Britain, Europe and India; while Australians were vitally concerned with the Pacific.[26]

This had been seen as early as the 1880s when Gladstone ignored the colonists' wishes over German and French moves in New Guinea and the Pacific. At a public meeting in Sydney in 1885 Sir Henry Parkes, ex-premier of New South Wales, had moved a resolution of loyalty to Britain, but protested against the 'apathy and unconcern evinced by the Imperial Government in respect to the interests of these colonies'. The British attitude, on the other hand, was expressed by the prime minister, Lord Salisbury, two years later when he remarked that the Australians were

> the most unreasonable people I have ever heard or dreamt of. They want us to incur all the bloodshed and the danger, and the stupendous cost of a war with France ... for a group of islands which to us are as valueless as the South Pole.[27]

The fact was that 'neither the Pacific, the New Hebrides nor Australia were that important' to Britain. It is not surprising therefore that Chamberlain's suggestion at the 1897 conference for imperial federation and a coordinated army met with a blank response in Australia.

The British, however, were worried by their declining world position after the unification of Germany. Britain wanted a greater contribution from the white colonies towards their own defence; to withdraw from 'unnecessary' commitments overseas—including what they called 'the Far

East'—and to make a series of agreements with foreign nations to protect her colonies. These policies presented problems for Australia. While the British were negotiating the Anglo-Japanese Alliance in the second half of 1901, the Australians were formulating their *Immigration Restriction Act*—against Japanese as well as other Asian nationalities. G. F. Pearce, later Australian Minister for Defence, remarked at the time that the British government might 'not always have the best interests of this part of the Empire at heart'.[28] It could hardly have been expected to, for the interests of Britain and Australia simply did not coincide. The Australian response in the years before the war was to support Britain for emotional and security reasons, but at the same time to try to influence imperial policy to suit Australia's own needs. This double policy led to complexities and conflicting viewpoints in the same person or group.

The Labor Party, for example, had attracted anti-imperialists, yet was itself influenced by the growing imperial sentiment, which it had to placate if it wished to win power. Pearce may have spoken in his maiden speech in 1901 of putting Australia first 'and the Empire very much second', but the party had to face strong public feelings on this issue, and therefore backed off from its demands to abolish, or appoint Australians to, State governorships, and settled instead for a policy of 'self-sufficiency within the Empire'. At the same time, Labor could join conservatives in demanding the right to consultation, by which Australian statesmen could hopefully make British politicians see their point of view, or at the very least be informed if major decisions were about to be made. 'But the suspicion was to grow that the British were being less than frank . . .'[29]

This suspicion was justified. The channel of communication ran, as we have seen, through the governor-general to the Colonial Office, which was a bugbear to generations of Australian leaders.

> The urbane and scholarly men of the Colonial Office brought the air of an Oxford college or London club to their mahogany and leather-furnished offices at Whitehall. They were certainly impressive at close quarters, but at long distance they could often be infuriating.

They also adopted a patrician tone towards the colonials in their memoranda and the scribbled notes they wrote to each other about them. As one commented, 'The Australians, who have never had to face any diplomatic difficulty, seem to think we can treat France like a Tonga.'[30]

All these issues arose in the 1902 Colonial Conference, summoned for the coronation of Edward VII, but used to discuss major policies with colonial leaders. The British government was preoccupied with the strategic situation in Europe, so when it spoke about 'imperial' foreign and defence policy, it really meant 'British', and increasingly looked to the colonies for support. Its problems were threefold: money, men and the need to maintain strategic control.

The British complained of the cost of empire, and saw no reason why the colonials, who gained the benefit of the *pax Britannica*, should not

also contribute towards its expense. 'Less than one-half of India's and
Australia's and New Zealand's trade was with the United Kingdom, yet
the United Kingdom paid more than seven-eighths of the cost of the naval
forces in Eastern waters.' Admiralty officials met before the 1902 conference
to discuss the requirements of the Australia station, and to seek a *pro rata*
contribution per head to its cost.[31]

At the conference Chamberlain therefore appealed to the colonies to
assist Britain to bear the burden of defending the Empire:

> The weary Titan staggers under the too vast orb of its fate. We have borne
> the burden for many years. We think that it is time that our children should
> assist us to support it.[32]

And he went on to offer a share in deciding imperial policy proportional
to the amount of assistance offered. The proposal was promptly vetoed by
Canada and South Africa, both of whom were less afraid for their security
and had powerful non-British minorities in their population. Australia,
however, was not so divided, and she felt vulnerable with the rise of Japan
in the Far East, and was therefore more open to Chamberlain's wiles.

"MY BOYS!"

The British attitude to the colonies, as portrayed by *Punch*, 28 February 1885.
To the English artist, NSW is Australia, and the Canadian government's permission
for the British authorities to recruit at their own expense is equivalent to Dalley's
offer of a fully paid contingent. Whatever their colony, all cubs look alike.
Inglis, *The Rehearsal*: 20.

The British wanted to create a reserve force, which could be sent to any crisis in any part of the world, as they thought fit. As Chamberlain saw it, the upsurge of imperial patriotism generated by the Boer War was a perfect opportunity to create such an imperial force. In Britain some planning had taken place in the Colonial Defence Committee, admittedly a low-level body,[33] for an expeditionary force of 160,000 men—40,000 of whom were to come from the colonies. Concern was expressed at the likely colonial reaction, but Hutton had advised the British that Australians would consider an imperial defence scheme, and New Zealand had suggested military reserves for the Empire. Nevertheless, concern at this idea had been expressed during the parliamentary debate on the first Australian Defence Bill in 1901. It flared up again in 1902, when parliamentarians were warned that the idea would be discussed at the forthcoming Colonial Conference.

In grand strategy, the Admiralty accepted the argument of A. T. Mahan,[34] that in the age of dreadnoughts a powerful navy should not split its strength, but concentrate instead in vital areas—such as the English Channel and North Sea—to defeat the main enemy battle fleet and win 'command of the sea'. The Colonial Defence Committee also believed in a centrally planned army for the Empire, and viewed Australian problems from a British perspective. Like Winston Churchill in 1942, it was prepared to sacrifice temporarily what were to it peripheral areas—such as Australia—to protect the centre. Yet Australians could not, in the nature of things, be expected to see the matter in this light. Pearce was to attack an 'imperial' report of July 1906 for remarking that any enemy could expect only 'transitory success'. Australians could not afford 'to be the victims of those "transitory successes" and it is our duty to see that we are not made the victims'.[35]

As for the 1902 conference, the idea of a centrally controlled imperial defence force to which Australia would contribute troops had split the Australian Cabinet even before the delegates met. The Australian prime minister, Edmund Barton, therefore suggested to the British government that the matter be discussed in private before the full conference; when Chamberlain ignored his plea, he joined Canada in flat opposition. He knew the trouble he would have had to face if he publicly agreed with the idea, for while the conference was in progress there was 'a remarkable outcry', led by the major newspapers and J. C. Watson for the Labor Party. The most that Barton therefore dared do was agree to standardise military organisation and equipment. The only colony to support Chamberlain's idea of an Imperial Reserve Force, specially trained, to serve anywhere in the world, was New Zealand. Australia and Canada simply promised to consider the matter when needed, and when General Sir Ian Hamilton was insensitive enough to suggest in December 1903 that the Australians contribute 3000–4000 mounted troops to help the Japanese (then preparing for the Russo-Japanese War) against Cossacks, the response was predictable.[36]

As far as the Royal Navy was concerned, the problem was to interest the Dominions more in naval matters and get them to contribute more

money, without threatening the Admiralty's control or making it keep
to what Jacky Fisher described as a 'ludicrous' distribution around the
world. Barton in the 1902 conference agreed to increase the 1887 subsidy
for the auxiliary squadron of the Royal Navy in Australian waters, and
it was now free to operate in either the Australia, China or East Indies
stations as required. This led to much Australian criticism, which was
given added point by the steady redistribution of British naval power that
occurred under Admiral Fisher from 1905 onwards, as a result of the
alliance with Japan and the growth of the German threat. Five battleships
were withdrawn from the China station to strengthen Britain, and 150
small craft scrapped. But as far as the Admiralty was concerned, this was
still not enough; the British government should have abandoned the
'paltry' Australian subsidy, and gained freedom to control its own navy
as it thought fit.[37]

The Committee of Imperial Defence (CID), consisting of the relevant
Cabinet ministers and the heads of the defence departments, had been
established in 1902 and re-formed in May 1904, but it concentrated on
technical matters and never really coordinated strategy. Nor was it really
'imperial'. Dominion ministers were not included until 1909, and even
then they attended only by invitation when they were in Britain, to hear
lectures on the British view of the world. Only the Imperial General Staff,
and the Admiralty and Hankey, really thought in imperial terms, and
it was easy to hide the decisions being made from the Dominions. Indeed
Richard Jebb argued in *The Times* that the CID was created largely to
safeguard British ascendancy within the Empire.[38]

In Australia, Major-General Hutton was 'an abrasive personality who
soon clashed with his Ministers' and informed his friend Hamilton that
Australians had lost confidence in War Office methods and 'view with
something of contempt all that emanates therefrom whether personal or
written'. His plan for an imperial reserve, called the Imperial Australian
Force, was watered down in the Australian Cabinet and omitted from the
*Defence Act* of 1903. The name would resurface, slightly altered, in 1914.
Hutton left in 1904, after a row with ministers, who then abolished his
position of commandant and replaced it with a Military Board. The
British connection continued, however, through his protégés, Major W. T.
Bridges and Lieutenant C. B. Brudenell White, to be immortalised by the
Anglo-Australian, C. E. W. Bean.[39]

In Britain, the review of imperial defence for the House of Commons by
A. J. Balfour, Prime Minister in 1905, made concentration 'at the centre of
the Empire' the basis of general strategy. This was highly significant for
Australia, and was formalised by the new Secretary of State for War, R. B.
Haldane, in his reformed organisation for the British army in July 1906.[40]

The twin issues of defence and consultation therefore surfaced again
in the Colonial Conference of 1907. The Australian delegates raised the
matter of the convention with France over the New Hebrides, and
protested at the sacrifice of their interests 'to the exigencies of Imperial
diplomacy'. Informed opinion back in Australia strongly supported this

stand. The *Round Table* demanded that Britain maintain greater naval power in the Pacific, in face of 'Japan's rapidly increasing industrial, naval and military strength'—a Japan which it 'identified as the real menace to Australia'.[41]

At the conference Deakin, once again Australian prime minister, proposed an Imperial Council with a permanent secretariat—away from the Colonial Office. That body had long been his *bête noire*. The idea was defeated by the opposition of Laurier of Canada and Botha of the Transvaal. All that was agreed was that henceforth the Colonial Conferences would be called Imperial Conferences and that the great white colonies should be styled 'the self-governing dominions beyond the seas'—which inevitably became shortened to 'the Dominions'. Nevertheless, though a secretariat was set up, it was still inside the Colonial Office, and used its staff—who could be considered 'sound'. The Colonial Office was simply divided into three departments, one of which was now named the Dominions Department.[42]

In defence matters, Haldane suggested that his new British General Staff should become an 'Imperial' General Staff, sending British officers to General Staffs in the newly designated Dominions, and accepting their officers in London. His aim was obviously to create an 'imperial' army, centrally controlled from London, as had been suggested at the 1902 Colonial Conference. It was never likely to appeal to Canada, South Africa or Ireland, but in 1907 Deakin led the demand that the Imperial General Staff should be an advisory body only. He did not want it to exercise central control over Australian forces; though he was willing enough for it to advise him on the measures of military defence he was about to introduce.[43]

As for the navy, the Admiralty did concede the usefulness of Dominions having small naval forces for their own defence. It therefore began to state its case to the Australian government early in 1908. Deakin then engineered, before informing the British, the visit of the American 'Great White Fleet' in August–September that year—to a rapturous reception in Australia. It was not surprising that he was not popular among the Whitehall mandarins, nor was his request for a powerful British fleet to visit Australia. 'Australia does not deserve a visit' was one comment, and 'They must have gone off their heads' another. In return, Deakin was scathing about the Colonial Office.[44]

## IMPERIAL NEUROSES

Then in 1909, with news of the German battleship building programme and British newspaper hysteria which it provoked, the Admiralty finally changed its mind about the Australian squadron. Now afraid that it was being out-gunned by the Germans, it began to encourage the Dominions to develop their own naval forces for the defence of the further parts of the Empire—as long as it retained final control in war.[45]

This reinforced Australian trends since the Japanese triumph over Russia in 1905, for most newspapers had at first dismissed the idea that Japan could be a threat, but the professional naval and military advisers, such as Hutton and Sir William Creswell of the Naval Board, thought otherwise. Their concern spread slowly to the parties, press and public. The newspapers were deeply involved: their picture of a Japanese threat, combined with the British naval scare of 1909, led to a predictable public campaign. 'Australia was caught up in the empire-wide panic of the dreadnought crisis' that followed. But the Australian National Defence League, unlike its British originator, regarded Japan and not Germany as the enemy, and C. H. Kirmess, in *The Australian Crisis*, recast the British war scare novel, *The Invasion of 1910* as a Japanese invasion of the Northern Territory. C. E. W. Bean echoed this panic, remarking that the three million British in Australia were 'within a day's sail [of] . . . eight hundred million Orientals'. Australians therefore were not comforted when British officials and politicians, such as Winston Churchill, pointed to the Anglo-Japanese alliance as the protector of British interests in the Pacific. The alliance was with Australia's main perceived potential enemy.

Various politicians were swayed, promoted, or stood to gain by, the new attitudes. In the ALP, Pearce abandoned his previous opposition to 'militarism' and 'imperialism' and became concerned with Australian defence. He declared later that it was the Japanese victory that made him change his mind.[46] W. M. Hughes—who appears extensively in this book and whose background will be discussed later—used the language of the most ardent imperialist. On the other side of politics, Deakin organised the 'Fusion' of the three non-Labor groups, and adopted a more imperialist foreign stance to appeal to his conservative allies. There was therefore little difference between the ALP and the Fusion parties on this issue: all gave Japan as a reason for their policies. When New Zealand offered Britain a dreadnought, New South Wales and Victoria threatened to do likewise if the federal government hesitated. In this way, the British 'dreadnought crisis was a catalyst in mobilizing a conservative political reaction in Australia to embrace imperial defence policy'.[47] It coincided with the mounting fear of Japan.

A special Imperial Defence Conference was held during July and August 1909. Here, it was finally agreed that the Australian government would create a naval unit, controlling the ships, while the discipline would be that of the Royal Navy. In time of war or emergency they would come under the Admiralty. The Australian government then invited Admiral Henderson to visit Australia in 1910 and discuss details of the vessels. One commentator writes that the 'new cooperation was a far cry from the old idea of colonial military forces guaranteed for imperial service'. Perhaps, but there were hidden implications nevertheless. The Australian government still placed limitations on its military commitment, and did not accept a comprehensive imperial military plan, although it did agree to standardise organisation, training, weapons and equipment, and to develop the Imperial General Staff.

Fear of Japan, however, drove the Australians further. In September 1909 Deakin suggested a 'Pacific Pact' between Britain, France, Holland, China and the United States to apply a Monroe Doctrine to the Pacific. The British bureaucrats poured scorn on the idea, and answered correctly but coldly, and Deakin soon after fell from office.[48]

The Labor government which replaced him turned to Australian self-defence instead. It considered the Swiss idea of compulsory military training for young males, and proposed to drill all boys from the ages of twelve to eighteen, and provide them with annual training with the citizen forces for a period thereafter. This was extraordinary, since it was applied in peacetime, and no similar scheme existed in any other Dominion or in Britain herself, although the Australian National Defence League was based on Lord Roberts' National Service League in Britain. So by 1914 Australia, if Gammage is to be believed, had 'over 200,000 males under arms of some sort, and a defence expenditure of 25 shillings per head, the third highest in the world after Britain and France'.[49] The government invited Field Marshal Lord Kitchener, then Commander-in-Chief in India, to visit Australia and New Zealand in 1909–10, to give advice on defence.

## KITCHENER IN AUSTRALIA, 1909–1910

Kitchener's visit to Australia was perhaps the most spectacular of those by British dignitaries. The general public reacted with an excitement similar to that seen during the visit of the Great White Fleet. Large crowds gathered to see 'the hero of Omdurman'; the *Sydney Morning Herald* said his name had become a household word; and a British officer remarked that Australians 'mobbed him wherever he went and feted him to an alarming extent'.

Nevertheless, behind the public facade, different motives were revealed by the parties concerned. Deakin was primarily interested in Australia's national defence: Kitchener (and Lord Haldane, Secretary for State for War in Britain) in military cooperation between Australia and New Zealand and their contribution to an imperial army. So sensitive was that issue, however, that Deakin and Cook, the leaders of the Fusion government then in office, felt obliged publicly to refute an article in the Melbourne *Age*, which had bluntly stated that Kitchener's mission was mainly concerned with an imperial field force. Nevertheless, the discrepancies in Kitchener's final memorandum suggest that the paper was correct. After all, in the same year Major-General Sir Alexander Godley became the commander of the Territorial scheme in New Zealand. Briefed by the British military that war with Germany was inevitable, he was to establish an infrastructure upon which a New Zealand expeditionary force could be organised.[50] As John Mordike argues, this suggests that Kitchener's hidden agenda was indeed to formalise Australian cooperation in imperial defence. This would also explain Haldane's comments in Britain before Kitchener visited Australia that they were in sight of common plans for the defence of the whole Empire— and why Kitchener was so keen to reduce Australian pay to the British level.[51]


## THE 1911 CONFERENCE AND ITS AFTERMATH

Nevertheless, there were still mixed feelings in Australia. Prime Minister Andrew Fisher seemed out of touch with public opinion as led by the press and some in his own party. Kitchener's visit and the upsurge in newspaper and public interest and imperialist hyperbole had hardly ended when the Imperial Conference of 1911 was summoned. When the newspapers printed Fisher's remark that Australia was free to decide whether or not to join England's wars, or even end the association with England, a wave of indignation made him repudiate the report. He accepted that when England was at war Australia was *de facto* at war too— but still asserted that the extent of her cooperation was for her to decide. In this matter Fisher was trying to adopt the policy of Canada, or indeed the Liberal government of Britain, who were bound to the French, but protested their freedom of action. Australian public opinion, however, egged on by the press, was in no mood for such subtleties. Nor were they accepted by all his subordinates. Pearce met imperial leaders at the 1911 Imperial Conference and was very taken with them (especially Lloyd George). It finalised his movement to the right and preoccupation with defence.[52]

Pearce did not yet speak for the rank and file of the Labor Party, however. The new ALP government still had nationalist and isolationist elements in it, who suspected imperial federation in another guise. So strong were these fears that the Australian Labor Cabinet changed its mind while Fisher was overseas, and forbade him to support even a foreign relations Advisory Council, lest that committed them to decisions.

Moreover, the promised consultation with the Dominions had still not materialised. The British government had ignored them in making the alliance with Japan and the ententes with France and Russia, nor had it asked their opinion on any of the international conferences. So when the New Zealand premier, Sir Joseph Ward, proposed an Imperial Parliament of Defence or Council of State, which would also have overseen foreign policy, together with a single imperial navy financed on a per capita basis, there were numerous interjections and great opposition.[53] The debate became bogged down in detail, but the idea was inevitably doomed by Asquith's insistence on Britain's sole right to control foreign policy, the praise of General Botha for decentralisation, and Sir Wilfred Laurier's flat refusal to agree to a joint policy-making body which would commit Canada. Perhaps by then it was too late anyway: 1907 seems in retrospect to have been the last real opportunity for such a scheme.

By 1911 the Colonial Office attitude to the Dominions had become deeply entrenched. In 1907 Deakin had clearly intended his 'imperial secretariat' to be outside Colonial Office control, but the eccentric first head of its Dominions Department, Sir Charles Lucas, who had sought its increased independence, had been forced to resign.[54] Colonial Office leaders feared a threat to their position. Their answer was a combination of arrogance and special pleading, as when Sir William Harcourt, then Colonial Secretary, remarked, 'It would never do to *say* we are too good for them, and they are not good enough for us', while one of his senior officials commented that 'Australia's Department of External Affairs could not even translate an ordinary letter in French correctly.' At the same time, they argued that as long as Britain paid for diplomacy and defence, the organisation of 'imperial' foreign policy was the sole preserve of the British government. So the latter held a conference in London with the major shipping nations without consulting the Dominions at all and, amongst other issues, discussed foodstuffs, which formed a large proportion of Australian trade. Asquith therefore only reflected his civil servants' views when he told Dominion leaders that his government was not prepared to surrender any share in the control of foreign policy. The civil service was divided, however, on whether refusal to discuss foreign policy with the Dominions gave them the right to opt out of decisions.[55]

Meanwhile, Dominion nationalism in Canada and South Africa had become, if anything, more touchy. The Australian Labor leaders in London were nearer the British than the Canadians, but because of their Cabinet colleagues in Australia had to be careful. They were, however, particularly worried by the Declaration of London which resulted from the conference, and Hughes was also concerned with the navigation laws. They therefore once again demanded some form of consultation. As Fisher put it,

> Being a family of nations they thought the time had arrived when they should be informed, and, if need be, consulted, before arrangements were entered into with other countries by which their interests were affected.

Sir Edward Grey, the Foreign Secretary, promised much more advanced consultation before the next Hague disarmament conference, and Fisher pressed him to agree to extend that to other treaties, which provoked Laurier. The British could always rely on the Canadian reluctance to become too involved,[56] for it provided a perfect excuse for their refusal to consult the Dominions effectively.

This weakness was illustrated when Grey gave a survey of foreign affairs at a special meeting of the CID. He gave the dangers facing the Empire as the reason for renewing the Anglo-Japanese alliance, but added that the British government was not bound by entanglements in Europe which tied its hands. This prevarication seems to have convinced Fisher of Australia and dithery old Ward of New Zealand—both overwhelmed by the illusion that the British had at last taken them into their confidence—but did not impress Hughes back in Melbourne.[57]

## AUSTRALIA AND BRITISH DEFENCE PLANNING, 1911–1914

Nor did the British government show any signs of a new willingness to consult the Dominions in 1911. They did not discuss the Agadir crisis with them, even though it occurred while the conference was meeting. In Australia Hughes protested against the rumour that Germany was to be compensated for loss of interests in Morocco by islands in the Pacific, and W. H. Kelly, prominent Member of the Australian House of Representatives and the Round Table, declined to pressure his colleagues into accepting the British plan, despite the urging of Philip Kerr, member of Lord Milner's 'Kindergarten' and the Round Table group in London. Where Australian and Round Table 'imperial' interests appeared to conflict, Australian members of the Round Table followed Australian interests.[58]

The era was one of uncertainty, and mixed opinions were held by all the protagonists. Discussion was largely at the initiative of the unofficial Pollock Committee[59] on imperial reform and the Round Table movement in London, not among the Dominions, where there was much apathy on the issues. If Dominion politicians had really been concerned about consultation, they would have helped to strengthen the CID. The conference had agreed that ministers should attend the CID when matters concerning their Dominion were discussed, and in 1912 Sir Robert Borden, then Premier of Canada, proposed that they be given permanent seats on it, so that they would receive more accurate and complete information. This idea was not supported by Australia, South Africa or Newfoundland.[60] Pearce who was by then preoccupied by the defence issue, and as Minister for Defence claimed that he received more practical advice from the CID than from the full Imperial Conference meetings, did not carry his Cabinet colleagues with him. Australia therefore did not follow Canada in appointing a permanent representative to the CID in 1914. Fisher, who maintained old labour ideas, would not allow the Australian High Commissioner to accrue the authority to speak for the government or commit it to unspecified action. Ironically his successor, Hughes, felt this even more strongly when Fisher himself became Australian High Commissioner. Meanwhile, Dominion public opinion was usually more concerned with internal development than the complexities of the European situation.

The Imperial Conferences were poor instruments for imperial consultation and debate. They lasted only a short time and were held at long intervals. While they were in session, members hurriedly raised highly complicated issues—between dinners, banquets and ceremonial occasions. As the *Round Table* put it, the meetings were conducted in 'an atmosphere of mutual admiration and social festivity'.[61] The brief and simplistic discussions were all too often the means whereby British politicians managed to convince colonial leaders of the correctness of British policies and hide the dangers and difficulties inherent in them. Meanwhile, the governors-general, the Colonial Office and British leaders saw a threat to themselves if the Imperial Conferences and the position of High Commissioner were allowed to develop too far, and took no initiative in any of these changes.[62]

In 1911 the Admiralty renegotiated its naval agreement, allowing the Dominions to have their own navies. The Royal Australian Navy (RAN) was to be regarded as a 'sister member' of the King's navy, with which its training and discipline were to be 'generally' uniform, as officers and men were to be largely interchangeable. It was to be under the control of the Australian government, except in time of war, when it came under the Admiralty, and was liable for service anywhere in the world. Discipline had always been an important consideration, for the Admiralty feared that an irresponsible colonial naval officer might commit acts that plunged Britain into war over a minor matter in a far part of the world. As for the civil authorities, it has been argued that

> British acceptance [that Dominion] governments should have the power to bind their citizens beyond their territorial limits when serving in naval vessels marked an important step in the establishment of extraterritorial powers of these governments.[63]

This seems, however, a little far-fetched. Moreover, as a result of the agreement the RAN became closely tied to the Royal Navy, while the purchase of equipment from Britain and the recruiting of British officers 'contributed . . . subtly to Australian dependence upon the Mother Country'.

For a while, however, the Dominions seemed to have been given a little extra freedom, and in 1912 there was much talk of forming an 'Australasian' fleet unit by combining Australian and New Zealand vessels. The New Zealand Minister for Defence, Colonel James Allen, wanted closer links with Australia, and his sentiments were echoed in Australia by Fisher, Pearce and Admiral Sir George King-Hall, the commander-in-chief of the Australia station. The Admiralty under Churchill, however, was worried by this sign of local independence; it ordered King-Hall to desist, and declined to reply to the New Zealand suggestion. Meanwhile, public opinion in New Zealand was wary of coming under the dominance of Australia, while Allen on a visit to Britain in 1912 was pressured by the Admiralty and clashed with Churchill.

In fact, the Admiralty was changing its mind once again, so that relations between it, Australia and New Zealand deteriorated. Churchill, convinced that Germany was the main potential enemy, was determined to concentrate British resources in European waters. The Admiralty therefore regretted the agreement with Australia, and in 1912 proposed to lend only Royal Naval Reserve and merchant officers to the RAN, a move which led the commander-in-chief of the Australia station to remonstrate.[64] Then in 1913, the year the Australia station was formally transferred from the Royal Navy to the RAN, Churchill postulated in his speech to the Commons on the estimates for 1913–14 an 'imperial squadron', built around a proposed Canadian nucleus, to be based on

Gibraltar, to protect any threatened part of the Empire. He gave the game away, however, when he admitted that it could reach Vancouver in 23 days, Sydney in 28 and New Zealand in 32, 'and the Channel a very much shorter time'. It was one more sign of Admiralty concentration on Germany and neglect of the distant parts of the Empire—an attitude that 'was far too well known to the governments and peoples of the various dominions for them not to penetrate easily the verbiage of the First Lord'. It was typical that New Zealand had not been consulted, despite the fact that her gift warship would be involved and she was obviously interested in such a new departure. Allen dismissed Churchill's idea, reminding the New Zealand parliament that 'it was very long way from Gibraltar to the South Pacific'.[65] As it happened, the refusal of Canada to cooperate ended the matter.

In his long career Churchill never understood, let alone sympathised with, Australasian needs or fears.[66] In his naval estimates on 17 March 1914 he criticised the idea of separate Dominion navies and reverted to his concept of an 'imperial' naval squadron, to which the Dominions would contribute their heavy ships. He had apparently sidestepped the naval agreement by putting obsolescent ships on the China station, and restressing the Anglo-Japanese Alliance. He insisted on the orthodox doctrine, that 'The situation in the Pacific will be absolutely regulated by the decision in European waters.'

Not surprisingly, the Australian press was up in arms, while its government sought British assurance that the naval agreement was still in force. It was so incensed that the Minister for Defence, Senator E. D. Millen, tabled in federal parliament a memorandum which included 'the sharpest criticism of the British made by any Australian politician, in public or private, since Federation'. It accused the Admiralty of abandoning the 1909 agreement, sabotaging the basis for the RAN, ignoring Australian needs and views (especially over the treaty with Japan), and totally failing to consult, or even notify, the Dominions. As in the 1940s, Australians doubted Churchill's assurances of a speedy despatch of a British battle fleet. The Australian government therefore pressed on with the development of its own fleet, while the Labor Opposition—and indeed the Australian members of the Round Table—totally supported Millen's memorandum.

Gordon remarks that 'This formidable indictment of Admiralty policy was perhaps the most significant in the history of the emergence of the dominions from imperial tutelage.' He probably exaggerates. It *would* have been significant, if World War I had not turned attention to Europe and obscured the lessons of the crisis, which had to be learnt all over again in the 1940s. For Churchill's unilateral abandonment of the 1909 naval agreement revealed his Anglocentric attitude to the Empire, while talk of superiority in vital (i.e. European) waters hid Britain's weakening power in the Pacific, and inability to protect her Empire there. The outbreak of the world war, however, prevented this fundamental disagreement from being resolved. Behind it all remained the other issue, the failure of the British government—despite its promises—to consult the Dominions where the latter's interests were likely to conflict with those of the British.[67]

Consultation did occur, however, when the British wanted direct Australian assistance. W. T. Bridges, 'a trusted imperialist' and now a colonel, had been left behind as Australian representative on the Imperial General Staff after the 1909 conference. The War Office, with the continuing series of crises, was keen to have Dominion assistance in the event of war. In 1911 the population of Australia was just under four and a half million, Canada just over seven million, and New Zealand just over one million. There were reserves of manpower available, therefore, that the War Office was desperate to tap.

It considered first of all allotting each Dominion a 'sphere of action' in the world, though it admitted that the real value of the Dominions would come only from being under War Office orders and available anywhere. The 'sphere of action' idea had been put to the full Imperial Conference in 1911, after Haldane had ordered a revision of the document to make it even more vague than it had been originally. It was carefully designed to hide from the Dominions what was going on. (An attack on the Gallipoli peninsula had been considered as early as 1906, while joint planning with the French to block a German thrust through Belgium had been under way since 1909.)[68] The Imperial General Staff would handle all technical details—'hopefully thereby escaping the attention of dominion governments'. One wonders what Bridges, Australia's representative, had gleaned of all this during his short time in London in the second half of 1909. He was certainly reluctant to return to Australia and it seems likely that Bean's account of an enthusiastic Australia which—by chance—rallied to the cause and ended up at Gallipoli is, to say the least, naive.

At the 1911 conference Ward of New Zealand was cautious, declining to commit his government beforehand.[69] The Australians, however, were different. At private meetings in the War Office, Pearce assured the British that Australian volunteers would be available in the event of war. He was going beyond his brief, and revealed the dominance of defence worries over his early labour reformist ideals, which had led to a widening gap between him and rank-and-file ALP members. He therefore added that the Australian General Staff needed a clearer idea of what the British were planning, and asked for mobilisation schemes.

Realising the significance of this bombshell—from a leading member of the previously dreaded 'anti-imperialist' Australian Labor Party—the Chief of the Imperial General Staff pressed Pearce to clarify his implied offer of an expeditionary force, and Pearce duly promised that the Australian General Staff would send their plans to the War Office. He also agreed that the utmost secrecy should be maintained, so the War Office paper was withdrawn and no report of the discussion appeared in the official proceedings of the conference. Thereafter, Pearce stressed fear of Japan as the rationale for defence spending. For himself this may have been true, but it was also politic: the government would hardly have relished a public discussion on the need for Australia to become involved in a European war. Once such a war broke out, however, a wave of imperial patriotism could be expected to sweep Australia. Till then, the less said the better.

Back in their Dominions, the respective military leaders copied their counterparts in Britain, and planned expeditionary forces as if they had full political and public approval. As a result, defence in both countries was further integrated into the British imperial mould. In New Zealand, Godley approached Allen with his ideas for an expeditionary force, even mentioning Egypt as one possible area of deployment. In Australia, Bridges, now commandant of the officer training establishment at Duntroon, approached the War Office privately to select imperial officers as instructors, despite a government decision to make appointments on an open competitive basis.[70]

A conference between Australian and New Zealand representatives followed in November 1912, primarily to discuss an expeditionary force of at least one division, comprising men from both countries. Amongst other things, the possibility of sending conscripts overseas was raised, although restrictions imposed by the Australian *Defence Act* made it difficult for the Australian government to promise the British an exact number of men. Pearce looked for ways of overcoming this limitation, but realised the controversial nature of the suggestion. He therefore instructed the conference secretary, Brudenell White, who had been on exchange duties at the War Office 1908–12, not to keep notes on any plans for an overseas force. The issue was too sensitive, and could be left to public support when war came. Plans for mobilising a volunteer expeditionary force, however, were drawn up. The paper on this appeared in August 1913, and, despite the use of the world 'defence' in its title, in the text it stressed the need for the offensive in war, and thus 'a field army capable of acting as a mobile expeditionary force'.[71] Sir Ian Hamilton himself toured the two Dominions in 1914.

Thus the War Office had succeeded in influencing Australian and New Zealand defence planning and integrating them into its system. It had drawn the Australasians—like the British themselves with the French— into at least a secret moral commitment if war came. The stage was set for the creation of the Anzac legend.

## BRITISH RACE CONSCIOUSNESS AND THE AUSTRALIAN PERSONA

Other factors, however, also affected the outcome. With the advent of social Darwinism there had been a revival of imperialism and racism towards the end of the nineteenth century. Australian leaders and newspaper editors had come to talk of the 'British' or 'Anglo-Saxon race' (which included the United States). There was much stress on white superiority and 'a new Britannia in another world'. As Lloyd Robson has remarked,

> Once it became almost totally accepted, as it was by about 1900, that Australian nationalism was compatible with membership of the Empire, a form of imperialism became a component of that nationalism.

So the *Bulletin* could rage against the British aristocracy and British greed, while glorying in 'the British race', and the Rev. W. H. Fitchett, headmaster of Melbourne's Methodist Ladies' College, wrote numerous Empire thrillers, including *Deeds That Won the Empire*, which was in its twenty-ninth impression of the seventh edition by 1914. Most Australian leaders saw themselves as both British and Australian—or, to use Deakin's phrase, 'independent Australian Britons'. So 'There was no clear line between English and Australians . . . One was subsumed in the other, like relations in a family.' Thus during the Boxer Rebellion the Senior Naval Officer at Woosung visited the Victorian ship *Salamis* and told the men (to cheers) that they were 'the British Contingent from Australia'. It is not surprising, therefore, that Deakin in his 1905 'Imperial Federation' address used the word 'nation' seven times, but only once with reference to Australians.[72]

Nevertheless, as Gammage has written, the dual nature of Australians led to psychological tensions:

> They vaunted their sunlit land, and drew snowmen on Christmas cards. They proclaimed their achievements in sport, and feared whether the British race degenerated in the antipodes. They heralded a new society, and venerated the English King.[73]

Where their ultimate loyalty lay varied with the individual. General Bridges had been born of an Australian mother in Scotland, and gave his main allegiance to the Empire. W. M. Hughes, on the other hand, was more divided in his loyalties. Although born in London of Welsh parents, he had sailed for Australia in 1884 and been in the country for thirty years when war broke out. He added sympathy for the working classes gained while an elementary school-teacher in London, and his experiences as a trade union leader in Australia, to imperialism. As he said in 1909, 'A man may be a very loyal and devoted adherent to, and worshipper of, the Empire, and still he may be a very loyal and patriotic Australian all the time.' This was not unusual: J. G. Legge, the Australian general who became highly critical of the British during the war, had also been born in London.[74]

In reverse, C. E. W. Bean, the future war reporter and official historian of Australians in the war, was born of English parents in Bathurst, New South Wales, while his father was headmaster of its school, but went back with him to England at the age of ten, and was educated at Clifton College and Oxford University. He returned to Australia at the age of twenty-five and promptly fell in love with the country, especially admiring what he thought were the archetypal Australians, the bushmen. He held the current social-Darwinian views of race and was convinced of the superiority of the Anglo-Saxons. He therefore painted a picture of the country Australian as 'a Briton reborn ... a Briton with the stamina and freshness of the 16th century living amongst the material advantages of the 20th century'.[75]

## MONARCHY AND MILITARISM

Coupled with this British race patriotism towards the end of the nineteenth century went—as in Britain—a growth of the more showy kind of militarism and a renewed loyalty to the British monarchy. The increased popularity of Queen Victoria towards the end of her reign, her association with imperial pomp and Australian federation, the tour of her grandson, the Duke of York, and finally her death that January, all 'focused the attention of a large section of Australia upon the institution of monarchy'. The subsequent death of Edward VII in 1910 led to the second royal funeral and coronation in ten years and provided the popular press with ample material to whip up royalist fervour. Support for royalty had so far increased that the King was eulogised by sections of the press as widely different as the conservative *Sydney Morning Herald*, the apparently radical *Bulletin*, and the Victorian *Labor Call*.[76]

This imperial loyalty, mirrored in New Zealand, was so pervasive that one commentator has claimed that 'the flame of Australia's imperial loyalty ... was then burning more strongly than at any time since Federation', while George V in 1913 was convinced that Australia's support could be counted upon.[77]

## EDUCATION, THE CHURCHES AND PROPAGANDA

Loyalty to crown and Empire was partly the result of newspaper propaganda, and partly that of Australian education, which followed similar movements in Britain, since Australian schools gained most of their personnel and teaching materials from the United Kingdom. Shakespeare and other English authors were widely taught, and patriotic English songs sung. The *Boy's Own Paper* was popular, and often carried stories of young Englishmen who courageously and honourably carried 'the white man's burden'. It therefore influenced generations of adventurous young male Australians.

Primary education provided the basic reading skill which made pupils more vulnerable to the opinions and emotions propagated by the press, but propaganda for the Empire was part of school teaching itself. Schools aimed to give their pupils 'proper' ideas of right conduct and attitudes, using even nature study and Wattle Day to that end,[78] and from third class onwards lessons on civics and history stressed the children's duty to the Empire.

Australia itself had so short a white history, with few exciting episodes, that it was not thought a suitable medium to inculcate patriotism or national unity. Teachers therefore taught British history, with its long and interesting past and extensive literature. The language later used in the *Anzac Book* reveals the authors to have imbibed schoolboy British history.

*Drawn by F. R. CROZIER*

"Wandering spirits, seeking lands unknown,
Such were our fathers, stout hearts unafraid."

The idealised view of British history. This painting by Frank Crozier, *Our Fathers*, 1915, was published in *The Anzac Book*. (AWM, Art 00010.)

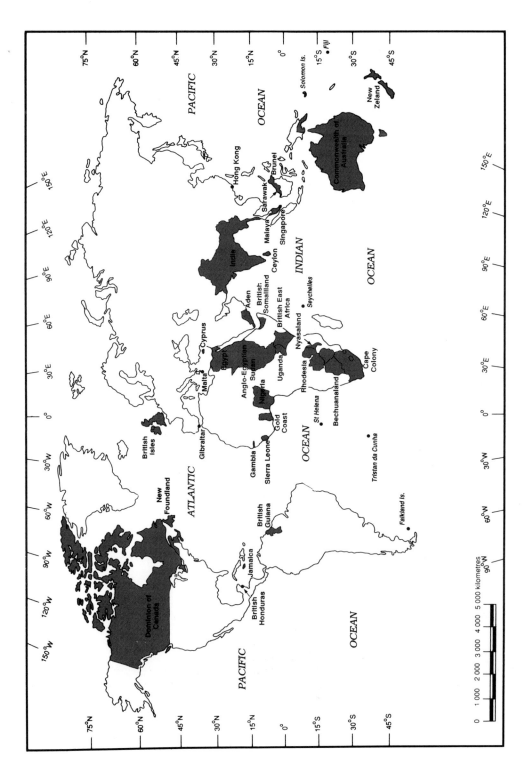

Map 1   Main centres of the British Empire in 1914.

Pupils were liable to be asked to write an examination answer on why they were proud to be members of the British Empire, the meaning of patriotism, Britain's place in history and Australia's obligations to her. The *Commonwealth School Paper*, published monthly from 1904 to 1915, expressed certainty about the British race and pride in the Empire. It aim was to encourage patriotism, distinguishing between Australian patriotism and that of the whole Empire, and it laid great stress on defence. Stories of British explorers and conquerors were used to rouse hero-worship; while geography could reveal Britain's power, using maps of the world with her Empire shown in red—in Mercator's projection which exaggerated its extent. Schoolchildren saluted the Union Jack, while patriotic numbers of the school papers were issued for Empire Day by the education departments of all States. Indeed, 'the annual celebration of Empire Day on 24 May ... was the highlight of a year-round emphasis on Empire loyalty and patriotism.' Children 'marched, produced patriotic displays, gave patriotic concerts and listened ... to addresses'.[79]

Secondary education, which was a separate system, was provided almost entirely by churches or individuals on the English pattern, in particular using the curricula, morals and educational ideals of the English public schools. A minority of pupils then went on to university, preferably in Britain for more British education, but if not, in Australia. Even there, however, most academics were from British universities, and the Australian academic scene was dominated by the British model.[80]

The lessons of the education system were supported by the churches, especially the Anglican Church, which linked itself closely to State and Empire. Most Anglican clergy were British, and stressed militant Christianity. The *Church Standard* declared in 1913 that the 'Empire is a trust for development from Almighty God himself' and even a Presbyterian minister argued that 'the Royal Australian Navy [is] a symbol of our sense of Empire'. Churchmen linked loyalty to the British Empire with Christian virtue and 'acted as if they were the official guardians of patriotism'.[81]

The impact of all this must have been overwhelming. For the lessons they learnt in the schools were reinforced in pupils' minds by public attitudes outside.

> British imperial propaganda poured into the colonies and captured the public schools and popular press. The rising generation through universal, compulsory education was socialised into the creed of Empire.[82]

In a speech to a lunch-time crowd in Martin Place on Empire Day 1907, W. W. Oakes, Member of the New South Wales Legislative Assembly, said that if the time came for Australians to show their loyalty, they would be ready 'to the last man and the last shilling'.[83] Andrew Fisher's famous statement in 1914 seems to have been merely an echo of an Empire Day commonplace.

## AUSTRALIAN PUBLIC OPINION ON THE
## EMPIRE RECONSIDERED

Despite this, we need to exercise some caution. The picture relies heavily on written evidence: newspapers, parliamentary debates and other printed material, letters and written recollections, school curricula. In particular, the newspapers dominate the evidence that survives, yet they created public opinion as much as reflected it. They were the only means the average person had of gaining news, and their ideas spread throughout the community.

Yet it may be dangerous to place too much reliance on them. For example, they stressed 'imperial solidarity', and reported great interest in military parades during the celebrations of federation in 1901. It is not clear, however, whether the crowds gathered because they accepted the ideas of 'imperialism' and 'militarism', or merely to enjoy some colour and excitement before the age of television and film. Probably the military parades did indoctrinate the public to glamorise war, and overlook the squalor and brutality that always attends it, but they cannot be taken as an automatic sign of 'militarism'.

Too many historians, however, have succumbed to the temptation to accept the surviving evidence uncritically. They have stressed enthusiasm for the Boer War, gone on from that to deduce widespread support for the Empire throughout the Australian community, and written of Australian acceptance of imperialism and British race pride at the turn of the century. Charles Grimshaw wrote that 'from the 1890s, when Australia was caught up in the wave of imperialism sweeping Europe, public opinion favoured Australia's continued active membership of the Empire'.[84] Yet, as we have seen, support for the Empire was politically motivated. The celebration of Empire Day was the result of a concerted campaign, largely inspired by one man, Francis Boyce, Archdeacon of West Sydney, but backed by a socially prestigious pressure group, the Australian branch of the British Empire League, which also strongly supported commercial interests in the Empire.[85]

C. N. Connolly has argued, however, in two thoughtful and perceptive articles, that the situation at the time of the Boer War was complex and reveals the crosscurrents between imperial propaganda and local Australian reactions. To start with, the offer of the Australian contingent to Britain for the Boer War was manipulated by Chamberlain and Milner. It was not spontaneous. Telegrams were sent to the mayors of all Australian capital cities asking them to organise meetings, and pressure was put on the Queensland government to offer 'volunteers', an offer which was then used to influence the other governments to follow suit. Most colonial governments were reluctant. They doubted the justice of Britain's cause and were wary of the likely costs of involvement. They would support Britain, but *in a time of crisis*, and they did not regard the situation at first as a crisis. In short, some Australians were capable of independent thought: they did not share British concepts of 'the Empire in danger' or the need to expand constantly. Milner was heavily implicated in the final New South Wales offer which presaged Australian involvement.

With British reverses and disasters in the war, however, and newspaper coverage, aggressive jingoism gradually became prominent, so that by Christmas 1899, when a second Australian contingent was discussed, only three members of the labour parties in the different colonies continued to oppose Australian participation. By then politicians clearly believed that public opinion supported the war, and opponents accepted that they were in a minority. The two dominant ideas at that time were loyalty to Britain and the belief that Australian participation revealed the growth of Australia as a nation. This last sentiment had been increased by federation in 1901, and illustrated by a torchlight procession and meeting in Queensland in 1902. The most striking example of the change, however, is Hughes himself. He had previously regarded the Boer war as being fought for financial interests, describing it as 'the machinations of a band of buccaneers' and an 'infamous war'. It was only when he joined the federal parliament, and British preoccupations left Australia apparently insecure in the Pacific, that his views changed, and he began both to demand an Australian navy and to stress the need for defence by the British fleet.[86]

After the war was over, however, histories of the conflict 'attributed the imperialist fervour of early 1900 to the governments and people of mid 1899', and in this way became the basis for imperialist myths. They had begun to be promulgated earlier, however. Chamberlain, Milner and others could use the war in a multi-national propaganda campaign for Empire, to whip up popular opinion at the time and strengthen imperialism afterwards. Thus when the first Australian contingents were about to sail, 'the Governor of New South Wales told Chamberlain that a 'spontaneous expression of thanks' from Queen Victoria would be "very deeply appreciated in Australia." '

Too much therefore can be read into newspaper reports. Leaders of the middle-class elite of Anglo-Scottish descent organised the patriotic rallies and bushmen's contingents—and were naturally impressed by the unity engendered by the war. Imperialism was their ideology, and they owned, managed or edited the newspapers, besides the fact that the latter received their news from British cable services and often copied articles from their British equivalents.

But it may be unwise to assume that this 'vocal minority spoke for the overwhelming majority of Australians who have left no record of their views'. Open opposition to the war was usually confined to alienated groups, but the most common response was probably neither support nor opposition, but mild concern mixed with apathy. It has been said that in New Zealand the 'Empire belonged to an official rhetoric, to newspaper editors, to school teachers, to politicians, to Governors and Governors-General' but 'for most people [it was] no more than an abstraction'.[87] One suspects that it was a fairly dominant abstraction, but whether Australians would feel obliged to support it depended on circumstances—and they were in the process of changing.

The *Round Table* remarked in 1911 that although Australians might refer to Britain as 'home', that was a trick of speech. Britain

> is, after all, a far land, even a foreign land, to the majority at least of the native-born, while Australia is the real 'Home' ... The empire is there, certainly, and we are proud of it ... But, except in the time of some stern crisis, or when some great world event ... catches at the nation's heart-strings, it is too distant, too formless, to excite any very strong enthusiasm.[88]

Nor was Australia as homogeneous as it appeared to be, or as the myth of an egalitarian country which was 97 per cent British has since made out. Hidden divisions existed, three of which were to be thrown into relief by World War I.

To begin with, the term 'British' hid the different traditions and memories of the English, Welsh, Scots, and the large minority of Irish Catholics in Australia. The Irish in particular were deeply alienated from the Anglo-Saxon supremacy by their religion as well as their historical traditions. This was seen in their educational system. The majority of Catholic schools had been founded by Irish orders, and 'did not teach the same patriotism, the same literature, or the same version of history' as the public school system. Catholic schools taught that a pupil's duty lay to God first and then Australia, rather than the British Empire. They were more cautious in dealing with Empire Day than the public schools, stressing St Patrick's Day and—to avoid charges of being unpatriotic—Australia Day.[89]

Secondly, wealth was not distributed as equally as the myth would have us believe, and certainly not between these four groups. Finally, there was a deep difference between recent migrants and the older-established Australians. Power and initiative in the colonies rested with the new arrivals from Britain. The elites in the country, the pastoralists, bankers, leading businessmen, politicians, were British orientated, if not of English descent.[90] Hughes was London Welsh; Pearce had English parents; Henry Fulwood, who became an 'Australian' war artist, was born in Birmingham; A. W. Jose, author of the naval volume of the official Australian war history, was born near Bristol. Andrew Fisher, prime minister of Australia when the war broke out, was a Scot of poor descent who had arrived in Queensland in 1885; W. A. Holman, premier of New South Wales, was, like Hughes, a Londoner. Native-born Australians were not to dominate Australian politics until the 1920s.

Nevertheless, there were subtleties and undercurrents in attitudes to the Empire that make generalisation difficult. For example, the New South Wales politicians who sent the contingent to the Sudan were nearly all Australian-born and W. B. Dalley, the acting premier, also came from Irish Catholic parents. Indeed, despite the increased rate of immigration, the proportion of Australian-born in the population continued to rise, and was over 82 per cent in 1914.[91] The Australian-born tended to see themselves as a new and better white race in the antipodes and therefore to jeer at Pommie 'new chums' and to talk of 'an effete, poverty-stricken, and caste-ridden England'.

Meaney has argued that they 'unwaveringly insisted on maintaining an exclusive political control over their own affairs' and sensed that their 'economic, political and strategic interests were so different from those of the Mother Country that union was impossible. And therein lies the answer to the riddle of Australian nationalism.' That may be so, but they also felt that Australia was vulnerable to the 'hordes of Asia', and so stressed the 'British' or white race as a whole, asserting that Australians were 'the pick of the British breed'. It left a strain of schizophrenia in the Australian psyche, but was useful because Australian ethnocentrism protected various interests and groups: against British capital or migrants, European or Asian threats, or internal opponents.[92]

Support for the Empire therefore firmed in the decade before 1914, partly as a result of British propaganda, but also because of fears roused by the Japanese triumph over Russia in 1905. Australians came to feel that they needed to support the British more wholeheartedly, for both they and Britain were threatened. This may explain why aggressive British nationalism was so pronounced in Queensland, where Anglo-Saxons were a smaller percentage of the population, and nearer 'the hordes of Asia'. If so, fear of invasion coalesced with social Darwinism to make Australians more open to imperial propaganda. At the same time the New Imperialism provided an ideal of progress based on Britain which had an enormous appeal to the Australian middle classes, most of whom were living basically British lives in the cities, and increasingly strove to do the 'British' thing—hence the very real sense of 'dual loyalty' in many Australians at the time.[93]

Some Australians also had conscious or subconscious political and social motives. Those who feared unrest from the poor looked to a closer political union of the Empire and an even more dominant educational system. 'Education and Empire' became their slogan, and was pushed by groups such as the Royal Colonial Institute, the Victoria League and the League of the Empire. The latter organised a pen-pals scheme and, after 1904, Empire Day, which was proclaimed in Australia in 1905, and culminated in a massive celebration in 1911—although significantly it was not officially accepted in Britain itself till 1916.[94] Conservatives stressed Empire Day to counter the perceived threat of socialism and republican nationalism. It could unite the new settlers in Australia in one nation; but it also enabled the ruling elites to maintain the system and their place in it. They thus used appeals to 'the Empire' to support their own policies, as the *Argus* in Melbourne did in 1915 when it opposed Hughes' referendum to increase Commonwealth powers. Meanwhile the labour parties, with the failure of the 1890 strikes and the depression of 1893, had become increasingly cautious and anxious to gain respectability. They turned for support to the small farmers, employers and middle classes, and ended their open criticism of Britain.[95]

By 1913, therefore, there was widespread public support for the Empire throughout Australian society, which explains the overt public reaction to the outbreak of war. The old divisions and differing interests, however, remained hidden below the surface.

CHAPTER TWO

# The Bugles of England

The bugles of England were blowing o'er the sea,
As they had called a thousand years, calling now to me:
They woke me from dreaming in the dawning of the day,
The Bugles of England—and how could I stay?

J. D. BURNS,
*'To England!'*

## THE RUSH TO WAR—AUGUST 1914

Burns, a pupil of Scotch College Melbourne, revealed the effect that British-orientated education and the climate of opinion, discussed in the last chapter, had on so many young men in 1914. His poem and subsequent death on Gallipoli[1] mark the starting point on the long slow road to Australian disillusionment—both with the war itself and the British handling of it, and the subsequent change in attitudes to the British relationship.

Recent research has cast doubt on the idea of a 'rush to enlist' in Britain in the first days of the war, and pointed instead to the reservations and mixed motives that existed.[2] In the same way, Australian reactions were more complex and subtle than has generally been recognised. Australia was not a sovereign state, and had no option but to go to war. When the time came neither she nor any of the other British Dominions were consulted—but neither was the British Cabinet or parliament. As A. J. P. Taylor has noted, 'the war came as though King George V still possessed undiminished the prerogatives of Henry VIII'.[3] For Australia, it was enough that her King had declared war. She too was therefore at war. The extent to which she participated was—in theory—a matter for debate, but in the climate of the time, such debate was bound to be almost nonexistent. Immediately before the war, as we have seen, there was widespread loyalty to Britain and fear for security in the Pacific. Both loyalty and fear could be used by the patriotic press and the leaders of opinion in 1914.[4] When therefore Britain sent a warning cable on 29 July, the Australian government placed its ships under the control of the Admiralty and offered an expeditionary force of 20,000 men. Peeved by being beaten in the race to prove its loyalty (for Canada had already offered men and New Zealand

40

was considering doing so), the Australian Cabinet felt that the despatch of its troops was urgent, and the only discussion was about the composition of the units to be sent. The British had simply suggested a number of brigades, which they could then join piecemeal to any of the larger formations in their army, but the Australian government wanted to send a recognisable national unit. It therefore offered its men as a division, the smallest section of an army which has its own separate administration. This turned out to be an important and far-reaching decision.[5]

Meanwhile, politicians of all Australian parties vied with each other to express their utmost loyalty to Britain, for a general election campaign for both houses of parliament was under way, and candidates could not resist the temptation to make extravagant rhetorical flourishes to gain popular support. Joseph Cook, the Liberal prime minister who was facing electoral defeat, immediately declared that whatever happened Australia was 'part of the Empire to the full ... when the Empire is at war, so is Australia at war ... All of our resources in Australia are in the Empire and for the Empire.' The Labor leader Andrew Fisher replied the same evening with the famous remark that 'Australians will stand beside our own ... to our last man and our last shilling.' This may have avoided the danger of the war becoming an election issue, but it also meant that voters had no choice in the matter of war and peace. In Perth the longest-sitting MLA described Australia as 'a suburb of the great British Empire'. But the prize for the strangest response must go to Hughes who, despite the fact that Labor was tipped to win the election, demanded—albeit ambiguously—that it be cancelled, and Cook remain as government leader. It was not. Labor won, and Fisher became Prime Minister with Hughes as his deputy leader. Even then, Labor members could not help taunting the opposition about their loyalty, for the the ALP 'had successfully promoted itself over its opponents as the party for running a war'.[6]

As could have been expected, the Australian press presented a united front. The *Sydney Morning Herald* as early as 11 July had remarked that when real trouble came, 'for better or for worse, in victory or in disaster, whether it means eventual success or absolute irremediable ruin ... we are in it with the rest of our race'. Most of the papers, however, as in Britain, greeted the war quietly, and there was no immediate anti-German sentiment. That came later. The common agreement, even from Irish nationalists, was steady support for the Empire. It was only after 6 August, when British and Australian involvement was clear, that a new more strident 'patriotic' note appeared, as

> community leaders organized patriotic demonstrations and public meetings at which politicians, mayors, bishops and others made stirring speeches ... [and] whole audiences rose to sing 'Rule Britannia' and to endorse with acclamation the proposal that Australia should send an expeditionary force to Europe.[7]

Churchmen were prominent in this campaign. The Methodist *Australian Christian Commonwealth*, whose editor was Welsh, stressed loyalty to the throne and the King personally, and a total conviction of the righteousness of the allies' cause. In this it was supported by the Methodist General Conference. The Presbyterian Assembly expressed its loyalty to the King and confidence in the British government, while the president of the Evangelical Lutheran Synod in Sydney did likewise, although the Lutheran Church may well have been nervous about its German origins and wished to head off criticism. The Church of England hierarchy, overwhelmingly British-born, naturally believed that it was a just war. The Anglican Dean of Sydney remarked in St Andrew's Cathedral that no one then present in the building would wish for peace at any price, 'certainly not at the price of British honour'. Even leaders of the Catholic Church, such as Archbishops Carr in Melbourne and Kelly in Sydney, despite the troubles in Ireland, supported the allies in the early days. The oldest Catholic newspaper in Australia, the Sydney *Freeman's Journal*, boasted that at last Australians were really a nation, with one heart and soul. In the opening days many Catholics joined the 'Australian Imperial Force' (AIF) that was about to be sent to the support of Britain: some did so from loyalty, while others hoped their action would help the movement for Home Rule in Ireland.[8]

Similar widespread support for the war, 'with almost indecent enthusiasm', was revealed in schools throughout the land. Schoolchildren drew maps of the war area, cheered troops as they marched off, and raised staggering amounts of money in fund-raising activities. Indeed, 'patriotic efforts became an important part of the ... school syllabus'. Private schools varied slightly. Protestant schools, even those founded by the Quakers, emphasised the Empire more than either state or Catholic schools. Anglican schools naturally laid great stress on it, but all were affected by the spirit of the time, and pupils from all schools volunteered for the forces. Private schools had been deliberately formed on British models to promote 'the values of honour, duty, sacrifice, patriotism, obligation to Britain and pride of race', sentiments which were expressed on Empire Day. Moreover, attendance at cadets was compulsory and most schools had a Cadet Unit.[9] Their reaction to World War I is hardly surprising.

The accepted picture of the Australian public is that reported by the governor-general, Sir Ronald Munro Ferguson—'indescribable enthusiasm'. It is one of crowds in the streets, patriotic funds heavily subscribed, young men rushing to volunteer and older men standing and singing the *Te Deum* in the Sydney stock exchange. As one historian puts it, 'Australians hailed England's declaration of war on Germany with the most complete and enthusiastic harmony in their history.' When the recruiting offices opened on 11 August a mass of men jostled for position, and by nightfall 3600 had enlisted in Sydney alone. Within two weeks 10,000 more had applied, especially from country towns where long marches, with nicknames like 'the Cooees', 'the Kangaroos', or 'the Wallabies', were organised to bring the men to the capital cities. Others walked vast distances, while on the Nullarbor Plain workers on the transcontinental railway 'downed tools the day they heard of the war and headed for Kalgoorlie to enlist'. By the end of the year 52,561 men had enlisted. Robson sums up the picture with the words, 'Although complete unanimity is not attained among millions of people, the response of Australians at the beginning of August 1914 was close to it.'[10]

Nevertheless, as in Britain, there were mixed motives. Public speakers stressed emotional loyalty to the homeland of themselves or their ancestors, and the lessons of British history. They argued there was a need to preserve the British race and the Empire to which all belonged. 'The Bugles of England' were calling. Or, as Graham McInnes puts it,

> This ship of state, sailing on through Australian hearts, heavily barnacled with innumerable individual emotions, dragged these young men in its wake as surely as if they had been tied with cords. The emigrant vessel was coming home . . .[11]

Imperial loyalty, however, was supported by material arguments: that Australia depended on Britain, and a British victory, for her security.

Nevertheless, despite all the emotional loyalty and euphoria reported in the press, doubts remain. The constant barrage of propaganda in newspapers and books, from pulpits and public meetings, the compulsory military training and the stress on Empire in the schools, certainly had a considerable effect.[12] But neither of the accepted explanations, that by C. E. W. Bean with his postulated Australian national character, or S. G. Firth and the influence of socialisation in schooling,[13] seems *completely* satisfactory. Bean, the romantic English-Australian, never understood working men, whether they were civilians in the bush or front-line soldiers, while the 'influence of the schools' theory presumes that the latter were effective, and ignores the fact that many of the volunteers had been educated under the old dispensation, or not at all.

To explain the phenomenon, we have to abandon the search for one overriding reason and look instead for many interrelated causes. Individual motives must have varied. Moreover, it has been said that 'the motives of men who fight in armies may be quite different from the official rhetoric that, from above, urges them on'. The soldiers themselves rarely mentioned the reasons for their enlistment, either at the time or afterwards. Talk about 'self-sacrifice' and 'Empire', imperial relations and foreign and defence policy, belonged to politicians and preachers—men who did not expect to have to go themselves. Such language was not used by the men who enlisted; they sometimes down-played their action by talking of the desire for adventure and travel. More often than not they would answer questions by simply saying that it seemed the thing to do, which indeed implies an emotional response to the predominantly expressed public opinion—and peer pressure—on the outbreak of war. It may therefore be significant that, as in England, much of the enthusiasm was deliberately manipulated in crowd situations.[14]

Many old soldiers who had served in the Boer War or other crises, and militiamen, joined the AIF, so previous military experience, and the taste for adventure and war, had some influence. The 1st Division included 6332 Australian militia or former British regulars, making up 43 per cent of the total. Unlike the New Zealand expeditionary force, the AIF had a large minority of British-born in it, a fact often overlooked by the purveyors of the Anzac legend. They were 13.3 or 15.64 per cent of the Australian population, but either 18 or 22.25 per cent of the AIF for the whole war, depending on whose figures are taken. They were more numerous in some formations, however, being 27 per cent of the first contingent, and 50 per cent of the 28th Battalion, from Perth. Overall, about one in five of the Anzacs were British born, compared with two in five of Canadian troops. Other British migrants, however, finding they could not gain a commission in the AIF under the age of twenty-three years, paid their own way back to England to enlist in the British army. According to Pearce, 8000–10,000 Australians had done so by the end of the war. In this they followed a tradition going back to 1815, when an Australian-born English lad was present at Waterloo.[15] Such were relations between Britain and Australia, and the British and Australians, during World War I.

Whatever figures are accepted, the British-born clearly volunteered in higher proportions than the Australian-born, and considerably higher in the opening days of the war. For example Robert Antill, a young English cabinet-maker, did not mention 'Empire' in his letters, but only 'England'. This reaction seems entirely natural. Australian-born historians under-estimate the bonds of the homeland, partly homesickness, partly sheer loyalty to the country of birth, which only a migrant can feel. They created a conviction in these men that they *had* to be back in its time of crisis. Another 'Australian' hero, John Simpson Kirkpatrick, 'the man with the donkey', who transported wounded soldiers from the lines at Gallipoli and died doing it, was in fact not Australian at all, but English. He was born in Tyneside, had been travelling round Australia for only four and a quarter years, and planned to return to England. In more exalted circles J. Talbot Hobbs, commander of the 1st Australian Division in 1918, came from Chelsea and had entertained Lord Kitchener in his home. Other examples can be found in the files of the Imperial War Museum in London. It is doing these men less than justice, therefore, to suggest that they looked on the war simply as a means of a free trip home.[16]

There were also class differences in the reasons for enlistment. The middle-class recruit may have been moved by abstract motives like loyalty to England, duty, or the Empire. Working-class motives on the other hand may well have been 'social mobility, steady employment, good money, friendship, the opportunity to break out of unsatisfactory personal relationships, and the chance to see the world'. One motive that was not heroic was—as in Britain and Canada—unemployment, which doubled across Australia (and quadrupled in Queensland) in the first months of the war. Even that most patriotic paper, the *Sydney Morning Herald*, mentioned unemployment, which ran particularly high in those trades which the war had disrupted. The official estimate was that half of the

5500 unemployed in the Sydney area had taken up 'military work', and in fact 'of the 54,000 recruits who enlisted in the first five months, 43 per cent were unionists, well above the proportion of unionists among adult males in Australia'.[17] Such men could see the war as an escape from their troubles because they had no idea how deadly it would be. As a result of the brief European wars of the nineteenth century, most people expected this one to be short, and many volunteers feared it would even be over before they could see action.

Moreover, the proportion of men who enlisted was not as high as the public excitement suggests. The figure of 52,561 by the end of 1914, mentioned above, though at first sight impressive, came from a total of approximately 820,000 who were eligible: it constitutes a mere 6.4 per cent. Historians who make much of the 'rush to enlist' might therefore do better to ask why *93.6 per cent of eligibles did not enlist.* Some could not meet the physical standards,[18] but the truth is that in Australia, as in Britain, voluntary recruiting was not to provide sufficient manpower, and, apart from the surge after Gallipoli, the numbers soon fell. A New Zealand historian has noted a similar phenomenon, stating that only 38 per cent of all men of military age enlisted, compared with 39 per cent in Australia. He does not say to what period of time these figures refer, but the inference is clear. Ken Inglis' question, why 'all those men [came], voluntarily, all that way, and kept on coming', therefore misses the point.[19] Most men did *not* volunteer, and they did not 'keep on coming'. The important questions are why, and whether the development of divisions within Australian society, divisions which were hidden by the predominantly British newspaper and power elites and the excitement of the time, and which social historians have since largely ignored, played a major part.

The Australian reaction to the war was more divided, and more hesitant, than most historians have been willing to admit. As Evans writes,

> Between the fervent British-Australian loyalists . . . and the dedicated opponents of the war . . . the majority of Australians remained, much quieter and more confused, less certain . . . A deeply ingrained affection for the Empire and an innocence of war's harrowing impact encouraged most to lean more readily towards assertions of war's promoters . . . but the bravado of many was seriously tempered by regret, anxiety and bewilderment.[20]

But even this may be too strong. Apart from those who harboured reservations in principle, many must have simply been worried by the unpredictability and killing and retreated into what may be described as 'defensive apathy'. The very shrillness of the recruiters suggests that they faced this response. In November, B. R. Wise, educated at Oxford, commented on 'the strange indifference of our peoples to the momentous issues of the present war.' Though the pro-war party was overwhelmingly dominant, therefore, most of the population was probably 'acquiescent'. While there is no data on which to test this hypothesis, it seems plausible, and would account for the events of the next few years. Middle-class leaders simply took for granted that their feelings were shared by the mass of the people; but the leaders of the intensive recruiting campaigns were soon to discover that many Australians were less committed to the war than they had believed.[21]

Compared with the widely reported pro-war sentiment, publicly expressed opposition to the war was certainly minute, but newspapers often declined to report opposition, which was suppressed anyway by government regulations, which were part of imperial censorship.[22] Officially backed 'public opinion' probably intimidated opponents of the war, while most Australians were concerned with their own lives, and— like other peoples the world over—had no great or abiding interest in foreign policy. Most knew little about Europe, and cared less. Such people could very easily retreat into 'acquiescence'.

Yet there were some open dissenters. The *Bulletin* began by being cryptic about both sides, although with a new editor it changed to aggressive advocacy of the war. The labour press was reluctant, as befitted those with socialist pretensions. The *Australian Worker* in Sydney expressed deep regret. It thought there were no extenuating reasons for war, and no principle or vital issue at stake. Australia had to be defended, but the *Worker* hoped that no 'jingo lunacy' would sweep the land. 'God help Australia; God help England; God help Germany; God help us!' In Victoria the *Labor Call* also regarded war as barbarous, but remained loyal.

In the early stages, the only outright opposition to the war in the labour movement came from the Industrial Workers of the World and others on the far left. They were swamped by the prevailing patriotic feeling, noisily promoted in the press, but they were not entirely alone. Apart from individuals such as Adela Pankhurst and followers of Shaw, the Quakers adopted their age-old stand, joining the small pacifist movement. Among the Catholics, the question of Ireland simmered below the surface. The Coadjutor Archbishop of Melbourne, Dr Mannix, spoke for them when he was insensitive enough to raise the issue on the outbreak of war. A shrewd observer should therefore have guessed that the continued loyalty of Irish Australians depended on attitudes in Ireland itself and British treatment of that country. Mannix did not condemn Britain openly then— but more was to be heard in due course from this 'troublesome priest', as we shall see.

Most of those who had reservations naturally kept them to themselves in the climate prevailing at the time. They were to become more public, however, during the conscription referenda in 1916 and 1917.[23]


## THE OPEN COMMITMENT

As Inspector-General, William Bridges was given the task of creating the expeditionary contingent of 20,000 men. It was he who named it the Australian Imperial Force, perhaps after Hutton's earlier suggestion, but certainly with his own attitude and experience at the War Office in mind.

Both he and White were pleased when their old confidant Pearce, who had been won over to the British view of the world at the Imperial Conference in 1911, became Minister for Defence in the new Labor government in 1914.

It was hardly surprising, therefore, that after the rush of volunteers the Australian government decided to offer a further force of 50,000 men— leading to somewhat wild talk of a second corps, and even an army— and put the lot at the complete disposal of the War Office. It only reserved the right to administer, pay, clothe, equip and feed its troops.[24] It was naturally concerned with security in its near neighbourhood, and when the Committee of Imperial Defence (CID) in London proposed that Australia organise forces to capture Yap, Nauru and Rabaul, promptly did so.[25] But as for the main areas of operations, Europe and the Middle East, the Australian government did not wish to take part in strategic decisions, or debate where or how its volunteers were to be used.

## EGYPT: PROBLEMS OF AUSTRALIAN COMMAND AND DISCIPLINE

The need for leadership of the AIF was another problem that the government was slow to face. The training school for regular officers, Duntroon, had not graduated its first intake when war began, and Australian society did not provide sufficient numbers of men who were educated, in the widest sense. The problem was probably made worse by Bridges' early death, just when he seemed to be establishing a supremacy for himself,[26] but even without that, the Australian army was almost inevitably dominated in the early days by British, or at least Anglophile, officers.

The British commander on Gallipoli, General Sir Ian Hamilton, had seen much of the Australians during the Boer War, and as Inspector-General of Overseas Forces had visited Australia early in 1914. He protested to the governor-general that he wanted to promote Australian officers but time was needed to train them. He rather spoilt the effect, however, by adding that true commanders of men were created as much by birth as education.[27] This was typical of the attitudes current at the time, so it is not surprising that Bridges' replacement was not an Australian officer but an ex-British Indian Army man, and protégé of Hamilton's, General Sir William Birdwood. He formed around him a British imperial officer group which with Brudenell White dominated the AIF till 1918.

Slightly lower down the scale, in the middle ranks there was much bitterness and intrigue. Such officers, to be promoted, had to be 'sound on the Imperial connection'—as was written of General Sir H. G. Chauvel, who began the war as a colonel representing Australia at the War Office. This made people like Colonel (in 1914) J. G. Legge and Lieutenant-Colonel H. E. ('Pompey') Elliott too bitter to judge their effectiveness dispassionately.[28] There was also a desperate shortage of good junior officers, as the governor-general constantly complained, with a resultant lack of leadership and discipline in the camps in Australia and on the troopships going out, both at sea and especially in the ports of call, such as Colombo.[29]

So it was a force with mixed characteristics which arrived at the Suez Canal and had its first sight of the trappings of the British Empire. Cheered from the other ships already there, the Australians felt proud of being part of a great enterprise. Unfortunately, this first impression did not last. Naive and untravelled, the Australians had high expectations of the British, and were, if anything, a little nervous whether they could reach their high standards.[30] They were therefore vulnerable to disillusionment when faced with harsh reality.

To start with, the British Territorials did not *look* like the troops who had fought in *Deeds That Won the Empire*. This was not just an Australian prejudice, for New Zealand troops reacted in the same way.[31] It was of course unfair to the British. Apart from the 29th Division, there were no professional soldiers of crack units such as the Guards: they were all in France. Instead, the Anzacs met only poorer British troops.

This led to an ambivalent attitude: reverence for Britain while jeering at the troops they met. On Gallipoli Oliver Hogue ('Trooper Bluegum') was to display typical loyalty to the Empire while making caustic remarks about 'the fool English'.[32] Australian hostility was also roused by the airs and graces British officers gave themselves (monocles being an immediate butt of satire), and even more strongly by the rigid and caste-ridden British army discipline. Robson wonders whether this Australian reaction reveals a more democratic and manly spirit, or 'a form of adolescent emotional immaturity'.[33] It certainly reveals lack of experience.

Once in camp in Egypt, the Australian troops, who included a number of very rough characters who had not been properly disciplined, sought relief from the monotony and hard training by indulging in the fleshpots of Cairo. Drunkenness and high spirits, combined with the racism common in Australians then, turned noisy celebrations into rioting, looting, and ill-treatment of natives. The most notorious incident involved the destruction of the Wazza, a red-light district in Cairo, where the men started to burn down the brothels, and then turned progressively on the fire-fighters and the military police. There have been various Australian attempts to blame the New Zealanders or minimise their own action. In his official history Bean dismissed the riots as little worse than university pranks—though this is not what he wrote at the time—and more recently Kevin Fewster has suggested that what began as retribution for grievances turned into a full-scale revolt against army discipline. But neither is convincing.[34]

Partly, it was due simply to the mundane fact that the Australian soldiers received more pay, and so could become more drunk and cause more trouble than the British troops. It was also, however, caused by weakness in the junior Australian officers and a failure of foresight by Bridges and White. They had not realised the need for an Australian military police, so when the AIF first arrived in Egypt, the only military police it possessed were a few in the 1st Australian Division and the Light Horse Brigades, supposedly to control the men in the field. As AIF numbers swelled, they were hopelessly inadequate to control the leave centres of Alexandria and Cairo, and responsibility was passed over to the British Corps of Military Police, the hated Provosts—known as 'Provos' or 'Redcaps'. It was a recipe for disaster.

The heavy-handed methods used by the military police in the British army for even minor offences were calculated to rouse Australians. Even the Australian police refused to cooperate with the British Redcaps and had to be allocated duties away from them. An entirely separate Australian military police force was finally raised in April 1916, but by then the damage had been done. Short cuts were taken, some undesirable characters were enrolled and had to be removed, and the tone was set for the rest of the war. As a result, the men lost all sense of proportion, ignored the causes of any trouble, and even turned on their own police. These incidents were followed by more despicable actions towards the natives, including murder, which went unpunished. Australian racism was revealing itself.[35]

Australian indiscipline inevitably involved relations with the British, not only their officers and Redcaps but the other ranks. The ordinary British soldier was not impressed by the Australians, especially if he was obliged to act as a piquet to control them. A corporal in the Lancashire Territorials thought they were

> a disgrace to the Army, nothing but an undisciplined mob ... and we are all confined to Barracks through them. They are all mad drunk having their Easter holidays but we dare not do as they do, they do as they like.

The poor pay and savage British discipline, with twenty-one offences involving the death penalty in 1914, prevented British troops emulating the Australian example. But New Zealand soldiers, who, despite some exceptions, were much better disciplined, were also contemptuous of the Australians, some thinking that the sale of liquor throughout the AIF in Egypt should have been stopped. One described the town Australian as 'a skiting bumptious fool', while another simply commented that 'These fellows seem to have a tremendous hooligan element among them.'[36]

The stories told of Australians and British officers are legion. They refer mainly to a refusal to salute, but Australians were also roused by British assumptions of superiority, and reacted by adopting the pose of being bovinely laconic. R. G. Casey, later governor-general, told of a British major who came across an Australian in a trench on Gallipoli, and brightly asked him what he would do if the Turks attacked. The Australian obviously thought he was dealing with an idiot, and the following conversation resulted.

> 'Well, boss, there ain't room for all of them in here.'
> 'No, no—I mean to say, what would *you* do if the enemy attacked in force?'
> 'Why, sit on the ———— parapet and shoot the b————s, did you think I'd start to open me tin of bully?'

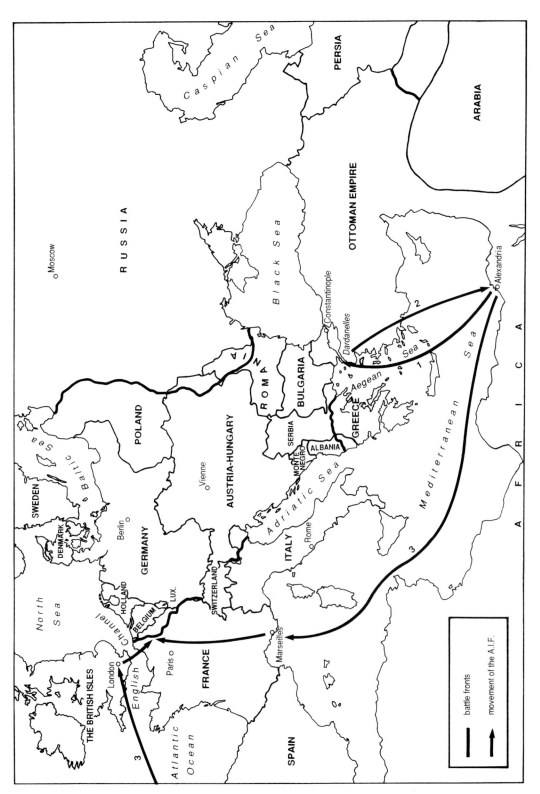

Map 2    The main battle fronts of World War I. The fronts moved their location during the course of the war.

Casey's comment was, 'And so the English learn the Australian!'[37] A similar total lack of 'respect', however, was also applied to Australian officers who stressed their rank. While such stories are scandalous to British ears, and cause amusement in Australia at the 'bucking' of authority and the naivety of the soldiers, general misbehaviour in towns and mistreatment of natives could only be irritating at the time and a sign of the vandal spirit. Such men had to be disciplined or removed, and both Bridges and Godley of New Zealand did send the worst troublemakers, and venereal disease cases, home. It remained to be seen whether the remainder would prove an obedient and competent fighting force when the time came for action.

## GALLIPOLI

The general apathy towards the study of strategy and tactics in Australia is reflected in the exaggerated stress on the Gallipoli affair. Strategically, Churchill's plan was sound enough: to drive Turkey from the war, or open up a way to supply Russia and so put more pressure on the Germans on the Eastern Front. But the tactical problem remained: how to break through a narrow seaway defended by minefields and coastal forts and, if a landing were made, to breach trench lines of barbed wire backed by machine guns and rifles. It was not strategy, but tactics, which bedevilled World War I. In addition, amphibious operations have always been the most hazardous of all military enterprises, and only the success of the landings in Europe and the Pacific in World War II have obscured this truth. Those landings, however, were the result of massive military and air superiority, surprise, a high level of military intelligence and expertise, long preparations and technical developments such as self-powered boats, floating harbours, and amphibious armoured vehicles. None of those factors applied in 1915, and the outcome could have been expected.

The operation was ill conceived and poorly planned, the result of Churchill's penchant for large-scale maps and grandiose strategic gestures, which were to cause similar disasters in World War II. The Australian troops were inexperienced, and so attributed to the affair a uniqueness it did not have. Not that campaigning on the peninsula was pleasant; the awful terrain, the flies, the hand-to-hand trench fighting, dysentery and British command bungling saw to that. But the trauma pales in significance when compared with the horror of the Western Front: the enormously increased bombardments, gas, and the sheer scale and destructiveness of the war. Those Anzacs who survived the peninsula and went to France accordingly testified to the worsening conditions.

The euphoria over Gallipoli in 1990, though understandable, therefore does less than justice to the men who fought on the Western Front. To give only one example, though casualty figures for World War I are notoriously unreliable, the general picture they give is clear. The Australians were only a minor proportion of the forces engaged on

Gallipoli. Australia suffered between 7600 and 8141 dead. Britain lost four times as many; the New Zealanders 2431 and the French 9798; while the Turks suffered more than 86,500. Nor does the Australian casualty list compare with their losses on the Western Front, where six times as many Australians were killed. None of this is to mention the horrendous French, German and Russian losses in numerous battles during the war. The truth is that Gallipoli was a minor sideshow, both in its location and its scale.[38]

Nevertheless, the Gallipoli campaign is interesting from the point of view of this book, since it saw a new development in the relationship between Australia and Britain. There was much Australian incompetence on Gallipoli, the classic occasion probably being the charge at the Nek. As mentioned in the introduction, it was an Australian officer, Colonel Antill, who insisted on the pointless attacks continuing. Keith Murdoch, so well known for his criticism of British officers, was equally critical of Australians in September 1915, arguing that there was 'a lot of murder through incapacity'.[39] Another example was Lieutenant-Colonel C. H. Braund's defence of Russell's Top on 27 April. Contrary to the praise Bean heaped on Braund in the Australian official history (which was followed by the British series), the New Zealand Lieutenant-Colonel W. G. Malone was scathing about the state of the Australians and bitterly criticised Braund for ignorance and poor tactics, such as 'the murderous notion that the only thing to do was to plunge troops out of the neck of the ridge into the jungle beyond'. Malone was so incensed that he seriously considered asking for Braund to be court-martialled for incompetence. Later he remarked in his diary, 'It is a relief to get in where war is being waged scientifically and where we are clear of the Australians.' This was probably unjust: the best of Braund's junior leaders were dead, and his men were exhausted and poorly trained. Nevertheless, the chaos and confusion of his command is disquieting. It only reflects, however, the confusion of the troops after the landing.[40]

The Australian soldier, however, rapidly earned a reputation for himself in battle. Even Chauvel, who had been deeply critical of their behaviour in Cairo, warmed to the men. British officers and onlookers as wide apart as Generals Maxwell and Hunter-Weston, W. F. Scott (a Royal Navy chaplain) and an 18-year-old midshipman, used the word 'magnificent' commonly, remarking on the men's intelligent obedience in battle. Hamilton, the British commander on Gallipoli, did so too, and wrote to the King's private secretary that the Australians 'although hopeless from our point of view as regards punctilio ... and although also having, to put it mildly, a very good opinion of themselves, yet ... are indubitably splendid fighting stuff'. The praise of the senior officers was to be expected: they received medals and commendations for the valour of their men, but it is too widespread to doubt. In his report to the King on the state of the peninsula, General Sir Charles Monro, who had replaced Hamilton began, 'The troops on the Peninsula, with the exception of the Australian and New Zealand Corps, are not equal to a sustained effort.' Australian fighting ability, however, received the ultimate—and ironic—accolade from Churchill, who 'produced figures to show that the "wastage" of recent attacks could readily be replaced by Australians and others who had recovered from wounds or illness'.[41]

In contrast to Egypt, reporters and onlookers began to mythologise the Anzacs, sometimes for ulterior motives of their own.[42] The Australians were probably not as bad as horrified commentators, accustomed to rigid British discipline, believed in Cairo, or perhaps as good on the peninsula. Certainly their discipline improved—probably due to reduced opportunities for misconduct. In battle, like all troops they varied. Even good soldiers will not fight, or fight well, on some days, and Bean himself admitted that the Anzacs sometimes had to be driven forward at the point of a revolver. Another characteristic, played down by Bean but which struck contemporaries, was a disinclination to take prisoners, and mistreatment of them once taken—in contrast to the New Zealanders.[43]

On the other hand, Australian illusions about British military competence were shattered. To start with, the medical facilities were disgraceful, paralleling those of the Crimea. Both the Australian and British heads of the medical services were grossly unfit, the only difference being that the Australian was too old and doddery, while the Briton was arrogant, idle and incompetent, and had to be *ordered* to accept an offer of help by the Royal Navy. The medical staff had grossly underestimated the number of casualties they would have to deal with, and the arrangements for transport were scandalous. Wounded were obliged to lie for days on the beaches under shellfire until a ship could be found to take them, and only the numbers of the dead solved the problem of overcrowding. The 'dirty, verminous transports', without doctors or stores, carried their cargoes of the dying and the dead from ship to ship in an effort to find accommodation. On one ship there were between 400 and 500 wounded, with only one bedpan, while wounds, untreated for seven days, suppurated. Arrangements ashore were equally chaotic. The first Australian Stationary Hospital at Lemnos was sent elsewhere, and it took the authorities four weeks to realise the need for another within short range of the peninsula, and to establish it at Imbros. Even the British official historian called the muddle 'indescribable'. In Egypt squabbling between the various authorities was the prelude to bitterness between Australians and British over the treatment of the wounded. British leaders resented criticism, and Lieutenant-Colonel C. A. K. Johnston, Commanding Officer of 1st Division base, took his complaints to Sir John Maxwell, Commander-in-Chief of British forces in Egypt, who naturally supported his British officers: both men then wrote to Australia. There, the secretary of the Department of Defence was sure that Johnston's complaints had been dismissed because they had come from 'a damned colonial officer', and Pearce and the Cabinet agreed. Enquiries were made, but—as could have been expected—found that Johnston had exaggerated. Disturbing reports, however, had reached even the governor-general from other sources and he cabled England. He too was assured that the War Office had done everything possible.

Stories of the muddle reached the press and roused Australian women in London, and the Australian government sent Lieutenant-Colonel Fetherston on a fact-finding mission. He urged that an Australian officer, Colonel N. R. Howse, should be appointed as director of Australian medical services. The War Office was reluctant, arguing conformity of procedures, and it was not until January 1916 that this was done. Two years later, at the Dardanelles Commission, Howse remarked

> I personally will recommend my Government when this war is over, that under no conceivable conditions ought they ever to trust to the medical arrangements that may be made by Imperial authorities for the care of their sick and wounded.

Nevertheless, despite a public exposé of the scandal in Australia by the *Age*, it had little effect on the Australian parliament, public opinion or government. The British authorities used the censorship to suppress the story for a long while, till the continuing slaughter on the Western Front weakened its impact. If it had come out immediately it might have seriously strained Anglo-Australian relations. As it was, the Australian government simply relied on the British medical arrangements and lines of communication on the outbreak of war, and showed no independence.[44]

British staff work in general was also noticeably poor during the campaign. Guy Dawnay, an aristocratic young staff officer, who in fact was rather amused by the Australians and was to take action against Hamilton for inefficiency, was described by one prejudiced Australian critic as 'the most bumptious, objectionable and incompetent bastard on Hamilton's staff'. Monash, then a colonel and CO of the 4th Infantry Brigade, wrote that the watchwords at Lemnos were 'inefficiency' and 'muddle', and Australian rumour held that when the campaign was over 'all these gallant gentry are to get three clasps to their war ribbon respectively for Imbros, Mudros, and Chaos!' Howse's comments have been noted.[45]

Gallipoli therefore began the long road of Australian loss of innocence. Faith in the might and wisdom of the British Empire and the idea of war as a glamorous adventure could not survive Gallipoli. British planning errors were noted with amazement. The Australian G. J. Johnston, General Officer Commanding Royal Artillery (GOCRA) 2nd Division, reported that his officers were puzzled.

> For years I have been teaching them that ships have little chance against forts, and in the whole history of war have never done anything against them when the conditions have been at all equal, yet here we see this extraordinary attack . . .

He blamed Churchill, 'who imagines he is the world's greatest general, admiral and politician rolled into one'. He thought it was madness to allow the navy to attempt the task alone, and some people in England should be hanged 'for allowing such an ill-prepared force to take on such a job after the Navy had failed'. The main culprits were in London, but they would probably be promoted. 'On the one hand you have the wretched soldier who loses his life, on the other the politician who carries on for ever.'[46]

Johnston was an educated soldier with a knowledge of military history, but lower down the ranks others—without his background—suspected bungling. Casey passed from a naive feeling of excitement and adventure to bitterness at failure. He was particularly caustic about the inadequacies of naval gunnery. In his diary he recounted that General Walker—who had objected most strenuously to Australian troops being used for the expedition—remarked that when the Royal Navy hit a target in peacetime exercises they put it in despatches. Casey added sarcastically that a naval battle couldn't be terrible, because 'I can't imagine one boat being so strikingly accurate in her gunnery—as to hit *another boat* [sic!]'. His third stage was resignation and depression, which he tried to cure by plunging himself into the technicalities of the task. In his diary, however, he confided, 'This game gets very sickening. I get fits of rather severe depression at times. It all seems so hopeless and endless and sordid . . .'[47]

Those attitudes were not uncommon. As the long muddle of Gallipoli continued, the Australians developed an increasingly good opinion of themselves and poor one of the British. British officers from Hamilton downwards were the butt of savage criticism. Nor was Birdwood exempt.

> Much has been made of the Australians' 'love' of 'Birdie', but it was nothing more than the tolerance they granted any 'decent enough bloke'. Birdwood and the Australians came from opposite ends of understanding, and all they had in common was a form of English language, limited and crude in the case of many of the Australians, stilted and artificially affable in Birdwood.

Talking to them in his condescending avuncular way about keenness 'to have a go at the Turk with the bayonet' only irritated them, especially after his gross bungling of the attack on Hill 60. But Birdwood had no grasp of tactics, which was to prove disastrous in France.[48]

Apart from administrative and tactical incompetence, the main thrust of both Australian and New Zealand objections was to the caste distinctions in the British army, and the gulf between the officers and the men. They 'had been taught by their parents, or had otherwise acquired, a strong dislike of the speech, manners and attitudes of the higher British classes'. It was possibly the latter's nonchalant sense of superiority, combined with lack of sensitivity to the sufferings of the troops, that infuriated the Anzacs most.[49]

Australian criticism of the ordinary British soldiers, begun in Egypt, was also reinforced, particularly after the failures on Gallipoli at Cape Helles and Suvla Bay. The latter fiasco was crucial in establishing a firm belief among the Anzacs that they were better than the British troops, whom they accused of running away and losing trenches which the Australians had captured, and which they then had to go to the trouble and danger of recapturing. In Egypt, the Australians had accepted, self-deprecatingly, the title of a 'ragtime army', but never again—'after the poor miserable crowd we have been with'. Some distinguished between effective and ineffective British troops, especially in the New Army, 'and

God help England if she relies on these last ... this war has made me intensely British and absolutely Australian'. More dourly, another remarked that Kitchener's men 'knew as much about fighting as a goose about God'. These views were echoed by Monash and *The Anzac Book*, which was probably a reflection of Bean's own developing Australianism. They were reinforced in Egypt when British troops fled from Romani, the Yeomanry officers leaving luxuries behind them for the Australians to find. This was ironic, since those officers had been some of the most 'disparaging critics of Australian indiscipline'.[50]

The Australians in fact went too far. They developed the paranoia of the inexperienced that they were doing more work and facing more danger than others. Legge wrote that he had come 'to the conclusion that Australian troops were already taking on rather a lion's share of the hardships here'.[51] It was a sentiment that was to recur later. They also developed the 'blame the British' syndrome for whatever went wrong. Many of their criticisms of British troops, such as Bean's comments about 'little, dumpy, smooth-faced Lancashire and Yorkshire youths' and 'the dregs of England's cities', were unfair. Physical size and appearance are no criteria for military effectiveness and courage, and the failure at Suvla was the result of confused planning, difficult terrain, and Turkish strength rather than the weakness of the British soldiers. The Anzacs would have done no better.[52]

From the point of view of this study the fact that the men held such opinions is more important than their accuracy, for they presaged a new attitude to themselves and the British. This was illustrated by Bean, who moved from his earlier imperial viewpoint to a complete, almost indiscriminating, admiration for Australian soldiers, and a new vision of Australia in the Empire.[53]

Australians and New Zealanders also came closer together. New Zealand troops also had a poor opinion of the British soldiers they saw, waxing bitter over their 'cowardice', for which they blamed the death of their comrades. Some suspected the race was deteriorating. But as a result of the fighting on Gallipoli, they no longer regarded the Australians just as loutish troublemakers, but began to respect them. Though still noting their brashness, they began to develop an admiration for the Australians that was to last. Whereas they had seen themselves in Egypt as a separate force, the idea of 'Anzac' took a hold. So too the Australians now clung to their distinctive uniforms until they were in rags, and by late May the wounded in Cairo objected to using the British Soldiers' Club because of its name.[54] It was a significant development in Anglo-Australian relations.

## ASHMEAD-BARTLETT AND THE MURDOCH LETTER

Meanwhile, in London, scandal was about to break. Ellis Ashmead-Bartlett had been selected to represent the British press on Gallipoli, and it was his despatch which roused Australian pride. As he described the landing,

The Australians rose to the occasion. Not waiting for orders, or for the boats to reach the beach, they sprang into the sea ... Then this race of athletes proceeded to scale the cliffs ...

Ashmead-Bartlett's eyesight, as one cynical commentator has remarked, 'must have been brilliant', since he had 'watched' proceedings from a battleship at sea before going ashore briefly later in the day. But that was not known in Australia. His report, coming from a 'British' source, was all the more acceptable.

Disillusionment rapidly followed for Ashmead-Bartlett, however.[55] He ran foul of Hamilton's staff and became increasingly pessimistic and critical of the way the campaign was being waged. He visited England in June, saw Prime Minister Asquith and presented him with a memorandum which roused the CID and the Dardanelles Committee, especially Sir Edward Carson, its chairman. When he returned to the peninsula, he found that the military censorship had tightened. The arrival of Australian journalist and newspaper entrepreneur, Keith Murdoch, provided Ashmead-Bartlett with his chance.

Murdoch stayed four days, and despite his specific promise to Hamilton that he would submit all material to censorship, was convinced by Ashmead-Bartlett's criticisms and agreed to carry a despatch to Asquith. Which of the two men instigated the idea is unclear, but they discussed the matter carelessly and were overheard. Hamilton was tipped off, Murdoch intercepted and the letter seized at Marseilles.

Murdoch, however, was a dangerous man to cross. In Australia he was a friend of Fisher, Hughes and Pearce, and had entertained some of them in the past. He was travelling to London as managing editor of the United Cable Service, while his contacts in England included Lord Northcliffe, owner of *The Times*, and Dawson, its editor. Once in London, therefore, he wrote an 8000-word letter to Fisher, with 'the massive overstatements which were typical of his writing in controversy', savaging the staff work on Gallipoli. It has been described as 'an amazing document—a mixture of error, fact, exaggeration, prejudice and the most sentimental patriotism'.[56]

It came at a crucial moment. Debate was then raging in key circles about the correct strategy to pursue. Carson, Lloyd George (then Minister of Munitions) and the Colonial Secretary Bonar Law were by now openly critical of the handling of the campaign, while others, like L. J. Maxse, owner of the *National Review*, were concerned about the possible impact of the developing fiasco on Dominion loyalty and enthusiasm. Even the critics, however, were hesitant about the effect a withdrawal would have on Dominion loyalty, now that Australia and New Zealand had committed their men, had received rousing reports of their heroism, and lost so many in action. Hankey discussed the matter with Bonar Law, who wrote to the governor-general.[57]

Murdoch therefore arrived at a crucial time. He saw Dawson, Carson, Northcliffe and Lloyd George—who suggested he send a copy of his letter to Asquith. The prime minister smelt trouble. Although he thought

Murdoch's letter was 'largely composed of gossip and second hand statements and the antecedents of the writer are not such as to command confidence', he also thought it might do mischief in Australia, and—more importantly—give ammunition to his critics in Britain. Guy Dawnay was then in London on behalf of fellow officers anxious about the mismanagement of the campaign, seeing the King, Asquith himself, Lloyd George and others. Murdoch was all too useful to the hawks in the British establishment. He later claimed in a letter to Pearce that he had been urged to act by Bonar Law and Lloyd George, but from the correspondence in the Lloyd George Papers, Murdoch himself seems to have taken much of the initiative, and was pushing his letter as far as it would go. A note to Lloyd George includes the sentence, 'I have just arrived from the trenches at Anzac'—a remark the emotional Welshman could hardly be expected to resist. Bean thought that 'patriotism' was Murdoch's main motive, but added that he also 'dearly loved the exercise of power'. Asquith accordingly played safe: he headed off his critics by taking the unprecedented step of having Murdoch's letter printed as a Cabinet Paper.

The aftermath was predictable. Evicted from Gallipoli, Ashmead-Bartlett returned home and had his story published in the *Sunday Times*. The Dardanelles Committee was deeply and bitterly divided, but finally decided to recall Hamilton—despite his dignified, though somewhat pedantic, rebuttals.[58] Kitchener then visited the peninsula and the troops were successfully withdrawn—the only effective part of the whole operation. The Anzacs were not the last troops to leave the peninsula. They were evacuated on the night of 18–19 December 1915; other British and allied troops remained on Cape Helles until 8–9 January 1916.

Ashmead-Bartlett, meanwhile, was *persona non grata* with the authorities. Sent from the peninsula, he was in urgent need of money, and first undertook a lecture tour of America, and then suggested another of Australia. This roused much concern. The British Naval Attaché and embassy in New York thought it was undesirable to allow Ashmead-Bartlett to tour Australasia because he was attacking the competence of British officers. Bonar Law agreed, but the governor-general cabled him that the tour could not be suppressed, and they had therefore arranged the strictest controls. Murdoch's letter had not been publicised in Australia—the censorship saw to that. By then Fisher had been replaced as prime minister by Hughes, who like Lloyd George was determined to wage war to the utmost, and did not wish to emphasise failure at Gallipoli. He was inclined to blame Hamilton for letting Murdoch visit the peninsula, and requested that in future no Australian pressman 'be allowed to visit the front without prior approval of the Australian government'. He cabled Bonar Law, who interviewed Ashmead-Bartlett. His tour of Australia went ahead, but it was closely watched: Ashmead-Bartlett had to submit copies of his talks beforehand and not the slightest deviation was allowed. Hardly surprisingly, his remarks were mild, and if anything, the governor-general thought, encouraged recruiting.[59]

Australian public reactions to Gallipoli were in some ways quite surprising. At the beginning, concern was felt whether Australian troops would behave creditably in battle. This fear turned to euphoria after Ashmead-Bartlett's opening despatch. Thereafter, helped by British censorship and governmental 'misinformation', Australians were slow to learn the tactical situation on the peninsula. Even that staunch imperialist, Governor-General Munro Ferguson, became so dissatisfied with the trickle of news that he approached London. There were delays in informing the Australian public of the casualty rate, and when that became clear, grief was mixed with pride and a naive faith that more of their own men would bring quick victory. The result was an upsurge in enlistment.

There was very little criticism of the campaign in Australia. Frederick Eggleston, the Australian intellectual later prominent in foreign affairs, wrote, 'There is no whimpering in Australia ... Nobody believes that we have conferred a favour on the Mother Country by fighting for her. We realise that the war is our war.'[60] The governor-general was at first worried, thinking that confidence in the British government had been shaken, and its prestige lowered, 'in those communities who were prone to think that Britain was played out and inferior to the younger countries of the Empire', but he expressed admiration in December, when there was still no criticism. Lord Stamfordham, the King's private secretary, thought this was 'splendid ... One almost took for granted that there would be some public outburst of criticism, if not recrimination.' Munro Ferguson agreed. 'The absence of carping here over the premature bombardment, and the postponed list of casualties, is beyond all praise.' Munro Ferguson, however, represented the British government in Australia, not the interests of Australians. But the latter were hardly represented by their own government either. Hughes' reaction to talk of withdrawal was to offer a further 50,000 men, without thinking of practical questions like the level of enlistments, and he dismissed out of hand a call for debate in federal parliament.[61]

This refusal to concern himself with strategy was a fatal weakness, but it reflected the public mind. Munro Ferguson thought there was no understanding of, or concern with, strategy in Australia: it was just a fight, as far as the Australians were concerned. This attitude was fed by the 'big-noting' that was promoted by the press in Australia, which touted Gallipoli as a 'tale of heroism that thrilled the world'. Self-congratulation abounded; Ashmead-Bartlett's and Bean's despatches were republished for use in schools; and a rash of short motion pictures emerged.[62]

The Australian public was in fact isolated from the war. The men at the front might have been on another planet as far as the Australian people were concerned. It was only with the lengthening casualty lists and the return of the wounded that some of the realities began to seep in. But the process was slow, and made slower by the reluctance of the returned soldiers to shock or horrify their families or friends. The government also did its best to prevent the truth emerging and to keep the public supporting the war through the use of censorship. In this it was aided by the press, while in the British parliament Sir George Reid, no longer High Commissioner but now a British MP, boasted of Australia's acquiescence.

## THE NEW ILLUSION: CREATION OF THE ANZAC LEGEND

All peoples need illusions to live by, or, in Sorel's term a 'myth' to unify them and give meaning to their lives.[63] As the illusion of the might, wisdom and military effectiveness of the British Empire was weakened by the war, another illusion was to take its place, that of the peculiar fighting quality of the Australian soldiers and the 'special relationship' of Australia with Britain. The development of this double myth is instructive.

Despite his eclipse, Bartlett had done much to create the excitement in Australia about the landing on Gallipoli, and set the heroic tone for the subsequent historiography. Murdoch took up the torch, and continued the creation of the Anzac myth in his famous letter, which gave full airing to the rumours current about weak British troops, as well as the incompetence of the British staff. On the other hand he praised the Australians as 'magnificent manhood, swinging their fine limbs as they walk about Anzac. They have the noble faces of men who have endured.' He also argued that they were disillusioned with the British. 'Sedition is talked round every tin of bully beef on the peninsula' and 'they much resent the sudden change in the attitude of the General Staff, which regarded them as criminals in Cairo, and now lavishly calls them heroes in Gallipoli'.[64]

Meanwhile, as a result of his observations of Gallipoli, Bean was developing his attitude to the Australian soldier as the epitome of the bushman, which formed the basis for his official history. He had personal reasons for being critical of the British authorities. The Army Council had adopted a very restrictive attitude to newspaper reporters at the beginning of the war: their numbers were limited and no photography was allowed. Offered only one post, the Australian Journalists' Association elected Bean just ahead of Murdoch. Nevertheless, the Army Council then forbade pressmen to enter the field of operations. This prevented Bean from reporting the landing before Bartlett, and subjected him to a period of intense frustration. It did not affect his feelings towards Hamilton, who allowed him generous access to Gallipoli, but it possibly left a legacy of subconscious bitterness towards the British authorities which surfaced later, as we will see. His point, that he was not the representative of some local British paper, but of the whole of Australia, was valid. After several appeals, the War Office turned the matter over to the Admiralty, where Churchill decided to have one press correspondent to represent *all* the Dominions. After further appeals from several quarters, and the advocacy of Reid, who was still at that time Australian High Commissioner, Bean was eventually allowed to join the Australians, but, much to his disgust, unlike the English journalists was not allowed actually to write anything. Finally, the Admiralty granted Bean full permission.

For their part, Australian national sensibilities were evident from the beginning. The Department of Defence decided that the High Commission should obtain 'for historical purposes' copies of censored correspondents' despatches. It did not approve of the (British) Federation of Northern Newspaper Owners using Bean as their correspondent, wanting to keep him exclusively for Australia. In the end it was agreed that Bean's despatches *could* appear in British papers, but one day after they had been printed in Australia. The Australian High Commission in London, however, saw their value as propaganda for Australia, and sent copies to all provincial papers. The censors countered this by insisting that Bean's reports be available for publication at first only in the evening papers— which were less widely read. The morning ones could not use them till the following day, by which time, of course, they were stale news.

Unlike the other newspaper correspondents, Bean stayed ashore on Gallipoli, talking to the men and trying to view the action from the front line. He was fascinated by individual heroism, and followed the rule of the censors, that it was no part of his duties to criticise the authorities, but simply to report. He therefore usually kept criticisms to himself. In this, he resembled many correspondents in that war. Even Philip Gibbs, who was so scathing afterwards, at the time was trapped by censorship, loyalty to the cause, and concern at what he saw. The habits Bean adopted as a reporter, however, led to a weakness in analysis; and this was to affect his later history.[65]

The Anzac legend, though it derived from Bartlett's despatch, Murdoch's letter and Bean's later writing, was developed by Bean at the time on the peninsula. *The Anzac Book* was peculiarly his creation, for of the 36,000–41,000 Australians who were on Gallipoli when the call for contributions came, only 150 responded, a return rate of 0.416–0.365 per cent. Even then, Bean rigorously excluded material which was different from his vision of an 'Anzac'. He intended to sell the book to the families of the men back in Australia, as well as the soldiers themselves, so some sanitising of the war was inevitable, but in editing it the way he did he descended into being a propagandist. Pieces which illustrated the grim reality of war, or mentioned cowardice, malingering, longing for beer, bitterness at officers or cynicism were rigorously excluded. 'The danger, the brutality, the suffering, the waste of life, and the dehumanising effects of warfare are conspicuously absent.' Nor was personal grief allowed to intrude. Instead, the material Bean chose, or wrote himself, stressed characteristics like humour, coolness under fire, contempt for mutilation.

As early as Gallipoli, Bean was emotionally committed to his vision of the Anzacs. After his return to Australia in 1904 he had travelled through outback New South Wales and thought he saw there qualities of independence and initiative that had been stifled in the industrial cities of Britain. He had encapsulated these ideas in two books in 1910 and 1911, *On the Wool Track* and *The Dreadnought of the Darling*. Fewster writes,

'The characteristics he perceived in the soldiers tallied with what had so impressed him in earlier years with the men of the outback.' To Bean, the Australian soldier was 'a bushman in disguise' and after only a few days on Gallipoli he commented that 'the wild pastoral life of Australia, if it makes rather wild men, makes superb soldiers'.[66]

Writing the way he did enabled Bean to ignore reality. For example, only 17 per cent of the AIF in 1915 were bush workers. He was also mistaken in his stress on 'mateship'. It was not peculiar to the Australians: the British talked of 'chums', but the idea was the same. All soldiers lean closely on those around them—they are forced to, to survive. Indeed, many of the attributes which Bean assumes were characteristics of the Anzacs were in fact common to many soldiers. To give a minor example, their habit of stripping to the waist and wearing only shorts when working was commonly adopted by North Country and Scottish troops too.[67] Most of all, however, he ignored the ugly face of battle, and the disillusionment and cynicism of the men.[68]

Although he professed to despise 'wretched cant' in newspapers, and the Australian public, 'which only tolerates flattery and that in its cheapest form', Bean did not hesitate to exploit the image he had created. Later in France in 1916 he reported an event at Fromelles as 'worthy of all the traditions of Anzac'. And in *Letters from France*, after describing a bombardment at Pozières, he commented: 'What is a barrage against such troops! They went through it as you would go through a summer shower . . .'[69] Such phrase-mongering leaves speechless anyone who has experienced bombardments, or simply interviewed a survivor of Pozières.[70]

The propaganda picture of the Anzacs on Gallipoli made an impact in Australia because of the delay before Australian troops took an active part in the war, the dramatic hand-to-hand nature of the fighting, the 'heroic' image presented by writers, and perhaps because 'the emotional poverty of Australian history had suddenly and substantially been enriched with drama for the first time'. It was an emotional generation and emotional times. Moreover, the fear that the Australian troops would not do credit to the nation was at last set to rest.

In all this the enormous sales of *The Anzac Book*, in France, London and Australia, played a part. Over 104,000 copies were sold by 1916, and they found their way into almost every home in Australia and New Zealand, as well as other parts of the Empire. The emotional response of relief and pride could be used for political reasons. The new 'glory' the Anzacs had won contrasted with the waste of such fine men, and provided a reason why the war had to be fought more effectively. It was therefore a vehicle on which Billy Hughes—like Lloyd George in England—could ride to power.[71]

For it suited all parties to accept the myth of Anzac. At the same time as the Australians gained a good impression of themselves, a wide range of British observers agreed with them. Guy Dawnay wrote to his wife full of admiration, and many other Englishmen did likewise. The press took up the story. To the British authorities, desperate for good news to give their people and some propaganda image to rally the Empire, the tale of the 'heroism' of the 'colonial sons of Britain' on the far-off peninsula was a godsend. They could hide blunders from the public and provide the heroic picture expected of warfare but so lacking on the Western Front. Even Bonar Law, for the sake of Australian public opinion gave an interview to Murdoch, whom he disliked, when the peninsula was evacuated, and then wrote to Munro Ferguson that the deeds of the Australians and New Zealanders 'bulk more largely in the minds of our people than those of their own men'.[72]

Birdwood too accepted the myth and was soon exploiting it. He wrote three letters to George V's private secretary, before and after the evacuation, expressing pride in the Anzacs, 'these magnificent fellows', adding 'I shall certainly spend the last day with my troops at "Anzac" ', and how he was looking forward to being with them in Egypt. He also wrote a series of letters to Kitchener describing in glowing terms the assault on Lone Pine and the conduct of the Anzacs on the withdrawal. At the Dardanelles Commission he asserted that his men behaved magnificently, and boasted that had they been at Suvla Bay, the attack would have succeeded. He then testified that the Australians and New Zealanders were reluctant to withdraw from the peninsula, since they regarded it as sacred, being the largest part of their military history. He cited the story of the man who —on going down to the beach past the lonely graves for the last time— remarked 'I hope they won't hear us leaving.' Outside the Commission, Birdwood wrote to Kitchener again, urging that more honours should be granted to the Australians. It is very difficult to avoid the impression that vested interest was deeply at work here, that Birdwood was concerned with his own advancement, and that had he spent on planning battles just part of the effort writing ingratiating letters to people in positions of power, more of his men may have survived.[73]

As it was, neither Birdwood nor the Anzacs could rest on their laurels, real or imaginary. The centre of action was about to move to France. Although some of the AIF were to stay in the Middle East, the majority were shortly to embark for the Western Front, where such idealism in their attitude to the British and the Empire as had survived Gallipoli, or been refreshed by new recruits from Australia, was to face new trials. Meanwhile, the politicians were to develop both Anzac illusions—the special relationship with Britain and the peculiar fighting qualities of the AIF—for their own purposes.

# CHAPTER THREE

# The War of the Politicians

'War cannot for a single minute be separated from politics.'
MAO ZEDONG,
Lecture, 1938

## THE COST OF WAR

The imperial relationship between Britain and Australia was bound to come under strain as a result of the war. As it dragged on, with great loss of life and the failure of the high hopes at its beginning, the enthusiasm of the opening weeks waned, the recruiting figures declined, and 'the sobering truth began to dawn that war involved little glory, and much sacrifice, suffering, and hardship'.[1] Inevitably, the idealistic—almost naive—relationship between Australia and Britain began to change.

The first hard truth driven home was the economic cost of modern war. The Australian government, full of enthusiasm and expecting a short and comparatively cheap war, had not only offered troops but also promised to bear the cost of their despatch and maintenance. The British War Office seems to have been generous in its estimates, granting Australia its military transport at a cheaper rate than Canada, and, after Gallipoli began, simply charging Australia a set cost per man per day. Nevertheless, although different figures are given by different 'authorities', by 1920 the war had cost Australia approximately £376,993,052. Of this, £262,507,829 had been raised from loans, and £71,087,125 from taxation, while £43,398,998 was owed to the British government for services and goods provided to the Australian army. With interest charged on war loans, repatriation and pension costs, the latter figure had risen to £831,280,947 by 1934.[2]

Australia, a primary producing nation in 1914, was bound to be deeply affected economically. The impact of war combined with drought to create depression: the mining industries contracted, workers were dismissed, and there were demonstrations against unemployment, which almost doubled in the first five months of the war, despite men enlisting. Simultaneously, as in Britain, prices rose alarmingly.[3]

64

To Australian State governments, the answer was a vigorous programme of public works. They therefore tried to borrow heavily on the London money market. But the British Treasury strongly objected to loans for civilian purposes, although it was willing enough to provide them to finance the war. Fisher as prime minister therefore decided to raise a common Australian loan for public works, and applied to Britain for £20 million. The Treasury refused, secretly citing the possible long duration of the war and the strain on Britain's finances. Fisher then avoided the impasse by asking Britain for £18 million 'for war purposes only'—the exact sum his government was prepared to lend to the States. The British were aware of Fisher's ruse, and the Chancellor of the Exchequer called Dominion High Commissioners and agents-general together three times in 1915 and insisted that British government loans were for war expenditure only. The Australian States would have to raise money on the open market to finance public works they had already started, though even that had to be approved by the British Treasury. New public works were completely forbidden.

It was an attempt to control Australian finances, made worse, from an Australian point of view, by the Treasury's habit of treating the other Dominions as single entities but Australia as six separate States and a federal centre. The Australian government therefore held a conference in November 1915, at which all States except New South Wales agreed to act through its agency. The British Treasury continued to try to rein in Australian expenditure—in vain. The States continued their huge borrowings throughout the war to fund public works, to the profound hostility of Munro Ferguson and the Treasury.[4]

## THE ILLUSION OF A SPECIAL RELATIONSHIP WITH SIMILAR INTERESTS

The appearance of imperial unity, created by the war, in fact hid deep differences of interest and opinion. In the first heady days few Australians reflected that—quite apart from the cost of warfare—placing their forces at the complete disposal of the British government implied also acquiescence in Britain's control of grand strategy and the conduct of the war. The common assumption was that the war would be over quickly, and that Britain's military, financial and diplomatic position gave her the right of unquestioned leadership. It was simply assumed that the Dominions would be consulted, as a matter of courtesy, when peace-making was to be considered.

These assumptions could not survive a long and bloody struggle, for Australians naturally cared how their men were used, what became of them, and so how the war was being run. As early as September 1914 Fisher was disappointed by the announcement of Lewis Harcourt, the Colonial Secretary, that no imperial conference would be held in 1915. Fisher argued that it would be a tribute to a free people to meet at such a time, but the British Cabinet did not agree, and quashed the idea by seeking the official opinion of the other Dominions—whose leaders were bound to have differing ideas—and then simply issuing a general invitation to Dominion Prime Ministers to visit London individually when they were able.[5] Fisher remained unconvinced: Australia and New Zealand were further from Britain than Canada or South Africa, and less present in British consciousness. In December 1914 Reid the High Commissioner, alarmed by the diversion of supplies from the AIF in Egypt to the Western Front, travelled to the Middle East to discuss the situation with the British authorities. He accepted the need at that time, but worried whether they could stop the diversion when necessary, and how Australian troops could be supplied.[6] In April 1915 Fisher sent his friend, the former prime minister J. C. Watson, to London to report on operations. Watson 'was worried by the British attitude to the war and the Dominions, and throughout 1915 urged Fisher to push for a conference'.[7]

British leaders, however, continued to operate on their old assumptions. Apparently they did not inform Fisher that the Anzacs were going to Gallipoli, although the governor-general knew. Meanwhile they used Australia to intern German citizens from South-East Asian and Pacific countries. One historian has even suggested that this was for Britain a revival of its transportation policies of the early nineteenth century, and for Australia a 'relapse into colonial dependency'.[8] This is an exaggeration: the British government was simply concerned with practicalities; and Australia could hardly 'relapse', for it was indissolubly a part of the Empire, and was anxious to help its war effort. But the incident does throw an interesting light on reflex attitudes in both Australia and Britain in the opening days of the war.


## MUNRO FERGUSON

The leading figure in the link between the two countries was the governor-general of Australia, Sir Ronald Munro Ferguson, who took office on 18 May 1914. A 54-year-old 'Scottish landed gentleman of established wealth and long descent', he had been first a Guards officer and then took up a 28-year parliamentary career. The new governor-general was a man with an impressive bearing and wit, and a wide range of interests. Naturally, he did not regard his position as that of 'a dignified rubber stamp', but instead 'an active imperial supervisor of one of His Majesty's overseas Dominions'. On arrival he was immediately faced with a tricky decision over a demand for the double dissolution of parliament, and during the resultant general election, while the prime minister (Cook) was occupied on the hustings, he cooperated with the Minister for Defence and the Attorney-General in organising the country for war.[9]

On paper the powers of the governor-general had been lessened. The British parliament's right to 'disallow' (i.e. veto) Australian legislation had never been invoked, while the governor-general's right to 'reserve' (decline to pass) Australian legislation had fallen into disuse, after a series of protests by Deakin. Moreover, an Australian federal public servant was now appointed to be the governor-general's secretary.

Nevertheless, the governor-general was still an impressive figure. He was not only the representative of the British monarch, but also protector of British interests and wishes with the Australian government. His secretary, Sir George Steward, was zealous for the office, and became head of the counter-espionage bureau, thus providing the governor-general with much information. Moreover, Munro Ferguson had his own cipher for communications with London, and as we have seen Australian governments had to communicate with Britain through him while the powers of the Australian High Commissioner in London had been restricted.[10]

Munro Ferguson was determined to maintain—and if possible restore—the authority of his office, and his period in Australia was to be its high-water mark. When the Admiralty dismissed the danger posed by the German cruiser *Emden* to the convoy carrying New Zealand troops to join the first AIF, he cabled New Zealand advising caution, and the British government endorsed his action. More officially, he reported directly not only to the King but also the British government. His voluminous

The King's representative in Australia:
Sir Ronald Munro Ferguson.
(National Library of Australia).

correspondence kept the Colonial Office informed in detail on Australian political, military and economic matters. His comments reveal the prejudices of a member of the British upper classes: hostility to trade unions; dislike of the White Australia policy; stress on the need for migration; and criticism of Australian government expenditure. He also forwarded secret intelligence reports—in much the same way that ambassadors reported privately to the Foreign Office. 'Combined, these functions made Munro Ferguson one of the most important and influential figures in the Anglo-Australian relationship during the war.'[11]

Moreover, as a British official he saw the world through British eyes. For example, he commented that the rush of Australians to enlist was 'highly creditable to the patriotism of the country';[12] for to Munro Ferguson 'patriotism' meant support for Britain and the Empire. More significantly, when Britain decided that the alliance with Japan was worth the price of Japanese expansion in the Pacific, the Colonial Secretary sent Munro Ferguson a cable 'for your eye only, and under no circumstances ... to be seen by anyone else', asking him to sound out Australian ministers and leaders of opinion. One historian thinks that in doing so Munro Ferguson 'irrevocably weakened' Australia's position.[13] Whether this was so or not, it is clear that the governor-general was serving British, not Australian, interests, as he was when he discussed the possibility of ceding all the New Hebrides to France. Even more seriously, in 1917, he refused to keep secret from the Colonial Office Hughes' attempt to get additional ships from America to transport Australian grain—thereby leaving Australia open to an equivalent reduction in British tonnage.[14]

He was insistent on the powers and prerogatives of his office. When Hughes as prime minister was in England in 1916, the governor-general pointed out to Cabinet the need to inform him of its decisions before the newspapers. Pearce, Minister for Defence and acting prime minister, was obliged to apologise, but was reluctant to grant the governor-general's request for reports on current events while he was in Sydney. The result was an acerbic statement of obligations, and a meeting concerning constitutional practice. For Munro Ferguson regarded his position as that of a constitutional monarch, with

> ... the right to advise, encourage or warn his minister on policy matters, even when such matters were but tenuously linked to ... 'Imperial interests'. It was a role which no governor-general since Northcote [1904–8] had attempted to assert and few of his successors imitated.[15]

It was also a role which more independently-minded Australians would be loath to grant him. Pearce ignored the governor-general when he could: Hughes—though an ally in waging the war to the utmost—was likely to undermine his power when he had the chance.

Nevertheless, Australian federal ministers sometimes found the governor-general a useful ally. He had noted the precarious nature of the infant federation, and firmly supported the rights of the federal government against the States. He insisted that he, not the State governors, should be the channel for information, and suspected that the Colonial Office was careless about this because in the past it had dealt with the States, and old habits died hard. There is a mass of papers in his files dealing with the subject, including an appeal in July 1915 to Hughes, then Attorney-General. The Colonial Office did indeed try to avoid being involved, though one member noted 'NSW's methods of carrying on war against the Commonwealth'.[16] Colonial Office neutrality was remiss but perhaps wise, for a major feud developed between Munro Ferguson and Sir Gerald Strickland, the governor of New South Wales, over precedence, control of the channels of information, and the occupation of Government House in Sydney. It was not helped by personal animosity, Munro Ferguson's wife apparently continually describing Strickland as 'the Dago'.[17]

Above all, Munro Ferguson was deeply concerned with the Australian war effort. He travelled round the country, attended ceremonial parades, visited camps and hospitals, and corresponded regularly with Pearce, Hughes, Birdwood and others. He was consulted on detail, such as the attempt to prevent Legge assuming command of the 1st Australian Division after Bridges' death. He was much influenced by his contacts, especially Birdwood, who made it a point to write him fulsome letters, and as a result prejudiced him in favour of White against Monash. He thus became the bulwark of the pro-British imperial establishment of the AIF. Finally, he became increasingly concerned by the Australian commitment to the war, giving active support to recruiting, being closely involved with Hughes in his conscription struggles, and afterwards bemoaning the loss of the referenda.[18]

Within eighteen months Munro Ferguson, helped by the war, had 'revived the influence of the governor-general' and 'established himself as a man of significance ... in Australian affairs', making him 'the most successful and active governor-general since federation'.[19] Ironically, the fate of his view of Anglo-Australian relations was sealed by the independently-minded man he regarded for long as his ally, William Morris Hughes.

## FISHER AND HUGHES

Hughes became prime minister on 27 October 1915, replacing the Scottish-born Andrew Fisher. The latter was a moderate, who accepted Australian involvement in the war but would not throw himself behind recruiting campaigns, and tried to take a middle position between the socialist left of the party on one side and those on the other who, like Hughes, thought the war overrode everything else. Munro Ferguson criticised Fisher,[20] but the latter's moderation appears similar to that of Asquith in England, and he shared a similar fate—to be overthrown by a fire-eating Welshman.

During 1915 a struggle developed within the Australian Cabinet, with talk of Fisher's 'ill health' and nervous tension. Fitzhardinge has suggested that the first signs of what today is called Alzheimer's disease had become apparent, but the truth seems to be that Fisher was wilting under stress and ambitious subordinates. As early as April 1915 Munro Ferguson reported to the Colonial Secretary that Fisher had vehemently denied a report 'which may have received encouragement in Ministerial quarters' that he wished to take the place of Reid as High Commissioner in London.[21]

Fisher was too much of an old-fashioned independent socialist. Writing to Pearce in August and September 1916 he thought the British conduct of the war incompetent ('If there is a way to go wrong it is seldom left untrodden') and dominated by the military. He appears more genuinely concerned for the personal well-being of the Australian soldiers— including prisoners and wounded, as well as allocation of leave—than Hughes. To this end he kept in close touch with Birdwood. He also made social comments that were completely missing in the responses of Hughes, who had abandoned his labour principles to be the 'great wartime leader'. Fisher, discussing stress, considered he had been right to give up the prime ministership, but wistfully thought of Australia and wished he could help the British Labour party in the conference it was then running.[22]

Despite Munro Ferguson's early distrust, Hughes won the governor-general's support by his fiery attitude to the war. Munro Ferguson described him as 'very small and nervous, very Welsh, able and determined'. He went on to liken him to Lloyd George, but he thought Hughes' judgement better. He wrote to Stamfordham, 'I put my Welshman a bit above yours.' Munro Ferguson found Hughes amusing, even intriguing, but also irritating. Certain elements of the larrikin in Hughes seemed to appeal to the Scottish laird, who often referred to him as 'my little Prime Minister'.[23]

## HUGHES IN BRITAIN, MARCH–JULY 1916

It was almost inevitable that Hughes would take up the earlier British invitation to visit the United Kingdom. Australian, and Hughes', prestige was also at stake. Sir Robert Borden of Canada had already visited Britain in 1915, and W. F. Massey of New Zealand was considering doing so. Moreover military, diplomatic, and economic reasons were at work.

Hughes had projected himself in Australia as a 'win-the-war' politician, who unlike others in the federal parliament was an effective wartime leader, capable of procuring victory and totally devoted to the imperial cause. He belonged to the combative type of politician who operates by waging campaigns against 'enemies'—'a constituency brawler'.[24] In the past, as trade union organiser and then Labor politician, his foes had been capitalists: now they were Germans. Hughes outdid the Kaiser in accepting war as the arbiter of nations, and passionately supported the imperial war effort. It was a popular stance to adopt at the time, and a closer connection in the public mind between him, Britain and the British government would help his own position against his Australian critics.[25]

After Gallipoli, he could hardly rest easy while the British government was noticeably failing to win the war, and causing heavy Australian casualties as well.

Moreover, he had been alarmed by the governor-general's hints at Japanese expansion in the Pacific, and was concerned about Australia's economic problems. Hughes was therefore in Britain for many different reasons in 1916: to achieve all his aims, he needed to visit the centre of Empire, be consulted, and be seen to be consulted.[26]

## TRADE PROBLEMS, 1914–1916

Hughes had attended the 1907 Merchant Shipping Conference in London, where he first met leading British politicians, and where his interest in defence was aroused and his support for economic reform and the White Australia policy increased.[27] When war broke out in 1914 British officials had suggested that Australia accept the 'business as usual' policy, yet prohibited trade with enemy countries and proclaimed a list of contraband items. They had, however, given some Australian products, such as copper for cartridges, preference on the British market. All this had been accepted in Australia and doubtful cases were submitted to the Colonial Secretary. Australia was part of the British Empire, and the British assumed their right to manage her trade.[28]

This 'neo-mercantilism' was supported by Hughes, who had fairly simple notions of trade between countries, and strongly advocated what later became known as 'total war'. Imagining a German conspiracy to control Australian trade, Hughes demanded that all German investment in the country be removed and launched a full-scale attack on German owned or part-owned firms in Australia—and Britain. He was backed in Britain by Northcliffe and his business allies and in Australia by the governor-general: not surprisingly, since the result suited British interests.[29]

Of more immediate interest to Australia, however, was the future of her main exports: wool, meat and wheat, which came under British regulations to prevent them reaching Germany. The interests of Britain and Australia naturally clashed over wool, a commodity of military importance since it was in short supply for uniforms. Britain needed cheaper wool: the Anglo-Australian and Australian woolgrowers and government wished to keep wool prices high, to improve personal profits, aid Australia's balance of payments and pay for the war.

At first, the British government had prohibited all wool sales except to itself, including merino wools (nearly 70 per cent of Australia's crop and not used for military uniforms) and then without warning planned to lift its own embargo on merino wool for resale to America. When Hughes protested, Australia was allowed to export her merino wool direct to America and some other neutrals, though crossbred wool still went to Britain only. The restriction meant depressed prices, and probably favoured British consumers, but in 1916 Britain agreed to buy and transport the entire Australian wool clip, 'on terms that were largely determined by the Australian government in consultation with woolgrower representatives and the major brokers'.[30]

This was odd, since as Australia's only customer Britain should have been able to dictate the price. But the Australian government could argue that without good returns on the wool clip, Australian prosperity would be threatened, and therefore her war effort weakened.[31] So while the British government paid its own growers the average 1913–14 price plus 35 per cent, it paid the Australians that plus 55 per cent—*after* Australian manufacturers had bought their requirements at a lower price, plus brokerage and handling charges. In addition, Britain paid the money whether it had the ships to import the wool from Australia or not. The Colonial Secretary protested, but the British bureaucracy did not have the knowledge or expertise to challenge the Australians, and he was overwhelmed by Hughes—to the considerable profit of the Anglo-Australian growers. It is difficult to avoid the conclusion that 'Empire loyalism took a back seat.'[32]

A similar but less dramatic development took place in meat sales. The British Board of Trade, on the advice of the Queensland agent-general, bought the entire surplus Australian meat supply, and when local companies seemed too keen on profits, the State governments in Australia either passed Acts or used administrative fiat to reserve all meat for Britain. In the first year of the war Australian exports of beef to Britain rose by over 49 per cent, while Britain imported 97 per cent of Australia's lamb and mutton. Australia's earnings from the former rose 117.4 per cent and from the latter two 22.4 per cent.[33]

The wheat trade had had a more chequered career, from crop failure in 1914 to a bumper harvest in 1915. Unfortunately, this immediately raised the problem of shipping. In London the High Commissioner and agents-general set up the London Wheat Committee to organise transport, but much shipping had been sunk, while the urgent need for troop transport and supply pre-empted the remainder.

This situation threatened Australian trade, which faced increases in insurance and freight rates. In contrast, Canada, Argentina and the United States also had large crops and a lesser distance to transport them, which meant that shipping was tied up for shorter periods. As with wool and meat, Hughes urged Britain to buy the entire Australian wheat crop, but though both the Chancellor of the Exchequer and the Board of Agriculture were sympathetic, it was impossible to secure shipping, and in September 1915 Bonar Law as Colonial Secretary was forced to reject Hughes' request.[34]

## THE SHIPPING CRISIS

Hughes reverted to the old threat, warning the British that lack of shipping would seriously damage Australia's prosperity, and therefore her war effort. He appealed to the patriotism of British ship-owners, and to the British government to requisition fifty steamers. Instead, the Admiralty requisitioned fourteen *Australian* ships for the Salonika expedition. (Perhaps it remembered that Australia had requisitioned twenty-six British ships for the transport of troops in 1914.) On Hughes' furious protest they were released, but freight charges escalated while only 400,000 tons of shipping could be chartered.

There was clearly a clash of interests between Australia, New Zealand and Britain in this matter. To Australia and New Zealand,[35] exports were essential to their financial viability, and therefore their war effort; to Britain, military transport and supply were the first necessity. Since German U-boats had closed the Mediterranean, Australasian cargoes had to come via the Cape of Good Hope, a voyage three times as long as that from Argentina. The turn-around time was therefore correspondingly higher. As the Colonial Secretary bluntly informed Hughes early in 1916, the 'absolute dearth of tonnage ... requires that it should be directed to nearest sources of food supply'. The British therefore set up the Shipping Control Committee to organise ships and allot them to essential services, which implied—although they did not admit it openly so it was not realised in Australia—transferring ships from the long Australasian route to the much shorter American one.

So while Hughes appealed for more ships, the Admiralty complained of the number of vessels the Australians had requisitioned to transport troops to Europe, and the committee in fact granted fewer. There would inevitably be a struggle between Hughes, seeking additional ships, and 'the Shipping Controller, endeavouring to withdraw from him, without undue offence, those ships which he had'.[36] On this issue Hughes was legitimately fighting for the interests of Australia and Australians, and was therefore justified, when he failed to bully or cajole more shipping from the Shipping Control Committee, in purchasing fifteen old tramp steamers on a bank overdraft. Of course the British reacted indignantly— the president of the Board of Trade talked in Cabinet of requisitioning them before the sale could go through—and Asquith had to mediate. Later, hearing that Lloyd George had made a similar remark, Hughes— then on his way back to Australia—threatened to return to London. The idea was promptly dropped! Hughes had his shipping, and founded the Commonwealth Line.[37]

## HUGHES AND THE PUSH AGAINST ASQUITH

The situation when Hughes had arrived in Britain on 7 March was ripe for intervention. Asquith's coalition government, formed the previous May, was divided and uncertain. It had not waged war effectively; it had avoided the issue of conscription; and it retained Lord Kitchener as Secretary for War despite his serious administrative failings, because his popular image made him difficult to remove.[38] Despite nineteen months of fighting on an unprecedented scale, there was still no sign of victory:

Gallipoli had proved a costly failure; German submarines were sinking a dangerous amount of British shipping with resultant food and other shortages; while the army in France was suffering unprecedented casualties without any noticeable success.

British public opinion therefore, though intensely patriotic, was volatile. The severe censorship prevented adequate news reportage: instead the nationalistic newspapers pumped out propaganda.[39] Behind acceptance of this, however, lay a deep-seated and widespread grief and depression at the losses; a growing confusion over the disaster that was developing; a collapse in recruiting and disillusionment among the workers; and a mounting demand for an effective win-the-war policy. The bloodshed, destruction and suffering were not what had been expected in the euphoric days of August 1914.

Hughes' attitudes to war and trade inevitably led him to intervene in the great struggles then raging between the strong personalities and leading groups in Britain. His experience, character and abilities made him a man peculiarly fitted to do so. His previous visit to England in 1907 had introduced him to English politics and politicians, including Lloyd George, L. S. Amery, Churchill and Asquith. His fiery temperament and strong opinions, and his ability to concentrate on one issue, with a grasp of detail that was amazing and which showed an almost photographic memory of the books and documents he had read, made him a formidable opponent.[40]

It was hardly surprising therefore that his was the most spectacular visit of any Dominion leader during the war. In just under four months he attended the Cabinet on occasions, met the rich and powerful in the British Establishment, visited the Australian troops in France, was delegate to the Paris Economic Conference (where the allies decided on measures of reconstruction and the protection of their trade and economies against the Germans after the war), and spoke to meetings up and down the land. He was lionised by the British press and people, showered with presents, gained the freedom of seven cities and several honorary doctorates, dined and travelled with the King and Queen, and had his speeches read throughout Britain.[41]

It was to be expected that Hughes would have a low opinion of Asquith, being deeply critical of the latter's policy of 'wait and see'. He thought Asquith knew little about the Dominions, 'made it a point of being a quarter of a century behind the times', and was, therefore, 'temperamentally unfitted to lead the Empire in war'.[42] Hughes was also unimpressed with the first Cabinet meeting he attended; but others before him had been driven to despair by Asquith's lax and inconsequential chairing of Cabinets.

Hughes' total devotion to the war effort put him naturally into the camp of Asquith's enemies. He thought more highly of Lloyd George and even Bonar Law, the leader of the Unionist Party, who as Colonial Secretary championed Hughes during his stay in England. Perhaps this came, as Fitzhardinge has suggested, from the attraction of opposites. As for Lloyd George, he and Hughes were two Welshmen who had similar backgrounds and temperaments, and Lloyd George had been much impressed by Hughes in 1907. On the surface they got on well in 1916. The two men were brought together by their 'Welshness', which set them apart from the English, especially Asquith, the epitome of the upper-class Englishman.[43]

But there were undercurrents at work in 1916. Lloyd George could hardly avoid seeing Hughes as a useful ally against Asquith. In a private meeting with newspaper magnates, when asked by Lloyd George what he thought of the British Cabinet, Hughes argued ironically that there were too many clever men in it, so it adhered to no coherent plan. It needed strong leadership from one man. Hardly surprisingly, Lloyd George agreed. When, however, Hughes asked him directly why he did not take control himself, he replied disingenuously that 'the time was not yet ripe'.[44] Hughes was fishing in troubled waters.

His attendance at the British Cabinet not only enhanced his power over his own colleagues back in Australia but also gave him prestige in England. Asquith was aware of the danger, and invited him to Cabinet meetings only 'at spacious intervals', lest his attendance 'crystallise into an institution'.[45] His dangerous prominence, however, was highlighted when several newspapers suggested that he should go to the economic conference that was to meet in Paris. Asquith had never really favoured the idea of an economic conference, and liked the idea of Hughes' attending it even less, but the combined pressure of the conservatives in parliament, the French, the newspapers, and in the end King George V himself, obliged him to give way. Hughes was an embarrassment, both in rousing the other Dominions to seek similar representation, and in what he might say. Bonar Law succeeded in handling the constitutional question, but completely failed to restrain Hughes.[46] It is difficult not to see in the campaign to have him at the conference yet another move to put pressure on Asquith.

Equally embarrassing must have been the whirlwind speaking tour upon which Hughes immediately embarked, accompanied by a fanfare of publicity. His 'programme of bellicose public speeches, urging a more energetic prosecution of the war against Germany and a penal approach to the German economy' after the war was 'heard by tens of thousands and read by millions in every part of Britain. They received unprecedented cover in every kind of newspaper, national and provincial', and extracts were printed as a pamphlet. At a farewell banquet Churchill, Grey, Bonar Law, Northcliffe and Rosebery vied to sing his praises, while there were demands for Hughes to return.[47]

Hughes' impact is not difficult to explain, despite the wonder of his biographer. Admittedly, he was a small wizened colonial Welshman, very deaf, often unwell, with a rasping voice. But there are a number of obvious explanations, foremost of which are his speaking style and his attitude to the war. For Hughes was a firebrand, who told the people what they wanted to hear, and blatantly appealed to their emotions. Even the printed speeches which survive suggest the power of the little man's oratory, which adopted the technique of the demagogue: simple emotional themes, in stark contrasts of black and white, constantly repeated. He inveighed against the pre-war illusions of pacifists and the evil of Germans, who he claimed had carefully prepared for a war. His speeches were therefore clarion calls to continue fighting with all resources to the bitter end. They offered 'neither argument nor exposition, but only the straight sharp jab at the emotions of the listener'. And since they were 'delivered with great emotional power and with the evangelical fervour of a "Welsh tribesman", there is little wonder that there was the atmosphere of a revivalist meeting about these gatherings'.[48]

Hughes also appealed to the interests of the business community, for he ranted against the preponderance of German industry in Britain and her Empire (which he attributed to the free trade policy) and demanded imperial protection. He called for America to join the allies and win a permanent victory—including economic victory—over the Germans. His ideas on economic war exactly matched those of the tariff-reform wing of the Unionist Party and businessmen in the Associated Chambers of Commerce—not to mention Northcliffe. Businessmen therefore supported Hughes and provided him with many of his speaking engagements,[49] which were given maximum coverage by the other centre of opposition to Asquith, the press.

Prime among the great newspaper magnates was Northcliffe, now owner of *The Times* as well as the mass-circulation *Daily Mail*, and a rabid imperialist, xenophobe and German-hater who was waging campaigns against conscientious objectors, aliens and the Asquith government. His attention had been drawn to the Australians by Murdoch's letter and the shambles on Gallipoli, which he was determined to end, but he was unsure whom to support as a new leader. He was doubtful about Lloyd George, but thought 'The war will disclose a genius.'[50] Hughes must have seemed the answer he was seeking.

Hughes' speeches appealed to Asquith's political enemies. His call for total war appeared in dramatic contrast to the casual attitude adopted by the government, especially as the tally of disaster continued. There were constant rumours of splits within the Cabinet, and Hughes' early speeches struck a chord with many people. Sir Henry Wilson at General French's headquarters in France, was 'obsessed by his desire to see Asquith replaced', and wrote to Milner on 22 March that he had read Hughes' speech 'with the greatest pleasure'. He 'comes along like a breath of fresh air'.[51] From King to the common people, Hughes struck a chord of popular need at that time.

Milner's Round Table group—Philip Kerr (co-founder, first editor of its journal and Lloyd George's private secretary); Sir Edward Carson (chairman of the Unionist War Committee) and Geoffrey Dawson (editor of *The Times*)—by March 1916 were discussing alternative possible governments at the 'Monday Night Cabal', which was occasionally joined by Sir Henry Wilson and Lloyd George. Maurice Hankey, the ubiquitous secretary to British government committees, suspected a plot.[52] But Milner had also returned to another idea of his, to link imperialism with social reform. Divisions within the British Labour movement and the death of Keir Hardie of the Independent Labour Party in September 1915 led Milner to believe that he could combat socialism *and* get the working classes to support not only the war but also a strengthened and unified British Empire. By January 1916 he had financial backing for a new 'imperial' Labour movement, the British Workers National League (BWNL), which published its manifesto ten days after Hughes arrived in the country.

Milner needed a keynote speaker and personality for his first public meeting. Hughes's sudden arrival fitted perfectly into the situation. His potential, 'as a Dominion leader, a Labour Prime Minister, a patriot, and an apostle of Empire clearly excited Milner'. So, to the disgust of the British Labour Party, Hughes in early May became the main speaker at the inaugural public meeting of the BWNL. There he repeated his old themes: and one spectator commented in his notes that 'The present Government. M [sic] Asquith's is His Majesty's Opposition to the Will of the People'.[53]

How deeply and knowingly Hughes was involved in Milner's movement is not clear. Stubbs, quoting Fitzhardinge, says that there is 'no direct evidence' for Milner being responsible for Hughes speaking at the inaugural meeting of the BWNL,[54] but this seems naive. Hughes was in close touch with Milner through several channels, including Leo Amery (whom he had also met in 1907) and Geoffrey Dawson, who regularly saw Hughes' helper, Keith Murdoch, since the latter had offices in *The Times* building. Milner wrote to Murdoch in December 1915 hinting at criticism of the government and expressing admiration for the Australians. Hughes dined with Milner on 16 March, the day before the publication of the manifesto of the BNWL, and the next day breakfasted with Lloyd George and discussed the representation of the colonies in the War Council, especially his own membership. He told the British Labour Party that 'An Empire policy will involve a change in British fiscal policy so as to secure National Safety, National Trade, and a real level of comfort for the worker and his family.' This was pure Milnerism, and the *Daily Mail* had a leading article that day on 'Labour and Mr Hughes', together with an article by Bean on 'The amazing Anzac Day landing'. Hughes later lunched with Milner.[55] It can therefore be taken for granted that Hughes was *fully* aware of Milner's activities, and was deliberately chosen by Milner as the keynote speaker for his vital inaugural meeting.

It is also quite clear that Hughes' speaking tour was fully supported by Lloyd George, who blatantly played up to his Welshness, remarking at Conway that he was

proud to think that he is a fellow-countryman of mine and that two Welshmen—I nearly said two young Welshmen (laughter)—should be working together in the same common cause, the cause for which we fought on these hills for centuries, the cause of freedom (applause).

This note was sounded again a fortnight later at the Trocadero Restaurant in London.[56]

Two great Welshmen: Hughes and Lloyd George. (National Library of Australia).

Donald Horne has claimed that 'Hughes was being used by Milner in his latest conspiracy . . . to provide background clamour to the replacement of Asquith by Lloyd George.' At the time, Bonar Law was of the same mind, informing Munro Ferguson that 'there is a great deal of discontent . . . and his outspoken views have been used as a "stick to beat the Government with" '. This view was widespread.[57]

To appoint Hughes to high office in the British government seemed the answer to the problems of many different groups and personalities. Lloyd George did not then command enough support to come into the open, and his energy was absorbed by the Ministry of Munitions. Northcliffe, angry at his failure to overthrow Asquith, decided that Hughes was the leader he had been looking for and put all his newspapers at Hughes' disposal—although Northcliffe's support was a commodity that could not be relied upon, as many men found out.[58] The fire-eating Admiral Jacky Fisher also wanted Hughes as 'war director' if not prime minister; Amery wanted to use Hughes to win back the Irish (and introduce conscription) and Churchill said that Hughes was head and shoulders above the rest. Many of the key players in British politics therefore gained from Hughes' tour. He 'reinforced the public feeling that the Asquith government must be replaced'.[59]

But Hughes himself also benefited. He gained international recognition and his speeches were cabled to Australia where they—and he—received maximum prominence. It was an effect that was fully intended, a public-relations exercise, designed to strengthen the position of Australia vis-à-vis Britain in terms of trade, and to bring Australia into the forefront of British thinking—indeed to make the British government *think* of Australia, instead of merely talking in vague generalisations about 'the Dominions'. Last but not least, it was intended to increase the status and prestige in both Britain and Australia of Hughes himself. As one commentator has remarked,

> To Hughes it mattered little if he was being used by the English media and by politicians alike for their internal political goals; he used them equally for his own purposes . . .[60]

## IMPACT AND SIGNIFICANCE OF HUGHES

The propaganda campaign putting Hughes forward as an effective potential leader of the British Empire inevitably had an impact on public opinion. Hughes himself later claimed that eighty-six members of the British parliament signed a request for him to stay in England and take a seat in the Commons and 50,000 women signed a petition to that effect. He also claimed that Northcliffe offered to put £50,000 into a trust account on his behalf if he would stay in England and join the British ministry, and that he was offered third position in the Cabinet by the government.[61]

The truth or otherwise of these claims is difficult to determine. The Northcliffe press at the time went so far as to hint that Hughes might be a fitting successor to Asquith. Murdoch was also working assiduously behind the scenes—unknown to Hughes, according to Murdoch—his only reservation being Hughes' poor health. It is not clear whether Hughes was romanticising when he spoke about 'the third position in the Cabinet', or whether the 'offer' came from Asquith or his opponents. But it is clear that only Northcliffe, Murdoch and the erratic and unreliable Admiral Fisher went overboard and supported him for the prime ministership. On his return to Australia in 1916 he told the governor-general that he could have sat with others around a table in London and given his opinion, but that was all,[62] which does not sound like the offer of a major position.

Presumably the serious suggestion was for Lloyd George to be prime minister, and Bonar Law or some other unnamed person Treasurer—leaving Hughes perhaps as Minister for War or Industry. If so, it is not surprising that he declined. Better be prime minister of Australia than third man—organising a bureaucratic department of state—in a British government under Lloyd George. Hughes was definitely not an administrator.

Hughes also lacked the breadth of vision, political subtlety and statesmanship to bring together the differing blocs of opinion in Britain. Without a power base of his own, he would have had to rely on deeply conservative forces. Moreover, the aggressive style of both Hughes and Murdoch had begun to arouse criticism. The Colonial Office noted Murdoch's actions, while Hankey called him 'a horrible scab', and even Bean admitted that his methods 'aroused some bitter hostility'—strong words indeed for that usually bland writer. Murdoch's ambition and self-praise[63] must have jarred on many English susceptibilities.

By May, Hughes was losing support. His poor health prevented him making a public appearance for nearly four weeks, and he had to cancel many engagements.[64] Perhaps this was why Northcliffe and others backed off from Hughes. He may also have been talking too much, for Hutchinson the publishers rejected the idea of a reprint of *The Case for Labor*, thinking that Hughes' vision of capitalists was superficial. By then Lloyd George was more sure of himself, even toying with the idea of forming a new party, and he and Northcliffe began to act together again. By the 27th *The Times* was talking of Lloyd George as 'the only man'. Northcliffe's brief flirtation with Hughes was over, and he had returned to his previous beau. Though the *Daily Mail* joined the panegyric of praise for Hughes as he left in June, it stressed his economic policy of removing German industry from the country, which was Northcliffe's continuing campaign. Meanwhile, Lloyd George was also coming closer to Milner's group. Thus began the movement which would overthrow Asquith and create the Lloyd George government the following December.[65] Hughes did well to return to Australia.

He had been a catalyst for the tensions and disappointments of the war and the struggle for power and influence that racked Britain's politicians and high command at the time. He came to Britain when the different groups opposing Asquith had not yet coalesced, so—for a brief moment—there was a power vacuum and Hughes was convenient to use. But that the contending parties should seriously consider him as an alternative prime minister is doubtful: they would always prefer a British politician to a colonial one.[66]

Nor is it at all certain that Hughes would have made a good British wartime leader. Early in 1916 he could express his views with a directness and freedom from responsibility which was impossible for any British politician. Once he was in power, however, he would have had to replace oratory with policies.[67] But the situation in Britain—especially concerning Ireland—was complex and enormously difficult, and Hughes had little talent for guiding a team in a situation where one man alone could not run the multiplicity of affairs. It is also doubtful how successful he would have been with the generals, if his power base in Britain had been no more secure than that of Lloyd George, while his military thinking was no clearer.[68] How capable he would therefore have been of solving the problems thrown up by the first world war is doubtful. Fitzhardinge believes that he was already beginning to question the assumptions of the Westerners, those who insisted that Germany could be defeated only on the Western Front in France, and opposed attempts to attack the Central Powers from Italy or in the Middle East. But there is little evidence of Hughes' thinking about strategy before 1918, and what there is, shows him to be quite conventional. As for grand strategy, the implications of the war passed Hughes by: for instance, he did not consider the position of Russia in the Middle East if the Gallipoli campaign had been successful.[69]

From an Australian point of view, Hughes was probably mistaken in taking such a prominent part in putting pressure on Asquith. The South African Jan Smuts later wrote to his wife that he did not wish to make the same blunder as Hughes; and Borden of Canada was 'rather shy after the Hughes campaign'.[70] More subtle diplomacy may have won Australia more favours, though it seems doubtful.

More important than his part in the cabal against Asquith was his struggle to improve Australia's trading position, which despite problems was largely successful. In addition, Hughes and his government had begun to realise that although their aim in the war was the same, British and Australian interests did not necessarily coincide, nor could British politicians and officials be trusted to see the world from the Australian viewpoint. There therefore needed to be change in imperial relations, or as Hughes put it to Pearce, 'the present system: under which the parliament of Great Britain determines our destiny—we having no voice, cannot, ought not to, continue'. Hughes did not apparently discuss this in Britain in 1916, and the Australian Cabinet came to no conclusions.[71] The issue would arise again in 1917, but Hughes was to be preoccupied by other battles in Australia then, so this next stage in the development of Anglo-Australian relations had to wait.

## KEITH MURDOCH

The pervasiveness of propaganda during World War I suited Hughes' temperament and methods as a demagogue. He was publicity-minded, and had long been interested in the press, having contacts with the Sydney *Daily Telegraph* in the 1890s and contributing regular Sunday articles to it between 1907 and 1911, as well as writing for various trade union journals. He always had a tendency to appeal beyond the party machines to the people—hence his statement on the outbreak of war.[72]

In the same way, he had three books on himself published in London in 1916. One, *The Day and After*, was a collection of his speeches with an introduction by Lloyd George, while the title of another, *From Boundary Rider to Prime Minister*, reflects both the hero-worshipping aims of its author and the posturing of Hughes himself.[73] Hughes then was well aware of the power of the press, was accustomed to use it to influence public opinion, and was careful to maintain friendly relations with editors and newspaper owners. His biographer writes of his prompt meetings with a large number of newspaper owners and editors immediately on his arrival in England.[74]

It was entirely in keeping with this approach that Hughes ignored his official liaison officer in London, the High Commissioner Andrew Fisher, and turned instead to Keith Murdoch. The latter, who became what today would be called Hughes' press agent, had since his Dardanelles letter gone from strength to strength and combined 'the functions of correspondent for the Sydney *Sun* and Melbourne *Herald* with that of unofficial spokesman and representative for Australia in general and Hughes in particular'.[75]

Murdoch was useful to Hughes, since he was not an official but a newspaperman who had contacts with British MPs, the government itself, and powerful men in the press, in particular Northcliffe. Murdoch 'became a constant intermediary between Hughes and Lloyd George, especially when they wished to bypass the Colonial Office.'[76] But he was a dangerous man for Hughes to employ, for he was not his servant but a free agent, who had wholeheartedly joined the group in London which demanded a 'strong' policy towards the war and sought to replace Asquith, as he in effect admitted to the Dardanelles Commission and boasted of later to Birdwood.

Birdwood and Murdoch both sought to manipulate each other. Murdoch indulged in a long correspondence with Birdwood, seeking to curry favour, and assuring him that he 'would never touch any AIF matter even at the request of the Government without telling you all about it'[77]— this despite the fact that he plotted to replace Birdwood also, as we shall see. He supported the death penalty for Australian soldiers, and the following year was deeply involved in attempting to get the troops to vote 'yes' in the conscription campaigns.

Birdwood on the other hand in May 1917 protested to Murdoch his

A famous photograph: Murdoch's official farewell when he left London to take up his
position as editor of the Melbourne *Herald*. Keith Murdoch, holding his farewell
presentation golf clubs, is on Lord Northcliffe's right, and Hughes is on his left.
(D. Zwar, *In Search of Keith Murdoch*, n.d.: 60.)

deep loyalty to the AIF. 'My one and only wish was to remain with it
to the end, irrespective of any possible advancement elsewhere.' And on
4 November he gave him a detailed account of his struggle with GHQ
to get all Australian divisions together. This seems an indiscreet letter for
a corps commander to write to a notorious journalist about his
commander-in-chief, but it was equalled by his missive to Hughes on
23 December 1917 in which he criticised Haig and said that he was all
right as commander-in-chief as long as he was surrounded by men with
brains, so that what he conspicuously lacked could be provided.[78]

Munro Ferguson broke into this cosy correspondence when he wrote to Birdwood and sarcastically referred to 'your friend Keith Murdoch', who had written an extraordinarily indiscreet article for the *Melbourne Herald* on the conduct of the war, command in the AIF and imperial relations. He added that he was 'one of the most ambitious amongst the Pressmen who set themselves up to rule over us'. This immediately elicited a reply from Birdwood which was critical of Murdoch's attack on the Colonial Office. Birdwood knew where his interests lay. Murdoch's request, therefore, to be able to visit France when the great German attacks were in process early in 1918, was stalled.[79]

Murdoch's main connection, however, was with Northcliffe, for he had an office in *The Times* building, and was on close terms with Geoffrey Dawson, the editor. His association with Northcliffe is an important aspect of Anglo-Australian relations in general during that war. He met him frequently on business, and the latter agreed to a daily column of Australian news in the *Mail* and a good space in *The Times*.[80] This link between Hughes and Murdoch, and their use of the press, was not unusual, and parallels the collusion in Britain between Churchill and Northcliffe which had led to Colonel Repington's article in *The Times* which had triggered the 'shell scandal', the Canadian prime minister's use of Max Aitken as unofficial Canadian go-between with the British government and Establishment, and Lloyd George's own efforts. The King's secretary, Lord Stamfordham, wrote of Lloyd George that 'the manner in which he uses the press is, to say the least of it, regrettable'.[81]

## THE FIRST ANZAC DAY, 1916

Typical of this PR mentality was the sedulous creation of the Anzac myth in both England and Australia for political and military purposes. As early as January 1916 Reid, no longer High Commissioner, stood for the British parliament as 'the first member for ANZAC', while Balfour at a meeting of the Empire Parliamentary Association to greet his successor, Fisher, praised the Anzacs and said that even those who knew the Western Front thought there had never been greater fighting.[82]

Government propagandists sought to create a heroic image of Gallipoli, helped by the fact that its proximity to the site of Troy suggested comparison with classical history. By their rhetoric they 'distanced and falsified the sordid reality of trench warfare, the inept staff-work and poor leadership, and the wastage of men and material'.[83] Bean's *Anzac Book* was redolent of this approach, as we have seen. It was not the worst example, however: John Masefield the poet, a member of the British propaganda team of authors operating from Wellington House, produced a book which 'chronicled the campaign like a medieval romance', with extracts from the 'Song of Roland' before each section.[84]

The first Anzac Day, London, 1916: the Anzacs march to Westminster Abbey.    (*Illustrated London News*, 29 April 1916).

The anniversary of the landing on Gallipoli on 25 April was therefore
too good an opportunity to miss, and great celebrations were prepared.
Before the day came, George V sent a royal message:

> Tell my people of Australia and New Zealand that to-day I am joining with them
> in their solemn tribute to the memory of their heroes who died in Gallipoli.
> They gave their lives for a supreme cause in gallant comradeship . . .[85]

On the day itself in London about a thousand Australians and 700 New
Zealanders, in five trainloads, arrived at Waterloo station, marched down
the Strand, through Trafalgar Square, along Whitehall to a service in
Westminster Abbey, attended by Kitchener and the King and Queen.
Thereafter, the Australians marched past Buckingham Palace to the Hotel
Cecil, where Hughes deliberately played on the emotions of his hearers
in his oratory. He forecast a new era in the history of Australia and New
Zealand, and praised the troops extravagantly: 'On the shining wings of
your valour we were lifted up to heights we had never seen: you taught
us truths we never knew.' The moral he drew was that his hearers should
do nothing 'unworthy' of such men and continue the struggle. Fisher
then spoke briefly, and Birdwood told anecdotes. McKernan comments
that 'No other body of troops, British, Colonial or Allied, was to be so
honoured during the war.'[86]

To the disinterested observer today, all this reeks of propaganda. The
inspiration for the ceremony would seem to have been Australian. The
New Zealanders were fewer in number, and did not march past Buckingham Palace but simply returned to their base, where they had held a service
in the 900-year-old village church that Easter Sunday.[87] The official march
in London, however, suited all other parties very well. For British government and propagandists it conveniently masked the fact that Gallipoli
was a disaster. For Hughes, it promoted his image as the leader of magnificent fighting men. For Milner, who attended the service, it advanced the
cause of Empire. Charlton is therefore probably right when he calls it
'an astute and cynical propaganda exercise'.[88]

Of course, Australians had watched events on Gallipoli with keen
interest: they had been thrilled by Ashmead-Bartlett's despatch, as well
as relieved that their men had done well. Those whose relatives were
involved naturally had been absorbed by the campaign, but it also had
a great emotional impact as news, and was therefore inevitably seized
upon by the recruiting officers, beginning with the chairman of Queensland's State Recruiting Committee. The Labor premier, T. J. Ryan, then
wrote to other State premiers and—bypassing the governor-general—
directly to London for the message from the King. Thereafter, whipped
up by the press, a public movement of support began to take off. Meanwhile, in Victoria, an 'Anzac week' was being prepared by churchmen,
moved by the fact that Anzac Day in 1916 was on Easter Tuesday.[89]

All this seems to have taken the federal government, then in Melbourne,
by surprise. As late as 15 April Pearce wrote to Fisher of 'informal' celebrations, and that neither the federal nor Victorian governments would

take official action, but wait till the war was over to see which event was 'more worthy of remembering'.[90] This would not satisfy the recruiting officers, the jingoes, the churchmen, the press—or Hughes in England. The governor and government of New South Wales took up the idea, and placed it under the theatrical entrepreneur, J. C. Williamson. They approached the Colonial Office, with the result that the Colonial Secretary cabled Munro Ferguson, asking what other celebrations were being held in Australia. The governor-general felt humiliated: this was the first he had heard of the affair, which had by then been discussed—without his knowledge—between Queensland, New South Wales, the Colonial Office and the royal household. When he replied giving details, therefore, he played down the significance of the day, stressing remembrance services.[91] In return he received the King's official message to 'my people of Australia'. It is clear from the sequence of events that the pressure came from the political leaders and 'recruiters' in both Britain and Australia.[92]

There followed a full-scale row between Munro Ferguson and Governor Strickland in NSW, for, to add insult to injury, the latter had changed the wording of the royal message on his own authority. Munro Ferguson was even more aggrieved to discover that the Colonial Office, in its desire to ensure the message got through, had cabled it also direct to each State governor. This was a direct threat to Munro Ferguson's monopoly of communication with Britain, and he called on the federal government for support, blaming the previous Colonial Secretary, Lord Chelmsford, and the Colonial Office.

Nevertheless, New South Wales had stolen the march, and when Anzac Day came round, both Munro Ferguson *and* the governor of Victoria felt obliged to attend the celebrations in Sydney. The governor-general's mortification comes through in the series of cables and letters he sent about the occasion, and which describe the shambles that developed.

He and his wife were jostled in the large crowd that had gathered. The parade of soldiers was preceded by a car with wounded soldiers in it collecting money in their caps—the blame for which 'Mr. Black, following the tradition of the Garden of Eden, attributes . . . on women'. There were two saluting stands. Premier Holman and Strickland took the salute on the first, and the Munro Ferguson on the second. Writing to Bonar Law, Britain's Colonial Secretary, Munro Ferguson added that he would never attend another march unless the army organised it and he thought that Holman was 'bossing the Returned Soldiers Association for political purposes', distributing voluntary funds and promising land grants after the war. He avoided a luncheon laid on by the Lord Mayor of Sydney at midday, informing Bonar Law, that the mayor was 'a dispensed with lawyer', who had been 'formally "chucked out" from the house of ill-fame kept by his wife, now "Lady Mayoress" '. But Munro Ferguson therefore felt that he *had* to attend a concert in the evening—and at it was promptly presented to the Lord Mayor and his wife! He indignantly told his secretary that in future any invitation he received had to have lists of the people who were to be presented to him attached to it.[93]

More importantly, he demanded that the Colonial Secretary support his status by routing all communications through him. After all, the royal message in Hobart had been savagely pruned and then announced as being 'to the people of Tasmania', while Strickland appealed to the Colonial Office to support his claims against Munro Ferguson, and Premier Holman proffered advice on military and diplomatic matters. Hardly surprisingly, Walter Long, the Colonial Secretary, decided that they had to support the governor-general and the federal government.[94]

The whole incident is vital to the theme of this book. Perhaps the Australian 'nation' was 'born' after Anzac, not in the mythic sense, but because for the first time people in the separate States were called on to think of 'Australian' soldiers rather than New South Welshmen or Victorians. Such an attitude was still not widely accepted, as can be seen from the separate State reactions to the first Anzac Day. It was only when the Japanese drove southwards in World War II that 'Australia' came into danger, and united thinking became more common. In the meantime, the Colonial Office drew the appropriate moral: Bonar Law was careful to pass a request from Strickland for information on Ireland through Munro Ferguson.[95]

The reaction to the first Anzac Day also revealed the influence of the press. In Britain, its cooperation had been wholehearted.[96] *The Times* announced the forthcoming parade on three occasions before the event. On 25 April the *Daily Telegraph* had a leading article, a full descriptive column and a map of the route through London so that Londoners could find suitable vantage points. The *Daily Mail* had first announced the programme on 15 April under the heading 'A chance to cheer'. Londoners for the first time since the war began would have the opportunity to see a triumphal march of troops and support the heroes. It backed this up with a Norman Lindsay cartoon, and stories on a wounded Australian and Hughes. Thereafter there was a veritable campaign of advertisement for the great day. The paper devoted 34 column inches to Hughes' speech at the Guildhall on 18 April: 'The British race has found its soul, and I as an Australian . . . rejoice that I am privileged to live', etc. Thereafter the matter was mentioned on 20, 22, 24, 25 and 26 April, with London readers encouraged to view the procession on the 25th.

The result was a propaganda triumph. Large crowds gathered, so thick in places that the formation was broken and the men walked in groups. The following day the *Daily Telegraph* had a photograph of George V leaving the abbey cheered by troops and the *Daily Mail* devoted 44 column inches to a glowing description, with girls throwing garlands of flowers to the troops from the open tops of buses in the Strand. *The Times* thought the crowds, two-thirds of them women, were the largest in London since the King's coronation.[97]

Despite the newspaper euphoria, odd phrases slip in that hint at other reactions. The *Daily Telegraph* talked of 'a heartfelt but not always very loud tongued greeting'; and the *Daily Mail* thought that the crowd in

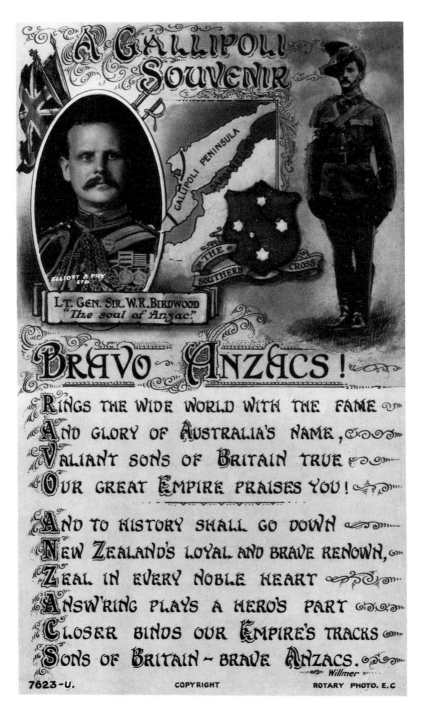

The imperial aspect of the Anzac legend: a Gallipoli postcard.
(AWM Printed Records Collection, 3DRK 6223).

the Strand was 'too utterly absorbed to make any clamour of welcome'. Perhaps the gauntness of many Anzacs reminded onlookers of the price of all this 'glory'. Although some Anzacs played up to the crowd, especially the young women, most soldiers disparaged the heroics. One West Australian wrote home that the Queen looked fatter than he had imagined, the King slightly dyspeptic and Kitchener red-faced.[98]

Meanwhile in far-off Sydney, the crowd of 60,000–100,000 people, moved by the sight of the returned Gallipoli men, many wounded, broke into the hymn 'Abide with me'. An onlooker described it as one of the most emotional moments of his life.[99] This is believable, but it could hardly have been the mood the recruiting sergeants or Hughes looked for. There was much grief in Australia in 1916. The regulations prohibiting the use of the word 'Anzac', meant to apply to firms, elicited a number of applications for exemption from ordinary people; heartbroken women whose sons had died at Lone Pine or husbands had fought on Gallipoli and were then in France, and who had named their house 'Anzac' in memory of them. The following year Munro Ferguson reported that the Anzac Day celebrations had a more serious character than any he had seen, and every church in Australia was full to overflowing.[100]

The reality: trench at Lone Pine, 8 August 1915. (AWM Official Photo No. A4029).

Official Australia had another attitude to and use for Anzac Day, and this continued in the years ahead, but it was built upon a deeper bedrock of emotional support for the day, support which Munro Ferguson had underestimated. Press propaganda, government attitudes and the continuing losses of Australian troops all strengthened this support, but the official celebrations subtly changed the message, from an emotion which could well have fuelled an anti-war movement or Australian separatism from the Empire, to one that acquiesced in glorification of the soldiers, if not the war itself, and the imperial connection. At the same time it could be 'used to redeem the British military reputation'.[101]

## HUGHES AND THE AIF

Hughes' stress on 'Anzac', and his stance as the leader of magnificent fighting men whose country had a special relationship with Britain, inevitably led him to visit Australian troops in France, and concern himself with the AIF. It was, however, an emotional, not an intellectual, response. He took every opportunity to speak to the men—in the streets, at his hotel, in camps and hospitals—was moved by what he saw, and demanded, and got, more rest for them in the immediate future. But he did not involve himself in the tactics of the fighting—except to try to have a quota of sixteen machine guns per battalion fixed for the AIF—and he did not go on to consider the adequacy of the British command and strategy, or the *use* to which the British put the Australian soldiers. Instead, in 1916 he assured Haig of his confidence and support.[102]

It was perhaps a little early for a different response. When Hughes arrived in Britain the bulk of the AIF was still being withdrawn from Egypt and redeployed in France. His farewell dinner was reported in the British press on 1 July 1916—the day the great British push on the Somme began. It was to take the disaster on that day, and the continued bloodletting as the battle dragged on, to force Hughes, like Lloyd George, to turn his mind to military techniques and strategy.

Instead, Hughes turned his attention to the administrative structure of the force and its place in Britain's armies. The AIF had doubled in size that January and February to five infantry divisions, and a rumour circulated that the Anzacs would be split up among British divisions. Hughes, backed by Pearce, saw Sir William Robertson, the new CIGS, at the War Office and demanded that Australians fight together and be commanded by Birdwood. Haig protested to Robertson that he had commanded Australians during the Boer War, admired them, and knew the value of *esprit de corps*. It had never crossed his mind to split them among other units of the British army.

Hughes, reassured, went further to support the idea of combining the Australian and New Zealand divisions into one Anzac 'Army'. The War Office however thought that was premature, and instead created two corps, one under Godley, the other under Birdwood, though it gave the latter administrative control of all Australians. Hughes took the argument to Haig in June. Haig reluctantly agreed that Birdwood should retain the administrative control of all Australians—though he thought the task too great—but argued that with five divisions the Anzacs were too few for an army but too numerous for a corps. He promised, however, to bring all Australians together later, if it were feasible. With this Hughes had to be content.[103]

# CHAPTER FOUR

# The Crucible of War: The AIF on the Western Front, 1916–1917

'The paths of glory lead but to the grave.'
THOMAS GRAY,
*'Elegy Written in a Country Churchyard'*

## FROM THE MIDDLE EAST TO FRANCE

Events in 1916–17 put to the test once again both Anzac illusions: that the Australian soldiers were recognised by the British as superior troops; and that as a result Australians enjoyed a special relationship with the British. At the time of their evacuation from Gallipoli a British private in the Medical Corps worried about the cleanliness and behaviour of the more lightly wounded Australians, while Guy Dawnay thought they had been 'so petted by the Press that ... they think themselves much finer fellows than they really are. They *are* fine fellows—but not fine soldiers'. They needed discipline and training before they would become the latter.[1]

Dawnay was obviously expressing the opinion current in British headquarters in Egypt, where by early 1916 approximately 100,000 Anzacs had been gathered. General Sir Archibald Murray, Commander-in-Chief in the Middle East, feared a return to the problems before Gallipoli. He described them as 'the most backward in training and discipline', and sent a letter damning them to the CIGS, General Sir William Robertson. Although noting their 'magnificent bravery', physique and fighting qualities, he was scathing about their lack of discipline and their 'enormous conceit in themselves', adding that out of 8858 cases of venereal disease in Egypt, 5924 were Australian. He also blamed the press:

> It has been so long the custom in the newspapers to laud the Australians as the finest soldiers in existence that it is very difficult now to convince them that they know very little of warfare.

The New Zealanders were much better.

This provoked anguished cries from the Australian corps commanders, Godley and Birdwood. The latter blamed ineffective Australian officers and bemoaned the fact that he could not get British ones because of the vast expansion of the British Army. Birdwood pointed to excellent Australian battle discipline, as seen in their absolute silence during the landing and withdrawal, and hoped that Murray would drop the comparison between the Australians and the New Zealanders. Meanwhile, he made frantic efforts to increase discipline, warning the soldiers they might not be accepted for France.[2]

The demand for men on the Western Front, however, was too high for the War Office to ignore 'magnificent fighting men'—even with poor discipline. By then, with survivors from the peninsula and reinforcements from Australia, there were four Australian divisions, and a fifth planned.[3] The first and second were grouped with the New Zealand division into I Anzac Corps under Birdwood and sent to France. A second corps under Godley was scheduled to go later.

So on 19 March, twelve days after Hughes arrived in England, the first troopship carrying the AIF docked in Marseilles. They were followed by II Anzac Corps in April–May. Their arrival in France showed how Murray's warnings had influenced British army authorities. They took stringent precautions: most men were kept on their ships till their transport was ready; no leave was given; and the troops were promptly entrained, usually at night, for northern France. It was all unnecessary. France was the land of dreams for most Australians. They contrasted its green fields with the sands of Egypt, were delighted to be there, impressed by European civilisation and on their best behaviour. A British officer remarked to Bean that the Australians had caused less trouble in Marseilles than any divisions he had seen.[4]


## THE WESTERN FRONT

Nevertheless, the British command at that time regarded the Anzacs as good fighting material but slipshod in their methods, a judgement that was soon confirmed. Placed in a quieter part of the line, several hundred were killed after carelessly revealing themselves and their battalion headquarters to enemy spotters. In addition, failure to obey orders led to the loss of two new secret mortars to the Germans.[5]

Australian weaknesses, however, were soon overshadowed by the bungling of the British command, under whom, as distinct from Gallipoli, Birdwood was now firmly placed. The AIF joined a British army in France in 1916 which suffered from serious defects. Its senior officers, due to the class from which they were drawn, as well as their education, experience and age, were not at home with the new technology. Moreover, the new 'Divisions' had not yet developed into teams of all arms, so the infantry, artillery and cavalry regarded themselves as separate, and there were no schools for developing combined tactical doctrine. Divisional and higher commanders therefore felt free to interpret the generalisations of the manuals as they wished, without help

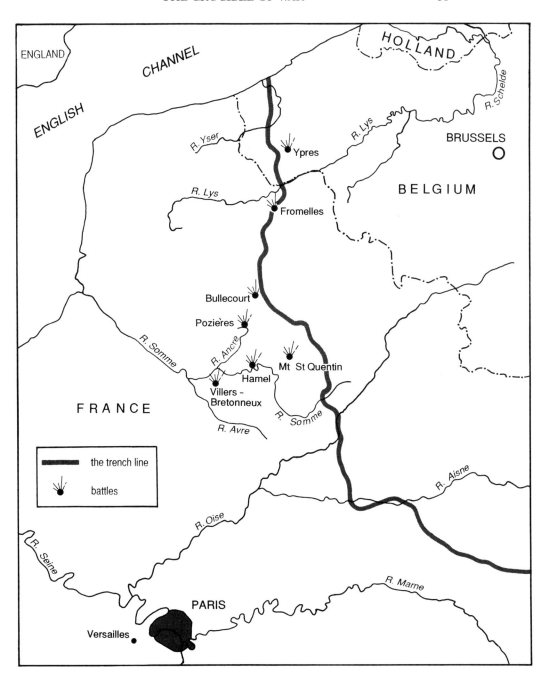

Map 3   The Western Front, 1916–18.

from Haig's GHQ until later in the war, provided they showed an aggressive spirit.[6]

The result was a chain of bloody disasters, which affected both Australian relations with the British high command and that high command's opinion of the Australians. The first occurred at Fromelles, which was notable for the crass incompetence of the planning by General Sir R. Haking, Commander of the British XI Corps, with confusion of aims, multiple postponements, and inadequate preparations. The attack was finally made in evening light, so the troops suffered heavily from German shellfire, while the British artillery was grossly inadequate. The Australians fought their way into the German line, and then back again, and in doing so lost 5533 men—68 per cent of the toll for nine months on Gallipoli.

The result was only to be expected: numbing grief, bitterness, and a deep disillusionment. In the past they had criticised the New Army, but consoled themselves with the thought that they would meet the cream of the British forces in France. That idea was shattered for ever at Fromelles. The Anzacs criticised the British 61st Division on their right for letting them down, and—more justifiably—Haking's command. Haking himself had 'nothing but admiration' for the Australians, and their 'fine fighting spirit', but his feelings were not reciprocated. H. E. ('Pompey') Elliott, commander of the 15th Australian Brigade, in a scathing account in 1920 told how he had shown one of the British staff majors his orders and persuaded him to go with him to no man's land. The British officer remarked that the attack would end in 'a bloody holocaust'.[7]

Bean was traumatised by what he saw the next day. His anger was only increased by the official British communiqué, which described the action as 'some important raids' and boasted of 140 German prisoners. He bitterly asked in his diary, 'What is the good of deliberate lying like that?' In his later history he added that the truth soon came out in Australia 'and went far to shake the confidence of part of the public in British official statements'. This seems unlikely. The censorship in Australia meant that British propaganda was probably accepted by most Australians in 1916, and few knew what had happened at Fromelles.

It must also be accepted, however—which Bean tried to hide—that apart from the bravery of individual infantrymen, the AIF—despite the mythology—did not stand out from ordinary British units at Fromelles. Australian staff work at Fromelles was also poor. The commander of 5th Division, General J. W. McCay, was so unpopular that his headquarters staff were unwilling to work for him, and there was another attempt to upgrade Australian middle commanders. McCay and H. Cox were re-placed. Whether their replacements would be any better remained to be seen.[8]

There followed even worse slaughter. Haig, thwarted in his early attack on the Somme, handed the task of capturing Pozières to his most bustling general, Sir Hubert Gough, who commanded the Reserve (Fifth) Army, and, after four failures, gave him the Australians. Gough was so keen

Pozières.
(*Top*) The results of the bombardment: the village as it was some months after the battle.
(*Below*) Carrying party of the 7th Brigade passing 'Gibraltar', a well-known headquarters dugout. No trace remained of the house which once stood here, but the cellar stairway had been thus fortified and its concrete covering is indicated by the slope to the right of the entrance. From the cellar some twenty steps led down to a still deeper chamber excavated by the Germans.
(AWM Official Photo Nos. E532, EZ98).

to use them that he decided not to wait for the Anzac Corps headquarters to arrive, but put the troops straight into the battle, a decision
described by General Walker—who was British—as 'the very worst
exhibition of Army command that occurred in the whole campaign'. If
by that he meant during 1916, the comment is just: Gough was to do worse,
however, in 1917.

At Pozières there was an argument with Gough to persuade him to
postpone the attack sufficiently to allow time for planning to occur.
Walker was supported by Birdwood and White, and managed to win over
one of Gough's staff officers to agree. This, together with the new tactic
of closely following the artillery barrage, enabled the Australians to win
a brilliant success on 23 July. It proved their undoing, however, since it
only encouraged Gough to demand more, and left them in a narrow
salient where they suffered some of the heaviest and most systematic
bombardments of the war, bombardments which have been compared
with those at Verdun. Seventy years later one old soldier was still
shuddering at them.[9]

Gough then persuaded Legge, then commanding 2nd Division, to try
to seize the remainder of the crest. A man of 'brash cockiness and flights
of fancy', Legge, like Gough, pushed the men under him, made
inadequate preparations, and ignored firepower. His troops suffered the
consequences. Even Haig, who always admired an aggressive spirit,
intervened. According to his diary, 'the Australians had at the last moment
said they would attack . . . without artillery support and that they did
not believe machine-gun fire could do them much harm'. White rejected
the allegations, but there seems to have been some truth in them. Within
six weeks the AIF had suffered 23,000 casualties—including 6741 dead—
and Bean commented later that the area was 'more densely sown with
Australian sacrifice than any other place on earth'.[10]

The author of a book on the battle has suggested that 'If Australians
wish to trace their modern suspicion and resentment of the British to a
date and place, July–August 1916 and the ruined village of Pozières are
useful points of departure.'[11] This is doubtful. Disillusionment had begun
on Gallipoli, been temporarily in abeyance in the opening weeks in
France, but revived after Fromelles.

Anger, however, certainly existed. Bean, usually most restrained, wrote
that 'some intelligent men' were convinced they were being sacrificed, and
that the Australian troops hated repeated attacks on narrow fronts, blamed
Gough, and disliked serving under him. Letters from the Australian
soldiers became more forthright. One wrote that his friends had been
'murdered' by the 'incompetence, callousness and personal vanity of those
high in authority'; another wrote, 'For Christ's sake, write a book on the
life of an infantryman . . . and by doing so you will quickly prevent these
shocking tragedies.'[12] After the war, Generals White and Gellibrand
criticised Bean's draft chapter of the official history on Pozières for
blaming Legge. 'Every senior officer in the Corps knew (ask any of them)
of Gough's constant insistence upon haste.' Legge had tried to fall in with

Gough's wishes, whereas, if he and his staff had been more experienced, he would have held out.[13]

Highly placed criticism was rare, however. White simply made a few comments in private to Bean, but that was all. The anger of the ordinary soldiers on the other hand was usually turned against their own immediate commanders. Birdwood's frequent assumption in speeches to the men that they had a keen desire to be back in action simply disgusted them. The numbed men realised by then that their chances of survival were virtually nil, and they became quiet and subdued, wanting only to be left alone.

## BULLECOURT, 1917

During the bitter winter of 1916–17 the Germans withdrew to their Hindenburg Line. Persuaded against his better judgement to cooperate with the French general Nivelle, whom Lloyd George had adopted as the man to win the war, Haig without any great enthusiasm began the battle of Arras in March 1917. The Australians, still under Gough and at the right of his command, were committed to attack in a re-entrant alongside the village of Bullecourt.[14] The characteristics seen at Fromelles and Pozières—rushed attacks and incompetent artillery preparations[15]—immediately reappeared.

Frantic to start as soon as possible even though the artillery had not yet caught up with the advance, Gough seized on the offer of eleven tanks and demanded an immediate attack. Despite the protests of Birdwood and White, it took place on 10–11 April. The tanks failed and the 4th Australian Division was left unsupported to break into the German line. It did so, but was obliged to withdraw, losing approximately 3000 men.

Gough remained unconvinced that the Germans were making a serious stand, and ordered a second attack, which began on 3 May. The left brigade fought its way once again into the German line, but the battle degenerated into trench fighting and ended by 10 May with the loss of a further 7000 men. The two battles had cost the Australians 10,000 casualties in nine days: ten times the daily casualty rate on Gallipoli.

They also ruined relations between most Australian commanders and the British. After the first battle of Bullecourt Australians bitterly blamed the British tank crews, and their hostility towards Gough was long-lasting and largely justified. Bean himself wrote to Brigadier-General Sir James Edmonds, the official British war historian, that Gough's tactics at Bullecourt 'were more criticised in the A.I.F. than any other plans or decisions in the war . . . and . . . the prospect of serving under him in the third battle of Ypres would have been depressing in the extreme'.[16]

Australian criticism continued. The photographer J. F. (Frank) Hurley wrote of the battle of Poel Cappelle:

God knows how those red-capped blighters in headquarters (60 miles from the front) expect their men to gain such a strong position when they're to

drag themselves through mud. Curse them! I'll swear they were not within
20 miles from the firing line when this attack was arranged, the ground is
impassable ...[17]

And Major G. Adcock wrote home: 'Everyone here is "fed up" of the war,
but not with the Hun. The British staff, British methods and British
bungling have sickened us.'

The Australians were not alone: an English reviewer wrote that
'Everyone who served in France knows that the Fifth Army, or at any rate
its staff work, acquired an ill repute in 1917',[18] and the Canadians too
were disgusted with Gough. The criticism, however, should have included
Haig, whose diaries reveal a total ignorance of the situation. Gough was
only carrying out the wishes of his Commander-in-Chief; the latter had
misread German intentions, both during their retreat and now they
had made a stand, and he continued to press his army commanders to
attack, even after 30 April when he had privately decided to wind the battle
down.[19]

Nevertheless, once again the Australians had also contributed to the
disaster themselves. Neither White nor Birdwood had stood up effectively to Gough or Haig to protect the interests of their men—which
illustrated the problems underlying Birdwood's relationship with the
British high command. He had remonstrated against Gough's more
ambitious objectives before then and occasionally had them curtailed, but
he was usually very reluctant to oppose his superiors. Neither Birdwood
nor White had protested against the heavy loss of life during Pozières.
And in February 1917, when—under pressure from White—Birdwood had
written to Gough about the Australian troops' need for rest, he did so
in such a half-hearted and ingratiating manner, warning Gough that
White would raise the issue, that it seems clear he was trying to serve
two masters, Britain and Australia, but was primarily concerned with
the former.

It is no wonder that neither he nor White succeeded in standing up
for the interests of the AIF, certainly if this was the tone of their
correspondence. At Bullecourt, Birdwood did not back White up strongly
enough: he was dependent upon Haig and the British army for his
promotion. Gough later wrote that he 'was always easy to work with'.[20]
White, in a later conversation with Bean, also revealed a desire to please
his British masters, but as a staff officer he hardly had the luxury of
resignation. As it happens, the next operational commander downwards who could have resigned was Major-General Sir N. M. Smyth,
commanding 2nd Division, but he also was British. Of the two brigadiers
involved, one, John Gellibrand, did resign after the battle: the other,
Brigadier-General R. Smith, was British and did not. From an Australian
standpoint, Bullecourt illustrated the absolute need to have competent
Australians in command and to gain at least a modicum of independence
from the British.

Not that it is likely that Birdwood and White could have stopped the
attacks: Gough dismissed the commander of the British 7th Division for

refusing to undertake a precipitate attack, and the Canadian General A. Currie was forced to go on at Passchendaele, despite the fact that as the representative of Canada he was unlikely to have been dismissed.[21] Even though Birdwood and White did not enjoy Currie's independence, they could have tried harder.

Moreover, Birdwood's and White's battle planning and tactics were also weak, and Australian staff work was poor. The artillery preparations for the second battle were grossly, if not negligently, handled: the possibility of using smoke was ignored, and the hour of attack was fatal. So Anzac command itself was almost as culpable as the British for the disasters at Bullecourt, though Bean avoided facing the fact while Birdwood flippantly and insensitively hid from Northcliffe that there had been any disaster at all.[22]

It has been suggested—once again—that Bullecourt 'destroyed any remaining confidence the troops had in the British high command', but it is extremely doubtful if any remained to be destroyed by then. The naive enthusiasm for Empire and battle that the Anzacs had revealed in Egypt and Gallipoli was long gone. Most of the Gallipoli veterans were dead or wounded, and though later volunteers hoped to live up to the traditions of Anzac, that too was an illusion on their part. The men of Anzac may have been gallant fighters, but they provided no model for those who faced the Germans on the Western Front. More scientific methods of fighting, a new attitude to war, and a more competent leadership were required, and they had not yet been provided. By mythologising the Anzacs, and avoiding criticism of Australian officers, Bean hid this from himself and later readers.

For the front-line troops, however, few illusions remained. As they saw it, the Western Front was worse than Gallipoli, and no commanders were competent. They vented their bitterness against the highest British officer they saw at close hand, Birdwood. Some described him as 'a bastard of a man', whose speeches on the theme of killing more Germans they derided.[23]

Birdwood was certainly not an effective corps commander. Many criticisms have been made of him on Gallipoli, while White commented on his concern with trivia and—later—that he had never once drafted a plan and could not remember much of what he had seen during his visits to the trenches. The latter seem therefore to have been simply PR exercises.[24] But he was not alone. Because Birdwood was poor at operations, they were left to White. His arrangements for the withdrawal from Gallipoli were excellent, but he seems to have been an indifferent battle commander, both at Pozières and the second battle of Bullecourt.[25]

There were also many British—and occasional Australian—comments on poor field officers in the AIF. One Australian told an Englishman that they would be all right under British officers, but that the Australian ones were 'bloody rotten'. Nor does Bean notice that if the Australian troops declared they only saluted officers they admired, and then saluted very few, that implied criticism of Australian officers as well as British.[26]

## THE BRITISH HIGH COMMAND AND THE ANZACS
## IN FRANCE, 1916–1917

As for the British commanders in France, they had mixed opinions about the Australians in 1916–17. They admired their courage and aggression in battle, but thought that their lack of discipline and ineffective leadership, which so often ignored the techniques needed for trench fighting and did not utilise the available technology with any flair, meant that too often a shambles resulted.

Haig noted in his diary their loss of mortars and machine guns in a German raid;[27] and although he recognised their potential, regarded them as desperately untrained. He did not like Birdwood, a protégé of Kitchener who was forced on him at the insistence of Hughes and others, and dourly—and accurately—commented that he was 'not much use for directing ops. His taste lies in making speeches to the Australian rank and file and so keeps [sic] them contented.'[28] He noted in July 1916 that their marching was bad, and when he sent them to Gough told him— of all people—to make sure they had only simple tasks and to go into the details of any attack carefully. During Pozières, although impressed by the fighting qualities of the Australian troops, Haig still thought the Western Front was new to Birdwood's HQ and insisted on replacing its artillery commander, Cunliffe-Owen, by one of his own men: 'I would be failing in my duty to the country if I ran the risk of the Australians meeting with a check through faulty artillery arrangements.' He insisted continually on the danger of machine guns and the need for artillery preparation. It was at this time that he encountered their dismissal of artillery planning, mentioned earlier, and thought they were 'very ignorant'. He saw Gough and his Chief of Staff, Neil Malcolm, after a failed attack and analysed why it happened.

> I impressed on [them] . . . that they must supervise more closely the plans of the Anzac Corps. Some of their Divisional Generals are so ignorant and (like many Colonials) so conceited that they cannot be trusted to work out unaided the plans for the attack.

White assured him that they had learnt their lesson and would be more thorough in the future.[29]

These remarks may irritate Australian readers, and some were undoubtedly unjust, but underestimation of German machine guns and artillery, together with the weakness of the Anzacs' own artillery work and slipshod planning of barrages, were key factors in the disaster in the second battle of Bullecourt, so it seems that some of Haig's criticisms were valid. Nor can Haig be accused of being anti-Australian. He wrote about Anzac artillery and planning in more detail than any other issue in his diary, using three pages in the original version. He seems to have liked the Australians and feared their potential would be thrown away by carelessness. In March 1917 he looked at the Pozières ridge they had helped capture, felt proud of Britain's 'Imperial Army', and was unusually benign when he later toured their units. This did not stop him reporting to Lady Haig in February 1918 that the Australians were not nearly so efficient as the Canadians—which once again he put down to Birdwood's search for popularity.[30]

Nor was Haig alone in criticising Australian staff work. Rawlinson, writing in his diary in December 1916, thought that the Anzac Corps was the weakest he commanded, and in the following February doubted their story that they had lost a trench because they had been counter-attacked. Then, reporting their transfer to Gough's Fifth Army, he commented that they were 'fine fighters but ... not soldiers—their Company and Battalion Commanders are lamentable ... I am really not sorry to lose them.'[31]

## DISCIPLINE AND MILITARY LAW

Another reason for the critical attitude of the British high command was the difficulty it had in accepting Australian attitudes towards discipline. The British army between 1914 and 1918 enforced one of the most rigid disciplinary codes in the war. The *Field Service Pocket Book*, 1914 edition, had seventeen offences for which the death penalty could be awarded. During the war approximately 346 British troops were executed, compared with 133 French, 25 Canadian and 10 American. German records have been lost, but even Crown Prince Rupprecht of Bavaria was surprised by the rigidity of British discipline, which appears to have become more rigid as the war went on.[32]

Australian discipline was modelled in general on nineteenth-century British discipline, but Section 98 of the Australian *Defence Act* 1903 stipulated that no Australian could be sentenced to death except for mutiny, desertion to the enemy, or treason, and even then the sentence had to be confirmed by the governor-general. This has been popularly attributed to a revulsion against the shooting of 'Breaker' Morant by the British during the Boer War, but in fact it dates back to the various Acts passed in the Australian colonies in the nineteenth century, based partly on a desire to control their own troops, and partly on opposition to capital punishment.[33]

Anomalies existed. One Australian was in fact shot during World War II: he had made the mistake of joining the New Zealand forces. Another was executed for murder under the civil jurisdiction.[34] Meanwhile, the *Naval Defence Act* of 1910 brought the Australian Navy completely under British naval discipline.[35] It is not surprising, therefore, that the problems associated with the AIF did not arise with the RAN. But for the AIF, with inexperienced officers and NCOs and all the distractions of the local civilian scene, the tone, set in the holding and training camps in Australia, was strengthened on the voyage out and reinforced in Egypt.[36] Fears of a recurrence then led to General Murray's letter from the Middle East and the precautions when the Anzacs arrived in France.

It is possible to read too much into this: the men boasted of their independence and the officers complained of the same, but both may have exaggerated. The tales of Australian 'larrikinism' are legion: some amusing, others revealing a more ruffian element that Australian historians seem to have underestimated. Australians were also moved by

Australian deserters jeer at the authorities: photograph of a group of ten Australian deserters which was sent to the Provost Marshal with the following letter:
Sir,
With all due respect we send you this P.C. as a souvenir, trusting that you will keep it as a mark of esteem from those who know you well. At the same time trusting that Nous jamais regardez vous encore.                    Au Revoir. Nous.
(AWM Official Photo No. A3862).

hostility to British discipline, which was only increased when the troops became battle-hardened. They were then likely to 'count out' officers who tried to exercise old-fashioned authority over them, even high personages such as the Duke of Connaught or General Allenby.[37] The Australians could be well disciplined when they saw the need for it: in battle, or when their interest was aroused, as during the first trip through France. But rigid formal discipline for discipline's sake did not appeal to them. Sometimes this cost them dearly, as when slovenliness in precautions against gas and trench foot left them weak in defence.[38]

More serious problems began to develop in France, however, with the increasing strain during and after Pozières. Anzacs suffered the same stresses and battle trauma as other troops, and—being free of the ever-present death penalty in the British army—reacted by malingering and being absent without leave (AWOL) and with outright desertion, which Bean played down. Until Pozières, 50 per cent of such offences reported to the military police were AWOL—usually men simply overstaying their leave because they were intrigued by Britain. After Pozières, however, desertion rates increased. The only penalty was imprisonment, which, despite the deliberately harsh regime in military detention centres, was naturally regarded by the men as preferable to death in battle.[39]

Figures vary, but whatever ones are used the AIF comes out badly in comparison with other sections of the British army. For example, despite their comparatively small numbers, out of 182 cases of AWOL on the Western Front in December 1916, 130 were Australians. Early in 1917 the three Australian divisions in the Third Army had roughly twelve times the number of AWOL convictions in the other twenty-two divisions. Indeed, in the first half of 1917 the Australian desertion rate was four times the average of the other Dominions. It has been estimated that 3803 members of the AIF were court-martialled for desertion, a rate of just below one in a hundred, though before 1916 they were mostly in Australia by men who had changed their minds about enlisting. This is not true thereafter, however, and some deserters infested the back areas, or the old battlefields, where they lived rough and jeered at the authorities. In March 1918 out of every thousand men, the British troops had fewer than one man in prison; the Canadian, New Zealanders and South Africans 1.6; but the Australians nearly nine. And in comparison with the size of their forces, Australian courts martial occurred almost twice as often as Canadian ones and more than three times as often as those of the New Zealanders.[40]

## ETAPLES

As the war dragged on, soldiers of all armies—British, German, Russian and French as well as Australian—reached their breaking point. In the British army, the result was a series of semi-mutinies, riots or strikes: such as the riot in the training camp at Etaples in September 1917. The

Australians—with the New Zealanders and the Scots—were involved in this affair, which was basically a revolt against brutal training, savage discipline and the Redcaps. The Anzacs presented the camp authorities with a problem: their friendship with the Scots provided the basis for joint action to remedy their grievances; and to fire on Australian soldiers would have precipitated a crisis in Anglo-Australian relations. Yet the authorities seem to have had few other ideas.[41] Perhaps typically of the Anzacs, however, it was not a politically aware mutiny against the war, its methods or its aims, but a riot about camp conditions and treatment of the men. Once they were improved, the trouble ended, and the Australians returned to the front.


## THE BRITISH HIGH COMMAND AND THE DEATH PENALTY

The Australian reputation for ill discipline naturally led to strained relations between the British command and Australians. It was easy to assume that the difference in discipline between the two armies was caused less by the character of the troops than the failure of the Australian disciplinary system. After all, the British soldier just did not have the possibility of adopting the cavalier Australian attitude to orders and rank—he was for ever faced with the existence of the firing squad.

Accordingly, there were continuous efforts by both British and Australian authorities to tighten Australian discipline. When the Anzacs arrived in France in 1916 the War Office considered a plan to keep their wounded out of England, and treat them instead in France, Egypt or Australia according to the seriousness of their cases. This was quashed, but the issue of Dominion troops mixing with British troops was considered by the War Cabinet on 12 September 1917. Unrest in Shoreham camp was then blamed on the Canadians, and it was suggested that colonial troops should be quartered in separate depots. Haig long 'considered ... [the Australian] easy-going attitude a permanent threat to the discipline of British forces', and worried lest they put revolutionary ideas into the heads of the troops; in 1918 he separated their wounded into convalescent camps of their own, away from other soldiers. At the War Office the Director of Personnel Services, Major-General W. Childs, found them a constant cause for exasperation.[42]

Australian commanders themselves were not satisfied with Australian discipline, and tried in a variety of ways to strengthen it. Lieutenant-General Sir J. Talbot Hobbs, then commanding 1st Division artillery, was admittedly of English extraction, but he 'told his unit commanders in May 1916 that he was "bitterly disappointed" in his efforts to make his men soldiers: their dress was slovenly, their march discipline atrocious, their failure to salute a byword'.[43] Australian courts martial frequently pronounced the death sentence as a deterrent, although it could not be enforced, and—contrary to Australian mythology—like other armies applied Field Punishment No. 1 (binding men to gun limbers or other equipment for hours on end)—though not in public.[44] The death penalties imposed on British soldiers were publicly announced, but amongst the Australians this had the reverse result to that desired: they felt disgust with the British army and pride that their own authorities did not allow it to happen.

In this they were too generous to their leaders, however. There was a demand in the Anzac Corps, from middle-ranking officers upwards, for the death penalty to be imposed on Australian soldiers too. It was only natural that the British high command should echo these ideas, which were entirely in accord with its own, and try to put pressure on the Australian government. This developed into a major issue in the relations between Australia and Britain.

Birdwood raised the subject with GHQ in March 1916, shortly after the Australians first arrived in France—allegedly to avoid any Australian being shot by the British before they realised the legal limitations they faced. He suggested that the Anzacs should be placed under the British *Army Act*, and that an approach should be made to the Australian government to that effect. The War Office and the Army Council agreed, and debate raged within the Colonial Office, where one official thought the governor-general's powers in the matter were 'absurd'. The Australian government, however, was at that time deeply concerned with recruiting and the proposed conscription referendum, and naturally regarded the proposal as fatal.[45]

The next attempt to change the situation occurred in December 1916, when Birdwood pointed out to Rawlinson of the Fourth Army headquarters that Australian discipline was likely to suffer because the law was still unchanged. This was like a red rag to a bull. The Fourth Army passed Birdwood's comments on to Haig, who thought the absence of the death penalty 'a menace to the efficiency of the Australian troops', mentioned desertions, and contacted the War Office, which passed his message on to the Colonial Office, which cabled Australia in January 1917. Rawlinson then reported high desertion rates among the Australians, arguing that he could not be responsible for their discipline unless the law was changed. Haig sent this to the Army Council, with the observation that absence from the trenches was 'assuming alarming proportions'. The Army Council thought the matter 'urgent'; the War Cabinet discussed the discipline of the Australian troops and decided that it created a difficult situation if Englishmen or Canadians could be shot while Australians could not. The Colonial Secretary then cabled the governor-general in Australia. Seeing the political situation in the country, however, it hardly required the recommendation of Pearce, Minister for Defence, against the proposal for the government to refuse to agree.[46]

The bickering dragged on during 1917. After the Anzacs joined Gough's Fifth Army on 14 February, he wrote that he had seen Rawlinson's letter and completely concurred. The death penalty had to be instated. In May— the month of the second battle of Bullecourt—Hobbs wrote to Birdwood urging that the death penalty be imposed on outstanding cases as examples against desertion, and Birdwood passed this request on the GHQ. Haig responded with a long letter on deficiencies in Australian discipline. He cited statistics purporting to show that in the first six months of 1917 the Australian divisions had an average desertion rate of 34.2 per division, while for the rest of the Britsh army it was 8.87. Unless the Australian government put its troops under the *Army Act* without reservations, he could not be responsible for the serious consequences that might result. The Colonial Office was worried by the distinction that had developed between Australia and New Zealand (where the death penalty did exist).[47] In July Godley agreed and Birdwood sent a letter of three foolscap pages to the Department of Defence in Melbourne summing up the correspondence, repeating Haig's assurance that they did not wish to impose frequent death sentences, only provide a deterrent, and suggesting that the role of the governor-general in confirming the death penalty should be abolished, and the Act amended as soon as practical after conscription had been introduced.[48]

Therein, of course, lay the rub. Hughes' government had enough trouble on its hands without buying into any more. The first conscription referendum had failed and recruiting had collapsed. The government could not hope to pass such a change without a major political row, which would become public and almost totally end recruiting, yet at the same time destroy any chance of winning a second referendum on conscription.[49]

The government therefore delayed dealing with the issue for months. In August it cabled that although it recognised the gravity of the situation, to make the change then would destroy recruiting altogether and force it to another conscription referendum which it would lose. 'It is imperative that until matters settle down the question of the death penalty should not be raised.' Pearce wrote to Birdwood that the government was 'convinced of the wisdom of the recommendation, but as Mr Hughes has explained to the British government, it could not come at a more inopportune time than at the present'.[50]

The year 1917 therefore passed with Haig, via Long, the Colonial Secretary, warning that the deterioration of Australian divisions might 'gravely affect the success' of British arms; the governor-general pointing out to Long that to introduce the death penalty might end recruiting and lead to the overthrow of Hughes' government; the adjutant-general spelling out the regulations as they stood; and Birdwood suggesting that the names of all deserters be published in Australia, to shame the men into action.[51]

## PROBLEMS OF CENTRAL AUSTRALIAN ADMINISTRATION AND COMMAND

Meanwhile, the relationship between the Anzacs and the British high command was reflected not only in the matter of discipline but also in the way the Australians were administered and fitted into the British military structure. As we have seen, the Australian army was an offshoot of the British army. Nobody thought it odd in 1915 that the Australian government wired London to confirm the appointment of Legge to command the 1st Division.[52] But the Australian government had also reserved the right to administer the AIF itself. It had therefore sought a national commander, and thought it had found one in Bridges.

Bridges, however, was a failure at many levels. He was far too British-minded, and although he saw Australia as part of the Empire, he thought in imperial terms, not Australian. He therefore hived off his administrative authority as far as he could, and left the AIF dependent on British administration more than it needed to be. Rigid and exacting with his men, he lacked the charisma of a successful leader. In addition, he appears to have been a poor battle commander. Finally he was studiously reckless in the face of danger, which led to his death within three weeks of the landing, leaving the AIF in a poor position. The Australian government then—partly as a result of weaknesses in Legge and partly from bickering among the other Australian brigadiers who wanted promotion[53]—missed the opportunity to reorganise the command of the AIF and appoint an Australian commander. Instead, it accepted Hamilton's suggestion that Birdwood be put in charge.

Sir William Birdwood was an Indian Army officer, who had quickly seen his advantage in stressing the independent role of the AIF with himself in command. His stance was to identify himself with Australia and the Australian troops. As General Murray put it to Robertson,

> He has a keen eye to his future, and would retain all that helps it. For instance, he wont [sic] willingly relinquish his charter with the Australian Government . . . He wants to remain at the end of the war everything to Australia and New Zealand . . .[54]

Birdwood spent much of his time writing ingratiating letters to all and sundry, as we have seen during and after Gallipoli. He had addressed Kitchener as 'my dearest old chief'. Now he regularly corresponded with the Australian High Commissioner, Andrew Fisher, and the Colonial Secretary, Walter Long, talking of 'my boys' and seeking support for his current projects. He even wrote to Lady Godley. His letters to Munro Ferguson were regularly eight foolscap pages of typescript long, and the one after the evacuation from Gallipoli reached fifteen. Even during the battle of Pozières, when one would have thought his mind would have been on other things, he had written to Fisher about 'the boys' and their 'magnificent bravery', who were 'in no way disheartened at not having succeeded in their first attempt' and threatening mutiny if they were taken out of the line first. He asserted a deep affection for the Australian soldiers, and declared that the one thing he wanted was to remain with them till the end.[55]

Birdwood's long correspondence with Senator Pearce is an important aspect of Anglo-Australian relations during the war. He discussed discipline, the Australian forces, and the appointment and promotion of Australian officers in detail. Nor did he hesitate to comment bluntly on

Haig, whom he thought lacking in any great human sympathies. He also discussed politics and pushed his own pet project, the creation of an Australian army. This was no doubt stimulated by his assumption that he himself would be chosen to command it, as Hankey (who seems to have been taken in by Birdwood) assured him on one occasion.

Birdwood wrote to Kitchener,

> I have now become so completely an Australian myself, that I feel myself identified with them ... and their interests, and I quite believe I shall have to go back to Australia with the Corps at the end of the war!! [sic]

He therefore took great interest in Hughes' stay in England in 1916, and his actions on the English scene as well as his trip to France. He obviously encouraged Hughes to speak to Haig about the possibility of creating an Australian army. Later, in 1918, when despite all this he chose to command the Fifth Army rather than stay with the Anzac Corps, he wrote to Munro Ferguson and Hughes protesting his closeness to the Australians and his desire to serve them in the future. To misquote Frederick the Great on Maria Theresa, 'he wept but he went'. Birdwood's ambitions were plain: he meant to achieve high office through his connection with the Australians, perhaps even the governor-generalship in due course (a fulfilment that was to be thwarted when in 1931 the then prime minister J. H. Scullin created Sir Isaac Isaacs the first *Australian* governor-general).[56]

But despite this Birdwood, no less than Bridges, was an *imperial* officer, and his first loyalty lay with the British army. A dapper little man, born in India of Indian Army parents and married to a baron's daughter, he owed his standing to his social status and charm, not military ability. In his numerous letters he never discussed Haig's strategy or use of the Australian troops with Pearce, the Minister for Defence in Melbourne, nor did he raise the issue with Hughes during the latter's visit in 1916. This absence of strategic or tactical thinking reflected not only Birdwood's lack of ability, but also his feeling that he was first and foremost a 'British' officer.

His appointment however had not stopped the arguments over the correct administrative structure. Birdwood had immediately fought Murray, who commanded in the Middle East, over the right to administer the men as well as lead them in battle. He and White wanted to set up AIF headquarters in London to administer the force, and with the right to communicate directly with the Australian government—though they would delegate some powers to Chauvel, who stayed in the Middle East in charge of the Anzac Mounted Division. The CIGS thought Murray himself should assume central administrative functions in Egypt—which naturally appealed to Murray.

Meanwhile, a struggle over independence in training occurred in Britain. On 1 June 1916 there was a serious clash between Brigadier V. C. M. Sellheim, commanding AIF HQ, and the Deputy Chief of the Imperial General Staff, who wanted the British army to provide instructors to train Australian troops, and the whole to be under Lord French. Sellheim was adamant, but the clash was hidden in the bland minutes.[57]

Birdwood had hoped that, once in France, he would be allowed to travel to London to put his case for the continuance of his control over the administration. Haig objected. He did not like Birdwood, with his Indian Army connections and closeness to Kitchener, and suspected his ambition, but tactfully left the decision to General Sir H. Plumer, in whose Second Army the Anzacs had been placed. The latter gave Birdwood permission to visit London, and two conferences were held with representatives of Australia, New Zealand and the War Office. It was finally decided that the AIF's administrative headquarters would be brought to Horseferry Road in London, and its commandant placed under Birdwood. It was left to Hughes to win Haig round, gaining at the same time a promise that all Australian divisions in France would be brought together if possible.

The independence of AIF administration from the British high command was thus formally secured, but whereas the Canadian and New Zealand administrations in London were to become large and effective with some initiative, the AIF headquarters in London remained purely an administrative body, and all policy decisions were referred to Melbourne. Moreover, since Birdwood was both controller of AIF headquarters and commander in the field in France as well, his time and attention was divided between the two posts, to the detriment of the administration in England. His only advantages were the right to communicate directly with Pearce, and the fact that he was helped by White in France and a large staff in London, and was in an area with good communications—unlike Chauvel in the Middle East.

He was not helped, however, by Hughes' personal appointment in April 1916 of Brigadier-General R. M. McC. Anderson to be commandant of AIF headquarters in London and the official Australian government representative at the War Office. A successful Sydney businessman, Anderson went to London to deal directly with the War Office on financial and administrative matters and be Birdwood's link with AIF training and holding depots in England. Despite time in the militia, Anderson was more a civilian bureaucrat than soldier, and was thoroughly disliked by both British and Australian officers. His tactlessness and penchant for sending rude telegrams was to cause problems for Birdwood. He was soon on extremely bad terms with the War Office, and the Australian nationalists demanded another Australian officer be officially appointed to liaise with that body. Birdwood, however, did not support that move, little as he liked Anderson—presumably because a really effective man in Anderson's place would be a threat to Birdwood's own position.[58]

Meanwhile, in the Middle East, battle raged over Murray's demand for an Imperial Mounted Division of mixed British and Australian units, to be commanded by a British regular cavalryman. Australian officers appealed to Birdwood, who naturally declined to be drawn into that hornets' nest: the War Office had approved of it, and Birdwood knew his own interests. Chauvel continued to press GHQ to give staff appointments to Australians, but he was not helped by Birdwood's refusal to allow Australian officers to be put on British staffs, which would have provided

AIF headquarters in Horseferry Road, London.    (AWM Official Photo No. D796).

training for them. The most Birdwood would accept later was for understudies to be appointed to all the lesser staff positions.[59] And there the matter rested, for the time being. The AIF was not fully integrated into the British army, but—due to Birdwood's position and interests—not fully independent either. It was an administrative and command structure that was fraught with difficulties, as was soon revealed.

Lower down the chain, the concern of the other Australian commanders for their relative seniority, and their jockeying for promotion, raised wider issues in the Anglo-Australian relationship. The Australian government had initially sent out Legge to replace Bridges, but this had caused 'a seething mass of resentment' among the senior Australian officers, especially Monash and McCay. The latter even argued that since the Australian government had put the AIF at the disposal of and under the control of the War Office, it had 'no more right to *appoint* [sic!] a Commander of a British or Colonial Division than it has to appoint a Battalion Commander'.[60] Fortunately for the future of Anglo-Australian relations, this argument was not accepted, because Australians already faced innate British prejudices. Although many junior officers had been drawn from other than the usual prestige schools and classes, and promoted from the ranks during the war, many professional soldiers remained convinced that officers were really created by birth rather than education, and that therefore 'colonial' ones could only be second rate. As the war continued, however, the desperate need for officers meant that such prejudice could not block appointments completely, although it did hold them back.

Nor was Birdwood a help. Pearce cabled him in February 1916 regretting that he had appointed two British officers, Cox and H. A. Lawrence, to divisional commands, instead of suitable Australians. Birdwood replied in great detail[61] and also wrote to the governor-general on the issue attempting to justify the appointments, but in truth he seems to have been reluctant to appoint Australians. After the matter had come to the attention of the Australian press, questions had been asked in federal parliament, and Pearce had written another letter, Birdwood finally responded in April 1917 assuring the latter that he understood the government's wishes. The Department of Defence however (stirred on by Murdoch in London and backed by Colonel T. H. Dodds, the Adjutant-General in Melbourne) then informed Birdwood that it had found the names of more than ninety officers in the AIF on 4 August 1917 who were not Australian, and asked him for a list of those who could be replaced.

This move was overdue. Dodds has been called 'aggressively Australian', but he was not exceptional by Canadian standards. Nearly two years before, in December 1915, Sir George Perley had stated that 'Canadians should always be given the preference in all positions in the Canadian forces' and 'It is naturally a source of proper pride that our Divisions are now under the command of Canadians who are recognised by everyone to be fit and capable officers.'[62] Australia was late in making her demands.

The Army Council fought a rearguard action: it wanted to keep British officers in the AIF, so that the army generally should be regarded as 'an Imperial organisation in which officers of the Dominion and British forces shall be considered interchangeable'. The Australian government was disappointed by this response and requested that a staff officer be specifically delegated to represent it at the War Office. To this Long replied on 11 August that Birdwood already represented Australian interests in London, so no separate additional appointment was necessary.[63]

## AN AUSTRALIAN ARMY OR CORPS?

The second—and potentially even more disruptive—issue, was the desire that all Australian soldiers should fight together, perhaps even forming an Australian army. This went back to the original offer of Australian troops to Britain in distinctive Australian units rather than simply being blended into British forces. A fear that this might happen arose for a while after Gallipoli, together with nervousness that the Australian soldiers would not see action in France.[64] The latter concern was ended by the transfer of the AIF to the Western Front—but the former continued to strain Anglo-Australian relations.

As early as February 1916 Birdwood was writing to Kitchener's private secretary that the more he thought about it, the more he was convinced that they should create an Australian army immediately. On being informed of this correspondence, the CIGS Sir William Robertson was sympathetic: he foresaw practical difficulties but was prepared to try to accommodate Australian wishes. The next month Birdwood wrote to Munro Ferguson in the same vein, adding—in case the governor-general had missed the point—that his senior officers regarded him as 'a suitable link in the imperial chain with the whole army'. His ambitions were plain. He also wrote to Murdoch on the subject, even talking this time of a Dominions army, and in a letter in 1918 to the governor-general he called it an Australian and New Zealand army, to cover the future defence needs of the two Pacific Dominions.[65] Indeed, from a letter he wrote to Hughes it appears that in December 1917 there had been a discussion about his 'permanent transfer to Australia'. There is no other trace in the files of the discussion, but Birdwood perhaps revealed more than he intended when he assured Hughes that 'my whole interests are centred in the Australian troops'.[66]

Meanwhile, a civilian group in London was also demanding a separate Australian army. Its prime coordinator would appear to be C. E. W. Bean, who hid his involvement when writing the official history, and attributed the leadership to Murdoch.[67] At any rate, as early as June 1916 he had noted in his diary his distaste for Godley, 'with his all-British staff', and in 1917 he wrote to Lloyd George urging that all Australian units should be brought together. Bean was allied with Murdoch, who stressed these demands in August 1917, when he got George V's private secretary, Clive Wigram, to write to Haig's Chief of Staff, Lieutenant-General L. Kiggell, suggesting a sympathetic response to Australian desires for a single corps or army. Murdoch then approached Kiggell directly, offering to see Haig, forewarning him of an approach the Australian government would make, and offering to act as intermediary with them. He was simultaneously lobbying hard and successfully to provoke the Australian government to action. There were few limits to Murdoch's machinations. Hughes himself was much taken up with the idea, writing to Haig about it in June 1916. Hughes wanted an Australian army and Birdwood to command it, but if—as Haig argued—their numbers were not large enough, then at the very least all Australians should be brought together, under Birdwood's command, into a purely Australian corps.[68]

The War Office, Army Council and British high command, however, preferred to think in terms of an 'imperial' army—in which the units from different areas could be moved around at need, like the Scottish or Welsh regiments, or the Australian squadrons in the Australian Flying Corps or Australian sailors in the Royal Navy.[69] When challenged, the British went further and argued that spreading the Australians around would make them think less of Australia as separate, but more as a part of the British Empire. This attitude was seen in the Middle East early in 1917, when Murray created the Imperial Mounted Division from two Australian and two British brigades, much to the disgust of Anderson, who wanted all four Australian Light Horse Brigades brought together in one Australian division. (It is noticeable that on this issue—where his own interests were not involved—Birdwood adopted the imperial line and was unsympathetic to Australian objections.) But Murray went further, and in August grouped the divisions and some other units into the Desert Mounted Corps—and put the lot under an Australian, Chauvel, who proceeded to place proved Australians in key administrative appointments. It was the 'imperial' theory in action.[70]

In France, Plumer wanted—once the third battle of Ypres wound down—to create two Anzac corps, each having one English division in it, but in London Walter Long, the Colonial Secretary, whose son had been killed, strongly sympathised with the War Office and echoed its ideas. On 12 September he cabled Munro Ferguson that the grouping of divisions in France depended on tactical requirements and had to be left to Haig's discretion. He then repeated the Army Council's argument for interchangeability of staff.[71]

Munro Ferguson had, however, been warned by Birdwood that these arguments were being put forward. The next move was to get Pearce, the Minister for Defence, to cable Hughes and the Colonial Office. Hughes was asked to repeat the request, and the Colonial Office was informed that

> it is strongly desired by Commonwealth that all Australian troops should be grouped together under command of General Birdwood and . . . commanded and staffed by Australian officers . . . This would appeal most strongly to Australian national sentiment . . . [I] should be glad if this matter could be referred to my colleagues in Imperial Cabinet.

The reference to the Imperial Cabinet was suggested by Murdoch, after a hint from Lord Milner.[72]

The Army Council was still reluctant, and tried in October to quash the idea by sending the correspondence to Haig and asking him whether it were practicable to group the Australians together. Haig predictably replied in the negative, arguing that to put all five Australian divisions into one corps would be 'unwieldy and cumbersome', and repeating the need for 'interchangeability of officers'. He therefore regretted that Birdwood had declined to transfer Australian officers to British staffs.[73] With the failure of the conscription referenda and the declining numbers of the AIF, White and Birdwood realised that the idea of an Australian army was dead, and instead suggested to GHQ that one division be withdrawn from the line to create a reserve for the others, until the strength of the AIF increased, and that the other four should be combined into one corps.

Political pressure, however, continued. Two days later, on 31 October, Hughes cabled Prime Minister Lloyd George that Birdwood should command all Australian troops and again requested that the War Cabinet consider the suggestion. This led Lloyd George to make enquiries, discover the previous correspondence—of which he had not been informed—and tell Long bluntly that his reply was unsatisfactory, since Hughes had specifically asked for the matter to be put before the Imperial War Council:

> It is obvious that the Cabinet cannot ignore a request of this kind ... The delay which has already occurred is discourteous to the Australian Government and may, I fear, cause some trouble.

He therefore insisted that the question should come before the Cabinet at once.

The opposition gave way. In London, Long in the Imperial War Cabinet supported the idea of a united Australian force, on the somewhat specious grounds that it would aid recruiting; and in France on the same day Haig accepted the suggestion that the four divisions be combined. II Anzac Corps disappeared, becoming the XXII Corps (with the New Zealand division in it), and I Anzac Corps became The Australian Corps. Back in London, the British Cabinet agreed, and did not even object to an Australian representative in the War Office, though it saved Haig's face by still giving strong support to the idea of an interchange of staffs.[74]

Lord Derby finally wrote and informed Haig on 9 November (what he already knew) that they were having trouble with the Australians,

> and I am afraid, for various reasons, we must look upon them in the light in which they wish to be looked upon rather than the light in which we should wish to do so. They look upon themselves, not as part and parcel of the English Army but as Allies beside us ... The Australians have got an implicit belief in Birdwood, and are quite determined that he shall be their Chief in the Field. I do not know what your feelings are with regard to his military capacity but I am afraid in this respect we shall have to humour them.[75]

He went on to remark that if the second conscription referendum succeeded the following month perhaps they could form a sixth Australian division, creating an army of two corps of three divisions each, with Birdwood as its overall Commander. This was in fact following the Canadian lead, but despite this, the War Office still clung doggedly to its imperial ideals. On 2 December it informed Haig that not only did it hope the Australians would maintain their divisions at full strength— it had all along thought that the Anzacs were 11,000 men short, to the consternation of the Colonial Office—but also strongly supported the principle of interchangeability of officers.[76]

The evidence however suggested that the War Office was wrong. All Canadian divisions fought together as a corps, which had a Canadian, Currie, as its commander from June 1917. The independence and cohesion of the Canadian Corps, and the fact that Haig was prepared to consult with its command before giving them their assignment at Passchendaele, was closely linked to their outstanding reputation on the Western Front. Yet the British were not mollified by Canadian success, noting instead how the system limited their flexibility in the use of the Canadians. They therefore did not recognise that creating the separate corps had led to increased Canadian morale and effectiveness. The year 1918 was to provide them with further proof.

CHAPTER FIVE

# The End of Euphoria:
# Anglo-Australian Political and Economic
# Relations, 1916–1917

'Now is the winter of our discontent...'
SHAKESPEARE,
*King Richard II*

The enthusiasm of August 1914 had ended in the bitter disappointment of Gallipoli, and the growing trauma of war in 1916 and 1917 wore down the enthusiasm of even the most optimistic. Deepening rifts had appeared in Australian society, and between Australia and Britain. Under the the long agony of World War I, old relationships were bound to change.

## THE DARDANELLES COMMISSION

Just before Hughes returned to Australia, in July 1916, its government received the news that in London Fisher had been invited to sit on the Dardanelles Commission. The government was unhappy about this, for it did not wish too much inquisitive attention to be paid to the Gallipoli affair. Pearce thought the commission a sign of weakness, and agreed only reluctantly, provided the Australian government itself was not involved, so 'Asquith confirmed the appointment on the basis that Fisher was a nominee of the home government and did not represent Australia.'

The major Australian newspapers, faithfully echoing government sentiment, were hostile to the idea, the *Age* putting it down to a 'series of intrigues, engineered by a group of mischievous political busybodies'. This attitude was echoed by White and Birdwood in France, who were anxious that the AIF should not be involved. There was therefore little Australian input into the enquiry. Fisher himself attended only thirty-seven sittings out of eighty-nine, rarely questioned witnesses or took part in the discussion, and was not present when Birdwood was questioned.[1] In the House of Commons, George Reid, now a Unionist MP, hoped that extenuating circumstances would be revealed. His attitude provoked one of Asquith's critics to complain that Australians appeared satisfied with everything about the Gallipoli campaign: aims, methods, medical arrangements—'the whole of Australia is satisfied with it'.[2] This was an exaggeration, but a natural one seeing the stance adopted by Australian leaders. Even Hughes' Labor opponents made no parliamentary reference to the enquiry. Perhaps they thought that criticism of the Gallipoli campaign would appear to be criticising the Anzacs, and would rebound on themselves. If so, the government by its propaganda had limited the parameters of debate.

This is not surprising, for from the Australian government's point of view the timing of the commission could hardly have been worse. It came after the celebrations of Anzac Day and coincided with difficulties in recruiting and a planned conscription referendum. At such a time serious revelations of British incompetence could only be harmful. The government therefore gave the commission the cold shoulder. In London, Fisher's declining powers were probably another factor in the totally inadequate Australian response. On the several occasions when a potential for a clash between Australia and England existed, it did not develop. Fisher bemoaned the fact that Australians relied on British ministers knowing more about the war situation than Australians did—and the British sympathised with him. Heavy criticism developed over the medical arrangements—but many British felt bitter about those too. The most likely flashpoint was the questioning of Keith Murdoch on 5 February 1917. British officials stressed the impropriety, not to mention immorality, of his actions—such as carrying Ashmead-Bartlett's letter, and his own letter criticising the management of the Dardanelles campaign, after he had signed an undertaking for Hamilton. Fisher defended Murdoch, emphasising Australia's 'separateness' from Britain, and arguing that Murdoch carried a mandate from Australia as a 'self-governing Dominion' directly concerned with the Gallipoli campaign. This was a most interesting—and significant—argument, but was not developed. The interview ended with Murdoch accusing the British army of making senior appointments from motives of friendship and personal influence, which highly offended the British officers present, especially as Murdoch, though proved wrong on detail, obstinately stuck to his opinion.

These 'exchanges marked the height of Anglo-Australian tension in the commission'. Fisher did not sign the report, on the ground that his other duties had prevented him from assessing the evidence. This was an amazing admission, but acceptable enough to Hughes' government. In contrast, New Zealand adopted a far more critical stance: there had been bitterness in the country over Gallipoli; and its High Commissioner, Sir Thomas McKenzie, insisted on including a supplementary report since he held strong views on the findings.

When the preliminary report was published in March 1917 it received widespread coverage in the Australian press, including the criticisms of the planning and conduct of the campaign. But, apart from journals on the left of the political spectrum, newspaper editors were reluctant to condemn Britain's conduct of the war and editorial comment was much milder than in Britain. Australian reputations were not at stake, and Lloyd George was by then in power. The editors hoped for much from his new government.

Robertson thinks that, although the Australian public must have formed a lower opinion of Britain's wartime leaders, 'in 1916 and 1917 most Australians in a position to inquire into the mistakes at Gallipoli consistently refused to do so'. Some did not wish to admit to 'pointless slaughter', others were 'imperial minded' or did not wish to harm recruiting. Others were moved by the fame of the Anzacs or their imagined nearness to success. Whatever the reasons, 'the campaign never became the subject of a violent, widespread controversy of the type seen . . . during the Vietnam War'.[3] The commission probably confirmed critics of the war and the government in their judgements, and strengthened their opposition to conscription, but probably had a mixed effect on the general public. In this it was similar to New Zealand, where Massey was sharply critical.[4]

## DIVISION WITHIN AUSTRALIA

Australian opinion was becoming increasingly divided. The early enthusiasm had gone; unemployment and price rises fed a growing disillusionment; and the lengthening casualty lists appeared 'on ferry terminals and railway stations; in the notice cases at the local post office or police station; in clubs and factories and shops and offices'. Such was the price of imperial loyalty. The marchers at the second Anzac Day celebrations in 1917 were fewer than one-third the number of those in the first; even some churchmen were beginning to doubt; and the returning wounded also had an effect on public opinion. At the same time the censorship of news and letters from the front fed rumour. Despite frantic efforts by recruiting committees, fewer recruits presented themselves, while demands for conscription produced fear in some and fanaticism in others. The community became divided, and 'Hughes' personal power base . . . started to disintegrate.'[5]

This last was inevitable. Hughes' preoccupation with the war and abandonment of Labor policies—such as the promised referendum on price controls—led to deep disillusionment among Labor voters. Hughes had gone to Britain in 1916, been fêted by the rich and powerful and 'obviously [felt] at home in the company of the conservative politicians, barons of business and media moguls of Great Britain'. Many therefore began to wonder about the causes of the war and British motives, and the old hostility to imperialism, passionately expressed by Frank Anstey in the House of Representatives in 1914, grew. It was voiced most clearly by the IWW. Even moderate Labor supporters who were still loyal to Britain also felt that Australia had separate interests of her own. These mixed attitudes and motives led to what one writer has described as 'the bitter, divisive, faction-ridden and erratic nature of politics in Australia'[6] as the war continued.

## CONSCRIPTION

Matters came to a head over the conscription issue. Hughes had earlier declared total opposition to the idea, but had since then become prime minister, discussed the subject with the governor-general, and begun to equivocate. In early December 1915 he remarked that so far as he knew and hoped, 'no circumstances will compel the adoption of conscription'.[7] Then he went to Britain to demand a firm war policy, just at the time when the need for total conscription was being widely debated there. Hughes could hardly support conscription in Britain and resist it in Australia, nor—as he secretly cabled Pearce—could Australia easily maintain her voluntary system. Pearce agreed, and cabled Hughes, then on his return voyage, that a draft scheme for conscription had been drawn up, but he would await Hughes' return before making it public.[8]

There followed the first conscription campaign in Australia. The Labor Party split and a new Hughes 'National' government was formed from twenty-three erstwhile Labor members and the Liberals. The bitterness that these events engendered, and the pamphlet, media and pulpit warfare they provoked, inevitably involved attitudes to Britain and the British. For Hughes could not resist comparing Australia with Britain, and appealing to the British authorities to add their weight to his arguments.

He began by declaring that Britain had put one-tenth of her population under arms, while Australia had only put one-twentieth.[9] Meanwhile the War Office—accepting casualty statistics and manpower needs provided by Birdwood after Pozières—suggested disbanding the 3rd Division, or simply borrowing men from it to make up losses in other divisions. Anderson, the commandant of AIF headquarters in London, had this cabled to Australia and got the Army Council to request a special draft of 20,000 infantry plus the normal monthly reinforcements to bring the 3rd Division up to establishment, while Colonial Secretary Bonar Law discussed the matter with Murdoch. The Army Council also demanded 16,500 men a month for three months to keep the 3rd Division in the field. Since voluntary recruiting in Australia was then running at an average of 6000 men a month, these were impossible demands. But that was deliberate: they arrived most opportunely on the day of the crucial Labor Caucus meeting.

Birdwood and White suspected a drive to help Hughes' conscription campaign, and cabled both the Army Council and the Australian Department of Defence in Melbourne, simply asking for more reinforcements, which in fact the Army Council also sought when it sent the 3rd Division once again to the front. Meanwhile, Hughes himself asked Lloyd George for a public statement that the war would last a year or more and the Empire had to increase the pressure. He also wanted information on the British war effort and requests to other Dominions, and even had the gall to appeal to British Labour leaders.[10]

But the most dramatic move was to try to influence the Anzacs, as the heroes of the first Anzac Day, to give a lead to Australian public opinion.

This involved the British high command, first in accepting Anderson as returning officer, and then—more contentiously—in supporting the campaign. Murdoch was the linchpin in this matter, even putting pressure on the CIGS, Sir William Robertson, to send a stirring message to the people of Australia. When the latter's message was not strong enough, he asked for it to be changed. Robertson, however, was nervous about interfering in Australian politics, and refused to strengthen it.[11] Murdoch had more luck with Haig, who when asked to do so issued a message to Australia in support of conscription. Haig noted in his diary afterwards, 'I sent the message as requested', but he baulked at allowing officers to address political meetings, as did the War Office. The most that he would accept was that civilians could talk to the men. Murdoch wrote that 'It was only by fighting his whole staff that I got him to agree to allow any meetings.'

Birdwood, meanwhile, had refused to send a cable direct to Australia, but did issue a message, which worried him. Birdwood resisted an almost unbelievable letter from Frederick Young, agent-general of South Australia and secretary of the London group in support of conscription, who wanted pressure put on the soldiers and a man at each divisional headquarters 'looking after our interests'. Birdwood replied suavely that 'it would be quite impossible for us to have anything like any political propaganda or canvassing among the men here by either side'. He then cited a dislike of the proceedings by GHQ. But when Hughes cabled urging him in the interests of Australia and the Empire to use his influence with the troops, Birdwood gave way. He told a friend that he much disliked doing so, as he opposed soldiers mixing themselves with politics, but Hughes' appeal was so strong that he felt compelled to oblige. But he added that he had 'tried to avoid doing the politician, and apparently issuing orders to the men as to how they should vote'.

Hughes had produced a printed manifesto to give to the Australian soldiers. Birdwood worked on a cautiously worded message to the troops, but, forced to fall back on platitudes, produced an emotional plea in favour of the 'yes' case, without actually saying so. He appealed to the troops to vote 'according to their conscience, for the good of King and country, the honour of the Australian people and the safety of their wives and children'. The governor-general sympathised with Birdwood in the situation in which Hughes had placed him, and thought he had extricated himself well. But Birdwood then, after another urgent message from Hughes, postponed the referendum for three days, to enable Murdoch's civilians to address the men.

The Australian soldiers however received the civilian speakers with hostility. On being told by Young that if they voted 'no' they would lose status in British eyes, they revealed clearly that

> they did not care whether Australia came first in the opinion of Great Britain or not—they desired that a sufficient number of Australians should be left after the war to develop their empty country.[12]

The stress on the soldiers' opinion was a two-edged sword. When the first 10,000 votes were counted and suggested a 'no' response from the troops,

Murdoch reported that GHQ wanted the Army Council to cable Australia to merge all the totals. He repeated the story later, but one cannot help suspecting that Murdoch himself was the instigator, frantically back-pedalling. In the end, the soldiers voted 'Yes' by a very narrow majority, largely from the troops in bases and probably the Middle East, rather than the front line in France, and to the sorrow and surprise of George V.[13]

The part played in all this by British leaders, and their relationship with Hughes, is interesting. Lloyd George had supported Hughes' first plea to Birdwood to issue a message to the men; Murdoch and Birdwood both discussed the matter with Lloyd George in his rooms, while Bonar Law worried that the war was weakening imperial ties. Meanwhile, in Australia, the governor-general strongly supported compulsion and exercised no restraining influence on Hughes. He informed the Colonial Office of the complex divisions within Australia and the details and ramifications of Hughes' battle for office. As the war went on, therefore, Munro Ferguson ceased to be an impartial adjudicator, and became strongly linked to Hughes. He supported Hughes' retention of office: both in 1916, even though he had a minority in both the House of Representatives and the Senate; and in 1917, despite his promise of another election if he lost the second conscription referendum. In this Munro Ferguson was backed by the Colonial Office, which regarded Hughes' retention of power as important to the Empire. To use modern idiom, it was not a level playing field in Australian politics in 1916–17. The dice were heavily weighted against those Australian politicians and parties who opposed involvement in the war, or even wanted to subject it to independent thought.[14]

Nevertheless, Hughes' tactic of pointing to requests from Britain to explain his policies[15] was a two-edged sword. It made the government appear an unthinking puppet in the hands of Britain, and so provoked independent Australians. The first conscription referendum, on 28 October 1916, was accordingly a narrow defeat for Hughes. From the considerable debate in Australia on the motives and reasons, and analysis of the figures, it would appear that loyalty or disloyalty to Britain was not the main motive. Australian voters commonly vote 'no' in referenda: it is one way to irritate a government and politicians they are displeased with. And in 1916 the voters had reason enough to turn on Hughes. The only surprise is that so many Australians voted 'yes'. Hughes nearly got his way; and four months later in February 1917 Holman's government in New South Wales ran a snap election on a win-the-war ticket—and won handsomely. Three months later again Hughes held a federal election and also won impressively. So the 'no' vote was not necessarily a vote against the war itself.[16]

Hughes tried to draw back from too close association with Britain: he was careful to decline an offer by the secretary of the Board of Trade for a message to the striking coalminers of New South Wales, and he promised not to introduce conscription without another referendum.[17] Nevertheless, the issue would not go away. The British *were* short of men, and became increasingly so as Haig continued the bloody assaults on the Western

Front. At the same time recruiting in Australia—as in Canada—collapsed. Hughes had cabled the British government vehemently opposing any participation in the Stockholm peace conference, so negotiation was ruled out.[18] Smuts' suggestion in July 1917—to use Australians, New Zealanders and South Africans in the Middle East only—would have saved shipping problems and released British troops from there to the Western Front, but rearranged the existing troop dispositions rather than provided more men. In any case, the British Cabinet disagreed, on the grounds that hope of seeing Britain was a major attraction for Australian recruits.[19] Another attempt to tap Australian manpower resources was therefore inevitable, and a second referendum was called for 20 December 1917.

Once again, Hughes looked to the British for support. The governor-general wanted the Army Council to provide an 'independent' estimate of how many troops were needed.[20] Australian leaders did not even hesitate to interfere with military operations in their need to secure a 'yes' vote from the troops. Pearce cabled Birdwood about this, adding that therefore 'it is imperative that they should be kept out of firing line or given best possible conditions until end of year'. Birdwood cabled back that the Anzacs were in comfortable quarters, and asked that a list of exemptions and the promise that conscription would be only for the duration of the war be sent out urgently. It was.[21]

Despite its best efforts, for complex reasons not relevant here the government lost by a slightly greater margin than before, and the bitterness and deep divisions provoked by the referendum put fresh strains on Anglo-Australian relations.[22] Even Murdoch now accepted that differing attitudes existed.

> Australians do not and cannot feel the same way towards the war as Englishmen. They are prepared to go . . . but the instincts of self-preservation . . . which fire the English in this war do not come into it.

In an analysis about the same time he thought that though most Australians supported the war and Britain, they were also becoming more national, putting Australian before imperial considerations. He thought that 'the sentimental tie with Great Britain tends to disappear with every new generation, and . . . the Empire of the future *must* have other ties'.[23] It was a long way from the euphoria of August 1914 and Eggleston's quiet assurance that this war was Australia's war also.

British reactions to the events in Australia ranged from sympathetic analysis by Stamfordham (who blamed lack of hospitality in England for the Australian troops) to criticism of Hughes, who seems to have lost prestige in British eyes.[24] Meanwhile, in Melbourne, the governor-general changed his attitude to Australia after the first referendum, from belief in the community's loyalty, to criticism of it as 'in the main the most irresponsible, self confident & inexperienced in the Empire'. He accused Australia of contributing less than her fair proportion to the war effort, and her troops for missing the early fighting.

These opinions were shared by the more militaristic Australians, for the country was more deeply divided than at any time until the Vietnam War in the 1960s. Hughes, like Lloyd George in Britain, had thrown his energies into winning the war, split his party, and then formed a new government with his erstwhile enemies. In doing so, he had abandoned his old friends and now led a party dominated by conservatives, leaving the intense bitterness of those who felt betrayed behind him in the Opposition.[25] His action inevitably left the leadership of the ALP firmly in the hands of men who were, if not hostile to, then at least critical of, Britain—and her governor-general. As Fitzhardinge puts it, 'Predictably, more of Hughes' followers were of English or Scottish birth (forty per cent against 27.9 per cent), though some in both cases had come to Australia as children.'[26]

More importantly, the ideological lines that divided the parties became more distinct. Ironically, Labor supporters included in their repertoire material from Britain, such as that produced by the various pacifist groups.[27] Their criticism roused all the emotionalism of the loyalist elements, usually of British parents, who regarded it as treason to feel that Australia was any less involved in the war than Britain, France or Belgium. Prominent among them were the Protestant churches, especially the Anglican Church, which was 'overwhelmingly imperialistic in its loyalty' and argued that

> The person who says that 'you can put Australia first, the Empire second', is arguing that Australia can be considered apart from the Empire ... [and] is a knave—or fool—perhaps something of both.[28]

The 'alignment of Protestantism with Imperialism was an important feature of war-time society in Australia', and these Anglican views were shared by many who supported Ulster's freedom from Home Rule. They were particularly influential in the Baptist, Methodist and Presbyterian churches, which propounded a frantic patriotism, with singing of the national anthem, flags draped across the pulpit and the names of volunteers read out and appeals for further recruits. The extent to which patriotism dominated proceedings and affected every aspect of church life was remarkable. Thus one Baptist minister assured his congregation that they were born Britishers as part of the will of God, while Methodist churches resolved unanimously that Australia, 'as part of the Empire, should bear a full share of the Empire's burden'. Church leaders came very near to compromising their message by adopting a religion of patriotism—though many of their congregations obviously did not follow them. Meanwhile, the members of the Round Table group felt ashamed that Australians did not recognise the moral debt they owed Britain.[29]

The loyalist element in Australia was constantly appealed to by Hughes, with remarks like: 'We stand for the Empire because in no other way can we stand for Australia', together with references to the sale of primary produce to Britain. The government therefore was careful to support the Returned Soldiers and Sailors Imperial League of Australia (later the RSL). That organisation avoided expressing the sentiments of

some ex-soldiers, who were critical of Britain and British leadership
during the war and wanted a more independent Australia. There was also
a renewed drive to inculcate imperial patriotism in the schools, while
racialism and intolerance seem to have deepened.[30]

## THE LABOR PARTY AND THE IRISH

Hughes' stance was politically expedient, for it placed great strain on the
Labor Party and ensured its defeat in elections. After the referenda he
could brand the remaining Labor members as unpatriotic or even traitors,
especially because, as a result of the split, most of their new leaders had
been born in Ireland or were of Irish Catholic parentage.

The government propaganda picture, however, hides an oversimpli-
fication. An analysis of the seventy-five Labor members of the federal
parliament in 1914 has suggested that twenty-three were imperialists,
while fourteen saw Australian glory in the war, making a total of thirty-
seven who supported Australian involvement. On the other hand, thirty
were more or less neutral and eight definitely opposed it, i.e. thirty-eight.
The party was therefore probably more confused by the war than most
historians have thought, and the split was not caused just by conscription,
but by underlying differences in attitudes to Britain and the war itself.[31]

Another basic division was caused by the problems in Ireland. Catholics
who were Irish or Irish extraction formed approximately 23 per cent of
the population, which had its own separate schooling, was led by an Irish-
manned and Irish-trained episcopate, and was strongly represented in the
Labor Party. The leadership advised Catholics in 1914 to assist the Empire:
for Britain had promised Home Rule to Ireland and they hoped to win
State aid for Catholic schools in Australia. So in early April 1915
Archbishop Kelly, Irish by birth and training, spoke in the language of
imperial patriotism, and every major Catholic newspaper except the West
Australian *Record* supported conscription.[32]

The first reaction to the Easter Rebellion which broke out in Dublin
on 25 April 1916, was therefore disapproval, for Ireland had much to hope
from the changes that had been promised. Church leaders denounced it
as 'an act of folly by political lunatics'. But as British repression continued,
with courts condemning Irishmen to death while British officers who shot
men without trial were exonerated, and the promised Home Rule was
'postponed', a groundswell of sympathy for the rebels developed. Archbishop Duhig of Brisbane condemned the 'wholesale executions', and the
British claim to be protecting small nations seemed increasingly thin.
Duhig and other Catholic leaders may still have supported conscription,
or had mixed feelings about it, but many ordinary Catholics, coming from
the working classes, would not have supported conscription anyway, and
British repression in Ireland only strengthened their opposition. It
'insulated [them] from much of the emotional impact of Imperial
patriotism'. They maintained their old opinions and tended to side with

those who believed that Australia's contribution to the war should be decided on national, not imperial, grounds. Archbishop Mannix had been associated with the phrase 'Australia first and the Empire second', and Hughes' language and attitudes only hardened the stance of many Catholics, who felt alienated from the community. The war had ended the temporary consensus of 1914.[33]

Irish opinion was not united, however. Those from northern Ireland were intensely loyalist and continued to volunteer for the army. Even Catholic Irish opinion was divided, at least in the first referendum, when Mannix, Hughes' great opponent in the second campaign, was still moderate. It seems therefore that repression after the Irish uprising confirmed, rather than caused, Irish opposition. Incipient Australian nationalism joined hostility to Britain over Ireland and many other motives.[34]

Australian politicians therefore watched events in Ireland anxiously. Both the federal and New South Wales governments cabled for information about alleged wholesale shooting by the British, to the indignation of the Colonial Office. Premier Holman was dissatisfied with the British denial: he asked Archbishop Kelly to support conscription and got both NSW agents-general in Britain to scurry around seeing Irish and British leaders in a desperate attempt to bring the parties together.[35] Pearce cabled Hughes, who was then on his voyage back to Australia, a suggestion made in the Australian Cabinet that he could give assistance to the British government on the question. This idea, oddly enough, had been floated by Amery in May, as part of the push for Irish conscription. The reasoning behind it was that Dominion leaders would be detached and sympathetic to the Irish.[36] It came to nothing, and Hughes—on the high seas— declined to be involved. After the referendum, however, he blamed the Irish. Contemporaries differed on the truth of this, but Hughes seems to have believed it.[37] He telegraphed Lloyd George in December that the Irish problem was an imperial matter, with profound effects on Australia. He could attend the projected imperial conference in London only if Lloyd George could settle Ireland. Lloyd George replied reasonably enough that

> I fully appreciate your difficulties, but you will recognise that it is not possible for me to settle Irish question just as I please. The consent and cooperation of the Irish Parties are essential.

He then listed the complexities and difficulties they faced, and suggested Hughes get the Australian Irish to put pressure on Irish leaders to be reasonable. The wording had been suggested by Philip Kerr (one of Lord Milner's 'Kindergarten'), but was no more practicable than Hughes' message.[38]

Faced with the election of May 1917, Hughes feared an Australian Irish backlash. On 8 March the Senate sent a resolution to the King, supporting the prompt grant of Home Rule to Ireland.[39] Four days later Hughes asked Murdoch to see Lloyd George and impress on him the effect on Australia, and to support Asquith's suggestion of an imperial conference of Britain,

Ulster, the Nationalists and Dominion prime ministers. Hughes would then seek to postpone the Australian elections and attend. He added that the 'Irish have right to local self-government'. Lloyd George would not have been impressed, especially as Hughes suggested Murdoch discuss this with Lord Milner and Amery, the two erstwhile conspirators against Asquith. Some have thought that Hughes' presence at the conference would have helped, for he was 'known to have an interest in settling the Irish Question, but [is] already proclaimed by English Tories as a great statesman'.[40] This seems doubtful, for Hughes was no conciliator. His reaction when faced with opposition was revealed in July 1917 when he tried to get the Foreign Office to approach the Vatican to silence Mannix.[41] On the eve of the election, Murdoch in Hughes' name begged Lloyd George to make some reference in his speech on Ireland to Hughes' efforts to promote Home Rule.[42] But that didn't work either.

## THE LATER FINANCIAL AND TRADING RELATIONSHIP

Financial relations also became tense. By 1917 Britain's resources were becoming strained, and it seemed to her leaders that Australian governments were spending money recklessly. The Treasury therefore suggested that the States borrow money from America.[43] Hughes was very reluctant, arguing that this would weaken Australian ties with Britain, a plea which roused the support of George V, Long and Stamfordham. The latter wrote of 'the consideration due from the Mother Country to her children'. This 'consideration', however, was not shown later in the year by Munro Ferguson, who sabotaged the Australian government by giving as his opinion that Britain had made credit much too easy for Australia, that she would borrow all she could, and that her workers were not suffering from the war—sentiments which Long duly passed on to Bonar Law.[44]

In fact, the Australian balance of trade does seem to have improved, the surplus of exports over imports rising from £26.75 million to £34.16 million—though gold and silver bullion exports fluctuated wildly. By now the war had proved an economic boon to Australia. Unemployment had remained around 6 per cent as State governments continued their borrowing to maintain public works. W. A. Watt as Treasurer remarked in his budget speech in 1918 that 'The prosperity of Australia is remarkable.' He praised Britain's generosity, and hoped it would continue till normal trade was resumed, for he was 'deeply impressed with Australia's dependence, not only alone for safety, but also for material progress, upon our Home-land and Empire'. It was a just comment.[45] What may give food for thought to today's economists, however, is that Australian prosperity was built on tariffs, overseas loans, government spending, and negative finance.

The prosperity was the cause of another betrayal of Australian interests by Munro Ferguson. In January 1918 he dutifully passed on the government's message that because of war expenditure it found difficulty in paying the full war debt to Britain, and requested to be allowed to pay £1 million a month for five months and then interest on the balance. He then wrote to the Colonial Secretary, however, that although 'Thanks to Britain this country is financially prosperous at the present', that might not continue, so the British should consider whether larger repayments might not be better. This eventually led to unseemly squabbles over payment for ammunition used by the AIF,[46] but more importantly it revealed once again that Munro Ferguson's loyalty was to the British, not the Australian, government.

Meanwhile, the wool agreement worked smoothly. Wool which Britain did not use herself was sold at cost to third parties if for war purposes, and for a profit if for civilian use—such profit to be shared equally, after costs had been deducted, between Australia and Britain. Australia gained from the sales and the British could control the flow of wool. Meat sales also went well.[47]

It was a different story with wheat and shipping. Informed that the American wheat crop would be poor, the British changed policies and sought the entire Australian crop—but on condition that they controlled the shipping. Despite Hughes' frantic negotiations to avoid being totally bound to Britain, he at length agreed—for a higher price. Early in 1917 however, unrestricted submarine warfare led to a further tonnage crisis, so the wheat Britain had bought was left to moulder on Australian wharfs—and provoke a gargantuan plague of mice and weevils. At the same time the Admiralty threatened to requisition even ships registered for the Australian coastal trade; Hughes threatened his own requisitions, and after similar difficulties with Canada the British government agreed in May 1917 that each part of the Empire could requisition ships on its own registry. The British promptly requisitioned their ships on the Australian coastal trade and the Shipping Controller also appealed for coastal vessels to replace the desperate shortage that faced Britain. Despite its own difficulties, the Australian government reacted sympathetically, released seven steamers immediately, and after another appeal eventually provided thirty-three ships from its coastal trade by the end of the war.

This shortage of shipping disrupted Australian industries which had been developed specifically for the British market, but by the end of the war Britain had bought the bulk of Australia's wool, wheat, meat, metals and dairy products, and so provided for Australia's commercial security.[48]

Nevertheless, what is striking is the inevitably different viewpoint of Britain, facing the German army across the channel, and Australia, 15,000 kilometres away on the opposite side of the globe. The problem with shipping was typical. The Australian government saw the transportation of its foodstuffs as a primary task, without which Australian financial and economic life would collapse. Britain saw the primary task as the transport of troops and war supplies, and therefore tried to import necessary food from the nearest and easiest source. The interests of the

two countries differed, and only loyalty, compromise on both sides—
though stretched to the limit on occasions—and sometimes British
secrecy, prevented a complete rift. Thus in the dispute over three German
steamers seized by South Africa in 1914, the Sydney Chamber of Commerce
asked Reid to remind the Colonial Office that they themselves were 'not
enemy subjects'.[49]

## JAPAN

The deepest division of opinion between Britain and Australia, however,
occurred over Japanese expansion in the Pacific. In 1914 the British, with
an inadequate fleet in the east and the threat of German battleships, turned
to their ally Japan to escort the AIF on its way to Egypt, protect their
interests against German raiders, and seize German coaling and radio
stations in the Pacific. This last was partly a defensive move against
German raiders, and partly the traditional policy of seizing possessions
which could be bartered at any peace conference that ended the expected
short war.

Although the British government tried to limit Japanese territorial
claims, it soon realised that Japan would take advantage of her position
and demand the Pacific islands north of the equator. This was most
embarrassing, and resulted in an attempt to hide the truth from Australia.
A prepared Australian expedition to Yap in the Caroline Islands was
cancelled, and a thoroughly evasive cable was sent to Australia about the
Japanese occupation of Pacific islands. It spoke of Japanese 'policing'
and left the question of ownership to be settled at the end of war. In fact,
there was a bitter dispute in the British Cabinet between the Colonial
Secretary, Lewis Harcourt, and the Foreign Office over what information
should be given the Australians. Bonar Law and Lord Lansdowne refused
to be involved, and Edwin Montagu, Financial Secretary to the Treasury,
bluntly, indeed callously, argued that

> the Japanese have been far more useful to us in this war than the Australians
> ... I would rather cede Australia to the Japanese than cede to Australia
> anything that the Japanese want.

So when the Australian government asked if an agreement had been
reached between Britain and Japan, the British categorically denied it,
while at the same time, as mentioned earlier, Harcourt privately cabled
Munro Ferguson to keep to the public policy that the matter would be
settled at a peace conference after the war, but 'prepare the mind' of his
ministers for Japanese gains then. The doubts this raised were probably
behind Fisher's suggestion for an imperial conference and the British
avoidance of the same. Harcourt however also instructed Munro Ferguson
that no 'anti-Japanese agitation should, during the progress of the war
be allowed to arise in Australia'.

Nevertheless, as rumours of Japanese intentions leaked out, Australian suspicion increased. In 1915 the Japanese wanted Australia to adhere to the Anglo-Japanese Commercial Treaty of 1911, which alarmed Hughes. As for the Pacific islands, although he was willing to wait at first for the peace treaty, there was a danger that they would become minor pawns in negotiations, so when he became prime minister he 'judged that the time was decidedly overdue for consultations with the British'. These occurred in London, when he saw Grey and the Foreign Office followed by a meeting with the Japanese ambassador to Britain. Hughes was not reassured, however, and his fears began to amount to an obsession, 'the more powerful because it could not be publicly expressed'. To a man of Hughes' temperament, the absolute necessity to hold his tongue would have been traumatic.

So when the question of Japanese control of Pacific islands was raised again in 1917, Hughes replied that Australia would not object to Japan occupying those in the North Pacific, and quibbled only about some which he—mistakenly—thought were near the equator. He was preoccupied in forming a new government at the time, and so 'acquiesced under duress' in accepting Britain's promise to support Japanese claims. The Colonial Office was greatly relieved, for otherwise it would have been obliged to provide a full account of Anglo-Japanese discussions for the Australians.

Australia could not really claim the islands in the North Pacific, which were too far away, but they were useful bargaining counters, and the trickle of information from Britain had made Hughes suspicious. Fitzhardinge thinks that fear of Japan lay behind the conscription campaigns: a conviction that after the war Japan would challenge the White Australia policy, Australia would need the Empire's help, and could only claim it if she had contributed outstandingly to Britain's war against Germany.

But there was not much sympathy for Australia in Britain's ruling circles. Balfour agreed with Grey that they could hardly forbid Japan to go into China, if she was excluded from America, Canada, Australia and New Zealand. Balfour was one of the originators of the Anglo-Japanese Alliance. Lloyd George argued that the question of Japan's colonial acquisitions should be treated after the war from an imperial and not a local (i.e. Australian) viewpoint—so much for consulting the Dominions![50]

### THE 1917 IMPERIAL CONFERENCE AND THE EMPIRE

Another possibility of influencing British policy, however, soon arose. As the war had progressed, the need to organise the resources of the Empire, and to that end perhaps change the imperial constitution, began to be widely felt. Various peace moves and the attempt by President Wilson of the United States to get the belligerents to clarify their war aims also added urgency to the belief of many of Lloyd George's supporters in a federal empire with a new imperial parliament.[51]

Lloyd George as a practical politician was more concerned with his own power base, and on taking office created a small inner executive Cabinet of five members, which did not include the Colonial Secretary, Walter Long. Long was naturally disappointed; he stressed the importance of the Empire and raised the thorny question of the fate of ex-German colonies. To allay Dominion concern Lloyd George cabled the premiers assuring them of his government's determination to carry on and win the war. This was not quite what Long wanted—a place in the inner Cabinet would have suited him better—but the first full Cabinet discussed the need to consult the Dominions on possible peace terms. Moreover, as Lloyd George admitted, they needed more men from the Dominions and could hardly therefore avoid consultation. He gave a flowery interview to Murdoch in which he spoke about Dominion sacrifices and the unity yet independence of the members of the Empire.

Accordingly, it was agreed to summon the Dominion Premiers. After some confusion it was decided that the body which discussed the war would be named the Imperial War Cabinet, although unlike a normal Cabinet its members were neither chosen by the prime minister, nor responsible to one parliament, nor required to resign if they differed from the majority opinion. More general debate on long-term issues of the Empire would take place in the Imperial War Conference, the chairmanship of which Lloyd George gave to Long. The 'Welsh wizard' thus in his usual fashion solved many problems at once.[52]

The summons, however, came at an impossible time for Hughes, who was then negotiating with Cook to form a coalition government of his ex-Labor followers and the Liberals. He then faced a general election in which his future hung in the balance. He could hardly leave Australia for several months once again, and in addition be cut off at sea for weeks on end. He therefore enquired as to Lloyd George's intentions, to receive a flowery cable from Long, who stressed the urgency of the discussions and earnestly requested his presence—but if not, a suitable substitute. Neither idea appealed to Hughes. He cabled Lloyd George, to settle the Irish question, and Murdoch, questioning the exact functions and likely practical effectiveness of the meetings. He clearly expected much talk and political posturing, but few practical results.

Murdoch assured Hughes of the importance of the intended meetings, and feared that if Fisher represented Australia, he would be dominated by Smuts. He also added that a weak conference 'might dangerously encourage "jingoistic English Imperialism" injurious to Australia.' It was an interesting thought, but unfortunately he did not elaborate on it. Milner, Lloyd George and Northcliffe all urged Hughes to come, but if not to 'send the most authoritative and representative alternative possible'. Hughes tried to stall, organise an early election, or postpone the British meetings—in vain. In the end he neither went himself nor sent a representative, his distrust of Fisher no doubt influencing him in the latter decision.[53]

The Imperial War Cabinet and Conference met from March until May 1917. Its members considered postponing important matters until Hughes arrived and Smuts suggested a message that imperial consultation would not be a reality without an Australian representative, but the Colonial Secretary stressed the difficulties in Australia while Sir G. Fiddes of the Colonial Office thought it would only have a bad effect on Hughes. Cabinet discussed the possibility of sending out the documents circulated during the meetings, hesitated when Lloyd George worried about security, but in the end did so. It sent a cable regretting Hughes' absence, while Stamfordham thought it 'deplorable'.[54]

It has been argued that the conference was really a clever tactic by Lloyd George to seem to grant consultation, while in fact granting little, and committing the Dominions, especially Canada, to support his policy of striving for victory in Europe.[55] This seems true enough, but it was nevertheless unfortunate that Hughes could not attend the meetings, for he missed a valuable chance for self-education and to put Australia's case.

He could not respond when Borden stressed Canada's great contribution to the war by detailing Australia's help. No wonder Australia was given less credit in 1917 and 1918. He did not hear the British point out that it was twenty-one days by ship to Argentina but forty-two days to New Zealand—with the obvious implications—and Massey's bitter retort that this was 'a sorry requital for all New Zealand's sacrifices in the common cause'. He missed the early discussion of the League of Nations and on Resolution IX, which defined the status of the Dominions as autonomous nations of the Commonwealth. This 'summarized the impact of the Great War upon the British Empire and forecast the transition to the postwar British Commonwealth of Nations'. It also seemed to abandon the idea of a federal empire, as Smuts pointed out.[56]

Moreover, the future of the Pacific Islands was discussed in the Curzon Committee. In this, Massey of New Zealand raised antipodean concerns and sought a definitive statement, but in the absence of Hughes got nowhere and was silent in the Imperial Cabinet meeting. As a result the committee's report stated that it had been agreed 'with the concurrence of the Governments of Australia and New Zealand' that the German Pacific islands north of the equator should be retained by Japan. This would not have passed so easily if Hughes had been present. Nor would he have missed the significance of Massey's bitter remark that 'in the past the Dominions had been willing to share the burden of Empire, but had no voice. That would not occur again.' Finally, he might have turned his attention to the *conduct* of the war, instead of just continuing it.[57]

In short, despite the ambiguity in Lloyd George's Imperial War Cabinet, Hughes missed a vitally important opportunity. Thereafter he had to be content with British official cables giving detail without explanation or debate—such as on the submarine campaign in September 1917—or generalisations on German colonies and the grand strategy of the Empire through correspondence with Amery.[58] Together, they may have lulled Hughes into a false sense of security.

## THE CREATION OF PUBLIC OPINION: CENSORSHIP

All governments in the war limited and arranged the information they provided others, in order to influence public opinion. Hughes, more than most, should have recognised this. The first—negative—method, was by censoring the information that the public received. Bean's despatches, for example, were very tightly controlled by the military censors. They were not only vetted, but it was stipulated on what day they could be published and whether in the morning or evening papers.[59]

Australian censorship of mail, newspapers and cables was established by a directive from Britain, and was 'nominally under the control of the Chief Censor in London, who delegated authority to Deputy Chief Censors in all British Empire countries'. Nevertheless, when the governor-general became involved in 1914, the Colonial Office protested that they would not presume to judge Australian censorship, which was a matter for the local authorities. In 1918 they twice declined to intervene, and pointedly noted that the governor-general on one occasion had acted without consulting the Australian government.[60] So Australian censors exercised their own initiative and came directly under their own government. The Deputy Chief Censor in Melbourne not only had 'direct links with London', but was also responsible to the Australian Minister for Defence. To help recruiting, he therefore accepted Hughes' request during the Gallipoli campaign to delete references to inadequate hospital treatment, camp troubles or criticism of the military planning.

The British *Defence of the Realm Act*, and others, were sent to Australia, and sometimes British decrees were copied word for word, irrespective of their applicability to Australia. The Australian *War Precautions Act* was 'the main instrument of wartime government' creating a censorship which was 'a devastatingly effective form of ideological constraint upon all viewpoints in any degree critical of the war effort or the righteousness of the Allied cause'.[61]

Robertson argues that the 'censorship did not prevent Australians from obtaining an accurate impression of the horrors of the fighting', but it seems clear that it did prevent a realistic appraisal of the conflict by Australians in general, and lessened their political awareness. For example, the failure on Gallipoli might have been the basis for separatism in Australia,[62] but news of the stalemate arrived slowly. It was not until August that the *Age* printed Ashmead-Bartlett's judgement that the result was unfavourable to the allies, together with reports from the London press criticising the campaign. And it was almost six weeks before the failure of the August offensive was accepted. The papers adopted a 'patriotic' tone when news arrived of dissension in the Asquith Cabinet, and were so ill-informed when Hamilton was replaced as commander that they could not make intelligent comment, and even they began to complain of their lack of background information. Churchill's resignation from the Cabinet in November attracted much attention, but the press was divided over the evacuation, printing some criticism of the British but in the main stressing the bravery of the Anzacs.[63] There was more bitterness in Britain than Australia over the Gallipoli failure.

Because of the censorship, Australians just did not know enough. Bonar Law asked Hughes to suspend judgement on Ashmead-Bartlett's letter, and prevent publicity. Hughes obliged. Ashmead-Bartlett's letter was impounded, and Murdoch's letter was not published in Australia until 1968. Later, as we have seen, when Ashmead-Bartlett came for a lecture tour he was obliged to produce the written text of his lecture beforehand, and officials attended to ensure he did not deviate from it, on pain of being removed from the platform. While British newspapers therefore branded Gallipoli as 'a bloody fiasco', the most that was admitted in Australia was bungling, and 'the imperial connection was in no way threatened or besmirched'.[64]

Nevertheless, the all-pervasive censorship was noted. Even the Round Table commented on the constant restrictions imposed 'at the request of the Imperial Government', or as a result of information from the War Office or Admiralty. It considered Australian independence lessened, and even thought that this would lead to a reconsideration of future relations.[65] It did not note that the initiative for much of the censorship came from the Australian authorities themselves.

## THE CREATION OF PUBLIC OPINION: PROPAGANDA

Combined with the censorship, moreover, was propaganda. Australians, like the other peoples of the Empire, were subjected to 'a constant barrage of indoctrination', most of which had British origins. The obvious example was the use of British songs such as 'Rule Britannia' and 'Sons of the Sea' at patriotic meetings, or the tidal wave of postcards which were printed and sent at the time, or the many films that were produced, especially recruiting films, some of which were British and some Australian. Australian censors were so rigorous that they would appear to have damaged the chances of this new propaganda medium, while Hughes embarrassed the Colonial Office by enquiring whether there was any truth in newspaper reports of a German 'corpse factory' in Belgium.[66]

In Britain the private group, the Central Committee for National Patriotic Organizations was soon replaced by more official bodies. In September 1914 a meeting at Wellington House in London of leading poets, novelists and publicists (such as Conan Doyle, G. K. Chesterton, John Masefield, Sir Henry Newbolt) created the War Propaganda Bureau, headed by C. F. G. Masterman. This sent articles, cartoons, photographs and 'news' to allied nations and the Empire, and fed them into the major cable services. In this way stories of 'Brave Little Belgium', fabricated German atrocity stories, emotional diatribes about the sinking of the *Lusitania* and the shooting of Nurse Cavell, reached Australia.[67] Meanwhile, the War Office organised tours of the front for selected writers, such as Masefield and John Buchan, who stressed the heroism and cheerfulness of the troops. Conan Doyle and Buchan wrote popular histories of the war while it continued. Indeed, Buchan was allowed to continue his *Nelson's History of the War* after he had been appointed to Haig's intelligence staff! Anzac Day 1916 has to be viewed against the background of this propaganda effort.[68]

The parallels with Australia were close. Bean's writing was in the tradition of the heroic war accounts of Wellington House, which carefully avoided the strategic aims of a campaign or battle, concentrating instead on the heroism of the soldiers. His *Anzac Book* has been discussed earlier, but what needs to be added here is that it was suggested by a British intelligence officer when the evacuation had been planned. Its format corresponded closely with the War Office's 'Notes on Propaganda' (a large number of articles, interesting to read, with no obvious propaganda use, but portraying the soldiers as cheerful and happy, etc.). In addition, an article by Edgar Wallace (of the Wellington House team) was inserted without Bean's knowledge. Although not directly commissioned, the *Anzac Book* was therefore an example of British propaganda techniques, and when Bean ran into difficulties about publishing photographs in it, he appealed to the Colonial Office, and Bonar Law asked the Army Council to grant permission.[69]

The Australian authorities also used Anzac Day celebrations to inculcate a feeling of pride. They painted a picture of heroism and a united Empire, with the Dominions coming to the aid of the motherland. This pride in the Anzacs and grief at the deaths could be used to prevent any critical analysis of the campaign, for that would appear to question the need for the men to have died.

In the same way, academics in Australia rallied to the cause. This is hardly surprising. Most professors were British by birth or education. G. A. Wood, Challis Professor of History at Sydney, had been born in England and was Oxford trained. Sir Ernest Scott (later author of Volume XI of the official history) had also been born in England. He was Professor of History at the University of Melbourne, and 'reflected the pro-imperial, Anglophile outlook of the staunch war supporter'.

G. C. Henderson, Professor of History of the University of Adelaide, although born in New South Wales had been educated at Oxford. Similarly, Archibald T. Strong was Acting Head of the Department of English in Melbourne. His life was akin to that of Bean. Born in Australia but travelling to England at the age of seven with his father, he later attended Oxford University and then returned to Australia at the age of twenty-five. Rejected for war service on account of ill health, he threw himself passionately into 'war work'. The disappointment was reflected in his writing during the war, which was sometimes quite virulent, depicting all Germans as a 'race of devils', who had 'deliberately manufactured the present war as a preliminary to the enslavement of Europe and the downfall of the British Empire'. He argued that the war therefore affected Australia as much as Britain, and opposed a negotiated peace with the 'hideous Teutonic menace'. His appeal to the working classes echoed Lord Milner's sentiments.

Those in the sciences went into war production or sat on technical committees, but those in the arts also had their place. War committees were set up in all universities, and organised patriotic meetings and conscription rallies in the country. Strong was particularly active on the latter. This reflected the totally British orientation of the universities at the time. The historian of this movement, John Moses, is careful to point out that Professor Wood consulted the available documents, but fails to note that these were *British* government compilations, and therefore part of British propaganda output.[70]

The exact effect of all this on the community is difficult to gauge. Many schools became even more imperial-minded, with patriotic rituals such as saluting the flag, although Catholic schools often adopted a more questioning spirit. The all-pervasive propaganda, however, filtered down to the young,[71] which was the intention.

## THE PRESS

Murdoch, meanwhile, after noting that the sentimental ties with Britain weakened with the passing generations, thought that one need was for more information about the Australian army. He blamed the British GHQ, and demanded more news for the papers.[72] The newspapers

> dominated the channels of public information ... and their roseate representation of the war, their impression of imminent victory, their suppression or minimization of the losses, defeats, squalor, misery, and horror, must have influenced the public greatly.[73]

They certainly provided no check on the military authorities or their governments.

Individual members or controllers of the press tried to influence governments, or overthrow leaders on occasion, as we have seen, and the latter were constantly worried by them. The governor-general bitterly attacked Murdoch for criticism of the Colonial Office and described him as 'obviously one of the most ambitious of the pressmen who set themselves up to rule over us'.[74] But the 'natural rulers of the Empire' protested too much. They themselves used the press to destabilise opponents, exercise influence, or even seize power, as well as censor information that put their policies or themselves in a bad light, and pump out misinformation about their own side.

As we have seen, when war broke out, the British authorities had begun by trying to limit press access to news, which led to Bean's troubles. But the Australian government adopted a similar attitude, and blamed Hamilton for allowing Ashmead-Bartlett to go to Gallipoli: it argued that unofficial reporters devalued the Government Press Service, and requested that in future permission should not be granted to any Australian press representative to visit the front without the prior agreement of the Australian government.[75]

Australian newspapers used British cable sources and press reports, and so echoed the slavish support for the high command and unrealistic reporting of the British press. They therefore provided no check on the government, or information to make informed judgement on the war. Nor did Australia loom largely in the British press. The *Daily Mail* in 1915 mentioned the French, the Gurkhas, the Scots, the Royal Fusiliers and the Worcestershire regiment, but—apart from Ashmead-Bartlett's reports —rarely the Australians.

Moreover, the use of heroic-romantic language masked the horrible realities of the war. Ashmead-Bartlett's famous despatch from Gallipoli was therefore not unusual, and he repeated it in even more flowery terms in September 1915. Such language was commonly employed in the *Daily Mail*, and it was only Australians' lack of experience that prevented them from recognising the genre, so that they took his praise at face value.

The Australians themselves continually complained about press bias, especially the use of the word 'British'. One pointed out in the overseas *Daily Mail* that victories were 'English', whereas defeats or disasters were 'British'. A perusal of the columns suggests this was hardly fair; indeed the governor-general thought that one reason for the failure of the first referendum was that exaggerated praise for the Anzacs made Australians think that they had done enough. But the *Mail*'s account of the evacuation clearly reveals the propaganda line. Avoiding the fact that the expedition had been a failure, it stressed the heroism of the troops. Nor were the Anzacs particularly singled out: the phrase 'English yeomen' was bandied around as praise was distributed among many divisions.[76]

Interestingly, there seems to have been a concerted effort to play down Australian achievements in 1917. Lord Riddell, owner of the *News of the World*, confided in his diary his protests against 'booming' the deeds of colonial troops while soldiers from the British Isles were ignored: 'No one grudges the colonials their publicity. The objection is the suppression of all reference to the doings of the home units.' It could hardly have been coincidence that three days later the *Daily Mail* had a leading article on dissatisfaction among British troops at praise for Canadians and Australians. A further article appeared in October on the neglect of the old English regiments, with statistics to support its argument that the majority of troops in the British army were in fact *English*.[77]

Tension between the Australian press and British elites does not seem to have lessened by the end of 1917. Thereafter, however, the Anzacs were reorganised into a united corps at last, and embarked on the run of triumphs with which they ended the war. It remained to be seen whether that affected relations with the British.

# CHAPTER SIX

# Anzacs and Brasshats: The British High Command and the Australians

Ludendorff: The English soldiers fight like lions.
Hoffman:    True. But don't we know that they are lions led by
            donkeys.

FALKENHAYN,
*Mémoires*

## THE REBIRTH OF THE AIF: FRANCE, 1917–1918

Bullecourt was the nadir of Australian military competence in World War I. Shortly afterwards the AIF began its most intense period of practical and relevant training, which bore fruit for II Anzac Corps (the 3rd and 4th Australian divisions and the New Zealand division) in the third battle of Ypres, under Plumer at Messines in August 1917. It was a training they desperately needed, and they improved immensely, but even so, when Haig insisted that only the best troops be used for the main attack, he still did not include the Australians.[1] The weather then broke, and the whole affair became bogged down in the horrendous mud for which it has remained famous ever since.

But success or failure, the result was the same: they suffered 38,000 more casualties, and by the end of 1917—seeing that two referenda had rejected conscription—were facing an insoluble reinforcement problem. In October Birdwood informed Haig that none of the four divisions of I Anzac Corps could be counted on for a further offensive operation.[2] The obvious need for rest for the Australian divisions placed him in a cleft stick: he felt honour bound to demand rest for his troops, yet if he did so, his claim to command an 'Army' looked even more thin. He began talking about the need to disband one or more divisions, and disperse the men to bring the numbers of the others up to full strength. He was bluffing: the move was to disband the fourth *battalion* in every infantry brigade—but even this provoked great opposition from the men and reluctance from their leaders.[3]

## BIRDWOOD'S PROMOTION AND THE FINAL
## ADMINISTRATIVE STRUCTURE

Considerable administrative changes were occurring within the British
army in 1917, under the impetus of Canadian demands. The Canadians
insisted that their force was one entity, whose separate existence should
be respected, firmly under civil control and autonomous from the British
War Office.[4] The Australians lagged behind the Canadians, but they too
were finally united under the command of Birdwood on 15 November
1917, and the corps was renamed the Australian Corps the following
January.[5]

Then in March 1918 Ludendorff took his final gamble. (General Erich
Ludendorff held the position of First Quartermaster-General, but he was
Hindenburg's right-hand man and the effective German commander-in-
chief on the Western Front.) With Russia out of the war, he launched
the first of four tremendous attacks in an effort to break the allied armies
before the Americans were deployed in large numbers. The weight of
the first attack fell on Gough's Fifth Army, which promptly collapsed.
Many units fled, their officers failing to give leadership, and the men
surrendered in similar proportions to the Italians in the North African
desert in World War II. There followed near panic, with Churchill talking
of a 'levée en masse', Haig issuing his 'Backs to the Wall' appeal while
considering breaking with the French and retreating on the channel ports;
and recriminations between him and the British government. Haig
avoided immediate trouble to himself by sacking Brigadier-General J.
Charteris, Chief Intelligence Officer, and Gough of the Fifth Army.
Birdwood, as the most senior corps commander, was offered the army
command.[6]

This created a real problem for Birdwood, and stimulated a further
reassessment of the Australian command structure. Birdwood could not
simultaneously command both the Anzac Corps and the Fifth Army in
the field, so his immediate military promotion seemed likely to damage
his ultimate future in Australia. He protested mightily that he wished
to keep his connections with the Anzacs, and argued somewhat speciously
that he should still retain administrative control of Australian forces, as
General Officer Commanding AIF in London.

The Australian nationalists, however, had long held reservations about
Birdwood, and wanted an Australian to command the corps. They noted
that in April he had insisted on sending forward a plan of attack despite
White's firm opposition to it, because—according to White—he did not
want it thought he wished to keep the Australians out of the fighting.[7]
He seemed more concerned about his own standing with the British high
command than the well-being of Australian troops.

The lead was taken once again by Keith Murdoch, who argued strongly
that the interests of the AIF were too widespread, while Birdwood had
visited the Salisbury training camps only twice in a year, and then only

for short periods. (Another of Pearce's correspondents thought that Birdwood had not spent forty-eight hours in the Australian training depots in England since the war began, and argued that 'his very position as an Imperial Officer would preclude him from standing up to the War Office'.) Murdoch compared the Australian with the Canadian system, and noted that the Australian government could have no control over Birdwood while he was army commander:

> Australia's interests inevitably involve conflicts with British officials. . . . In strategy we have suffered deplorably by British mistakes . . . General Birdwood becomes now an even more close and absolute servant of G.H.Q. His past has been British, and his present and future lie completely in their hands.

He thought that to safeguard Australian interests the AIF should be totally 'Australianised', and command in the field separated from administration in London.[8]

That however raised the problem of who was to fill each post. White, ever loyal to Birdwood, had agreed to go with him to the Fifth Army as his Chief of Staff, and with Haig's support Monash had been appointed to command the Anzac Corps. This provoked a cabal, led by Bean and Murdoch, and including Fisher, to lobby Hughes and the Australian government to put White back in command of the corps, and Monash to command the AIF post in London, on the mistaken assumption that White was the more able commander. Birdwood's reaction was to write on the matter to both the Colonial Office in London and the Australian government in Melbourne, which brought Watt and Hughes into the debate.[9] Hughes, however, was a man with definite ideas of his own, and could not be manipulated easily by any of the parties. By this time he was critical of British management of the war and increasingly identified with 'the Diggers'. The issue therefore now raised in acute form not only the simple matter of army command, but also the relationship between Britain and Australia.

Monash, the new commander of the corps, was both an Australian nationalist *and* one who could get on well with the British—since he had been a protégé of Hutton. His commanders were also men who had been born in Australia or had lived there for many years. Typically, therefore, he arrived at his first divisional commanders' conference in what had been Birdwood's Rolls-Royce, but flying an Australian flag on its bonnet. His pride in the Australian character of the corps comes through in his letters to his wife; but this did not stop him having a close rapport with George V, helped by Monash's meticulous organising of the review of his troops by the King.[10] Monash was determined not to relinquish command of the Anzacs in battle until he—and they— had proved themselves.

The Australian nationalists and Hughes, however, were equally determined that command in the field should be separated from the administration of the AIF. Hughes cabled his government:

No man can serve two masters. Remember Birdwood is now commanding an English Army. He looks to War Office for his orders and preferment for the maintenance of his position. Where interests of Australia and Britain clash—and that they do clash and have clashed in military matters is certain and that interests Australia have suffered—for which will he stand?

Hughes went on to argue that the Australians had more than their fair share of the fighting, and compared their fortunes with those of the Canadians, who had their own corps commander in the field and a separate Canadian general in charge of administration in London. He thought therefore that in view of his past services, Birdwood should be given a choice of positions.[11]

That left Birdwood with a dilemma: whether he should relinquish command of the Fifth Army and become GOCAIF again, or retain his army command and abandon the Australians. Typically, he tried to avoid it and have the best of both worlds. He had the sympathy of Munro Ferguson, the governor-general, and was in correspondence both with him and the Colonial Office, complaining of the machinations of Murdoch. The Colonial Secretary, Walter Long, was sympathetic but would not take sides. Birdwood then sought Haig's opinion. The latter advised him to accept the GOCAIF—no doubt thinking he would be rid of Birdwood if he did so. Birdwood accordingly informed Hughes that he would be available—after 30 November.[12] The war, however, ended before that date arrived.

Monash being knighted by George V. (National Library of Australia).

## THE AIF ON THE WESTERN FRONT, 1918

While these debates were raging, on the Western Front the soldiers whom the commanders were to lead were reaching the peak of their effectiveness. During the great British retreat the Australians came into their own. The Canadians insisted on remaining together: both General Currie and the Canadian government protested against their units being split up or mixed with British ones. Haig borrowed Lord Derby's phraseology after one meeting and remarked, 'I could not help feeling that some people in Canada regard themselves rather as "Allies" than fellow citizens in the Empire!' He added that though they held a wide front near Arras they had not yet been in battle, whereas the Australians had allowed themselves to be moved in separate units to the areas of greatest need, and were spread out from Albert to Amiens.[13]

Used in that way the Australians, as they marched to fill gaps in the line, saw evidence of a breakdown in British morale, and their contempt for the British Tommy, and pride in their own abilities, increased correspondingly. As Liddell Hart later wrote:

> They exulted in the freedom of open fighting and in the feeling that they were saving the situation, a feeling enhanced by the impression of the British troops as exhausted and drifting.

Whether this was fair to the British troops—many of whom did not break—is beside the point. Dour Australian orders to their men not to surrender or retire reflected their cocky self-assurance that they could hold the Germans, and that they were different. A British Hussar officer reported Australian 'jubilation' as they packed their kits to move. All 'the men I saw are in great heart and fairly had their tails up'.[14] With their high morale came a new willingness to contradict British commanders if necessary. In stark contrast with Fromelles (1916) and the second battle of Bullecourt (1917), when Brigadier W. Glasgow was ordered in 1918 to make a counter attack before Villers-Bretonneux near sunset, and told that it was the order of the corps commander, he retorted 'If it was God Almighty who gave the order it could not be done in the daylight.' His demand that the assault be postponed till darkness was granted.[15]

Moreover, the German attacks had broken the fighting into open country once again—which suited the Australian temperament. Small bodies of them infiltrated the German lines, seizing captives and dominating no man's land, in 'peaceful penetration'. The historian of the Fourth Army, the later CIGS Montgomery-Massingberd, paid glowing tribute to the Australians in this kind of warfare and stated that the Australian dominance 'had a very important effect on subsequent operations'.[16]

Finally, the uniting of the corps, and the appointment of Monash and his team to lead it, provided the Anzacs at last with competent commanders. There followed the brilliant little success at Hamel on 4 July and the triumph in conjunction with British and Canadian forces

Australian troops about to attack Mont St Quentin. (AWM Official Photo No. F.31439).

in the larger battle of Amiens on 8 August, which Ludendorff regarded as 'the black day of the German Army'. The great improvements in technology and firepower helped to win these victories, but the expertise of the troops, and the efficiency of their commanders, also had much to do with it, as did the horrendous losses of the German army in their great attacks. It was a very depleted force that met the Australians from July onwards, and 'Rawlinson reported to Haig that German officers were now saying frankly that their men would not face the Australians.' After the spectacular capture of Mont St Quentin by the physically and numerically weakened Anzacs which has been described as 'the greatest infantry exploit of the war' and left Rawlinson 'totally incredulous', the Australians finally broke into the Hindenburg Line itself, before being withdrawn for rest on 5 October.[17] The armistice came before they returned to action.

## HOW GOOD WERE THE AUSTRALIAN SOLDIERS?

If Australian public opinion was divided on the war, on one thing it was united: the merits of the Australian soldier. His prowess was first celebrated by Ashmead-Bartlett's ringing despatch on the landing on Gallipoli, with phrases like 'this race of athletes'. The theme was taken up by Bean on the peninsula and permeates his official history and other writings. He 'idealised [the] Australian as a reincarnation of the 16th Century Briton', and claimed that there was 'overwhelming evidence that

the AIF, like all the other armies from the British dominions, was found
to be amongst the most effective military forces of the war'. For his part
Monash in 1918 added his weight to the paeon when he described the
Australian corps as 'the backbone of the Allied Armies'.[18]

In the 1960s Bean's work and the Anzac tradition was revived for modern
readers by Bill Gammage and others. Gammage stressed the heroism of
the Australians, especially during the British retreat, and disproportionate
captures and advances they made in the last seven months of the war.[19]
Ken Inglis has accepted this view and written extensively on the impact
of 'the Anzac legend' on Australian society.

More recently, however, a new school of historians has begun to cast
a cynical eye on what appears to be 'big noting'. Murdoch's account of
Gallipoli has been savaged, and they have pointed out that Bean
understated factors such as weapons and leadership, exaggerated bush
influences, and by his use of language 'heroicised' the fighting.[20] Educated
in an English public school and university, mixing with officers, and with
the privilege of freedom of movement, Bean in many ways did not
understand the ordinary Australian soldier.

Of course, all nations praise their own soldiers. Canadian authors have
been no more backward than the Australians, one putting the Canadians
among the top British divisions in 1916 without mentioning the
Australians at all.[21] Modern readers are therefore left undecided whether
to believe the stories of the first AIF or not.

Partly this stems from problems inherent in generalisation. Some
characteristics were extremely common in the AIF, a larrikin streak and
inveterate gambling being two of them. This sometimes helped in battle.
Frank Hurley the photographer described Australian ammunition drivers,
frustrated by being held up while a road was under shellfire, whipping
up their horses to dash along it, while the onlookers bet on their survival.[22]
Stories of refusal to salute British officers, and indeed jeering at them,
are legion.

Yet all generalisations have their exceptions, and hide complex truth
with simple statement. The AIF, like all armies, contained a mixture of
men: good and bad, efficient and inefficient, conscientious and careless,
brave and cowardly. It would have been very unusual if it had been
otherwise. At the second battle of Bullecourt the 6th Brigade under
Gellibrand was brilliant, while the 5th Brigade under Smyth was poor.[23]
The tunnellers were greatly praised throughout the Second Army and by
Haig in 1917, but he still had reservations about other Anzacs.

Bean's adulation of the Anzacs on Gallipoli and his tendency always
to soften judgement on Australians, prevented him from frankly admitting
that the quality of infantry officers and the higher staff, and the leadership
they gave, was *vital*, and varied enormously. But his reluctance to judge
between good and bad Australian officers, together with his partiality for
Birdwood and White, in whose small coterie he felt at home, weakened
his analysis. By painting all his picture in bright colours, he prevented
himself from distinguishing between light and shade.[24]

Officer: "Why do you not salute?"
Anzac: "Well, to tell you the truth, digger, we've cut it right out."

The Australian reluctance to salute. *From the Australian Front,* 1917: 38.

The Anzacs also improved with time. They did well in the admittedly easier Middle East conditions,[25] and in France they came into their own in the last eighteen months of the war. Once the German attacks had been held and began to peter out, the Australians went on the offensive in 'Peaceful Penetration'. Small bodies of Australians—or indeed individual soldiers—raided the German lines and outposts, and dominated no man's land. As Bean was careful to point out for English readers of *The Times*, some German commanders, in an almost petulant tone, complained that

> The enemy, who has grown up in the Australian bush, wriggles to our posts with great dexterity from flank and rear . . . It has often happened that complete pickets have disappeared from the forward line without trace.[26]

There has been a tendency in Australia, derived from Bean, to antedate this efficiency, and attribute to the Anzacs earlier in France, and even on Gallipoli, the skill displayed towards the end of the war. Yet the truth seems to be that they were raw and relatively untrained on Gallipoli. Too often their officers were inexperienced or too old, and they suffered heavy losses accordingly.[27] The official British war historian, Edmonds, twice pointed out the improvement to Bean in 1928, when commenting on Volume III of the official history: 'You must differentiate between 1916 and 1918, in which latter year the Australian leading and staff work are classic.' In 1916 they were 'distinctly amateurs, in 1918 they were finished artists, not only in fighting but in staff work'.[28] But Bean ignored the point, except in minor asides and the privacy of his diary. For example he admitted that they were 'half-trained, at Pozières', and in a talk to the Royal Australian Historical Society in 1927 he let slip that they were '—at any rate towards the end of the War—the most effective . . .'. But he usually evaded the issue and in 1935 was still arguing with Edmonds about how 'Colonial life' produced better soldiers.[29]

The evidence is overwhelming, however. The scrappy methods of the Anzacs when they arrived in France in 1916, resulting in the loss of life and trench mortars, have been noted, as also their disregard of German firepower at Pozières and incompetence at Bullecourt. Carelessness after the first battle of Bullecourt allowed the Germans to overrun Australian guns at Lagnicourt[30] so that a British artillery officer thought they were good in attack but lazy in consolidation and did not work on their entrenchments, especially wiring. He added that they were prone to panic, a remark that threw Bean and White into a flurry![31] Yet there was a steady improvement at the end of 1917, which was noted by Haig.

There followed Hamel and Amiens, in which the Australians excelled in infantry–tank cooperation. A recent study has confirmed this, and pointed to a comment in the current *Weekly Tank Notes* that the Australians worked particularly well with tanks. Indeed, they appear to have been the troops who were pre-eminent in infantry–tank cooperation—one British sergeant calling them 'the finest fighters in Christendom'.[32] From the British collapse in March 1918 till the withdrawal of the Anzacs from the line, for a little more than 21,000 casualties, the Australians had captured 29,144 Germans, 338 guns, 116 towns and villages, and engaged 39 enemy divisions, 6 of which were as a result disbanded. This represented about 22 per cent of captures made by the British army, although the Australians formed only 9 per cent of its troops and, according to Terraine,

> is a testimony . . . to the pre-eminent fighting qualities of the Australian soldier . . . and . . . to the collective . . . efficiency of the . . . Corps. I doubt whether there is a parallel for such a performance in the whole range of military history.

All this sounds somewhat exaggerated, but at the time Rawlinson's thanks were equally profuse, talking of 'the discipline and high organising capacity of the Australian Corps'.[33]

## REASONS FOR IMPROVEMENT

This great change came from a variety of reasons. Partly it was a matter of comparison. The armies of the major powers had by then bled themselves white. It has been estimated that any army will mutiny when the numbers of its dead equal the number of serving soldiers in it. Such a mathematical formula, though perhaps too rigid, contains an element of truth. At any rate, that time came for the Russian and French armies in 1917 and the German army in 1918.

The British, like the Germans, were also weakened by their heavy losses as the war dragged on. Those who doubt the fierce courage of many British troops in 1915 and 1916 should read Philip Gibbs' *Realities of War*. But the continual slaughter, during those years and in 1917, meant that by 1918 the British army, like the German, was not what it had been. It was the great error of the British generals to assume that they could suffer such losses without fatally weakening their own army as well as that of the enemy. They had lost too many good men for the survivors to face more battles with relish.

And the German army too was not the same instrument that had withstood the British on the Somme in 1916 or at the third battle of Ypres in 1917. Constant bloodletting, culminating in Ludendorff's loss of shock troops during his attacks in early 1918, had killed the best soldiers, and the Australians faced the old, the very young, and demoralised units. Rawlinson noted this, and it was reinforced by instances of single Australian soldiers or small groups coming back with large numbers of German prisoners.[34] This is not to say that certain German units were not capable of putting up a dangerous resistance, as they revealed on several occasions. The German army was never an enemy to underestimate, and the Anzacs needed all their skill and training to dominate it, but it seems that they were beginning to do so by 1918.

In the last year of the war the Australians could claim to be elite troops. Their new unit organisation led to success at Messines, and the 'Australianisation' of the corps increased their morale and efficiency—though Edmonds could not accept that point. For it came with the equally vital improvement in Australian officers. For example, Major-General W. A. Coxen became the new commander of the artillery. He was not only Australian but also much more efficient than Brigadier-General W. J. Napier, the previous GOCRA, if the surviving records are anything to go by.[35] Most important of all, however, was the improvement in the Australian high command. Bean's greatest weakness in his official history was failure to accept his own mistake at the time, and stress the competence of Monash and his team, compared with the tired duo of Birdwood and White. Monash had many British admirers, and his strengths and weaknesses have been analysed before: his stress on training, meticulous planning, use of every technology available to him, coordination of all arms, wide-ranging conferences, ability to picture ground, all made him stand out from other commanders.[36]

Of course he was not alone, nor should all his later claims for origi-nality be accepted. Canadian staff work under Currie was also excellent, including the widespread use of conferences.[37] Moreover, Monash had advantages. The nature of the war had changed, to the great benefit of the Australians, for the German army was not only weaker, but fighting in open country again. But the role of *training* and *command* in the improvement of the Australians in 1918 has been rightly stressed by a recent historian.[38]

## HOW DIFFERENT WERE THE AUSTRALIAN TROOPS?

All armies claim that they are superior to their enemies or allies, and this claim is a reflection of their self-confidence or *élan*. In World War I, colonial troops naturally compared themselves with the main British army. Yet that army was weakened by constant changes between corps, whereas the colonial troops increasingly fought together. One English colonel reported that his division was in five different corps and three different armies in one month. He went on to comment that the Aus-tralians and Canadians therefore had a great advantage, while another writer pointed out that constant reorganisation prevented the corps commanders taking responsibility for training.[39] Indeed, the King's secretary, Lord Stamfordham, remarked to the Australian governor-general that for this reason the Australians and Canadians were more homogenous, and therefore more valuable as fighting units. British leaders, however, did not draw the obvious conclusions. They had another example in the Scots if they had wanted one, for the Highland Division also fought together, and developed a fierce reputation, until, sick of heavy duties, their commander deliberately mixed them with English units.[40]

The Canadians also gained a reputation as one of the most effective fighting corps on the Western Front, being more experienced than the Americans and backed by more reserves than the Australians. A Canadian historian attributes its excellence to breaking with the traditions of the British army and increasing independence.[41] He sounds like an Australian historian writing of the Anzacs. Indeed, many of the characteristics that Australians like to consider their own appeared in the Canadian corps. The later Field Marshal Montgomery of World War II wrote that 'The Canadians are a queer crowd; they seem to think they are the best troops in France and that we get them to do our most difficult jobs.' He added that he was disappointed in them. They were 'magnificent' at 'plain straightforward fighting', but were 'narrow minded and lack soldierly instincts'.[42]

As one Canadian historian notes, however, the idea of natural fighting abilities, or 'soldierly instincts', is a myth, and the Canadians had to learn the trade of war 'in a bloodbath of confusion and misdirection . . . at the cost of heavy casualties and setbacks'. The style of the corps under Currie was very similar to—and preceded—the Anzacs under Monash: meticulous planning; extensive use of technology and matériel to save lives; and an equal tendency to dislike officers. Like the Australians, too, the Canadians triumphed in the last 100 days, and like them suffered heavy losses—over 30,000 men in that time.[43] What is different is the heightened sense of independence revealed by the Canadians earlier in the war.

Finally the New Zealanders, so often in Australia the forgotten part of ANZAC, also had the reputation of being as effective as—and sometimes more reliable than—the Australians, with less of their larrikinism. Many British therefore preferred them to Australians.[44] So it would seem that although the Anzacs had certain characteristics in a perhaps exaggerated form, and were among the more effective of the allied troops in 1918, they were very similar to other units and the mythology should not be accepted completely at face value.

In three ways, however, the Australians were undoubtedly different from other allied troops on the Western Front. They stand out as being the *only* force composed entirely of volunteers even until the end of the war; moreover—especially in the early days—they were accepted only after rigorous physical standards had been applied.[45] It is therefore unfair to compare them with the great mass of Britain's conscript army. Finally, it is possible that the compulsory military training many of the Australian soldiers had undergone prior to 1914 gave them a great advantage, which Bean underestimated.[46]

Perhaps the greatest difference between colonial and British troops, however, derived from the colonials being *outsiders*. The Australians, for example, came from a distant continent on the other side of the world, and acted almost like tourists—an attitude that as time went on they may have deliberately exaggerated in order to distance themselves from the horrors around them. Moreover racism, based on social Darwinism, was a deep-seated Australian characteristic, and could easily be applied to the British as well as Egyptians, particularly when they thought of the 'ill-nurtured people of [the] industrial slums' of England.[47]

Care, however, needs to be exercised. Many of the AIF *were* British. Thus Corporal O. S. Blows, 28th Battalion AIF and proud to be a member of it, had been born in England and had emigrated with his brother in 1910.

He was not unusual. Some estimates suggest that 40 per cent of the AIF were British, and one can find comments like 'Next to me I found an experienced soldier of my platoon . . . an Englishman.' Moreover, many AIF *officers* were British—a point which Bean makes—and where they were not, had often been trained in British training schools.[48] All this makes the stress on the difference between the Australians and British all the more confusing. Photographs of Anzacs taken at the time show ordinary men, tall and short, fat and thin, tanned from Egypt and cocky from their group experiences, but not radically different in appearance from any other group of British soldiers.[49]

Nor were their attitudes always different, despite Australian mythologists. For example, stress on the Anzac informality of dress on Gallipoli—wearing shorts and stripped to the waist, etc.—would seem misplaced, since in the gruelling heat many troops adopted such garb.[50] Again, all troops—Dominion and British—had in common the background of popular entertainment in the music halls, the stress on sport and the code and language of 'sportsmanship'. Most Australians—despite Bean, who argued for the superiority of the bush-bred countryman[51]—were townsmen. Men from agricultural pursuits probably amounted to under 14 per cent of AIF recruits, for Australia was 'already one of the most highly urbanised societies in the world'. Nor was promotion in the Australian army as democratic as Bean makes out. Promotion was from the ranks, since no other avenue was open, seeing that Australia lacked the English-style upper classes and AIF casualty rates were so high. Nevertheless, officers came disproportionately from Protestant, non-manual backgrounds, such as commerce, the professions and clerical work.[52] The British army also promoted from the ranks, though not to the same extent. Finally, most British troops were either 'Kitchener's men' or later conscripts, and not regular soldiers. They, as much as the Australians, were 'civilians in uniform', often bitterly critical of the regular British army and its formal codes, and with them too the 'hard cases', and the men least amenable to formal discipline, were often outstanding in battle. As we have seen, however, the iron British discipline prevented them showing the independence of spirit of the Anzacs.

## AUSTRALIAN AND BRITISH DISCIPLINE: COMPARISON AND REFLECTIONS

The problems with discipline continued into 1918. Australian mutinies occurred in that year, and not only over the disbandment issue. The 59th Battalion refused to go forward twice in September 1918 because it felt it had been too long in the line without relief, and the 1st Battalion did so once. The issue became mixed with the refusal of several battalions to be amalgamated owing to the heavy losses and lack of recruits from Australia, and the AIF was saved further embarrassment by the collapse of Germany and the end of the war.[53]

Meanwhile, the troubles both in Australia and between Australia and Britain continued. When the government took up Birdwood's suggestion that the names of deserters be published in Australia, there were complaints in federal parliament, where Watt managed to hide the high rate of desertion in the AIF.[54] In 1918 a battle developed over Hughes' desire to have Australian courts martial composed of Australian officers only.[55] In May the Adjutant-General tried to sneak a great strengthening of the Act in at the same time as he remedied an obvious omission, the death penalty for plain murder, for which two Australians were then being held,[56] but the Cabinet spotted this and would have none of it. Moreover, it was in no hurry to amend the *Defence Act* anyway—probably foreseeing trouble if it tried. In this it was undoubtedly correct, for even in December 1918, after the war had ended, federal parliament declined to change the Act, and the authorities then had to try to provide penal servitude for life for murder. The matter dragged on into 1920.[57]

Both Hobbs and Monash had modified their views by 1918, realising the nervous strain many of the men were under.[58] Even by the end of the war, however, Haig had not changed his mind. Meeting Dominion journalists in September 1918, he could not resist showing them a table which revealed that nearly one Australian in a hundred was in gaol *'because Capital punishment is not allowed'* [his emphasis] compared with British units in which only one man in a thousand was in prison.[59] The fact that the Anzacs had proved so successful in the last 100 days, and the light that might throw on old-fashioned British 'discipline', completely escaped his attention.

There is no evidence that the rigid British discipline produced a more effective fighting army. Those Australians who doggedly stuck it out in 1917 and 1918 eventually became a key part of the British forces. Compulsion and discipline may drive troops to the front, but it cannot make them fight with verve and determination once they are there. For that the British needed men imbued with patriotism and enthusiasm for the cause; and as the war went on the numbers of such men dwindled. Sir Maurice Hankey, the ubiquitous British public servant to the Cabinet, remarked:

> It is this meticulous clinging to our obsolete, undemocratic standard of what they are pleased to call discipline—saluting etc.—that has made the English Army so rotten that it has never achieved one successful offensive in the whole course of the war.[60]

Hankey's father had run a sheep station in South Australia for a time, his mother was Australian and his wife South African. Hankey therefore had strong 'Empire' sympathies. But British officers who saw the Australians at close quarters often admired their fighting qualities. Hamilton praised them on Gallipoli, and Major-General S. S. Butler thought them 'simply superb, scorning danger and death', but he was Birdwood's chief intelligence officer. Admiral Keyes, however, also overcame initial prejudices to admire them greatly on the peninsula, as did the Hussar officer,

Major-General Lord Burnham. Further from the front, stories of Anzac daring circulated in Britain.[61]

Monash argued that discipline was only a means to an end: to produce coordinated action for a purpose,

> not lip service, nor obsequious homage to superiors, nor servile observance of forms and customs ... the Australian Army is a proof that individualism is the best and not the worst foundation upon which to build up collective discipline.

Liddell Hart agreed: 'their deeds of 1918 provided ample vindication'.[62]

There are negative aspects to egalitarianism, however. Australian discipline depended on the personal qualities of its leaders to a much greater degree than the British, hence the numerous complaints about the quality of Australian officers in Egypt. Haig blamed Birdwood for seeking popularity rather than giving strong leadership,[63] but Birdwood preferred to appeal to the better natures of the men and the cause they were fighting for, and sympathised with those whose nerves had gone. In this he was in advance of his time: the concepts of battle fatigue and trauma are accepted today, and 'it is recognised that even the best soldiers may become ineffective after prolonged exposure to combat'. Most soldiers in World War I were in action long beyond what today would be regarded as acceptable limits, and *all* armies were affected in either 1917 or 1918.[64]

It is interesting, however, that Monash's division, the 3rd, was acknowledged to be far freer of disciplinary problems than any of the others. Monash appealed not to the men's 'patriotism' and what Bean called their 'finer feelings', but to old-fashioned *esprit de corps*. Bean was bitterly critical, and did not draw the obvious moral from Monash's success. Moreover, formal Australian discipline improved during the war. Birdwood's ADC, an Englishman, noted that they were much more punctilious in saluting in France in 1917.[65]

Differences between the Anzacs and the British army were also partly social in origin. Monash rejoiced in the fact that 'there was no officer caste, no social distinction in the whole force' while Bean argued that British officer discipline was based on 'strongly marked social differences between men and officers, which our men resented and Australians generally dislike'.[66] There was a gulf between the ordinary Australian soldier, or even officer, and the British command that was almost unbridgeable. Regular British officers of the old army came from the upper, indeed the landed, classes, with different education, background, experience and wealth from their men, with whom they had little in common and from whom they were rigidly separated—as indeed were the NCOs.[67] Australians, on the other hand, stressed comradeship between officers and men. Many of the officers had served in the ranks; all were volunteers, which affected their attitude, as it did many of the other Dominion troops. For example, a Canadian nurse told an officious British sister that she had not voluntarily travelled 3000 miles 'to be spoken to like that by anybody'.

Also, in contradiction to Bean, the fact that many Anzacs came from an urban and industrial background, with its tradition of trade unions and strike action, may have made them more likely to stand up for their rights. But even in this there were British parallels. In January 1919, after the war had ended and the threat of the death penalty appeared less, the 'strike' by the Service and Ordnance Corps nearly brought the transport and supply of the British army to a halt, and there was a series of soldier riots in England.

Perhaps the more endearing aspect of the AIF attitude to officers was their refusal to treat them as a separate caste. Thus Birdwood, bathing in the nude at Anzac beach, could be greeted by a digger who surveyed his ample stomach and remarked, 'My bloody oath mate, you 'ave been among the biscuits'![68] The British high command, however, tended not to have a sense of humour in such matters, and regarded irreverence as equivalent to insolence. Moreover, it still harboured reservations about the effectiveness of the AIF, reservations which were sometimes justified during 1917 and also reflected the tensions that existed in Anglo-Australian relations in the political sphere during that year. But they were definitely not applicable to the Anzacs' *annus mirabilis* of 1918.

## THE BRITISH HIGH COMMAND AND THE ANZACS, 1918

The great weakness of the British high command's complaints about Australian discipline, and demands for the death penalty, is revealed by the heightened efficiency of the AIF as the war ended. Even Haig commented in August 1917 that 'the Australians [in the 2nd Australian Division] have never looked better since they came to France'.[69] But he missed the implication of this. If, despite acknowledged weaknesses in their discipline, the Anzacs became one of the more effective units in the British army, how essential was that discipline?

Instead, as with the Canadians, British officers were upset by colonial independence. The British complained that the 'Canadian Corps is perhaps rather apt to take all the credit it can for everything, and to consider that the BEF consists of the Canadian Corps and some other troops.'[70] The speaker could have applied his remark equally to the Australians. To some British officers, the Empire existed to support the British system and only British ways were right. This did not apply to all, however. After the capture of Hamel on the Western Front, Rawlinson— once more the Anzacs' army commander and a great improvement on Gough[71]—produced a 19-page report with appendices and maps on the operation and attributed the success to several factors, including the skill and fighting spirit of the Australian troops. Haig much preferred Monash to Birdwood, and always had excellent relations with him. He had long considered giving Monash the corps command and was greatly impressed with his plans for Hamel. Terraine suggests that in discussing Monash Haig entered 'perhaps the greatest volume of unmitigated approval for any one man in the whole of his Diary'. The Fourth Army report on Hamel was later printed by GHQ and circulated to all units, becoming part of the British technique for winning the war. After the seizure of Mont St Quentin, Rawlinson is reported to have phoned Monash to describe how he wanted the Mont taken, and—on being told it had already been captured—retorted 'You spoiled a damned good battle!'[72]

This chain of success left the Anzacs at the end of the war with a reputation of being among the elite forces, together with the Guards and the Canadians. Liddell Hart remarked that 'they proved themselves ... [then] the best fighting troops of any army in the field'.

> In the later stages of the last war, the Australian Corps was by general recognition perhaps the most effectively operated of any; it certainly played a leading role in our victorious offensive.[73]

The change in Rawlinson's attitude can be traced in his diary. His criticisms of the Anzacs had continued during 1917, as he watched proceedings during the third battle of Ypres, although he did not personally command them until November, when he took over the Second Army for a while. Thereafter, he began slowly to comment favourably on their work, though still bland about Birdwood and White. Then, on replacing Gough in command of the Fifth Army, he noted 'the Australians and cavalry have fought magnificently', and before long was referring to them as 'my Australians' who 'will, I am sure, give a good account of themselves'. He especially praised Hobbs and Monash, 'who are both good Commanders' and the 13th Brigade 'which did brilliantly'. He still did not think much of Birdwood's planning, and though he thought White 'excellent' he looked forward to Monash taking command—an event which he specifically noted in his diary.

Thereafter, he used the Australians in a demonstration of infantry-tank cooperation for Haig on 31 July. To train the Americans, he put them with the Anzacs ('just to show them what a fight is like'). By then his tone was completely different. He even became amused by Anzac idiosyncrasies, describing in May how an Australian soldier, anonymous in a gas mask, rowed a small boat on the Somme during a bombardment to pick up fish stunned by the shelling. He noted their use of Christian names, and their casual treatment of a German officer. After 8 August he wrote that 'the Canadians have done splendidly and the Aussies [sic!] even better—I am full of admiration for these two Corps'. His valedictory order to the Australians caused a 'stir' at GHQ.[74]

The British high command, however, had also changed its attitude. Haig after an inspection in May 1918 reported that 'The Australian is a different individual now to when he first came, both in discipline and smartness.' GHQ therefore paid the Australians the compliment of using them to demonstrate the new infantry-tank tactics, and as instructors to the American army, and sent patrol leaders from the 5th Australian Division to train British II Corps, which was below par. Haig's papers contain a note on Australian Corps gains between March and July 1918, with the remark that: 'Throughout this offensive period, no less than 16 enemy Divisions have been encountered and defeated.'[75]

Afterwards the historian of the Fourth Army produced a commemorative book which is full of praise for the Australians, for example talking of their organising ability and discipline, and describing the Australian attack on 18 September as a perfect example of infantry–machine gun cooperation. He clearly considered the Anzacs to have been outstanding.[76]

Terraine habitually talks of the Australians as the 'spearhead' of the British army in 1918. While this has an element of truth in it, the term needs refinement. In Australia it has become accepted that the Anzacs were 'shock troops' (to use the idiom of the day). In 1918 in France they numbered only 10 per cent of British forces, yet held 30 per cent of the British line, and accordingly had the highest per capita casualty rate of any British contingent in the war.[77]

The British had begun by underestimating the Australians, and indeed all Dominion troops. When war broke out, Haldane suggested—and the British Cabinet agreed—to use them for garrisons, and not bring them to England. The war's almost insatiable demand for manpower, however, would not allow that attitude to continue. The praise heaped on the Australians during the Gallipoli campaign suggested they would form an important addition to British fighting strength. By January 1917 the British Cabinet drew up a comparison of the manpower and enlistments in Britain with the various Dominions. It noted untapped reserves in Australia, so; despite the failed conscription referendum, decided to ask the Australians to fulfil their previous offer of a sixth division.[78]

The British high command, however, was also anxious not to let the idea spread that colonial troops were either unduly used or unduly successful. In August 1916 Bean ran into difficulties in France, partly from the jealousy of other British correspondents, and partly because GHQ thought too much was being written about the Australians. The attempts to play down Australian achievements in 1917 were noted in the last chapter.

This became an important issue in Anglo-Australian relations in 1918. In that year, after their great assaults had failed, the Germans suggested that the British high command used colonial soldiers as shock troops, implying that the British 'were not only fighting to the last Frenchman, but the last Colonial too'.[79] This was just the idea the British high command had been desperate to avoid. The War Office therefore officially denied it. As Charteris insisted,

> Australians and Canadians are only a small fraction of the Army, and it is the units from Great Britain that are necessarily bearing the brunt of the fighting and winning through.[80]

In early 1918, therefore, when the Australian Press Association tried to gain permission for a representative to travel to France, it encountered not only professional jealousy from Murdoch and the United Cable Service but obstruction from Birdwood, in the name of GHQ or the War Cabinet. He talked of a 'conducting officer' while the representative was within corps bounds.[81] Such an attitude, and the suppression of news of the Anzacs, provoked a counter-move by the Australians. In April and May 1918 Murdoch complained that the Australian public was getting very little news of its men. He sent sycophantic letters to GHQ for access to France, and clashed with the censors. Birdwood was unsympathetic, but Monash took action to provide more news coverage.

In July 1918 the British Ministry of Information wrote to Bean on the matter, suggesting a propaganda booklet. Bean replied that there was an element of truth in the German claim, and a flat denial would do no good, since the Australian soldiers could see with their own eyes the comparative weakness of the British divisions alongside them. He put this down to the English being bled white by the war, and differences in education and conditions of life in the Dominions and Scotland. He insisted that Dominion soldiers were being used as shock troops, and ought to be, but the trouble was they also had to hold extensive sections of line at the same time. The aim was not to save British lives, for 'British commanders have never spared British troops', and 'all Scottish Divisions and a certain number of others', such as the Guards and the 7th and 29th British Divisions, were also shock divisions in fact if not in name. But it was not widely realised how 'done up' many British divisions were. He cited Major Neville Lytton as his authority. Bean's argument, however, did not appeal to either GHQ or the War Office.

Lytton wrote to Bean, agreeing with many of his points, but commenting that what he did not like was that

> Australian troops are telling the Americans that they and the New Zealanders, the Canadians and the Scottish can fight, but that the English troops are no good at all... Everyone... knows that the Australians are magnificent troops ... but they also think that they combine badly and are very free in singing their own praises and downcrying their neighbours.

He ruined his effect by adding, 'Unfortunately, some dud [sic] divisions have on one or two occasions been put next to them.' However, he thought it was bad team work and bad chivalry to boast of one's own superiority.

Bean had obviously struck a raw nerve, for Guy Dawnay, then a major-general at GHQ in France, wrote to him that casualties in British divisions involved in the retreat were twice those of Dominion forces. (His argument that this meant they had been more severely tested, however, was not valid— many of the British 'casualties' had in fact surrendered.) After further correspondence between Bean, Lytton and Dawnay (who by then had adopted a 'gracious' tone) the file closed, but it reveals what Dawnay called 'touchiness' about the whole matter. Not surprisingly, to counter German propaganda, the press in the next month produced a series of percentages to show that the English divisions bore the bulk of the fighting and losses.[82]

As a result of all this, the British public received mixed messages. In January and September 1918 there were British complaints about the emphasis on the Anzacs at Gallipoli. This did not prevent individual reporters praising the Australians in the field and though the *Mail* was silent on the part played by them in stemming the great German attacks in March 1918, it loosened up in May, provided a good account of Hamel in July, and continued reasonable accounts in August and October. The attempt to exclude references to the Australians had either failed or been abandoned.[83]

Moreover, Australian leaders inevitably became involved in the issue. Never a man to ignore publicity, Hughes in September invited British, American and French journalists and VIPs to visit the battlefields and talk to Australian soldiers, while Monash entertained journalists and demanded better press coverage.[84] Both men were notoriously hungry for publicity themselves, but also had quite legitimate reasons as well. Monash was concerned for the morale of this troops, and Hughes was gearing himself up for a major battle to protect Australia's standing in post-war Britain and to mould the peace conference to Australian needs. It was essential to him therefore that the Australian contribution to victory should be widely known.

Linked with this issue was the question whether the Australian troops were in fact used more than other British forces. In October 1918 Haig wished to return the Anzacs to the line, but there were rumours that two Australian divisions might refuse to return. When on the 24th the British Cabinet considered the matter, the CIGS reported fears that there would be trouble with the Australian troops if they were returned to the line, and with the British troops if they were not. He added that the Australian divisions had had *more* rest than the British—a claim which would have roused the Anzacs and Bean to fury if they had known of it.

The origin of the idea was a correspondence between the Colonial Secretary, Walter Long, and Birdwood himself. Long thought that the Australians, New Zealanders and Canadians were mistaken. Because their deeds were reported, whereas those of the British troops—due to the censorship—were not, they had developed the idea that they were being 'unduly employed'. Birdwood agreed, and blamed the prominence given Dominion troops by their press correspondents. He argued that in the great retreat the Canadians were unemployed and the Australians came into the line only when the German impetus had run out. So much for Long and Birdwood, both men who, in their official capacity, needed—and indeed claimed to possess—great sympathy for the Empire—not to mention the fact that Birdwood always posed as the arch-Australian. Apparently Hughes, when he had visited the troops that September, had promised them a long rest, a promise which had been followed within two days by orders to return to action. Birdwood thought the Australians lucky to have had the rest, and that they had not been used any more than the English divisions. However, he wrote to warn the CIGS of Australian complaints. The latter therefore brought the issue before Cabinet, which agreed that Long should keep in touch, and if Monash was not amenable, Hughes should be recalled from his speaking tour to London—presumably to give him orders.[85] The following day Haig listed in his diary the average casualty rates per battalion since 21 March as: British, 45 officers and 1088 ORs; Canadian, 42 officers and 956 ORs; and

Australian, 36 officers and 704 ORs. He concluded that 'The Australians have the least claim of any therefore for consideration on account of losses.'[86] It is impossible to assess the source or accuracy of his figures. He was wildly mistaken in some of his other statements in the diary (such as those concerning Bullecourt, which bore no relation at all to what actually happened), so these figures are not conclusive either.

The truth is complex and difficult to establish. As we have seen, in France Haig and his army commanders did not at first think highly of the Australians and therefore used the Canadians as their key fighting troops in 1916. Indeed, the Canadians were widely regarded as possibly the finest troops in the British armies.[87] Nor were the Australians used more heavily than any other division in 1917, either in the Arras battles or during the third battle of Ypres.[88] But a change had occurred by 1918. At the end of that May, the British III Corps had a frontage of 6000 yards, whereas Australian Corps covered 18,000 yards. Figures on frontages in Bean's papers suggest that on 1 July 1918 the 5th Australian Division covered a wider frontage than any other in the British army (one would need to assess the activity on its front) but the other Australian divisions did not. Figures for 11 August 1918 suggest that the Australian Corps then covered a wider front than any other—17,000 yards as against III Corps' 11,000 and the Canadian 12,000—but again the number of divisions in a corps varied, as well as the activity on the front. Terraine has published Haig's map of 25 September 1918, showing German divisions massed opposite Rawlinson's Fourth Army (in which were the Australians).[89] The statistics of the Fourth Army, however, show the Canadians losing more men (killed, wounded and missing) than the Anzacs in early August, and III Corps losing more between 8 August and 14 October. In *no* period were Anzac losses the highest of the corps in the Fourth Army. But it is difficult to assess the exact significance of these statistics. Bean gives casualty figures as a percentage of total enlistments: Australia 52.14, Britain 42.07, Canada 30.76, New Zealand 25.24,[90] but percentages are notoriously unreliable indicators, and the statistics for that war are 'rubbery', to say the least.

More important, however, were the attitudes that had developed. Clearly the Anzacs and their leaders believed that they were more effective troops, and that they were being used more often than others. This belief reinforced their attitudes towards the British high command and leadership generally.

## THE AUSTRALIANS AND THE BRITISH HIGH COMMAND

As Bean wrote—but discarded—for his official history,

> The Australian was never in complete sympathy with many of the British Staff ... [who] picked up the colour of his necktie or the shape of his collar, or the use of some form of speech that did not conform ... The Englishman thus shut himself into a different world in which the Australian did not wish to enter ...[91]

The third battle of Ypres, 1917. Men and pack mules round Idiot Corner, on Westhoek Ridge, amidst shell fire. (AWM Official Photo No. E1480).

Generals Birdwood
and White,
December 1916.
(AWM Official
Photo No. E94).

Most troops of course did not know their commanders—Englishmen or
Australians. They were gods beyond lowly foot soldiers, who avoided
them wherever possible. Majors were bad enough; a colonel a figure of
power. Anything above that was like an alien from another planet. As
one veteran remarked, with memories of Pozières in mind, they assumed
that Haig and the high command did not care if they were killed and
were using them as 'cannon fodder'. But they were fatalistic about it. They
expected to be killed; the most that they could hope for was 'Blighty'—
a wound sufficiently serious to take them out of the battle line, and to
England for—hopefully—a long period of recuperation.[92]

Despite the bland wording of Bean's official history, there were deep
differences of opinion and attitude even among the officers in the AIF.
At the other end of the hierarchy, senior Australian officers tended to be
British in their attitudes, either from their education, from training in
England before the war, or from socialising in higher British circles.

Birdwood and White represented the British origins of Australia and the
imperialist school of thought.

Though Australian-born, Brudenell White had been brought up in a
family of Irish extraction, with aristocratic and military traditions. Despite
Bean's defence of him, his pro-British stance and undemocratic attitudes
are evident. After joining the regular army, he became aide-de-camp to
Hutton, with whom he struck up a close friendship. White worked best as
an able adjutant to more public figureheads: Hutton, Bridges and
Birdwood. Like them, he was an imperialist and a conservative military
thinker. He was occasionally provoked into an outburst, such as after
Gallipoli, when he told Bean that he agreed with Murdoch's criticisms,
but that they should go beyond Hamilton to Prime Minister Asquith and
his supporters, who 'ought to have been put on . . . trial for undertaking
the expedition.' He told Admiral Keyes that if he had anything to do with
it, Australia and New Zealand would never again send an expeditionary
force overseas unless they had strong representation on the War Council.[93]

It took much to shake White's habitual discretion. Usually, he was
much more circumspect, and accepted British blunders with fortitude.
For to a man like White, the function of the Australian military was as
an expeditionary force in the British imperial army. This in return would
guarantee Australia's protection by Britain. It was typical of this way of
thinking that after the war White insisted on his correct formal title,
'Chief', not 'of the General Staff', but 'of the Australian Branch of the
Imperial General Staff'.[94] His and Birdwood's attitudes and thought
processes derived from the British upper class. Thus Birdwood, in his
introduction to *The Anzac Book*, wrote, 'Boys! Hats off to the British
Navy! It may be that thinking of the old "Anzac" Days, the words of the
Harrow School song will spring to one's mind.'[95] It is difficult to think
of a more inappropriate recommendation to the mass of Diggers on
Gallipoli. It must have jarred on the ears of the Australian nationalists.
Bean's *Anzac Book* itself, with its classical allusions and its pro-British
bias, was redolent of the English public schools, one of which Bean had
attended.[96] The soldiers probably bought it for those at home, partly out
of group loyalty, partly because it was all that was available, and partly
because it did not reveal to those they loved the sort of experiences they
were going through.

But it was not only English assumptions that offended. When the
Australians looked at the incompetence and folly of Gallipoli, they could
hardly fail to be disillusioned, and this feeling was further reinforced in
France. Whether they lost their illusions about the might of the British
Empire and the superiority of all things British on Gallipoli, or at
Fromelles, Pozières, Bullecourt or the third battle of Ypres, must have
depended on the individual Australian and his experiences. But closer
observation of the British army could only have soured them, and
increased their feeling of being different. Jarred by British attitudes, disillusioned by the war and with Birdwood and White, a few middle-ranking
officers went on to reject the very idea of an 'imperial' defence policy. Their

motives were mixed, naturally, with their own ambition, for they saw 'British' officers, and the friends of White and Birdwood, promoted. As a result, thwarted ambition, raucous Australianism and sound criticism blended together, so that it is difficult after this passage of time to distinguish the motives of the men and the rights and wrongs of each case. Perhaps the best-known examples are Legge, Elliott, and Gellibrand.

Legge was a university graduate, a veteran of the Boer War, who had been responsible for the introduction of compulsory military training in Australia. From 1912 to 1914 he was an Australian exchange officer at the War Office. On the face of it, he should have been an ardent imperialist, and whether he adopted the Australianist position from idealism or thwarted ambition is not clear. Outspoken and tactless, he had made many enemies, even among Australians, and his appointment to replace Bridges on Gallipoli after the latter died provoked a threatened mutiny. Sidetracked into commanding the 2nd Division, his alleged mistakes at Pozières gave ground for his return to Australia, where he became Chief of the General Staff till 1920. No doubt, as Clarke comments, 'Legge's vocal confidence in his own opinions was . . . irksome to British officers like Maxwell and Birdwood who nursed assumptions about their own professional superiority and the primacy of imperial interests.' But Haig himself had formed a bad opinion of Legge, perhaps to avoid facing squarely his own problems with Gough.[97]

More literary was 'Pompey' Elliott, whose account of Fromelles has already been noted. In 1918 he thought that Birdwood, beneath the veneer, disliked Australians. Their 'casualness and independence was gall and wormwood to him'. From time to time Birdwood implied that they were an undisciplined mob; he gave promotions and decorations to British officers, and when compelled to do so gave them to Australians who 'by attendance at Sandhurst or elsewhere had acquired what might be termed a lacquer of English Polish over their Australian interior'. Thwarted ambition is apparent in Elliott's account, but there was probably an element of truth in it. White's comment, when Elliott complained, that there was a 'greater reliability and higher standard of Honor prevailing on the average amongst British Officers', was hardly tactful, and goes far to exonerate Elliott.[98] His scathing denunciation of Birdwood and White at Bullecourt in the Australian federal parliament after the war[99] revealed the contempt he felt for them and his continuing anger at the bungling and consequent loss of life in France.

This last sentiment seems to have predominated with Gellibrand. Exactly one month after the opening of the second battle of Bullecourt he resigned from command of 6th Brigade, despite the fact that it had been the outstandingly successful one in the whole affair. Typically, Bean makes no mention of this in his account of the battle, but instead tucks it away in a footnote, 352 pages later, in a section dealing with a totally different subject. Also typically, he sheds no light on the matter. A letter from Gellibrand in the Australian War Memorial archives, however, reveals that he was deeply dissatisfied, and strongly hints at favouritism, the 'old boy network' and incompetence in both 5th Brigade and 2nd Division. It was very bitter.[100]

The same situation was revealed in the Middle East. Hurley noted in his diary a preponderance of British officers in the command level there, and, perhaps unfairly, thought Chauvel failed to look after the interests of his men. David Horner defends this as an 'approach of co-operation with the British rather than confrontation', but admits that it offended some of Chauvel's nationalistic subordinates.[101]

## ATTITUDE TO BIRDWOOD

Australian soldiers, however, reserved much of their vitriol for their own—Australian—officers. Several complained about superiors who volunteered their men for further action to gain glory for themselves. Birdwood roused bitter contempt for his constant enthusiasm for further 'stunts'. 'You old bastard' was the usual response.[102] It has been written of Birdwood that

> His popularity among his Anzacs was something of a newspaper myth. . . . it is doubtful if he ever really came to terms with his men . . . 'Talking to the rank and file his attitude was constrained and stiff, and his affability was obviously forced and unnatural' writes an Australian who was in an exceptionally good position to judge. 'His conversation with them was platitudinous and completely uninteresting. He bored the men and they bored him. . . . As time went by, 'Birdie's bull' became more and more the subject of ridicule among the men, and even the officers, of the A.I.F.[103]

This may have been behind a complaint by Birdwood in 1918 that a column of Australian troops, with officers, had not saluted his car as it passed. Monash argued that they did not recognise Birdwood's flag—but one wonders. A returned soldier wrote later that he had been 'infuriated at the utterly careless, slap-dash, don't-give-a-damn planning of Birdwood, Skene and White' for the attack on Chanak Bair, and that Birdwood was obsessed with the bayonet. He added that when the 1st Division veterans were given home leave in 1918, they sang before the troops paraded to see them off:

> Goodbye Billy Birdwood: Farewell Douglas Haig,
> Since we've joined the Army, we've been your bloody slaves.
>     Gallipoli was a failure, France a bloody farce.
> You can take the whole of the A.I.F.
>     And shove it up your . . .

He added that 'to Birdwood's fury, the song became popular and was sung at most gatherings of Australian troops right up to demobilisation'.[104]

Junior officers often sympathised with these sentiments. They were usually better educated than the rankers (though one should beware of exceptions), had a wider vision of the war, and often felt freer to express their opinions. But junior officer or other rank, the criticism extended to the whole of the British army and its ways, and sometimes coloured their attitudes to all things British, as we shall see in the next chapter.

# CHAPTER SEVEN

# Of Britain and the British

Bloody war and bitter experience weakened the affections of Empire.
Australians met the English during the struggle, and the acquaintance lifted
the veils of distance and ignorance, and qualified their old enthusiasms.

BILL GAMMAGE,
*The Broken Years*

## AUSTRALIANS AND THE BRITISH ARMY

With their increasing competence by 1918 the Anzacs came to look with
jaundiced eyes at the whole British army; from its high command, to field
officers and the ordinary Tommy. In the Middle East, the photographer
Frank Hurley noted 'a decidedly unfriendly attitude' between British and
Australian forces.[1] The Light Horse had been hostile to British concepts of
discipline in Egypt in 1915, knew of British bungling on Gallipoli, and
thereafter was disgusted by the luxuries they discovered after the 5th
Yeomanry Brigade officers camp had been overrun. They suspected soft-
ness, gross negligence and cowardice, and were made more bitter by what
they regarded as the disproportionate awards given to British troops and
staff officers after that incident. Their anger at British incompetence in
medical care and provision of fodder for horses was only increased by the
British withdrawal from the first battle of Gaza and the airs and graces the
British high command gave themselves. So the Light Horse not only
failed to salute Chetwode and his orderlies as they rode through their ranks,
but laughed aloud at their stiff and formal way of sitting on their horses.[2]
Even the replacement of Murray by the much more efficient General Sir
Edmund Allenby could not alleviate Australian contempt for the British
command, which unfortunately joined with hatred for the Arabs in
December 1918, when an Australian was killed and the Anzacs took a
murderous revenge on the local village of Surafend. They bitterly resented
Allenby's scathing comments on them, and laughed in his face. None of
this was helped by the deliberate British policy—for political reasons—
of giving recognition to Arab forces rather than Dominion troops.[3]

In France, as we have seen, the disillusionment of Gallipoli had been
reinforced at Fromelles and Pozières, and became even more bitter in 1917.

It is not surprising, therefore, that with the British retreat early in 1918 contempt for the British army increased. Hobbs, 'despite his upper middle class British origins, clearly identified himself as Australian' and said that he found the behaviour of the British higher command 'depressing' and that it had 'disgusted many of my officers and men'. He began to talk of the British, not as 'we', but 'they'. And Monash, orientated to the British Empire as he was, appealed to the Anzacs before 8 August to do their best 'for the sake of AUSTRALIA, the Empire and our cause.' In this appeal Australia was still part of the Empire, but she came first, and was put in capital letters. And quietly he wrote to his wife, 'Some of these Tommy officers are not worth the money it costs to put them into uniform . . . bad staffs, bad commanders.'[4]

In this, the Australians were not very different from the New Zealanders. Major-General A. H. Russell, who commanded the New Zealand Division, commented, 'It is impossible to get British Divisions as a rule to attack in the dark, tho the advantages are obvious.' [sic!] He then complained of a demand for a sudden attack, despite previous promises to the contrary, and added 'the Higher Command is oblivious of the difficulties of the lower ranks'.[5]

## THE WAR REPORTERS

Among the more vocal Australianists were the war reporters. They had come into direct contact with the British military bureaucracy earlier—and suffered it more continuously—than most Anzacs, and were exposed to petty restrictions and narrow-minded officials. Nothing was more calculated to turn them off the British army. Bean had had great trouble getting permission to land on Gallipoli, and was treated with arrogance by Major-General W. Braithwaite, Hamilton's chief of staff on the HQ ship, the *Arcadian*, which, Bean wrote, was 'swarming with staff Officers of the usual British type'. The whole staff then went to lunch, not bothering to invite Bean, whose chapter of miseries was completed when he was later snubbed for 'being so bold as to ask whether any boats were coming' by which he could transfer off the ship.[6]

This treatment of war reporters was not unusual, and when Bean thought of seeing Lloyd George, he was approached by Philip Gibbs, the British war correspondent, to ask the prime minister to relax the censorship. Bean also was asked by Australians to get more rest for the Anzacs and to lobby for their consolidation into one corps. Murdoch went further and wanted Gough removed. Bean did not get his interview, and wrote to Lloyd George arguing that GHQ did not understand the Australians, listing the obstructions he had had to face, and asking for the right to appeal to him in future.[7] The British GHQ had publicly relented, and was now usually polite, but still did not accept the need for war reporters, feared them, and hedged them round with restrictions. Bean saw the staff officer Guy Dawnay again in 1918, and described him as 'a rather spoilt-boy, dogmatic English University type . . . He was not intending to be patronising, but he was.' None of this was calculated to endear the British command to the accredited press representative of Australia, and it is not surprising that he became one of their critics.[8]

Bean later wrote on Pozières a passage which he did not publish in the official history. Gough had complained that the Australian soldiers were making a fuss about their losses, while the British had lost more men. Bean conceded this, and adds:

> But his attitude is typical—that it is presumptuous of the troops to complain of tactics by which they lose 9000 in a battle. Instead of searching for something wrong—which was that they were fighting a battle . . . without any attempt on the part of their leaders to devise suitable tactics . . . beyond merely hitting the enemy again and again in the same place. This was the leaders' folly— but it was the troops who were supposed to be wrong in complaining of it.[9]

In his diary, Bean drew a very cryptic picture of Haig, whom he considered widely read but cold with people, ambitious and inarticulate, and lacking an understanding of the need for the press in modern war. Even so, his view of Haig was much milder than that of Edmonds, who privately told Liddell Hart that Haig had no human side, was above—or below—the average in stupidity, and could not grasp things at conferences, especially anything technical. He, more than Gough, deserved to be fired in 1918. Compared with this, Bean's criticisms seem mild, if not downright weak. For example, he remarked that failure on the Somme was 'due to lack of sufficient precision of thought as to what the objects and methods of the . . . fighting should be'. And he commented that Haig was only responsible for Gough's impetuosity in that 'he did not exert his control when such very wrong things were being done'.[10]

He was much more forthright, however, in castigating the British *system*, where men like Gellibrand were not promoted because they were not sportsmen, and were too learned in their profession. This Bean took to be evidence 'of the hopeless defects in a system which elected a staff much on the principles of a hunt club'.[11]

## AUSTRALIAN OPINION OF BRITISH FIELD OFFICERS

Usually, however, Bean was kind to the British. After the war, he criticised Monash for attacking English officers, saying that many gallant ones fought with the AIF, and that once the Anzacs got to know them, and they the Anzacs, both sides admired one another.

Bean is not to be trusted on the attitudes of the AIF to officers. His account of Gellibrand, for example, has been rightly described as oozing 'admiration and affection' and his diary has references to 'old fashioned simple gentleman to the backbone' and 'a great type of man'. On another occasion he describes a fictional officer as a

> product, perhaps, of a culture which one would not desire to see established without modification in this country; but to me, and to some other Australians who met him over there, the finest thing on earth.[12]

This, however, was far from being a common Australian opinion. There had been much criticism of British artillery as early as Gallipoli, while Elliott was noted for his dislike of British officers, criticising those who led the 4th Division at the first battle of Bullecourt.[13] Monash described junior British officers as 'young men from the professions and from office stools in the English cities, who have had no experience whatever of independent responsibility and leadership.' He thought they were too 'comfort orientated and aloof'.[14]

Australian soldiers held similar views. One told the author several derogatory tales of British officers: one sexually harassing a French girl; and two others refusing to accompany him on a mission into no man's land. Anzacs were sometimes horrified by the way British officers treated their men; and petty disputes with British officers were not uncommon.[15]

The British army, in fact, was a product of Edwardian British society. Class and status mattered. So British officers, often chosen for their class or educational background, stayed aloof from their men, eating in separate messes even in the front line if possible. On the other hand, the 'Australian tradition was for the officers to take the same food and drink as the men' and a spirit of camaraderie between officers and men resulted. New Zealanders also told tales of British officers' callousness towards the comfort of their men, and insistence on petty discipline.[16] This last—and their stress on a separate status by enforcing saluting—was particularly resented by Australians. They also saw the well-connected receive rewards and those far more worthy ignored, and sometimes 'from devilment saluted cinema doormen, railway guards, hotel porters, and any other civilian under a peaked cap'.[17]

## BRITISH FIELD OFFICERS AND THE AUSTRALIANS

In their turn, at least in the early days, British field officers thought the Australians vulgar. One wrote to Kitchener's secretary in 1914 that they 'seem a roughish lot'. A captain in 1915, after remarking that they were good fighters, added:

> but. . . there was hardly the slightest pretension to being gentlemen or civilised. Their faces were coarse and hard-bitten . . . the Australian manner . . . was blatant and self-assertive and the Australian voice likewise. I am afraid I never wish to meet any more Australians—there seems to be too much of the Botany Bay strain in them! My servant too complains that they are a rough lot.

Others thought their sanitary habits on Gallipoli 'just too disgusting and filthy for words' and that they had much to learn.[18]

English prejudice was revealed in a variety of ways. A Victorian farmer who had volunteered for the Royal Flying Corps noted that the colonel in charge of his school was a former Etonian,

> and not very partial to Colonials! . . . in his opinion Colonials, and especially Australians, weren't 'officer material'. The term officer, in his opinion, was

synonymous with 'gentleman', and while he might make officers of us, 'gentleman' was a term not applicable to us.

The Canadians were subject to a similar attitude on occasions.

Yet other British officers saw the fighting qualities and independence of the Australians, and admired them, and as time went on these came to be a majority. E. J. Rule reported on an English colonel (who admittedly had been an instructor at Duntroon Millitary College before the war) that 'Like many English officers who have had anything to do with our forces, he became fascinated with them, and I remember his telling us that we had records every bit as good as the Guards.' He was not alone.[19]

This admiration grew in 1918, as the Anzacs improved—significantly amongst the elite of the British forces who had seen the Anzacs in action.

> After fighting beside Brigadier Elliott and his men at Villers-Bretonneux ... the Chestnut Troop of the Royal Horse Artillery ... repeating the courtesy extended by the Troop to two regiments ... in the Peninsular War, invited

*Dear Old Silly.* "AND WHERE DO YOU TWO COME FROM?"
*Wounded Australian.* "WE'RE ANZACS, MADAM."
*Dear Old Silly.* "REALLY? HOW DELIGHTFUL! AND DO YOU BOTH BELONG TO THE SAME TRIBE?"

English ignorance of Australians, as seen by *Punch*, 10 May 1916.

Elliott and the officers of his four battalions to be honorary members of their
Mess as an open demonstration of their regard.[20]

The commander of the 1st Cavalry Division wrote to Monash, thanking
him and the Anzacs for their help during the German attacks in March,
adding that 'It was a pleasure and an honour to be fighting alongside
troops who displayed such magnificent morale.' And the English author
of a biography of Monash, A. J. Smithers, said privately that he wrote
the book partly because of 'the gallantry of Australia's 1914-18 soldiers
(which he learned of from his father, who fought beside them in France)'.[21]

## BRITISH TROOPS' ATTITUDE TO THE AUSTRALIANS

British troops themselves also had varied attitudes to the Australians,
depending on individual experiences. As we have seen, many thought
them a rough lot in Egypt, but thereafter a note of admiration crept in
for their fighting qualities, and—in France—their independence from the
harsh discipline to which the British Tommies were subject.

In the Middle East, four batteries of the Territorial Army Royal Horse
Artillery were attached to the Australians. 'So closely did the English and
Scottish gunners identify themselves with the mounted brigades that
they even sought permission, unsuccessfully, to wear the emu plumes in
their headdress.'[22] Back in France the author Frank Richards, with the
Australians for the first time, commented in amazement on an Australian
brigadier visiting his men: 'It was the only time during the whole of the
war that I saw a brigadier with the first line of attacking troops' he added
that 'there was also an excellent spirit of comradeship between officers
and men.' This parallels the surprise expressed by the medical officer of
the 2nd Battalion, Royal Fusiliers, when the head of the Australian
medical units arrived to check on the treatment of the wounded. He wrote,
'Was one of ours ever within the shelled zone when there was the greatest
need. . .?'[23]

But sour notes were also struck. There were complaints that the
Australians escaped fatigues and were the only ones to be fully rested.[24]
But as has been discussed already, the Anzacs' complaint was the complete
opposite. Edmonds wrote to Bean in 1932 that 'the home troops regarded
the Australians and Canadians as the spoiled children of G.H.Q., who
were given most rest, the pick of the fighting patches, and most of the
praise'. Bean in reply admitted that 'we all knew those things that were
said about us' but went on to point to Pozières and other battles to prove
they were untrue. But Edmonds' attitude has been accepted uncritically
by some later writers.[25]

There was certainly resentment at the high rates of Australian pay,
similar to the resentment at American army pay during World War II.
An Australian sergeant described how the Tommies looked on enviously
at Australians playing cards in a railway station 'and the six little heaps
of silver coins, which the free Australians seem to handle so carelessly'.[26]

It was not only the sense of injustice that rankled, however, but also the results. As one historian puts it,

> The 'fuckin five bobbers' brought home to the lowly Tommy, with his shilling a day, his relative poverty, while at the same time intensifying this by driving up prices behind the lines.[27]

The Australian authorities tried to alleviate the situation. One soldier reported that in August 1915 an order went out limiting the drawing of pay to two-fifths of the daily rate, 'to remove the distinction . . . between the British and Australian rates' and to encourage thrift. But many men got round it by drawing on their private funds.[28]

The problem would not go away. In August 1916 a CID paper revealed the discrepancies in pay rates. Whereas a British private received one shilling a day, South Africa paid its privates three shillings; Canada four shillings and two pence; New Zealand five shillings and Australia six shillings. South African troops in Europe, however, were paid British rates, and the Army Council, desperate for South Africans to volunteer, wanted the British government to supplement their pay. Despite the Chancellor of the Exchequer's worries how they would answer if they were asked why they were paying South Africans more than their own men, Cabinet agreed, but only once further South African troops enlisted.[29] Then, in March 1917 the matter was raised in the House of Commons, when Major-General Sir Ivor Philipps remarked:

> The subject of low pay is talked about every day by the soldiers. . . . These Colonial men had 5s and 6s a day, and they drank coffee and beer and went out to buy butter, cheese and eggs for themselves in the town . . . What chance had my men with their 1s a day . . .?[30]

In September of that year the War Cabinet again discussed the problem of colonial pay, and decided that Dominion troops should not be quartered in the same depots as British troops, and that it would review the latters' pay in due course.[31] The British Cabinet, however, was unwilling to increase the pay of British troops, despite the injustice to its own men. It did not augur well for a post-war 'land fit for heroes to live in'.

Resentment between British and Dominion troops was also caused by the censorship. The British authorities were determined to prevent any news of the position of individual units from reaching the Germans, and so rigidly removed all references to them in reports. This was overdone, for the Germans were quite capable of discovering from prisoners or the dead what units were facing them, and the boost to home morale—not to mention that of the units concerned—if a success had been scored would have outweighed any drawbacks. The British high command, however, was unhappy with war reporters, and did not know how to handle them or how useful they could be.[32] It would have preferred simply to have issued communiqués. The public was not satisfied with that, and least of all were the Dominions. Their authorities, faced with the need either to maintain recruiting or to introduce conscription, were determined that their men should receive recognition. Their reporters were expected to mention their men, and argued with the censor when he tried to stop them. As a result, the British complained that the exploits of their soldiers were inadequately appreciated,[33] while the Dominions complained that when their men achieved an outstanding success, it appeared in the press simply as a 'British' victory—masking their achievements and making it appear that British troops were better.

## AUSTRALIAN ATTITUDE TO BRITISH TROOPS

In fact, the Anzacs were convinced otherwise. Bean wrote that 'The Australian did not mix freely with the English soldiers of the ranks because they had an entirely different outlook', for as volunteers the Australians felt more independent and the social equal of officers.[34] British troops were predominantly English,[35] but it is interesting that the Anzacs always got on well with other groups from Britain, especially the Scots, who showed an initiative similar to that of the Dominion troops. This is not surprising, for the Scots also were heavy drinkers like the Anzacs, and were constantly running foul of the English Redcaps. Dawnay, when he met Bean in 1918, took offence at the latter's remark that the Scots were better than English troops,[36] but it was a common opinion among the Anzacs.

The Scottish educational system created a strong egalitarian and democratic spirit that appealed to the Australians, rather than the more class-conscious English. The Australians, like the Scots, were independent and curious about all aspects of the war, while the English soldiers left such matters to their officers. This 'struck the Dominion troops as curiously bovine, and, already unimpressed by their fighting performance, they were ready to make the "Tommy" a stock figure of humour.' They wondered why the British soldier accepted his lot, and sometimes urged him to stand up for himself—to the irritation of British officers.[37]

The poor opinion of British troops had appeared as early as four days after the landing on Gallipoli. The gulf then widened between the two sides. The Australians regarded the British as old-fashioned, incompetent and arrogant; the British looked at the more casual Australian discipline, and thought it made the Anzacs worse soldiers. Elliott's attitude was bitterly anti-British from the beginning—perhaps, as one old soldier surmised, as a result of events during the Boer War. He thought that 'no man did more to worsen relations between the Australian and English troops than Pompey'—describing one English regiment as 'the Scarlet runners', doubling a fine on Gallipoli because the man involved was a 'Pommy', and preventing Englishmen from being promoted in units under his command. During the retreat in March 1918 a British staff officer, whose men he had arrested for looting wine, complained to General Headquarters; while Elliott's orders to his men to shoot any British stragglers had to be countermanded by Hobbs.[38]

The Australians also revealed the ignorance and arrogance of the naive. To such men, their own experiences had to be more important, or serious, or difficult, than those of others. Thus, when the Anzacs first arrived on the Western Front they asked the British whether they had been fighting, or had been in France, 'in tones calculated to offend'.[39] After the battle of Fromelles, the Australians blamed the British 61st Division—quite unfairly—for not attacking with more verve, assuming from their own losses that they had a more difficult task. Their conviction that British troops could not be trusted to hold their own became firmly grounded, being repeated in April 1917 after Bullecourt.[40] They sneered at the British for adopting the 'Live and Let Live system': 'The cold footed hounds. The more one learns of the Tommies, the more one despises them. We shake [the Huns] up wherever we go.'[41] The most that the more generous Australians would admit was to think the troops all right, but their officers poor. Bean was restrained in his criticism, but reported that when the Royal Welch Fusiliers withdrew from Polygon Wood two officers visited the neighbouring Australians and apologised for the behaviour of their men. The Anzacs resented local British troops losing positions they had just gained, so that the Australians then had to recapture them. The British tank crews at Bullecourt drew scathing criticism in numerous reports, in which the word 'cowards' appeared. Lieutenant E. J. Rule (who kept a diary much quoted by Bean) reported—quite unfairly, seeing the primitive nature of the tanks—that 'it was not the tanks' fault; it was the chicken hearts who manned them'.[42]

It was so easy for the Australians to compare the somewhat wild Scots with the 'colourless, stunted, half-toothless lads from hot, humid Lancashire mills' or the 'battalions of slow, staring faces, gargoyles out of the tragical-comical-historical-pastoral edifice of modern English rural life'.[43] Comments about poor specimens from the industrial slums also began early. In late 1914 Bean thought that 'the little pink cheeked lads from the Manchester cotton mills . . . looked like children when compared with the huge men of the Australian regiments'. Yet Bean, like the Anzacs themselves, ignored the drastic weeding out of the unfit which had occurred in the recruiting offices. The later standards for the Australian soldiers were to decline.[44]

The Anzacs, however, also very soon felt that they were being given an unfair burden of the fighting. In November 1916 the governor-general reported to Long that the Anzacs were complaining about leave, and added that there was 'considerable discontent' in the AIF because of the soldiers' belief that many British troops were being held back in England. This provoked a highly unsympathetic response in the Colonial Office, where minute-makers wrote of the Australians' 'voyage to Europe' as if it were a holiday cruise. In May 1917, while the battle of Bullecourt was raging, Hobbs saw Birdwood and reported that the men of the 5th Division had been talking to the British 11th and Guards Divisions, and the former had been out of the line for three months and the Guards for seven weeks. Even though the assumptions may not have been valid,

Birdwood was worried enough to write to Gough, and his letter went up to GHQ, which replaced the Australians with a British division.[45]

## THE GREAT RETREAT AND ANGLO-AUSTRALIAN RELATIONS

The trouble reached its peak in March 1918, with the British withdrawal before the German attacks. Monash himself had difficulty in finding X Corps, which his division was under, and used his Australians to plug the line near Doullens. The timely arrival of the 4th Australian Division provided the support he needed, but revealed evidence of the breakdown of British morale, with a crying general and officers who had abandoned their duty.[46]

> Marching through the rear of the crumbling 5th Army it seemed to the Australians that they were the only units heading towards the front. The roads were clogged with retreating British foot-soldiers, labour troops, artillery, transport and staff cars.[47]

One later reported that, as the 4th Brigade debussed,

> they were met by streams of English troops pouring by, intent only on saving their lives. They were neither use nor ornament. [One group rounded up and put under a sergeant, ran away as soon as he turned his back.] As a result . . . the English have lowered themselves considerably in the eyes of the French population, and I may say also in our boys' too.

He put the difference down to poor English officers, too young and unseasoned, who did not look after their men, a judgement supported by Monash and many others.[48]

His experience was not unusual. The British 47th Division panicked, moved its transport back without orders, and chaos reigned. The Australians, trying to force their way through the retiring masses, were warned by 'staff officers retreating in great haste' that the enemy was not far behind, and 'a car containing nine red-tabbed officers speeding down the road in indecent haste received a volley of abuse from the "Diggers" going in the opposite direction'. An English medical officer noted they asked about the morale of his division, and wondered 'Is every Anzac sick at the failure of the [British] troops . . . to hold?' He later recounted how Australian troops, quartered by a fur-coated area commandant in a bare field, threw him in the local river.[49]

The British were also pouring reinforcements into France (110,000 by 4 April) sometimes using men just over eighteen, many poorly trained, to plug the gaps. As one Australian wrote in despair,

> English children; pink faced, round cheeked children, flushed under the weight of their unaccustomed packs, with their steel helmets on the back of their heads and the strap hanging loosely on their rounded baby chins.[50]

Much of this of course was unfair. The Australians had not had to face the hurricane gas shell bombardment by the Germans, or their sudden attacks on that first day of Ludendorff's offensive, 21 March 1918. Where they did so later, they too were capable of leaving the front line or mass retirement.[51] Many British troops fought hard, and suffered heavy losses. A recent study blames rather GHQ, Gough, British corps commanders, the inflexibility in the British command structure, and failure to understand or accept the German system of defence in depth.[52] But whether the comments were unfair or not is beside the point. Australian opinion was clear and has survived to this day. Elliott, as could be expected, was scathing. He had some admiration for the cavalry and the machine-gunners, but despised British troops and officers.[53] On this occasion, however, he was widely supported. Currie of the Canadians thought the same, and upset the British high command by saying so.[54] One member of the 4th Australian Division wrote:

> The road is a continuous stream of ... detached parties of 'Tommies' who have become 'lost, stolen, or strayed' ... Seems to me that the whole damn lot are more intent on getting back than getting up. They'll make a good advance guard—for the civilians' retreat.[55]

These attitudes came to the attention of the British government. The CIGS reported to the Cabinet that 'scurrilous and unfair allusions to the conduct of British troops were being made in letters written by Australian troops serving on the Western front' and extracts from Australian letters about British troops were read out. He wanted the Australian government, no less, to take action. The Cabinet decided to request the governor-general to do so. It agreed with the CIGS that the Ministry for Information should send the Dominions 'information with regard to the fighting performances of British troops for publication in the Dominion press'. It was then revealed that for the previous two years the War Office had organised articles on the doings of British troops to be sent to the colonies for publication—with 'most satisfactory reports of the results'. Cabinet decided that publication of any critical letters should be prevented in the Australian press, and the Ministry of Information should send out more material.[56] It is perhaps significant, however, from the point of view of this book, that by that time the British authorities were themselves using the word 'British' to distinguish English, Scottish, Welsh and Irish troops from Australians.

The British censorship surveyed 83,621 letters during the later days of the German offensive to 12 July. For the Australians, it reported: 'Adverse opinion as to the fighting qualities of English regiments was so freely expressed as to suggest the possibility of serious trouble between Australian and English troops in France.' It went on that the conditions under which the British troops retired were lost sight of, and perhaps Australian heads had been turned by their successes. Their accusations 'display at least a lack of the generosity which might have been expected from troops with whose fighting record the whole world is familiar'. On the other hand, the Australian troops were highly praised by English letter-writers.[57]

The trouble the censors and Cabinet feared slowly developed. In September, when—as previously recounted—one company of the 1st Australian Battalion refused to join a second attack on the same objective, the men complained they were not getting a fair deal and were being used for other people's work:

> There was a widespread feeling that British troops had repeatedly failed to keep up, and that the Australians, as well as fighting on their own front, were sometimes called on to make good their neighbours' failure.[58]

Long before this, however, the old complaints that Australian work was ignored in the press had become all the more bitter. Monash wrote to his wife that press correspondents were forbidden to mention the fact that Australians had held the gaps in March 1918, and several long cables had been delayed until their news was stale. The single report that got through was by Philip Gibbs in the London *Daily Telegraph*.[59] One historian has commented on the semantic problem, that the word 'imperial', which might have been assumed to imply colonial troops, in fact was used to refer to units from the United Kingdom, so that

> readers of newspaper reports of the fighting could gain only the vaguest impression of the respective contributions being made by the colonial divisions, and readers of *The Times* would never have known that the Canadians and Australians were taking part in the fighting in France at all.[60]

This point was made by Bean in 1939, when he discussed the 'serious misunderstanding ... between Dominion forces and the Imperial authorities'. He too thought the reason was partly semantic. The English press used the term 'British' to mean troops from the United Kingdom and the Dominions; the Australians read it to mean those from the United Kingdom only. Another term should have been used for Empire-wide troops.

All this was true enough, but it was not the only reason. As Bean himself added, the Dominion forces were the most effective in the British army, and were recognised as such by the Germans, so as we have seen the British authorities tried to play down the difference.[61] From the Cabinet discussion it seems that the censors were deliberately blocking any mention of Australian efforts in the press in both England and Australia. The reports by the Director of Military Operations to the Imperial War Cabinet on Hamel were very subdued. Despite the excitement in the Fourth Army, GHQ and Supreme War Council, he seems to have had no desire to praise them. Charteris, Haig's intelligence chief, insisted that British troops were bearing the brunt of the fighting—but were just not so impressed by publicity as the 'Colonials'. He was unsympathetic to requests that Australian pressmen should see Haig and extol the Anzacs, jeering at their assurances that this material would be used only in Australia.[62]

Birdwood meanwhile made frantic efforts to get the Australians to think well of the English. He circulated to divisions a warning that they

English, Scottish and Australian soldiers. (AWM Official Photo No. E3672).

must expect to be on continuous duty, and that British troops who left the areas near them were only going to other parts of the line. A second circular argued that

> depreciation of [our] kith and kin is not necessary for the full acknowledgement of the great work the Dominion troops are doing. We are of the same blood, and the creation of friction by criticism is only playing the Germans' game.[63]

## BRITISH ELITES AND THE AUSTRALIANS

The British elites followed the attitudes of the military and were convinced that the Australians had too good an opinion of themselves, and were made too much of. In Australia as early as 1916 the governor-general had complained that 'The public is but partially aware that there are other British Troops besides the Anzacs in action.' Indeed, he thought that Australia's contribution was much below her fair proportion, and tried to emphasise the role of the British. Fisher as High Commissioner was very upset by a sneering aside in the Commons that Australian patriotism rested on British loans, together with remarks about what Australia had done and was willing to do. Stamfordham wrote to Munro-Ferguson in 1917 that 'there is too much disposition in certain quarters to try to make out that the War has been run and won by Dominion troops' and he thought much mischief had been done in Australia by exaggerated press reports of their men. That this was the royal view is confirmed by Haig's diary: George V had read a minute by Lord Milner in the Cabinet papers, which confirmed his suspicion of 'the harm done by the repeated Press utterances in praise of the doings of Dominion troops, while there is almost silence as to British achievements and losses'. The Dominions naturally thought that they had done all the fighting, so their men no longer enlisted. The King thought that the prohibition on mentioning units should be lifted, and publicity given to British troops. The CIGS sent this on to Haig, saying the War Office wanted him to give it his consideration.[64]

GHQ's reluctance to give any information about events was ostensibly in the name of 'security'. Yet British troops also resented it when their deeds were not mentioned[65] and the suspicion remains that the secrecy was also used to cover GHQ blunders. Philip Gibbs wrote to Bean in 1917 that he was 'always being abused for writing too much about Australians and Canadians and New Zealand troops'. One would love to know who abused him, but clearly the pressure was on to play down Dominion successes.

It continued even more strongly in 1918. Long, writing to Birdwood in October, thought that the press had given the Anzacs so much reportage that they thought they had been overused. But the reverse was equally true. The Anzacs could well retort, as one writer asserts they did in the 4th Brigade, 'Whatever we do they'll say *they* won the battle; next time we'll let them win it.'[66] Monash made vehement protests to *The Times*, Rawlinson and Wilson, and argued that his appeal to the Anzacs was to the prestige of their arms, and if they received no recognition he would not be responsible for the maintenance of their fighting spirit.

He claimed great success, but seventy years later one old soldier was still deeply offended by English newspapers. As he saw it, after a particularly nasty affair the Australians would look for some recognition, but 'all we ever got were reports that "British" troops had triumphed'.[67] Bean himself made strenuous representations to GHQ on the subject, which reveal what George Orwell called 'newspeak' in the British high command. Bean wrote to Major Neville Lytton, the military head of the British press at Amiens, protesting at the use of the word 'British' in communiqués about the battle of 8 August. Lytton however replied that he realised that this might cause bitterness among the Australian troops, but it was necessary to restore American and French confidence in the British army. Bean then received a letter from Dawnay, on GHQ staff, protesting his admiration for the Anzacs, dating back to Gallipoli, and arguing that the term 'British' applied to all of them, and that no Englishman would ever think of using communiqués as a means of propaganda. He was anxious about the Anzacs' low opinion of British troops, and appealed for unity. Bean thanked Dawnay for this specious letter, but argued that the term 'British' would no longer suffice, since to Australians it implied troops from the British Isles and no others. He argued in several letters for a more open policy and giving of credit whenever it was due to the specific units that had deserved it. The communiqués in the Middle East always distinguished between British, French and Australian units, and the British people themselves had particularised the use of the word to a greater extent than GHQ realised.[68]

## 'BLIGHTY': THE ANZACS AND THE ENGLISH

At first, the British authorities encouraged Australian soldiers to have leave in England, in the hope that this would boost recruiting in Australia. The Anzacs themselves responded enthusiastically, for a desire to see England had been part of their reason for volunteering.[69] The Australian-born came mainly from the non-travelling class in Australia, so the letters and postcards they sent home were redolent of the excited and slightly naive 'tourist' attitude of many of the men. Their descriptions were often semi-articulate, as they sought for words to describe how they felt to those at home who had never seen England: 'The trip ... to Salisbury is beyond my description. You have no conception of the depth of meaning in the phrase "the green fields of England".'[70] Their language often echoed the magazines and texts they had read in school. It also depended on their time of arrival: if summer, they waxed lyrical, but if winter, then they were often glum. Sometimes they came straight to camps in England, where they arrived in cold and snow, and were hit hard by the British army's habit of siting camps in the most bleak and inhospitable

An Australian camp in Britain: the bitter winter conditions at Longbridge Deverill. (AWM Official Photo No. D386).

places. One Anzac was horrified to find water frozen in the tap. Another
wondered why the English had 'gone to so much trouble for this country.
It has such a vile climate.' Others, however, thought it more invigorating
than Australia's hot season.[71]

As we have seen, the men had many links with Britain. A significant
number were British-born (as many as one in four of the recruits in June
1915) and their parents or brothers and sisters were still living there. Others
had cousins, uncles and aunts or more distant relatives. The vast majority
took the opportunity to call on them, and see the home towns and villages
of their ancestors. If nothing else, it gave them a friendly fireside to visit
and interested and interesting faces to see. It was a touch of home. And
many found a delight in England: its countryside and old buildings, its
history and beauty. They were determined tourists, frequently overstaying
their leave to see the sights. Richard White suggests that the demand 'to see
England properly', and not just the wish to avoid battle, accounts for some
at least of the AWOL figures that so offended the British high command.[72]

The more highly educated, and those who came from the middle
classes, or had money to spend, naturally felt even more strongly bound
to England. The photographer Frank Hurley, on setting out for the
Middle East, wrote,

> I am deeply sorry to leave England, it has become a sacred and beloved country
> to me. The Old Piccadilly, Hyde Park and the Imperial [his hotel]. I shall ever
> think of them . . . As I write we're leaving Old England's shores. They lay down
> even now with a hazy skyline and as they grow dimmer, I seem to feel as though
> I've left a part of myself there. Dear old land, whenever shall I see thee more?[73]

Australian soldiers in Trafalgar Square.    (AWM Official Photo No. D710).

A party of Australian nurses and soldiers in London setting out to visit places of interest. (YMCA).

Reactions were intensely personal, depending partly on the man con-cerned, and partly on his experiences. They also changed over time. At first the men had high expectation of the land they had been taught at home and in school to love. But reality, and the mischances of life, changed many of their views.

The first arrival, usually after a long sea voyage, caught their imagi-nation: 'They had been prepared, imaginatively, by years of schooling and private reading, to invest this moment with a sense of mystery and awe.' They looked in wonder at the old houses, the fields and the farmlands of England. When they were on leave, London was their obvious first port of call, with the usual tourist attractions: the Houses of Parliament (and some listened to the debates), Big Ben, Westminster Abbey, St Paul's Cathedral. After that, a live show in a London theatre was a highlight for many, sometimes remembered seventy years later. London remained the hub and centre of the Australian British experience, stupefying the Australians, at least at first, with its size and complexity, including the 'moving stairways', then unheard of in Australia.[74]

Inevitably, the 'honeymoon period' gradually wore off. Driven by homesickness and loneliness, the Australians became more critical. They noticed, and commented on, the formality of the English, and the red tape of the British hospitals. They also noticed the soot and dirt of London, the pale faces of the people, and the indifference of the city. As time went on they became more familiar with it, and the contrast with France made it seem all the more attractive, though they never ceased to

The war brides embark for Australia.   (Patsy Adam-Smith, *The Anzacs*: 341).

show amazement at—and disapproval of—women working, and others despised the behaviour of crowds during the air raids on London.[75]

Naturally enough, however, being young men, they had an eye for the women. One reported a friendship with the cinema operator in the local cinema and spent his leave helping her show the films. The wounded often struck up friendships—and more—with their nurses. The Australians were lonely, and welcomed being brought into English homes and family life once again. Many English women preferred the Australians, with their higher rates of pay, to the more poverty-stricken Tommy. The only reminiscence the author has come across from the woman's point of view is a letter from a young woman who was 'nearly engaged' to an Anzac, and blamed herself for being so weak as having anything to do with Australians. He was 'a good looking apparition' but 'evidently a rogue'. However, he was sent to the front so the engagement was broken.[76]

The ill feeling on the part of British soldiers and male civilians—and gossip by the females—can be gauged by the attitude towards Americans in World War II. On the Australian side, though some thought that marrying an Englishwoman was unfair to the women of Australia, a large number of marriages did occur. By December 1918 Australian soldiers in England were marrying Englishwomen at the rate of 150 a week. There were 5626 'war brides', and in all 15,386 wives, children, fiancées and dependants returned to Australia with the AIF in 1919. Unfortunately, there were also a number of bigamous marriages. The respect of each side for the other waned, and some Australians became suspicious and critical of Englishwomen. They never got used to seeing them in public houses, or smoking, for example.[77] Many Australian soldiers therefore came to idealise the Australian women they had left at home.

This was only increased by another aspect of Anglo-Australian relations which was often mentioned and discussed: the large numbers of prostitutes, especially in London, pestering the men, who were highly paid by British standards. The number of prostitutes grew, and reports abound of them propositioning the men in restaurants and at bus queues. Brothels became a nuisance in London, Weymouth and Salisbury.[78]

There was also, naturally, an increase in venereal disease. This directly concerned the military authorities, not for the morality of the situation, but because VD took the men out of the firing line. In April 1917 Birdwood wrote both to the governor-general and Long about it, saying that unlike British troops the Anzacs had no homes to go to, and were pestered by the women of London. He had received letters from the parents of Australian soldiers about this. They had been prepared to give their sons to fight and die for the Empire, but they had not reckoned with this. Birdwood wondered if the Imperial War Council could discuss it, and perhaps the *Defence of the Realm Act* (DORA) could be invoked. This letter appears in several places in the files, so it seems to have circulated around the higher levels of the Australian government. Birdwood had suggested the use of DORA because the *Contagious Diseases Act* had been repealed in 1886.

It was a delicate matter. The British authorities were reluctant to act: neither the War Office nor the Home Office was prepared to take responsibility, even though the Colonial Office under Long was very worried by the complaints. The problem was particularly bad with Dominion troops. The ratio of VD cases to troops among the whole British army in 1917 was 34 per 1000 men; for New Zealanders it was 134.2 and Australians 144. As a result, unreported in Australia, some of the AIF were issued with condoms when going on leave (despite the explicit instruction of the Army Council) and brothels were arranged for them.[79]

The problem grew worse in 1918, however, 'when 60,099 British and Dominion troops were treated in France, an average of thirty-two out of every 1,000 men ... under Haig'. This wastage was the equivalent of a division a day, and 50 per cent of the cases had been contracted in England. It is not surprising, therefore, that there was finally a discussion in the War Cabinet in February 1918, and, when the matter was again postponed, Long wrote urgently to Lloyd George. The problem with using DORA, however, was that it was to be applied to the women only, and not the men involved. Long, however, argued that there would be grave trouble if they postponed action much longer: 'The Dominions are constantly pressing that instant action should be taken and I really cannot be responsible for the consequences if further delay occurs.' He then issued a further memorandum on the subject. The Dominions had urged 'in the strongest possible terms' that action should be taken. Borden remarked that Canada would never again send men overseas to any war 'unless we are assured that such conditions as have met our soldiers here will not meet them again', while the New Zealand government sent a telegram demanding an immediate answer.[80]

For the Anzacs, a change had occurred in their attitudes. They had expected to find England akin to Australia—after all, both countries spoke the same language. But it soon became apparent that they were not similar. With the climate went petty annoyances such as the refusal to accept Australian money, and more serious ones, such as the British class system, with which they had no patience. Thus privates or NCOs insisted on visiting restaurants where officers ate. The English regarded this as a sign of Australian arrogance; the Australians as English snobbery. They were quick to resent what they suspected was condescension, or patronising behaviour, and demanded to be treated as equals. They detested the English distinction between officers and men. They also noticed with distaste the gap between wealth and poverty in Britain and came all the more to regard Australia as 'God's own country'. The British could only dislike what they regarded as brash and arrogant Australians,[81] but Australian egalitarianism appeared in some very odd places. A. G. Butler, for example, who later wrote the medical volumes of the official history, came from Queensland of English-born parents. Educated at Cambridge University, he left natural history for medical studies, and returned to Australia only in 1914. From his background, he should have been an imperialist and lover of England, but he fully accepted the egalitarian principles of the Queensland of his youth. A colonel during the war, he insisted on wearing Digger's uniform and refused to join officers' clubs. In his diary he criticised England, railing against 'the hateful and ghastly luxury of the rotten wealthy people of England'.[82]

There was, then 'a growing mood of disillusion and disenchant-ment'. One letter-writer wrote that he hated England, and that 'they ought to give England to Germany and apologise for the state it is in'. Homesickness, the weather, and war weariness all contributed to the feeling, which was not restricted to Australians. A New Zealand writer thinks the Kiwis 'found the British excessively class conscious and the environment depressing'. The climate was terrible and snobbery rife. Though many were fascinated by the evidence of British history, and seeing the sights of London, meeting relatives and seeing their parents' birthplaces, on the whole Britain disappointed them. The climate was dismal, taxi-drivers cheated them, and the people were narrow-minded and untravelled. Frederic Eggleston, though an Australian intellectual, summed up the pilgrimage many more simple Australians made. Although 'enraptured' by the cathedrals, and the evidence of history all around, he found English society 'foreign' to him, and thought 'the term "British" described a generic racial and ethnic group ... "The English", on the other hand, were the often incompetent, residual rulers of the Empire.'[83]

Some Anzacs remained deeply attached to Britain to the end, but as McKernan puts it:

> For most Australians the land they had come to fight for had ceased to be 'home' once they experienced the reality as distinct from the myth they had learned at school and from their parents.

Moreover, to escape the battle trauma they had suffered, and the chronic stress under which they lived, they reacted as soldiers usually do, and indulged in fantasies about home. So they turned their eyes back to Australia as a source of sustenance, creating 'a highly idealised picture of their homeland', which they saw with new eyes.[84]

## THE ENGLISH AND THE AUSTRALIANS

A similar path of disillusionment was followed by the British. At first, the Australians were welcomed as 'heroes', like men out of the distant past. Ashmead-Bartlett's reaction to them on Gallipoli was echoed in London, where the Australians—promoted by British propaganda to hide the shambles on the peninsula—had the reputation of 'bronzed Gods'. The year 1916 was the honeymoon. Australian troops had first arrived in Britain; Billy Hughes was touring the country and stirring the people; and Australians were high in favour. Their wounded were greeted with praise; bishops talked of them; and the upper classes invited them into their houses and entertained them. McKernan calls it the *annus mirabilis*.

As we have seen, Anzac Day was celebrated in London and the Australians were given a magnificent reception.[85]

Like all propaganda, however, it triggered a backlash. Some thought that it was overdone, or simply 'Colonial boasting', more British troops being involved on Gallipoli than Australian. *John Bull* for example wrote that the 29th Division should have been in the first Anzac Day parade, and not just 'Colonial troops'. The criticism was unfair, for the celebrations were not of the men's making: there were British political motives at work, as well as honest admiration for the prowess of the Anzacs in men like the poet Masefield. But the impression remained. Sections of the press began to complain that the Anzacs were overpraised while the British army was neglected, and indeed the Anzacs themselves became embarrassed by the press.[86]

The Anzacs also had a reputation for making trouble, and as early as March 1916 one hotel proprietor refused accommodation to an Australian. This was reinforced by resentment at their brash and confident ways and their attraction to—and treatment of—British women. Australian press criticism of English war brides roused bitter resentment in England, and cases of bigamy led to a press campaign. McKernan blames their relations with women for the change in the ready welcome the Australians had first received: 'By 1917 they were seen, whether fairly or not, as amorous, dangerous, even lustful. ... The Australians, too, had formed rather stereotyped views about English women.' The Australians had played up to their image too often. The English became wary of them; and the Anzacs resentful. One Englishwoman told an Australian that she would sooner have 'Germans, or convicts, there than Colonial troops'.[87] Of course, the Australians were housed in large numbers in camps (127,000 passed through Weymouth) and the areas around army camps are notorious for disliking soldiers—of all nationalities. Yet the Australian military police cooperated well with their civilian British counterparts, and a charge by *John Bull* that Australian behaviour was serious cause for alarm was disproved by a subsequent investigation.[88] Gradually, however, the magistrates in Weymouth became harder on Australians, as their charges changed from petty misdemeanours, more the result of boisterousness and drink than serious crimes, to riots involving 300–400 Australians and civilians. Tension between both sides was growing, and was revealed at Salisbury, where the magistrates sentenced one Australian to twelve months' imprisonment with hard labour.

By now, 'the Australians had been transformed from heroes to criminals' in the eyes of British authorities, so that a riot in Epsom begun by Canadians was reported at first to be the work of Australians, while the British War Cabinet discussed Australian rowdiness and was advised that the Australians should be kept from London and repatriated to Australia as soon as possible. The Australians reacted in kind. The men on the final march past the King were aggrieved by not being allowed to stay in London for the night, so when the order 'eyes right' came, many looked at the ground or the sky or anywhere but right. At least one Australian onlooker was embarrassed.[89]

The Australian victory march passing Australia House, London, 25 April 1919.
(AWM Official Photo No. P212/01).

Yet, when all this has been said, many Australians retained a great affection for the English, and many of the latter kept their ties with Australia for years to come. Many soldiers afterwards reminisced about the delight in visiting England again in 1918, and the hospitality of the people. One, while talking about the 'stand-offish English way' still gave many instances of kindness and hospitality, while another corresponded with a family for years and sent them food parcels in World War II. The press farewelled the Australians nostalgically.[90]

## SCOTS, CANADIANS AND NEW ZEALANDERS

The Australians also had a particular affinity for the Scots. Many separate sources vouch for this. Bean himself commented on 'the quite remarkable friendship which ripened between the soldiers of the two nations'. This was based on Australian respect for the Scots as soldiers. Some Scots of course fought in the AIF, but there was admiration for the Scottish regiments, such as the Gordon Highlanders at Bullecourt. Indeed, the Australians said that the Jocks had never yet failed them. This respect combined with loathing for the English military police, the hated Redcaps. Stories were told of Anzacs and Scots combining in battle against them, and indeed this combination appeared in the riot at Etaples.[91]

Many Australians therefore made their way to Scotland on leave. This was partly because they could nominate a destination, so the logic was to go to the furthest point, to see as much as possible of the British Isles on the way. But it was more than that,

> because there was a special affinity between the 'Jocks' and the men from Australia. They fraternised on every possible occasion in France, and such friendly feelings were also manifested in Scotland towards any wandering Australian.[92]

One old soldier recounted two leaves he had spent in Glasgow, where he thought the people most hospitable and more relaxed than the English; another spent time with an aristocratic family in Edinburgh.[93] The relationship with the Scots was probably the warmest the AIF had with any of its comrades in arms.

They had few dealings with the Canadians. Some of those at Passchendaele in 1917 were not happy, but their cooperation in 1918, for instance at the great battle of Amiens on 8 August, was good. Meanwhile, on the civilian front, Bean was upset by being beaten in producing a photographic exhibition in London by Beaverbrook, the Canadian Max Aitken, who became Canada's representative, the British Minister of Information, and press lord in turn. He was also irritated by Beaverbrook's attempt to gain the services of the photographer Hurley, though Bean disapproved of Hurley's attitude to composite pictures and deliberately blocked his activities.[94]

With the New Zealanders the Australians maintained the love–hate relationship that had developed since Gallipoli. The Kiwis admired the Australians' fighting qualities, but thought them brash and undisciplined. They resented the fact that they were under-represented in the Anzac Day march in London in 1916, one writing that we 'didn't land on Gallipoli though you might have thought so once'. Nevertheless, on the battlefields, Godley personally liked Monash, constantly referring to him affectionately as 'old Monash' and was reluctant in November 1917 to sever his connection with the Australians.[95]

All these relationships were soon to come to an end, however, with the conclusion of the war and the making of the peace, when Australia and Australians were to face the problems of the brave new world that had been brought into being by the loss of so many lives.

# CHAPTER EIGHT

# A Peace of Sorts

Between the idea
And the reality
Between the motion
And the act
Falls the Shadow.
T. S. ELIOT,
*The Hollow Men*

## HUGHES IN ENGLAND, 1918–1919

When W. M. Hughes, the Australian prime minister, arrived on 15 June 1918 he took his place in the Imperial War Cabinet and the Imperial War Conference, which had been established the previous year. There he found some old friends, such as Leo Amery. An affinity of outlook existed between the two men, both in their attitude to political power and their desire to strengthen the British Empire. Amery, who had been in correspondence with Hughes, met him when he arrived in London and thought him 'a little older and more like the dormouse in Alice in Wonderland than ever'.[1] Hankey seems at first to have been amused by Hughes' eccentric ways. When the latter commandeered three government cars for himself on a trip to the Continent, Hankey commented that as a result the British government's highly secret papers were 'cruising about France in a lost motor car in charge of a French private soldier'. Lloyd George, however, was irritated: Hughes was beginning to pall. Even as early as 2 July, the British prime minister's reaction was to draft statements himself and ignore the Dominion premiers, and Hankey had to remonstrate with him.[2] It was a bad omen, especially as Hughes like Lord Northcliffe demanded that a hard peace be imposed on Germany. Lloyd George was swamped with work; he had no patience with Hughes, and could not tolerate him destabilising his government in the way he had done that of Asquith. There was less talk of Welshness in 1918—except as a term of abuse.

Hughes had been mistaken in not appointing a representative to the Imperial War Cabinet meetings in 1917. Australia would have had a voice, even if a minor one, in the deliberations, and Hughes himself would have received a more direct and detailed report of the discussions. Hughes, however, was poor at delegating authority to others, and distrusted Fisher, preferring to leave the position unfilled. As a result he had been isolated

190

The Firebrand and the Fossils
Asquith: "David, Talk to him in Welsh and pacify him!"

Asquith: Talk to him in Welsh, David, and pacify him!
Although this cartoon was drawn for his visit in 1916, the attitude to Hughes was very
much in evidence in 1918.    (National Library of Australia).

while the handling of the war deteriorated and new thinking developed.
Keith Murdoch told Hughes in 1918 that his 'personal hold on this
country lost a bit through your non-attendance at the Imperial War
Cabinet': Britain's leaders had become cooler, as they 'felt that you had
not made full efforts to have Australia represented'. Hughes, 'slightly
crestfallen', hoped to make up lost ground and that Lloyd George 'is not
unfriendly towards me'. Murdoch assured him that Lloyd George's regard
was as high as ever. That was an ambiguous remark, but the implication
was untrue, for Hughes had lost prestige by not attending and—as
Monash bitterly remarked in a letter—Australian interests had suffered.[3]

## MILITARY TACTICS AND STRATEGY

Hughes immediately got off on the wrong foot in 1918 by arriving too
late to attend the first three meetings of the Imperial War Cabinet, and
then repeating his earlier criticism of the British for not providing

information. By missing those first three meetings, however, he was absent during the dramatic debates when Borden, Massey and Smuts had attacked the mismanagement of the British army, the slaughter at Passchendaele, the failure to remove incompetent commanders, and the need to promote able men—if necessary, non-professional soldiers, as in the Canadian army. So in response to Hughes' outburst Lloyd George blandly stated that it had all been discussed in the three previous meetings, while Smuts bluntly remarked that lack of information was Hughes' own fault for not being present in 1917. It was an inauspicious beginning.[4]

Indeed, it was long overdue for Hughes to turn his attention to military matters. Till now his government had failed to discuss strategy and the use of the AIF, let alone the operational plans of the British commanders. When J. H. Catts in the Australian federal parliament in October 1915 had asked for 'some discussion' on Gallipoli, Hughes had replied that he was not responsible for directing the campaign. They should refrain from criticising the British, for Australia's task was 'to carry out the instructions of the Imperial Government, and to give that Government our hearty and enthusiastic support'. He added:

> I do not pretend to understand the situation in the Dardanelles, but I know what the duty of this Government is: and that is—to mind its own business, to provide that quota of men which the Imperial Government think necessary.[5]

Such an attitude was a dereliction of the Australian government's duty at the time, and became increasingly inappropriate as the war went on. It was only in December 1917 (after Passchendaele) that Hughes at last cabled the British that he was 'seriously disturbed' by the military situation, but even then he forgot to pursue the point when the British deliberately failed to respond.[6] It was not till March 1918, with the collapse of the British Fifth Army, that Hughes had his mind turned forcibly to British military incompetence. He then cooperated with Borden of Canada in the Imperial War Cabinet in probing it.[7]

Lloyd George, however, succeeded in turning Dominion unrest away from himself by setting up the Committee of Prime Ministers. In effect, he had coopted the premiers in his struggle against Haig. Hughes later told Bean that he and three other premiers had discussed Lloyd George's wish that they should initiate moves, but felt that the situation was too critical. They were 'loath to become catspaws for the removal of . . . Haig', but were deeply concerned about their troops. Borden lost his temper and told Lloyd George that if there was a repetition of Passchendaele, 'not a Canadian soldier will leave the shores of Canada' as long as he was premier. The real problem was Haig: whether to replace him at this crucial stage of the war, and if so by whom. Lloyd George even babbled later about using the Canadian Currie, with Monash as his Chief of Staff, but that cannot be trusted. Nevertheless, the Committee of Prime Ministers came to sensible conclusions, and might have led to the overhaul of the British high command and the establishment of political control over the military but for the collapse in German morale and the victorious allied advance that ended the war soon afterwards—to the utter surprise of both Hughes and the British leadership.[8]

Hughes' reaction to the problem that faced the British in June was to stress technology. He was very impressed by the Chief of the Air Staff's review of air policy and the potentiality of air power, and applied this to the manpower situation.

> We are not fighting this war for the sake of fighting, but for the sake of beating the Germans . . . our object is not merely to win . . . at all hazards by the sacrifice of the last man we have got, because if we win, we lose, we are barren.

It was a long way from 'the last man and last shilling'. Unfortunately, the discussion then became bogged down in a rambling debate—led by Lloyd George—on the relative importance of trained men compared with technology. The members of the War Cabinet had neither the knowledge nor education necessary to run a great war effectively. Hughes, however, was deeply worked up by his argument, for he repeated it almost verbatim to Bean, adding that the British had never conserved their men, and Haig would have gone on throwing them into battle indefinitely.

Hughes, in alliance with Churchill, continued to stress technology. For more than thirty pages in the minutes of a later meeting he posed highly technical questions which allowed Churchill to put his points. Hughes had obviously been primed, for his main motivation was not the technology itself, but concern for losses in the AIF. Talking with the men, he had heard—and taken to heart—their current jibe, that if the war continued in that way, the AIF would need only two ships to carry it home: one for the officers, the other for the identity discs. It had taken Hughes a long time to turn his mind from Australian politics and economics to the war, but now that he did so, his attitude was that of Churchill and Monash: every form of technology should be used—and they should wait for the Americans.[9]

Hughes' arguments were contradictory, however. He advocated the Easterner option—a strike against Austria—but also demanded a quick end to the war with the complete defeat of Germany, without losing too many lives; and he supported intervention against the Bolsheviks in Russia, though there were considerable advantages to Australia in encouraging Japanese expansion in northern Asia, instead of the Pacific.[10]

Hughes was being dragged into debates on the grand strategy of the war and being shown its complexity. Every possible solution presented difficulties. By 16 August Hughes and the other premiers were concerned by the effect that Lloyd George's idea of waiting for 1920 and the Americans would have on British and French public opinion. They need not have worried: Hughes seems to have noted the waning morale of the German army early, and, once this was confirmed by events in August, repeated his demand for the final defeat of Germany.[11]

Even this, however, led to mixed messages. For Hughes' deepest emotional concern was with the men of the AIF—and publicity for them, himself, and Australia. He had been enraptured by the Australian

Hughes with Australian troops, Belgium, 1919.   (National Library of Australia).

troops when he visited them in France, viewing them with the typical
authoritarian leader's emotional romanticism.[12] In August he was annoyed
by the attention paid to the Canadians, and sought information on
casualty statistics to use for publicity; but, apart from the wide discrepancies in the figures provided, he was told that it was not in the public
interest to make them known. He then volunteered some of the Light
Horse for the Western Front, but also demanded rest and leave for the
AIF. Despite these inconsistencies, he had moved—erratically—from
technology to a policy of 'conservation'.

   The inconsistencies continued. Hughes insisted that the AIF should
not be used in a major battle without his approval, and was therefore
deeply angry when he heard that the men had taken part in the battle
of Amiens. This quickly subsided, however, when their brilliant success
became apparent. Likewise, when he heard that the AIF was going back
into the line in November, he protested vigorously to the CIGS, Sir Henry
Wilson, on the ground that the men needed rest, but then, once the
armistice was announced, demanded that they be allowed to take part
in the occupation of Germany—though not permanently. This provoked

sarcasm from Wilson—'won't they be too tired?'—and a responsive explosion from Hughes. Meanwhile Rawlinson wrote of the need to put the Empire on a firm foundation, 'and crush self-advertising asses like Hughes'. This was hardly a just comment, nor was Rawlinson the man to make it. It is true that Hughes had used emotional support for the AIF as part of his public stance—Horne compares him with a trade union leader or a politician nursing a constituency—but his desire to protect his men from any further slaughter while giving them, and Australia, the honours they had won already by their hard fighting was quite legitimate. Hughes was equally critical of the generals, remarking that 'it would be to cover them with fulsome eulogy to say they were only one war behind the times.'[13]

His other aim was to gain maximum publicity for the Anzacs, and so help to raise Australia's standing in Britain, and perhaps influence any peace that was made. In this he was like the Canadians, whose policy has been described as 'directly related to the achievement of a new status for Canada in imperial relations'. Australia House was officially opened by the King on 3 August; and in September British editors and journalists were invited to inspect the area of France captured by the Australian army and talk with Australian soldiers. Hughes organised seven press parties, and wanted more Australian press representatives on the Western Front, with more facilities.[14]

In 1919 he insisted on a special march on Anzac Day ('The Day We Celebrate') when the Prince of Wales took the salute in front of Australia House. The War Office disliked Hughes' assumption that they would agree, but even worse occurred in the Dominions March on 3 May. Originally planned as a 'Colonial troops' parade, it was changed when the Canadians and Australians refused to march alongside coloured men. The Colonial Office thought this most deplorable, and likely to have a bad effect on India, but Australian racism was fuelled by determination to be treated as equals. Despite glib words by the British authorities, they did not so treat the coloured citizens of their Empire.[15]

## PROBLEMS WITH THE AIF

Criticism of this occurrence reinforced the long-standing suspicion of the Australians as larrikins and troublemakers. In the second Cabinet meeting after the armistice, when Austen Chamberlain reported that crowds had lit bonfires in Trafalgar Square with petrol, he could not resist adding that 'Australian soldiers had evidently taken a leading part in increasing the rowdiness of some of the crowds.' Long, never sympathetic to the Australians, remarked that it was important to get them out of London as soon as possible. There was a comment that there had been few excesses, but 'of these few, Australians were prominent participants', and

> the main difficulty was with the Australians, who apparently intended to make their behaviour in Cairo in 1915 a standard for future action. Steps are being taken to stop leave into London.[16]

English prejudices were showing. It was ignorance and ingratitude to recall the days of Cairo. The men of those days were mainly dead— or back in Australia wounded from fighting in England's 'Great War'. The survivors were not the same men they had been three years earlier— but the members of the Cabinet showed neither understanding nor sympathy.

Hughes had to combat those feelings, and at the same time deal with technical problems. The supply of shipping to repatriate the Australian troops led to several rows between him and the Shipping Controller; while the War Office suggestion of a committee to deal with post-war military forces led Hughes to suspect an attempt to create an imperial army, and together with Borden he got the Cabinet to veto the idea.[17]

Unfortunately, Hughes was so preoccupied with the soldiers that he did not consider another disadvantaged group, the Australian armaments workers in Britain. Approximately 6000 volunteers, they had received lower wages than they would have commanded in Australia, and often had to supplement them from their own savings. The War Office had tried to draft the men into the British army, and the Colonial Office had been obliged to issue them with exemption cards. At the war's end they were granted no medals, and British bureaucrats worried in case they gained preferential treatment that led British munitions workers to complain. The Treasury flatly refused to rebate British income tax; the idea of meeting the King fell through; and the War Office vetoed the suggestion that they could march behind the troops in the Dominions March. The most they gained was a free passage back to Australia for themselves and their families—if they applied within a month of the notice—together with five pounds towards the cost of resettlement. A polite thank you letter was eventually sent by the King to the governor-general. It was harsh and ungenerous treatment.[18]

## ECONOMIC PROBLEMS CONTINUE

Hughes' attention, however, outside the subjects discussed in the Imperial War Cabinet and the AIF, was preoccupied by economic matters. He vehemently repeated his old themes, getting the Imperial War Conference to reaffirm its 1917 resolution to make the Empire self-sufficient in food, raw materials and industries, and to establish imperial preference. Hughes supported Massey's moves against German settlers, compared with Borden's more moderate approach. He spoke at businessmen's meetings up and down the country, and claimed that the Treaty of Brest-Litovsk showed the German desire for the economic domination of the world. He demanded economic organisation and the alliance of capital and labour.

Hughes was trying to revive the crusade he had waged in 1916, and goad Lloyd George into a strong policy. But the latter did not appreciate instructions from Hughes, and they clashed over German access to raw materials. Hughes was supported by Long, who had lost sons in the war, but not by the mass following he had won in 1916. His forceful speeches alienated the free traders, but even among their opponents he was just one of many bitter voices at the time, and his pleas for Empire trade too obviously promoted Australia's own interests. Apart from *The Times* and the *Morning Post* the press was hostile, especially after a speech on 27 June in the London Chamber of Commerce. He was accused of being dictatorial, intellectually incapable of understanding the issues, and given to 'stupid vulgar abuse'. As the *Westminster Gazette* put it, the questions 'may seem very simple to an Australian who sees them from his own angle and vision', but they were in fact very complex, and Hughes' ideas, if put into effect, would check British progress, reduce foreign trade, and prevent the pacification of the world and the development of the League of Nations. The firm of Merton sued him for libel and cost the Australian government £6500; his publicity officer resigned; and Hughes appeared to have lost his touch.[19]

At the same time he was frantically trying to sell Australian produce, in very difficult circumstances. Lloyd George's war organisation had created 'an intricate network of controls and committees', and Hughes, refusing to delegate to others, plunged into the minutiae himself. He was accordingly sent from one branch of the bureaucracy to another—in his own words, 'like a clockwork mouse'—until he arrived eventually back at his starting point. British planners were no longer preoccupied by the threat of German domination of trade, but by the problems of Britain's financial and economic recovery: raw materials, shipping and finance. Once again, Australian and British interests clashed. Britain required supplies from the nearest country; Australia needed to sell her produce. Hughes wrote to Bonar Law that Australia had been generous, but now Treasury threatened to buy no produce at all, which would totally destabilise the country. The wartime demand for wool had ended, and growers in Australia were nervous about the prospects, while the wheat remained unsold.

The difficulty was the chronic lack of shipping. The British had offered to renew the contracts, but on condition that Australia hand over forty-seven coastal vessels. Hughes did his best, and thought he had won a wheat agreement, but the clause about Australian shipping remained. After he had appealed unsuccessfully to Bonar Law, the War Cabinet set up a committee under a reluctant Austen Chamberlain, who remarked that 'Hughes is such a difficult man to do business with.' The committee supported buying Australian copper and lead, 'not from an economic standpoint' but 'from higher political grounds', but discussions on wheat continued till 1919. Peace reduced the demands for shipping, while Hughes took his battle with the Shipping Controller to Lloyd George and also demanded German ships.[20] The basis of the trouble was not Hughes' personality and methods, which admittedly did not help, but simply the clash of interests of the two parties.

## IMPERIAL COMMUNICATION

British representatives used idealistic language, but were always tempted, when they suspected potential trouble, to avoid providing Dominion governments with information. 'Consultation' was therefore honoured more in the breach than the observance.

Hughes in August 1917 had sent a series of specific questions to Lloyd George, arguing that Australia's fate was as much involved in the war as that of Britain.[21] Canada felt so strongly about consultation that in the same year she had asked if she could be represented at the Supreme War Council in Paris. This had led to an anguished British Cabinet meeting, where it was thought undesirable to invite Dominion representatives, unless they came as 'British'. Yet, if the Dominions were *not* represented, consultation became all the more important. Debate then turned on to telegraphic communications and the date for the next Imperial War Cabinet meetings.[22]

This was a foretaste of 1918. In the Imperial War Conference Borden, perhaps hoping for an ally, began by regretting that Australia had not attended in 1917.[23] Thereafter, the first substantive matter to arise was the supply of information from and the channels of communication with Britain. Formally, as we have seen, they went via the governor-general to the Colonial Office, before being passed on to relevant British departments or ministers. It was a convoluted process which was liable to lead to delays. Sometimes this was due to simple bureaucratic complexity, as when it took six weeks in 1918 to get information from the War Office to the Australian government, via the Colonial Office and the governor-general, on the minimum number of men to maintain the AIF. On other occasions, however, there was obstruction at some point, as when Hughes' request in 1917 for the organisation of Australian divisions to be put to 'my colleagues in the Imperial War Cabinet' had been held back by Long. Amery thought that had been deliberate.[24]

It is not surprising, therefore, that the process of communicating directly with essential departments had begun earlier under the impetus of wartime exigencies. As early as August 1914 Pearce, Australian Minister for Defence, had claimed this right with the Army Council on AIF matters.[25] Moreover, the relationship between Hughes and Munro Ferguson had become strained in 1917. Provoked by Hughes' carelessness with secret documents, the governor-general had ordered the head of the Australian Counter Espionage Bureau to raid Hughes' home and 'retrieve certain papers'. It seems a fair comment that 'This episode must rank as the most arrogant illustration of Munro Ferguson's functioning as the British government's principal representative in Australia.' He even seemed a little ashamed of it himself. This did not stop him complaining that Hughes acted independently of him, and failed to inform him of decisions or actions taken, such as leaving for Britain in 1918 without informing him who was to be the acting prime minister. Long sympathised, citing Hughes' telegraphing Lloyd George direct through Murdoch.[26]

Hughes' ally in this matter was Amery, who sent a long letter to Lloyd George on 9 July giving the history of the Imperial Cabinet system, and arguing that it should be developed and there should be greater continuity of consultation after the Dominion prime ministers departed. Hughes agreed with Amery on the need to discuss the foreign policy of the Empire with the Dominions and bypass the Colonial Office[27]—the natural ally of the governors-general in this matter. But Hughes himself had not helped the flow of information by his refusal to appoint Fisher his representative in 1917.

Long tried to head off the demand for direct consultation, suggesting that instead they should appoint a Secretary of State for Imperial Affairs[28]— with himself doubtless as the first incumbent. Such a move would also have maintained the key roles of the governors-general and a British minister in the relationship between the Dominions and London. Not surprisingly, when the matter came up for discussion in the Imperial War Cabinet Hughes rejected it outright. He did not want another department, but a

> recognition of the fact that the Dominions were participants in the Councils of the Empire on a footing of equality. They were Governments, each sovereign or quasi-sovereign in its own sphere, consulting with each other about their common affairs.

He added that 'if the United Kingdom no longer professed to control dominion governments, there was no need for governors-general to represent the United Kingdom government as well as the sovereign'. They should therefore be appointed by Dominion prime ministers.

The debate raged over three meetings, but started to turn sour for Hughes. Borden supported him strongly, but was perhaps a little too flexible, suggesting permanent representatives of the Dominions in London, meeting British ministers, an idea strongly held by Massey of New Zealand. The latter admitted the practical difficulties privately to Hankey; but Hughes' attitude had been quite openly revealed in 1917. Lloyd George tried to be diplomatic: he accepted direct communication, and for the rest suggested that an informal committee of constitutional and legal experts be appointed to consider further cooperation. Hughes exploded! He said that 75 per cent of the Australian soldiers in France were opposed to having anything to do with the Empire in the future. If this were true, it was a most interesting comment on Anglo-Australian relations as a result of the war, but anger and fear of imperial federation seem to have been Hughes' main emotions.

Opinions on federation were deeply divided. There had been a renewed push for it by Lionel Curtis, who had brought out *The Commonwealth of Nations* in 1916, and Massey supported it. But in Australia even G. A. Wood had noted the deep labour hostility to the idea, and stressed the needs of Australian independence within a free Empire. What was needed was consultation. On this occasion, Borden pointed out Hughes' inconsistencies and Smuts soothed him down, but the embarrassment of the meeting comes through even the dry and censored minutes.

From reading them it seems that past commentators—even Fitzhardinge and Spartalis—have not fully understood the situation. The key to the scene is undoubtedly Hughes' deafness. What strikes the present author, having lived with an intelligent but deeply deaf person in the family for some years, is the tendency to anger (derived largely from frustration with the ailment), aggression, touchiness about personal standing, and liability to mis-hear statements and accordingly vehemently launch forth into an argument that misses the point under discussion. Thus in Britain in 1918 Lloyd George protested he did not mean 'federation', and Hughes—after a series of ranting non-sequiturs—asked Lloyd George to *restate his idea*. This is a complete give-away to someone who has lived with the deaf. He had not heard Lloyd George's original statement clearly! Lloyd George obliged, moderately, but deaf people in this situation cannot then admit to having misunderstood, for they feel stupid. So Hughes continued his objections—but in a falling key. The meeting was adjourned, but it— and other lesser incidents like it—had a serious impact on Hughes' standing in Britain and Anglo-Australian relations.

In the next meeting it was finally agreed that the Dominions had the right to communicate directly with the British prime minister on subjects of Cabinet importance, normally though the Colonial Office but directly in exceptional circumstances. The prime ministers could appoint a representative between the sessions of the Imperial War Cabinet. Hughes' explosion had, however, roused the fears of Dominion leaders for their independence: now even mild Massey talked of imperial federation, the Boston Tea Party and the revolt of the American colonies.[29] It was a pity, for while the war continued, the Dominion leaders had some chance of changing British attitudes: they had much less later.

Back in Australia, the governor-general was deeply hostile to the change. Munro Ferguson had suffered diminution of his power during the war. His attempts to extend his supervisory role over the Australian government through the Executive Council had been blocked; his admonitions to Hughes to adopt a more orderly and less ruthless administrative style were ignored; and the occasions on which he was overlooked increased. In short, his bid to make the governor-generalship the equivalent of the English constitutional monarchy—with added powers of initiative—was failing.[30]

He therefore bitterly opposed the changes that Hughes was supporting, and contacted the governors-general of New Zealand, South Africa and Canada. In doing so, he was indulging in direct inter-Dominion communication—which was more than the Dominion governments themselves ever did. He defended his formal constitutional position in a somewhat neurotic letter to Long. If direct communication were allowed, instead of Hughes being advisor to the governor-general, he would be advisor to the British prime minister. More practically, and with knowledge of Hughes to prompt him, he pointed out that the governor-general would be left in ignorance of government policies and actions. Another lengthy letter in October discussed the threat to the power, prestige and status of the governor-general, the only representative of the British government in Australia. He felt let down by the various Colonial Secretaries.

In this he was unfair to Long, who, after appearing amenable, quickly moved into full-scale opposition to the proposals, threatening resignation at one stage, and describing Munro Ferguson as 'probably one of the best Governors General who has ever represented the King'. He bombarded Lloyd George with letters and memoranda. But Munro Ferguson was humiliated by the appointment of the Australian Trade Commissioner in the United States without his knowledge, and horrified by Murdoch's criticism in the Melbourne *Herald* on 7 September of the 'crusted devastating bureaucratic inefficiency and ineptitude of the Colonial Office' and the 'general hatred' with which it was regarded—though that would hardly have been surprising, considering the arrogance with which the Colonial Office sometimes regarded the Dominions. Munro Ferguson almost resigned, but Long regarded such a move as 'a great disaster' and Hughes said he 'attached immense importance' to his staying in office. So he agreed to extend his term till December 1920, to cover the visit to Australia of the Prince of Wales.[31]

It was natural for Munro Ferguson to resist the change, and argue that by turning him into a figurehead it would diminish his office both as an internal umpire in Australia and a symbol of imperial unity. He was right. It meant a change in imperial relationships, but it was the almost inevitable outcome of Australian nationalism and British involvement in Europe.


## CONSULTATION

Communication, however, was only the means to an end. What Dominion leaders wanted was consultation on matters that affected them. The British accepted this—in theory. On 2 August 1918 the Foreign Secretary ostentatiously asked permission of the Imperial War Cabinet to continue treaty negotiations with Brazil, making unctuous comment about 'the definite recognition of the right of the Dominions to have a voice in the settlement of such questions'.[32] A cynic might note, however, that it was a very minor matter. Where life-and-death issues concerned Britain, there was a tendency to act first and consult the Dominions later. This rapidly became apparent in the months ahead, when the wolf of British policy peeped out from under the sheepskin of 'imperial consultation'.

Two things precipitated events: the Fourteen Points put forward by President Wilson of the United States; and the totally unexpected collapse of the German armies from August onwards. This last was most inconsiderate, for the Imperial War Cabinet of 1918 had officially ended, most Dominion leaders departed, and only Australia had its representatives, Hughes and Cook, in Britain at the time. Unlike 1917, Hughes was on the spot at the vital time, when peace terms could be decided.[33] It did him no good at all.

Despite the clear British promise to consult Australia on peace terms,[34] Lloyd George deliberately avoided bringing Hughes into the discussion. The reason for this can only have been that Hughes' aggressive manner had by then thoroughly turned Lloyd George against him. The outburst on 25 July over channels of communication, and the way the other Dominion leaders were influenced by him, meant that Lloyd George was bound to be nervous about involving Hughes in the initial discussions. He would be liable to disrupt the meetings and demand his own way. And his aims were well known: the economic destruction of Germany; a hard peace; and the acquisition of German colonies. None was supported by Wilson's Fourteen Points.

On 17 October, when German collapse seemed imminent, it was decided to hold a special Cabinet meeting to consider the armistice and the peace. Despite Hankey's warning him that Hughes, Long and Montagu (the Secretary of State for India) would expect to be present, Lloyd George, who did not trust Montagu either, did not inform them, and decided to hold, not a Cabinet, but an 'informal conference of Ministers'. Later in the British War Cabinet Lord Curzon joined Long in strongly supporting Hughes' right to attend all meetings and to discuss the armistice—in view of Australia's sacrifices, which were 'a good deal more than the Americans'. Hankey, backed by Bonar Law, urged Lloyd George to include the three men at all meetings, and the War Cabinet agreed that Hughes should attend its next session.

Lloyd George ignored them all. His attitude was disgraceful, for it amounted to the deliberate and continued exclusion of Australia's prime minister from a whole series of meetings, despite many previous promises. Hughes was in the country, and had given notice of his movements if they needed to contact him, so there was no excuse. Nor were Smuts and Hughes—the only Dominion leaders available the time—invited to the crucial meetings of the Versailles Council between 29 October and 4 November, though even more minor powers like Greece and Portugal *were* present.

But Lloyd George's policy was also highly unwise. An explosion was inevitable once the truth came out.[35] Hughes discovered what had been going on when the terms accepted at Paris were announced in the Imperial War Cabinet on 5 November. He vehemently protested, and on this matter was backed to the hilt by his government. Watt cabled his 'surprise and indignation' that the decision had been made—despite previous assurances—without consultation. He regarded it as a 'painful and serious breach of faith'. Hughes passed this message on to Lloyd George, and on 6 November spoke with great effect and bitterness. As far as he could see, the peace terms were settled: 'The British Government had declared war without consulting the Dominions, and now they are settling Peace Terms equally without them.' He went on to wonder what the functions of the Imperial War Cabinet were supposed to be: it was not executive, and they could hardly call it consultative. Lloyd George tried to bluff his way out by using clever rhetoric and special pleading.

He claimed that decisions on peace terms in general had been discussed in the 1917 meetings of the Imperial War Cabinet, to which he had begged Hughes to send a representative. Now, only the armistice had been decided, 'nothing had been done to prejudice Australia's claims', and 'The Dominions have by their heroic efforts won a place in the Great Council', etc. It cut no ice. Hughes' comment was unanswerable: 'We who have fought for four years as equals are treated like lackeys.' He regarded the British statement as a 'palpable evasion of [the] position'.[36]

He therefore made his complaint public, with an address at the Australia Club, a protest printed in *The Times*, and a letter and a speech at the British Empire Club. The official reply, also published in *The Times*, followed Lloyd George's arguments in the Imperial War Cabinet and appeared lame. Even Hughes' Australian critics supported him on this issue, while the British imperialists rallied behind him. John Latham, the young Australian lawyer and lieutenant-commander in the naval reserve who was officially assisting Cook, wrote to Philip Kerr that the basis of their cooperation depended on 'common loyalty and good faith' and events had cast doubt on their existence, or the ability of the British leaders to realise the significance of their actions. He cited past promises, and pointed out that the military situation was totally different from that of 1917, so reference to discussion then was simply irrelevant. It was a very strong letter for Latham. Amery thought Hughes right, and admitted in his diary that it was 'mainly because he is so irritating to most of them personally both on account of his deafness and aggressive manners'. He phoned Hughes, whose first response was that the time for talking was over, practically suggesting that the Empire had broken up. When he did meet Amery, he was in a 'very aggressive mood'. Amery blamed Lloyd George, and pointed out to him that if the Dominions were consulted, they would be more inclined to accept a single imperial foreign policy. He urged him to write personally to Hughes that Australia's rights would be protected, and in several memoranda argued that the Dominions should be represented at the peace conference, and that no subject, however minor, that was of concern to them should be decided without consultation. Sir Robert Garran, the Australian Solicitor-General who also attended the Imperial War Cabinet, thought the British exclusion of Hughes an 'extraordinary blunder'—an 'altogether inexcusable and damnable decision'. Lloyd George's eventual letter to Hughes, however, though it regretted the 'misunderstanding', still stressed that this was only an armistice which did not decide issues finally, and did not really amount to an apology for the lack of consultation.[37]

Behind Hughes' bitterness and aggression lay a deep distrust of British policy towards Japan. He had received numerous hints of Japanese expansion during the war, and did not trust the British to support Australian interests. Wilson's Fourteen Points, which talked of freedom and equality, roused all his fears, and he suspected betrayal. He attacked the British government for weakness towards America, and being 'dragged behind the wheels of President Wilson's chariot'.[38] By accepting the

Fourteen Points as the basis for the armistice, the allies had committed themselves to the terms of the peace.

Technically Hughes was wrong, but tactically he had a point. Wilson's ideas set the agenda for the discussion at Versailles, though in the event the allies could hardly be said to have followed their spirit. Moreover, the Imperial War Cabinet had never discussed Wilson's Fourteen Points. Hankey admired Hughes' stand, remarking that his critique on 30 December was 'a fine specimen of ruthless and pungent analysis of President Wilson's claim to dictate to the countries who had borne the brunt of the fighting', but most British spokesmen seemed to feel that Hughes was being a bore, and turned to other matters.

## REPRESENTATION IN PARIS

Hughes' answer was to visit Paris and enlist the willing support of the French against Wilson.[39] He also demanded the right to be present at the forthcoming conference in Paris. In this he did *not* have the backing of the Australian Cabinet, which echoed Amery's fear of the break-up of the Empire and thought his public protests amounted 'to hanging the British family linen on the line for the information and amusement of other nations, including enemies'. The Dominion position would be misunderstood or exaggerated, and the ties of Empire injured, if not broken. If Hughes had—temporarily—given up on the Empire, the Australian Cabinet had not. Nor did it support his claim for representation at Paris, but Hughes ignored it.[40]

Lloyd George at first thought that one Dominion representative should sit as the last person on the five-man British Empire Delegation (BED), and suggested that Borden would be most suitable. Again, Hankey warned him 'that he could not have Borden without Hughes, as Australia had made the same sacrifices as Canada. But the warning seemed to fall on deaf ears'.[41] Hughes declared roundly that no one Dominion leader could represent the others. Lloyd George's next idea was for a 'Dominions panel' to fill the last post, with the representative chosen from the Dominion most concerned with the matter in hand. It was not only that he objected to Hughes, it was also that, as he admitted, he thought that 'it was impossible to treat the Dominions as separate from the British Empire'. Amery was right: Lloyd George had still not got the message.

Hughes was supported by Smuts and Borden, both of whom had been present in London in 1917. Borden cabled Lloyd George on the need to give 'serious consideration as to representation of Dominions in Peace Negotiations', and Lloyd George replied that he valued his advice and earnestly hoped he could sail for England at once. It was a very different tone to that adopted towards Hughes, who, according to Smuts, got on Lloyd George's nerves. Nevertheless, Borden agreed with Lloyd George that the desire of Ward and Massey of New Zealand to attend the conference was 'absurd', and was willing to accept the position

Lloyd George planned for him, or even the idea of a panel of Dominion delegates.

Hughes flatly refused to accept either, and since he would neither be silenced nor compromise, in the end the Dominions got the best of both worlds, being represented in the BED, *and* having two delegates of their own at the peace conference—though they were allowed to vote only as part of the BED. Nevertheless, they were admitted as separate entities, comparable to such powers as Belgium and Portugal, were individual signatories to the treaty, and therefore became original members of the League of Nations. It was a great advance on Hughes' attendance at the Paris Economic Conference in 1916—where he had been merely a British delegate and as a result Australia had gained no increase in status.[42]

## THE PEACE OF PARIS

Three main issues dominated Hughes' attention in the Versailles peace conference: reparations; mandates, including the Japanese control of the Pacific islands; and the racial equality clause. Hughes demanded reparations to meet the total cost of the war to every allied nation, ignoring critics like Lloyd George who argued that this would either bankrupt the country that paid, or destroy the economies of those that received. Hughes then went on to the Cabinet 'Reparations Committee'. It has been suggested that in nominating Hughes as chairman of the committee Lloyd George was trying to silence his business critics. But a reading of the minutes reveals a marked reluctance by all members of the Cabinet to serve on the committee, and Hughes' prominent part made him an obvious person. His protest that he would rather stay outside and criticise only clinched the matter!

Hughes' biographer argues that, in this committee, Hughes appeared at his worst: dogmatic, hectoring and illogical. In a short time it brought down a report that demanded £24,000 million in reparations, and horrified many in the Cabinet. Bonar Law and Lloyd George thought it 'a wild and fantastic chimera'; Lord Milner warned against 'Bolshevising' Germany; Churchill worried about its impact on the British working classes, and Smuts about its encouragement of the French. Cabinet finally decided that the Allied Indemnity Commission should try to get from Germany the greatest possible indemnity 'consistent with the economic well-being of the British Empire and the peace of the world'. Hughes remained unconvinced, and delivered a scathing attack on Lloyd George's conversations with President Wilson.

He then went on to Paris and a full-scale row with the British. Inevitably, the Americans insisted on blocking any attempt to extract the full 'war costs', while Lloyd George rejected as too high the claim put forward in the memorandum of Hughes' committee, snubbed Hughes when he asked permission to give an interview to the London *Daily Telegraph*, and wrestled with the tricky problem himself. After a private conference he finally came to an agreement with the Americans and the French. Reparations were allocated on a priority basis of actual damage, but included war pensions and separation allowances. He was congratulated on all sides for this masterly display, except by Hughes, who was firmly in a minority of one and who resisted all attempts to win him over. The matter closed with a casuistical letter from Hughes, and a bitter response from Lloyd George. Anglo-Australian relations had seriously deteriorated.

Fitzhardinge and Booker think that the original sum suited Lloyd George's electoral stance in Britain, and gave Hughes a bargaining counter for his claim to the Pacific islands. But there is no evidence in the files of these motives. Hughes' arguments were simplistic; while Lloyd George seems genuinely worried by his demands, concerned by their economic consequences and disgusted by his intransigence. On this issue Hughes was isolated, though Lord Riddell pointed out to Lloyd George the vital help Australia had given Britain during the war.[43] The point was not appreciated.

## THE FATE OF THE PACIFIC ISLANDS

Surprising as it may seem, another matter now came to a head that made Anglo-Australian relations even worse. As has been recounted in Chapter 5, the Japanese had claimed the North Pacific islands and British leaders, needing Japan's assistance in the war, had accepted that claim and were unsympathetic to Australia. Early in 1917 the British had asked Australia to 'acquiesce' in 'some pledge on the subject', and Hughes had eventually cabled that Australia would not do or say anything that would make relations between Britain and Japan difficult. When Long persisted in asking for agreement to 'some such pledge', Hughes finally cabled back using the same words. As Spartalis notes, 'This surely was grudging acquiescence, more or less under duress; none the less it was given.'[44]

Fitzhardinge argues that these 'piecemeal revelations, and sequence of assurances, breaches and new assurances, inevitably undermined Australian confidence both in Japan's motives and in Britain's credibility'. Australian Intelligence officers thought Japan had given minimal help and used the war to further its own expansionist aims. Nevertheless, Hughes was also partly to blame. He had neither attended the 1917 conference himself nor appointed a representative. Had he done so, he or his agent would have seen the matter calmly analysed in the Curzon committee which dealt with the German colonies, and Australia's and New Zealand's interests considered. An Australian delegate could have helped Massey clarify some points, but instead he was on his own.[45]

Hughes meanwhile wound himself up with fear of Japan, and adopted his usual pose, as a 'constituency brawler' for his own side.[46] He had travelled to Britain in 1918 via America, where, according to Munro Ferguson, he had sought support from President Wilson, without success. While in New York he had suggested a Monroe Doctrine in the Pacific. This was designed to appeal to the Americans, and he repeated the suggestion in London, together with the idea of a federation of Pacific islands—including the French—with its headquarters in Sydney.[47]

Fear of Japan was the basis of Hughes' criticism of British failure to consult, but his attitude was one reason why the British *avoided* consultation. They knew there would be trouble. Scribbled on an agenda in the Lloyd George papers are the words, 'Mr. H may contest the right of Japan to islands in the Pacific . . . but we are irrevocably committed by the pact of 1917 and discussion should not be permitted.'[48]

Debate in the Imperial War Cabinet was confused, for several issues were mixed together: first, whether the islands should be handed back to Germany; second, who should get them; and third, under what terms. The first issue reflected differences of opinion between Britain and Australia over the treatment of Germans in New Guinea and was soon settled, for it was agreed unthinkable that the islands be returned. Debate on it revealed, however, that Hughes denied consultation about the agreement with the Japanese. It was a bad omen.[49]

On the second issue Hughes claimed that the surrender of German New Guinea to Australia at Rabaul in 1914 meant the surrender of German islands in the North Pacific too. This was technically correct, but he went on from there to demand that all German Pacific islands be ceded to Britain for administration by Australia. He glossed over the information Britain had sent Australia on the issue during the war, claimed to have acted under duress, and wrote to Lloyd George putting his case in detail.[50]

There was, however, no way that the British Cabinet could blatantly break their promises to Japan and also accept responsibility for the North Pacific islands, even if they had not involved the danger of a further, unwinnable, war in the Pacific with the Japanese. Lloyd George pointed to the various wartime communications with Australia, and agreements with Japan, including Hughes' acquiescence in the Anglo-Japanese Agreement of 1917.[51] Hughes received no support. Even Amery dismissed the Australian case, while Lord Robert Cecil in a memorandum insisted that Australia had been consulted, Long suggested seeking Pacific island opinion, and Borden suggested giving them all to America. Even the Australian Cabinet, whose ideas on both the Pacific colonies and the White Australia policy Hughes followed, was nevertheless concerned to maintain friendship with America and the 'relationship with Motherland'.[52]

The third issue—mixed in the confused discussions with the other two—was whether Australia was to gain the South Pacific islands, and whether under her direct rule or through a mandate. Hughes declared that if anybody wanted to shift Australia from the islands they would have to come and do it, and 'What we have we hold.' In this of course he was 'operating on a very simple spoils-of-war assumption' then unquestioned in Australia but increasingly challenged overseas. Reaction against the horror of World War I had led to a groundswell of opinion against what were regarded as its causes, hence the demand for the internationalisation of colonies.[53] It was this that President Wilson's call for self-determination tapped. But Hughes was by now completely out of touch with idealistic opinion everywhere.

The debate raged in Paris in January. Although Lloyd George brought the Dominions' case before the Council of Ten, a row broke out in the BED. Hughes was intransigent, and cited support for his position in the Australian parliament and Cabinet. After much debate, the compromise of C-class mandates was put forward—probably by a combination of Latham, Hankey (stimulated by Hughes), and Smuts, though other names have also been mentioned, such as Clement Jones, the Secretary of the BED, and Borden's legal advisor, Loring Christie. Whatever the origin, Lloyd George tried to persuade Hughes to accept it, in the end losing his temper and telling Hughes bluntly that he 'would not quarrel with the United States for the Solomon islands'. Hughes then threatened to appeal to *British* public opinion, and Hughes and Lloyd George descended to abusing each other in Welsh.

This was the most serious disagreement between Britain and Australia during the peace conference. Even after Hughes finally accepted the compromise—with bad grace—it left Lloyd George fuming that he would not be bullied by 'a damned little Welshman'.[54] Hughes had articles placed in *Le Matin*, as well as *The Times* and Paris *Daily Mail* (both Northcliffe papers). The latter reported an interview which suggested that the British delegation had been kow-towing to Wilson, the colonies resented it, and there was a danger that the British Empire would split up. Although Botha and Ward were also mentioned, Hughes was clearly 'at the bottom of the whole thing', as Lord Riddell noted. President Wilson protested and threatened to return to America; Lloyd George was furious. Amery tried to placate him, but he had 'worked himself into quite a fine temper . . . striding about and saying that Hughes was quite impossible . . . a regular little cad, etc.'. Amery had enough tact not to 'venture to suggest that one of the difficulties . . . was a certain similarity of temperament between both little Welshmen'. He called on Lloyd George's wife to soothe the ruffled feathers, and wrote to Hughes suggesting a personal meeting between the two men. Hardly had that blown over, when, to the distress of Hankey, Hughes appealed directly to the president of the conference—without informing the British—to give the mandate to Australia. Garran was deputed to speak to Hughes, who guaranteed that he would in future go via Hankey.[55]

Liberals like Edwin Montagu thought Hughes' selfish motives had jeopardised the peace of the world; but it was Hughes' personality which jarred as much as his policies. In fact, Wilson distrusted the Japanese almost as much as Hughes did, but this was hidden by the poor procedures of the conference and Hughes' abrasive ways. His deafness made matters worse: the celebrated occasion when he blithely assured Wilson that Australia would ignore the opinion of the whole civilised world is another instance of his affliction at work. Hughes had simply not heard the question. But there can be also little doubt that Hughes was deeply disliked by most of the British, and some Australians, for his aggressive ways and bullying manner. It is hardly surprising that Balfour on one occasion, when Hughes rose to speak, muttered '*Que je le déteste*'— how I detest him.[56]

## THE TREATY SIGNED

The bickering over the racial equality clause merely resulted from and perpetuated Hughes' disgruntled frame of mind in this phase of the conference. His obstinate refusal to accept the clause suggested by Japan, however watered down and moderate it became, dragged Smuts and the British into the issue. Massey, who equally feared Asian immigration, was prepared to negotiate, and did not publicly side with Hughes on the issue. In the end, tired of arguing, Lloyd George instructed Cecil that if Australia still refused to accept it, the BED must oppose it too. The clause failed.[57]

Hughes had also opposed the establishment of the League of Nations from the beginning, as the outcome of Wilson's Fourteen Points, which he despised, arguing that no nation would accept orders from an international body in matters that it regarded as its vital interests, such as the White Australia policy. He suggested instead 'an agreement between the United States and Great Britain which would ensure the peace of the world'. He continued taking side-swipes at the league in the midst of discussing other issues, and it was clear that he was deeply opposed to the concept. He could tolerate it if it was a pious aspiration and no more, but if it was to control the British Empire in matters of government and defence, he was absolutely opposed. On the other hand, there were divided opinions in the British government, as a rambling debate in the War Cabinet on the causes of war revealed.[58] It was ironic that in July 1919 the general secretary of the League of Nations Union in London invited Hughes to become an honorary vice-president[59]—oblivious of the fact that this was akin to inviting a wolf to become vice-president of a Vegetarian Society.

Despite all these squabbles, in the end the peace treaty was signed. After a memorandum by Borden, and some debate, it was agreed that the Dominions should become separate signatories. The British government then suggested that it could be ratified by the King on the advice of the British government—parliamentary approval could come later. Several of the Dominions had promised their parliaments the right to discuss the treaty first, and the Dominions, as separate entities, claimed the right to agree. The British government had still not woken to the implications of the new Dominion status. However, after a protest by Borden the idea was dropped. As for Australia, Watt had promised federal parliament that the treaty would not be ratified until it had considered the terms, though constitutionally the monarchy 'ratified' a treaty, while parliament merely 'approved' it. In the end, Hughes signed subject to the reservation that the Australian parliament had to approve the treaty. But the independent adherence of the Dominions to the treaty was the important point.[60]

## PARIS AND HUGHES SUMMED UP

It is not surprising that so many Australian authors have concentrated on Hughes in London and Paris 1918-19, for no other Australian leader till then had been so aggressively independent, and had dominated much of the argument at a major peace meeting. Anglo-Australian relations would never be the same again. Ignoring his Cabinet, he had fought for separate representation at Versailles and as a result he—and Australia— moved to centre stage for a brief while. Though many others shared his beliefs (such as Massey of New Zealand, which was keen to keep Samoa and Nauru[61]) and he did not by himself decide the terms of peace, at least by his stand—and stance—he had made British leaders consider Australia. Even Lloyd George told Wilson at the signing of the peace treaty that the Dominions were entitled to adequate press representation as a result of their contributions during the war. And by winning separate representation Hughes could pose as the leader both of an independent small nation in the League of Nations *and* part of the British Empire, with all its resources to support him, as need dictated. Australia itself could adopt a similar dual stance in the years ahead.[62]

Nevertheless, there is no question that Hughes had his weaknesses. Compared with the other Dominion leaders, he had come late to the debate, and due to his defective hearing and aggressive character tended to turn discussion on the great issues of state into personal battles. He thus become a figure of amusement for some, and aroused dislike and even deep hostility in others. It could be argued that by his abrasive and aggressive policies he threw away the goodwill won by Australian loyalty in the war and the fighting qualities of the AIF. Instead, British opinion was focused on the brashness of Australians and their failure to respond to international idealism. As Malcolm MacDonald was to write later,

> Greatly and genuinely as I like the Australian people, I am bound to say that the way to persuade an average Australian of the virtue of any principle is to show him what advantage he is going to get from its operation. It does not impress him much when he is told that someone else is going to gain from it.[63]

British leaders preferred quieter Australians, such as Latham and Garran, who worked well with the team in Hankey's imperial secretariat. Hankey and Amery were genuinely imperial-minded, and that Anglo-Australian relations remained as close as they did was perhaps attributable to them.[64] It was not attributable to Long, who was unsympathetic to the Australians on most occasions, except when they were demanding that harsh terms be imposed on Germany. He did not really look after their interests, or help to moderate Hughes' excesses.

It has also been argued that Hughes was useful to both Clemenceau of France and Lloyd George in toning down President Wilson's 'doctrinaire proposals', but Lloyd George was capable of modifying Wilson's ideas on his own, without the distraction of Hughes' intransigence. For example in a War Cabinet meeting he agreed with Hughes that the sacrifices of Britain and the Dominions entitled their views to be heard, but argued that the best tactics were to assume agreement, and to fight Wilson openly only if every effort had been exhausted. In other words, they should not begin with a fight, which was Hughes' natural inclination. However, there was much dissatisfaction in the BED that it was turning into a 'one-man band', and that Lloyd George was making all the decisions, so perhaps Hughes provided a much-needed counter-weight. He himself at a dinner party afterwards with Amery was 'thoroughly pleased with himself' and the outcome.[65] It is not surprising: he had demanded a hard peace, and had gained one.

What is more pertinent to this book is his attitude to the Empire. This was mixed. He felt that Australia needed the British Empire for trade outlets, money for development, and protection, but was determined to maintain absolute freedom of action. It was a stance of which many of his Australian critics would have approved.[66] He repeatedly argued that

> The British Empire is not Great Britain, nor any of its parts. ... Each Dominion is self-governing, as France is. And therefore each Dominion has its individual character, its special interests, its peculiar problems. I mention one—the future of the Pacific, which is vital to Australia.[67]

That Britain was not the Empire was a point that would not have been accepted by a wide section of British opinion, nor indeed the British government, which in 1920 accepted that for League of Nations purposes the 'British Empire' was the United Kingdom government. Despite a Canadian protest, it continued to do so.[68]

Stress on the Pacific highlighted the fact that British and Australian interests did not always coincide. Hughes therefore flatly rejected the argument of his Australian critics who said he should not have protested, and that Australia's interests were safe in British hands.[69] Instead, Hughes' vision was of an Empire which gave protection to its component parts, but allowed them maximum independence. If this occurred, there would be no clash between Australian nationalism and membership of the Empire. But Hughes, like his predecessor Deakin, realised the British tendency to regard the Pacific as a matter of distant—and therefore minor—importance. It was therefore absolutely necessary for Australia to consider its own interests, and nudge—or bully—Britain into supporting them. This would be difficult, as the British reluctance to stand up to Japan revealed. No wonder that on a shopping expedition for a signet ring his fancy was much taken up with one depicting Hercules grappling with the lion![70]

It has been argued that there were disadvantages to Hughes' double representation at Versailles. If the Dominions had simply been represented as small powers, they could have claimed that their separate existence as states had been acknowledged, but when they claimed also to be part of the British Empire, although they gained prestige as members of that Empire, their international status became ambiguous.[71] Yet this was exactly what Hughes wanted: dual status as autonomous units with independent interests in foreign policy; but still within the British Empire, so gaining economic strength and military security from it.

## HUGHES' EFFECTIVENESS

Seeing those were his aims, it has to be asked whether Hughes had strengthened and deepened the ties between Australia and Britain, or left Australia in a stronger position in 1920 than it had been in 1918, apart from the ending of the war. He had been faced by a difficult situation. Britain in 1918 was under a reasonably effective government. Although Hughes was useful to Lloyd George in his campaign to regain control of the generals, there was not the same opening for a rousing prophet from the antipodes, and his public stance gained less support.[72]

He was weakened by his ill-health (some commentators said he looked old, though in fact he was only fifty-four) his deafness—which seems from the surviving accounts to have been growing worse—and his narrow range of interests. Once he was no longer the centre of attention, he seems to have lost grip. A few issues roused him: but apart from them he was quiet for long periods during the discussions, and joined the debate only when one of his pet subjects was raised. He seemed casual about attending meetings, even missing the farewell address to the King by the Imperial War Cabinet in 1918, 'having apparently forgotten about it'. His aggression, when other Dominion representatives tried to be constructive, was notable. Stamfordham wrote, 'His presence here does not make for peace, either as regards the War or as far as Home Politics are concerned.'[73] His self-centredness, and his use of the tactless and pushy Murdoch, were irritating. For example, in organising Hughes' travel plans Murdoch managed to upset the Colonial Office, the Admiralty and even the prime minister's department, as he admitted, while Birdwood remarked that Murdoch was

> one of those curious people who think that the interests of Australia can be safeguarded only by blatant aggressiveness ... I find that by quietly and temperately representing ... our interests, we have been able to get practically everything we wanted ...[74]

Booker accuses Latham and Eggleston of being convinced of the 'superior wisdom' of British diplomats and civil servants, because their obvious disapproval of Hughes only encouraged British criticism.[75] But Eggleston was hardly blindly pro-British at this time, and one can support one's side without agreeing with the tactics used to do so.

It only remains to assess the position Anglo-Australian relations had reached by 1919, and the future implications of all the expenditure of blood and effort.

# Conclusions: The Post-war Years

'That's what I mean ... Myth. Sometimes, for *some* people, myth ... becomes
its own reality.'
'Like disinformation?'

DAVID MORELL,
*The Fifth Profession*

## THE WAR OF ILLUSIONS

To the victorious allies in 1919, World War I seemed to secure their position
in the world. After the Peace of Paris, the British Empire reached its
greatest extent, covering one-fifth of the earth's land surface, and
possessing the largest population of any state on earth. Moreover, its
Dominions and colonies had rallied to the 'mother country' and sent their
soldiers overseas to support her in her hour of need. The war seemed
therefore to be a triumph for the Empire, presaging new unity and
strength, and further development in the years to come. To Australians,
the war also seemed to support the idea of protection under the imperial
flag, especially as her sons had contributed so much to the victory. It
confirmed one of the patterns in Australian foreign policy: reliance on
'great and powerful friends'.

Yet the future was to reveal that these were all illusions. Victory won
at the cost of so many lives and so much wealth could only weaken, not
strengthen, the Empire; Britain's new territories extended her commitments over the earth, beyond her strength; and the war speeded up the
centrifugal tendencies apparent beneath the public rhetoric in the early
years of the century. Her resultant weakness led to years of indecision and
withdrawal in the face of the dictators in the 1930s.

The introduction to this book, however, raised certain specific questions
about the war. Were Australian soldiers more effective than others; if so, did
that ensure special treatment for Australia? To what extent therefore did
Australia enjoy a favoured relationship with Britain, and how did that
relationship change during the conflict? Finally, what light does this study
throw on the idea that Australia could rely for development and defence
on British support in the years ahead—and by extension later on America?

213

## AUSTRALIA: THE MYTH OF THE DIGGER

The question whether Australian soldiers were more effective than others
in that war, and their resultant treatment by the British forces, obliges
the historian to reassess a basic tenet of Australian history, the myth of
the Digger. This widely held belief in the special fighting qualities of the
Anzacs goes back to Gallipoli itself. Bean was moved by his experiences
and what he saw there to seek for a national identity. This began in *The
Anzac Book* and continued in his official histories after the war. As he
put it,

> The first question ... clearly was: How did the Australian people—and the
> Australian character, if there is one—come through the universally recognised
> test of this, their first great war?[1]

But taking this approach weakened Bean as an historian, for it slanted
his selection of evidence from the beginning.

He also had other weaknesses. He based too much of his writing on
the diary of his experiences (the sights he had seen and the conversations
he had held) as a war reporter. His prejudices and misconceptions at the
time, despite his care, therefore slanted some of his later views. Again,
his class background, education (public school and Oxford), rank and
position created an unbridgeable gulf between him and the ordinary
soldiers. In this he was not exceptional. The experiences of that war
separated the front-line troops from the rest of the community. The
governor-general, for example, called the wounded soldiers who refused
to re-enlist 'loafers'.[2] It is difficult to imagine a less appropriate description
for men who had gone through World War I battle. But the vast gulf
between the stipend, honour and lifestyle of a man like Munro Ferguson
and the soldiers prevented understanding, even more than the differential
in pay between officers and privates.[3]

With his background and position, Bean inevitably sympathised with
the world view of the senior officers. If he had not, he would have had
to adopt it, simply to get information on what was happening. Even so,
they told him only part of the truth and not the whole picture, using
him to further their own individual propaganda needs. Bean inevitably
felt grateful to them for bringing him into their circle, felt himself to be
one of them, and avoided criticising them wherever possible. It is true
that at that time a 'gentleman' would not criticise another publicly, but
Bean took that too far, for historians cannot operate if they make no
judgements. Yet, being in headquarters so much put Bean apart from the
ranks, so that he did not understand what occurred at the cutting edge.
In particular, his education prevented him from coming to terms with
technology, especially artillery, yet it was the development of technology
and tactics that changed the nature of the war. Instead, Bean idealised
the junior officers, increasingly so as they were killed in the continuing
battles. His history, therefore, is slanted history, despite his great strength—
his unrelenting search for the *factual* story. (This last is illustrated for

example by the acerbic exchange between Bean and Edmonds, the official British historian, in which the generally mild Bean remarked that Edmonds' account of some British units in 1918 was 'unrecognisable by anyone who saw them'; and the orderly British retreat in fact was more like a rout. They—'in plain English—ran away'.[4]) His growing Australian-ness, however, allowed him to criticise British more than Australian commanders and troops.

In truth, the Anzacs were far more diverse than has been accepted. They were more than larrikins: they ranged from thugs, heavy drinkers and gamblers to sensitive men and teetotallers, who were often deeply religious and patriotic. The overwhelming majority were at neither extreme, being simply decent honest men who volunteered for the war from a variety of motives, were traumatised by their experiences, but did their best and became effective soldiers by 1918. But their opinions were often ignored in the years to come, especially when they clashed with the image the authorities wished to create, as for example in the adoption of pacifism by some.[5] In general, however, they were more tough, hard-bitten, and cynical than Bean imagined, deeply critical of their own officers, as well as British ones.

The question whether they were better fighting men has been discussed in Chapter 6: some were, and others were not, but in general they improved as the war continued and reached their peak in 1918. One factor in this has also been ignored by the myth—the improvement in Australian officers. There had been grave weaknesses in many in the early days. The first ones were in many cases too old or incompetent, and were partly responsible for poor discipline in Egypt and blunders on Gallipoli. Birdwood's reluctance to promote Australians as staff officers prevented them from gaining staff training.[6] The purges and promotions, followed—after further fiascoes in France—by a new wave, were played down by Bean, but sufficient hints have survived. They, and the occasional British and Australian criticism of AIF officers, are suggestive, and have been noted in the earlier chapters.

It is time that Australians accepted all this, and by so doing looked again, with clear eyes, at the myths surrounding the Anzac legend. For in fact 'Anzac' was a myth in every sense of the word. Aspects of it were untrue; yet at the same time it formed the basis for a sense of Australian identity. Nevertheless, as a historian of Nazi Germany has written:

> If historical investigation undermines the founding 'myths' of one group or another, the scholar still believes that its members should revise their self-awareness and learn to live with complexity.[7]

## AUSTRALIA AND BRITAIN

This is applicable also to the corollary of the belief in the fighting power of the Anzacs: the special relationship with England which sprang out of that and our British ancestry.

In the early years of this century, Australia had the classic relationship with Britain—its 'motherland'. The vast majority of settlers had come from the British Isles; there were immensely strong links of emotion, blood and history with Britain; and Australia was bound financially for economic development, and legally under the Crown, to London. But as a result of the war, relations between Australia and Britain had undergone many changes.

In Britain, as McKernan has written, the Anzacs went from heroes to criminals. British authorities considered they had too much money and independence, were liable to misbehave in public, and should be returned at speed. Their reputation as effective fighting soldiers, however, lingered—until World War II.[8]

Australia's contribution to Britain's war effort had been considerable, but not overwhelming. It was consistently below that of Britain and Canada, or—taken as a proportion of population—of New Zealand. Among the Dominions New Zealand led, with nearly 20 per cent of her male population serving abroad. As a percentage of casualties to embarkations, Australia suffered 64.98, New Zealand 59.01, Britain 50.71, and Canada 49.74—but as a proportion of the total population, this represented percentage losses for Britain 10.91, New Zealand 9.8, Australia 8.5 and Canada 6.04.[9]

It is clear that the Australian contribution, though great, especially as it came from the only country that maintained voluntary recruiting, was not as overwhelming as the myth would have us believe. At the same time there had been economic strains, with Hughes—in his usual combative manner—being determined to protect Australia's economic interests, both then and in the future. But the economic interests of Britain and Australia did not necessarily coincide, any more than the strategic ones.

This was revealed very clearly in the discussions concerning peace at the end of the war, and the continued disagreement about the repayment of Australia's war debts to Britain afterwards. It has been argued in earlier chapters that Hughes won substantial benefits for Australia in his trade negotiations. The British Treasury at any rate thought so, and considered that Australia should use her surpluses in London to repay her debt to Britain. It was unwilling to modify the terms in Australia's favour.[10]

It seems clear from this study, therefore, that Australia did not enjoy a special relationship with Britain, at any rate more than any other Dominion of her Empire. There were many ties of blood and sentiment between the two countries, but the power-brokers in Britain—the press, government and civil servants—did not sympathise with Australia and Australians. They thought the Anzacs useful, but British snobbery meant that they were irritated by Australian 'brashness' (and accent), and being Anglocentric did not sympathetically understand Australia's separate needs.

As for Australian allegiance to Britain, the idealistic upsurge of loyalty and enthusiasm in the early days could not survive the rigours of a long, mechanistic war. As failures and weaknesses became apparent, Anzac disillusionment was inevitable. The same was true of the Australian public, especially as recognisably different interests became clear during the war. Australians were vitally concerned with the far South Pacific, but their men were dying in Europe. The reaction of the 'loyalists' was to use censorship and propaganda to whip up and maintain support, but this response in turn strengthened the doubts of their opponents.[11]

As a result, the war had a schizoid impact on both Australia and the Empire. On the imperial stage, this was increased by Hughes' attitudes and policies. After seeing the movement for conscription in Britain he supported it all the more aggressively in Australia, and the resultant political imbroglio kept him away from London in 1917, when important wider issues were being raised. He never regained his prestige when he returned in 1918, but remained an outsider, fighting against Britain for Australia's interests, rather than rallying Britain against Germany. Moreover, Lloyd George, by then firmly in power, had no intention of letting Hughes destabilise his government as he had that of Asquith. Hughes had served Lloyd George's purpose, and was now merely an irritant. Partly for this reason, and partly because he wished to avoid going into details on the fall of Asquith, Lloyd George later minimised Hughes' role in his *Memoirs*.[12]

The impact was even more far-reaching in Australia. The superficial result was strengthened loyalty to Britain. Some Australians moved back there after 1918,[13] while the Empire federationalists hoped that the loyalty revealed during the war, and the bonds of alliance, would bring the differing parts of the Empire closer together. At the Royal Military College at Duntroon the 'Imperial spirit' continued to be extolled, and officers who stressed the Australian ethos were criticised. 'We are Britons overseas and our Army is a British army.'[14] This stress on Australia as part of the British Empire, and protected by its might, was naturally taken up by Hughes and the political establishment in Australia, and supported by the RSL.[15]

But the imperial federationists were few in number in Australia, and the voices of those who extolled the old allegiance to Empire, though given prominence in press, pulpit and on the hustings so that extravagant support for Britain continued in the inter-war period, were no longer alone. The war, as we have seen, had led many soldiers to see Australia with new eyes, and consider her apart from Britain. As it progressed, Captain E. J. Rule's diary entries became more critical of the British high command and more complimentary to the Australians. By the 1930s Bean was writing to Edmonds, 'you Englishmen'.[16]

Those who thought like this were not as numerous in Australia as in Ireland, South Africa or Canada, but they did exist, for the war provoked nationalism, not only in Europe, but in the Dominions as well, and so began the process of turning expatriate Britons into Australians. And the returned soldiers' ideas had some status, for, after all, they had been to Europe.[17] These ideas were particularly strong in Canada. A Canadian historian has remarked that notions of imperial federation were 'in tatters' after the war, and noted that Borden changed from 'a devout imperialist to a determined nationalist'.[18] In 1919 the CIGS's idea of using Canadian and Australian troops to help garrison Germany was therefore flatly rejected by those countries, and in continuing imperial conferences in the inter-war years the independence of the Dominions was rammed home.[19] The split in Australian society, thus engendered, continued till the 1970s.


## ANGLO-AUSTRALIAN RELATIONS FOLLOWING THE WAR

The Australian Cabinet, though far away from the decision making and not agreeing with all of Hughes' ideas or attitudes, still supported many of his views, and was horrified that Australia had not gained more in reparations. They feared the taxation needed to meet the costs, and felt they had been ignored by Britain because they were distant. They also feared there would be an outburst of popular anger in Australia when the terms were announced, and that this would weaken support for the Empire.[20] This last did not materialise, because the media supported the government, but Australian public opinion had clearly been split by the war.

As for the soldiers, they had changed under the impact of the stress of war. They

> were not the same men who had embarked from Australia a few years before, bound happily for Armageddon; nor were their kinsfolk in Australia quite the same. As the heat of summer hardens a cicada newly emerged from ... the ground, so the heat of war ... hardened the Australian sense of identity. The British/Australian duality was still discernible, but not to the same pervasive extent as it had been in 1901.[21]

The early euphoria and idealism—not to say naivety—had therefore passed. The soldiers had now seen the British close up, and the romantic illusions of the pre-war days were ended. They realised that the British army had serious defects; and Britain herself appeared small and affected by class differences. The soldiers had lost their simple awe of the British Empire, and adopted a sometimes brash nationalism to replace it. They returned with a new pride in Australia, which they probably exaggerated because of the acute stress they had suffered. Besides battle trauma for the infantry, other Anzacs had endured uncertainty, constant change, different food, climate and customs; all of which made them look back nostalgically to their homeland, and idealise what their fellow Australians had done. Modern psychological theory suggests all soldiers indulge in wish-fulfilling fantasies about home, which may account for Anzac disillusionment with Britain. In this respect, the Anzacs reacted like other soldiers in other wars.[22]

But, in or out of armies, no one can come through a war of that magnitude and remain unchanged. Andrew Fisher, who had spoken of 'the last man and the last shilling', asked Lloyd George in 1918, 'If the D[ominion]s have not won a man's place during this war:—What are they expected to do to earn it at some future day?' At the same time, praise for the Anzacs in the press roused Australians' pride in their troops. There was a certain loss of prestige by Britain from which she found it difficult to recover, as Munro Ferguson noted, especially as the press stressed 'our Aussies' as 'the "spearhead" and "shocktroops" of the British Army'. This, together with the changes in channels of communication, gave the Dominions the status of allies.[23]

Two reactions, however, were possible: both soldiers and civilians could become more nationalist and independent. Their very homesickness and the xenophobia which that creates caused some Anzacs to praise all things Australian and denigrate the best of Britain and Europe.[24] Alternatively, they could become Empire-minded, convinced that Australia needed Britain for defence. The population was therefore divided between the British-Australians and the nationalists, who stressed a separate Australian identity.

This split was illustrated in surprising reactions. To start with, the British women who had married Australian soldiers sometimes received a hostile reception in Australia. According to Munro Ferguson, some 'were mobbed and pulled about by a crowd of factory girls [sic]; much capital was made of the presence among them of a few undesirables, and a vulgar and acrimonious correspondence on the subject of these marriages was started in the press'. His comment corresponds with that of an old soldier with a British wife, who recalled that they had to move from Sydney because of the hostility of their neighbours, and it took years for her to be accepted. This reaction was probably also helped by controversy in the British press, especially the *British-Australasian*, on the issue.[25]

Equally significant was the reaction of certain intellectuals. Eggleston criticised Lloyd George for being carried away by oratory and forgetting liberal principles. Bean was convinced that the Anzacs were on the whole better fighting men than the British, blaming the effects of the Industrial Revolution for that. For a while in 1917 he had muttered revolution, writing in his diary that if Lloyd George nationalised the railways, demolished the slums, struck at the British class system and abolished the monarchy, the masses would help him. 'Then we may come out of this war as a great Empire with a real chance of development in us— young, beginning, active, thinking.' He later reported with approval John Masefield's support for a revolution in England after the war. But this was Bean's reaction to the disasters of 1917. It was akin to the attitudes of those who later looked to fascism as a way of cutting out the rot in society; but Bean was too humane a man to go along that road.[26]

The government—and Hughes—survived this potentially dangerous period by stressing the valour of the Anzacs, officially mourning the fallen, and emphasising the glories of the Empire's victory, by which the policy adopted by the Australian government was vindicated. In line with this it even approved the guarantee to France against German aggression. In the event this lapsed, but continued Australian support for Britain on the Continent is striking.[27]

The discussion of soldier settlement in Australia, of both returning Anzacs and British ex-servicemen, paints a similar picture. Despite official reluctance in some quarters, Rider Haggard's tour of Australia in 1916 had roused great enthusiasm. Both Hughes and the State governments saw the scheme as a way of extracting development monies from Britain, while Churchill thought of redistributing the white population of the Empire. It was to result in the *Empire Settlement Act* in 1922. The early enthusiasm waned, but Australia still took the largest share, 43.7 per cent, of the British ex-servicemen and their families who went abroad under the scheme.[28]

In trade matters also Hughes felt vindicated. The German domination of the international metals industry had been broken, and the Australian company BHP, in conjunction with the British Metals Corporation, gained a share of the world market, as the only lead and zinc producers in the Empire, and the greatest in the world. Despite his troubles with shipping, Hughes had won good deals for Australia in the wool and wheat trade, which put her in a position to dominate the post-war markets. Meanwhile the governor-general worried about the possible diversion of Australian trade to America or Japan, the impact of tariffs, and the restoration of British trade after the war.[29]

Nor did Hughes change his attitude to imperial constitutional reform, despite the complex and unsatisfactory state of Empire inter-relationships that developed in Paris.[30] During the war Borden and Smuts had begun talking about a Commonwealth of Nations, and Lionel Curtiss had popularised the phrase in two books published in 1916. In 1917 the Imperial War Conference had talked of the Dominions as 'autonomous nations of an Imperial Commonwealth' in its resolution on consultation.[31] Hughes would have none of it. As he had prevented a committee of experts being formed in July 1918, so at the 1921 Imperial Conference he completely scotched the proposal of Amery, Smuts and others for a constitutional conference which would define the relationship between Britain and the Dominions. His motives were partly the internal political situation in Australia and partly his attitude to the Empire. He gleefully described this as his 'best work', but his shortsightedness was promptly revealed by the Chanak crisis in 1922, when Lloyd George appealed to the Dominions for support, in defence 'of soil which is hallowed by immortal memories of the Anzacs'. This was emotional blackmail.

The struggle therefore developed once again to ensure that the British really did consult the Dominions before committing them to any policy.[32] Hughes fell from office before it got under way, but there followed

> a new period in the relationship between Australia and Great Britain . . . in which the . . . Dominions sought to exercise an influence upon British policy through consultation—and in which the term 'British Commonwealth' gradually replaced 'Empire'.

This came about slowly and in stages, especially as Australia's new prime minister, S. M. Bruce, Australian-born but British-educated, remained convinced that Australia's security depended upon her membership of the Empire, and cautious in his attitude to change in it.[33] That indeed became the accepted truth of conservative Australian governments in the inter-war period. Its weakness was revealed in 1942.

Immediately after the war, Amery had suggested to Lloyd George that there should be an Imperial Cabinet of British Ministers and Dominion representatives. Hankey had high hopes that the secretariat of the BED could be transferred to London and become the permanent officials of this long-running Imperial Cabinet. This was part of imperialist idealism in Britain: Amery even suggested sending British students to Australian universities. But it all came to nothing. There was natural jealousy from the established British Departments of State,[34] and both Britain and the Dominions were preoccupied by the politics of reconstruction. The Imperial War Cabinet ended.

Nor did constitutional reform come easily. Hughes' suggestion of one Imperial Court of Appeal for both Britain and the Empire (rather than the House of Lords for the British and the Privy Council for the Dominions) was referred to the next Imperial Conference.[35] Perhaps the most far-reaching change was the reduction in the powers of the governor-general. Munro Ferguson had allowed the right to refuse a dissolution of parliament to lapse; he had been replaced as the channel of communication between the Australian and British governments; and—as Amery pointed out—in future the governor-generalship would more closely resemble the position of the monarch in Britain. His successor was chosen from a list of names submitted by Milner (the Colonial Secretary) to the Australian government.[36]

In the same way, the dream of powerful coordinated imperial defence ended. Hughes himself joined Canada in rejecting an Admiralty idea (backed by Lloyd George) for a single imperial navy, and Admiral Jellicoe then toured the Dominions to advise them on their naval requirements.[37] But it was already too late: Britain wound down her defence commitment to the so-called Far East. She scrapped fleet units; she allowed the Anglo-Japanese Treaty to end and replaced it with the Washington Treaties, which established battleship ratios between the major powers in the Pacific, in 1921; she ran down her defence establishment on the assumption that she would not be involved in a major war within ten years—the so-called Ten-Year Rule. Before long all countries were indulging in government economies.

This did not necessarily please the Australians. That Hughes really was concerned by the Japanese was revealed by his panic-stricken cable to Lloyd George when the Japanese fleet held manoeuvres in 1919, and his creation that year of the Pacific Branch of his Prime Minister's Office, under E. L. Piesse, to collect and analyse information on Pacific affairs. Piesse dreamed this would form the nucleus for an Australian Foreign Office, but the branch lapsed when Hughes lost power. The other option, which occurred to Latham in his memorandum for the Pacific in July 1918, was an alliance between America and Britain,[38] but the latter did not eventuate, and the denouement came in 1941, when the Japanese struck at Pearl Harbor, and for the first time in her history Australia was really under threat of attack.

The immediate aftermath of World War I in Australia, however, was less dramatic. The public was concerned with mourning the dead, and getting back as quickly as possible to peace—and hopefully economic prosperity. Hughes' election victory in December 1919, when the National Party was returned to power, coincided with the final report of the Gallipoli enquiry. This, though noticed in the press, was not given wide coverage.

Australian caution about criticising Britain, however, did not make the latter more open with her Dominion. The request by the Australian government in 1926-7 for a copy of the evidence presented to the Gallipoli enquiry was refused. At the same time, there was surprisingly little criticism of the war in Australia. The theory accepted by the vast bulk of the population, weary with the war, was that we had won a victory, even though the cost was grievous, and our prosperity and defence relied on the bonds with Britain. The Labor Party paid little attention to the final Gallipoli report; the RSL triumphed over rival—and more critical— organisations; and both nationalists and Empire loyalists used Anzac Day as their emblem. For it conveniently hid many differences of emphasis. There

> was a spectrum of feeling ranging from those who definitely adhered to anti-British aspects of the Anzac legend, to the great bulk who saw little or no tension and regarded Australia as a special case within the British Empire, and those who had strong, if not prime, loyalties to the Empire . . .[39]

## BETWEEN THE WARS: THE 'GREAT AND POWERFUL ALLY' SYNDROME

This book has looked at World War I through the prism of the Anglo-Australian relationship: its nature; the changes it underwent from 1914 to 1919; and the lessons for the future. In particular, it raises in acute form the problems of reliance on allies: their tendency to drag us into wars in which we might not otherwise be involved; their habit of assuming that their interests are those of Australia; and their failure to consult us when they suspect that there is a clash of interests.

World War I only continued the process of Australians assuming a separate national identity. Federation had barely begun it, but as the Great War continued, the soldiers came to see themselves as distinct from Englishmen, and the men from different States, thrown together, regarded themselves as Australians, instead of New South Welshmen, or West Australians. At the same time not only Hughes but less prominent Australians such as Bean and Murdoch increasingly noted the differing interests of Australia and Britain.

This lesson of the war was reinforced in the inter-war years. S. M. Bruce, prime minister of Australia from 1921 to 1929, had been in the *British* army during the war, came to Australia by chance, and all his life thought of himself as English. Yet that did not preclude him from regarding himself also as Australian, and fighting for Australian interests against the British government. For Britain's vision of the world, and her basic needs, were often diametrically opposed to those of Australia. As Sir Charles Lucas wrote, 'the standing problem of the Empire, how to reconcile unity and diversity, presented itself in the most direct and practical form'.[40]

The best example is the differing attitude of the two countries to the Pacific. That ocean was remote from Britain, and—despite imperial posturing—really of minor concern to the British government. Yet it was part of Australia's vital strategic area. In 1918 Australian leaders felt fear and suspicion of Japan, which was only made worse because Japanese and Australians could not meet and negotiate face to face, but had to operate through the British Foreign Office ('with its anxiety to placate Japan') and the Colonial Office (nervous of Australian reactions). More direct imperial communications helped a little, but what was really needed was an Australian diplomatic service charged with supporting Australia's own interests. That, however, had to wait till World War II, when Menzies' government appointed the first Australian minister abroad—to Japan—in August 1940.[41] By then it was too late.

The usual Australian answer in the inter-war years was loyalty to Britain —while stressing separate Australian interests. Thus Major-General J. H. Bruche, the Australian CGS, commented on a CID paper in 1933 which suggested switching defence priorities from the Far East to Europe,

> The detachment of this ... is admirable, from the British point of view, but what for Britain is merely the acceptance of a risk means for Australia the facing of imminent disaster. Australia ... is part of the stake, and is therefore not in a position to take a detached view of the question.[42]

It was true enough, but the government was determined to maintain its public stance of reliance on Britain, and ignored him.[43]

The reasons for this were many. Partly, vested interests were at work. For example, the RAN continued to be closely integrated with the Royal Navy; and the RAAF maintained its separate existence by appealing to the RAF in Britain and being linked with that force. But, more importantly, there was a long-standing absence of any strategic or tactical analysis by Australia's political leaders. Their failure to come to grips with strategy and tactics until very late during World War I is striking. Only the growing disaster in France had finally provoked Hughes to go beyond rhetoric and consider such matters, but the war ended too soon for the lesson to be thoroughly learnt. Thereafter successive conservative governments won elections on emotional support for Britain and minimal defence expenditure. Meanwhile British education continued to influence Australian youth until much later.[44]

There followed the Great Depression, when British businessmen and financial interests were seen as the prime causes, and World War II, when the Australian government once again sent troops to the Middle East, and was only provoked into realising that it had a responsibility to its soldiers and that strategy and tactics *do* matter, by the fiascoes in Greece, Crete and Singapore, and the threat of Japanese invasion. The result was a blazing row between prime ministers Churchill and Curtin, when 'all the deep British prejudices about Australians suddenly surfaced, such as the convict legacy and the large Irish component in the population'. The British High Commissioner then said Australians were 'inferior people', and Churchill thought they were cowards and came from bad stock.[45]

After World War II came the great wave of migrants from Europe, and as the years went by an increasing proportion of the Australian population did not come from the British Isles. In foreign policy, Australia turned to America for protection, while Britain became preoccupied by European concerns. In joining the Common Market, moreover, she abandoned the Australian industries and farms that had been set up to feed her and *forced* Australians to look elsewhere for markets and trade.

Australian 'independence' therefore did not come with the *Statute of Westminster* in 1931, as has been argued.[46] That may have been the *legal* date, but it was certainly not the emotional, political or military one.

Australian woman visiting war graves at Villers-Bretonneux, 1990.   (G. Dalley).

Many years were to pass, during which the lead was taken by Canada, Ireland and South Africa. Several wars later, the British retreat from their Empire, and the abandonment of Australia by a Britain preoccupied with Europe, together with Asian migration and economic decline have at last forced Australian opinion to change. The great dream of imperial unity—and even the old bonds of Empire, though they remain as a sentiment of warm feeling for Britain in many Australians and constitutionally in the links with the Crown—has now finally ended.

# Notes

## INTRODUCTION

1. There are an average of fifteen items per page on 393 pages of listings. Enser, *Bibliography*.
2. Adam-Smith, *Anzacs*; Laffin, *Damn the Dardanelles*. For comment, see Gerster, *Big Noting*: 254–8.
3. For Australia, see Fewster's thesis, 'Expression and Suppression'.
4. See Mearsheimer, *Liddell Hart*: 61. Hart himself remarked on 'the soldiers' lack of a sense of intellectual honesty', and how a true picture of the nasty side of the British higher commanders had not emerged. (Liddell Hart Papers, 11/1933/25 and 31). The Australian War Diaries also tried to hide disaster: e.g. after the second battle of Bullecourt, I ANZAC HQ War Diary says for 3 May 1917 that 5th Brigade had formed a defensive flank (WO 95/903); in fact it had been slaughtered by machine guns and German artillery. For Bean on the deficiencies of the records, 'Technique': 66.
5. Prior and Wilson, *Command on the Western Front* is probably the best recent example, which for the first time puts into perspective the tactical nature of the fighting, and the problems that the generals and lesser commanders faced.
6. A. J. Balfour, cited in M. Stephens, *A Dictionary of Quotations*, London, 1990. For example, the accounts of the Suvla Bay fiasco by Bean, Churchill, Moorehead, Rhodes James and Bush all use the exculpatory report written at the time by Lt-Col. Aspinall, or the same man's later official history. Prior, 'Suvla Bay tea-party': 25.
7. e.g. Inglis, 'Anzac Tradition' and 'Anzac and the Australian Military Tradition'; Gammage, 'Monash' and 'Anzac'.
8. Hastings, 'Writing Military History'; Andrews 'Bean and Bullecourt'; Nile, 'Peace'.
9. e.g. articles by Mordike and Crumlin. See also earlier work, such as Prior, 'Suvla Bay', and Winter, 'Anzac landing'.
10. Bean II: 617–20.
11. 8141 dead on Gallipoli, compared with 48,617 in France. See Chapter 2.
12. Terraine, *To Win a War*. More recent work has begun to remedy that deficiency. See Prior and Wilson, 'Manner of Victory?': 80–96; Wilson, 'Significance': 24–6; and especially Travers, *How the War Was Won*.
13. For a survey of Marwick's book, and a critique, see McInnes and Sheffield, *Warfare in the Twentieth Century*: 2–3.
14. In a way, this is also fair. The war photographer Frank Hurley commented on the much better chance for survival of the soldiers in the Middle East compared with those in France. Palestine was more or less a holiday in comparison. Hurley Diary, 31 Dec. 1917, p. 129, ANL MS 883.
15. HMSO *Statistics*: 762
16. See McKernan, *Australian People*: 11 for his part-German, Catholic, working-class aunt in ultra-loyal Melbourne University, and the dissimilar experiences of individuals in a time of war.
17. *Napoleon*: 16.
18. Parsons, 'Australia's contribution'.
19. Barnett, *The Swordbearers*: 235–6.
20. Quotation, McGibbon, *Path to Gallipoli*: 3; 'disastrous consequences', Pfeiffer, 'Exercises': 178.

21. Robertson, *Anzac and Empire*: 265-7. Cf. the Sydney *Sun*, 31 Oct. 1914, quoted in Crowley, *Modern Australia*: 225-6.
22. Even the authority on this point seems to find difficulty in deciding the exact date of Australian independence. Cf. Hudson and Sharp, *Australian Independence*: 138, which suggests either the *Statute of Westminster*, 1931 or our ratification of it in 1942, with 'Strategy': 28, which implies 1945.
23. This point was made by Andrew Fisher at the special meeting of the CID in 1911. He 'admitted that the United Kingdom could legally commit the Dominions to war, but insisted that any direct aid from Australia was a matter for the Australian Parliament to decide'. Robson, *First A.I.F.*: 16.


CHAPTER ONE   THE BRITISH EMPIRE AND AUSTRALIA

1. *The Times* 23 June 1897: 9; Morris, *Farewell the Trumpets*: 21; *Whitaker's Almanack*, London, 1897: 325-7, 334.
2. MacKenzie, *Propaganda and Empire*: 69-73; Cannon, *Long Last Summer*: 6; Inglis, *The Rehearsal*: 27 .
3. Blake, *Papers of Douglas Haig*: 248-52.
4. Gordon, *Dominion Partnership*: 194, 200, 210; Cross, 'Colonial Office and the Dominions': 142. For the Foreign Office, Hudson and Sharp, *Australian Independence*: 22. For horsemanship, Reader, *At Duty's Call*: 39.
5. Summers, 'Militarism in Britain': 104-23.
6. Harvie, *War and Society*: 127.
7. MacKenzie, *Propaganda and Empire*: 5-7, 16-34, 48-50, 68-72, 98-9, 106-7, 160-2, 181-5, 202-7, 243-6, 254-5. Parker, *The Old Lie*: 18, 56-7, 125-7, 133-7. For Northcliffe, the Unionist Party and the press campaign against Germany, Haste, *Keep the Home Fires Burning*: 5-20.
8. In Victoria Charles Gavan Duffy and John Dunmore Lang had been moved by intellectual motives, regarding Britain's wars as 'generally unjust and unnecessary'. Hall, *Australia and England*: 103-27.
9. Blainey, *Tyranny of Distance*: chs 8, 9, 12; Meaney, *Under New Heavens*: 391-2; Inglis, 'Imperial Connection': 35-7.
10. Inglis, *The Rehearsal*: 15-19; Serle, 'Australia and Britain': 10.
11. Crowley, 'The British Contribution': 55-88; Reader, *At Duty's Call*: 38-9; *Yearbook of the Commonwealth of Australia*, No. 1: 906; No. 7: 1032; No. 12: 1169. 'Precis of Proceedings of the Imperial Conference of 1911', Cmd 5741, June 1911: 43 in Pearce Papers, ANL MS 1827/16.
12. Quotation, Hudson, in McKernan and Browne, *Two Centuries of War and Peace*: 32. For birthplace, *Yearbook of the Commonwealth of Australia*, No. 1, 1908: 145. Meaney, *Search for Security*: 3-4.
13. Fitzhardinge, *Little Digger*: 15; Cannon, *Long Last Summer*: 4; L. F. Fitzhardinge, interview with author, 17 Dec. 1986.
14. Hudson and Sharp, *Australian Independence*: 19, 38; Clark, *History of Australia*: 331; Grimshaw, 'Australian Nationalism': 168; Hobson *Evolution of Modern Capitalism* and *Imperialism*; Fieldhouse, *Theory of Capitalist Imperialism*: 54-9.
15. Hudson and Sharp, *Australian Independence*: 47.
16. Eggleston, 'Australia and the Empire': 538.
17. Grimshaw, 'Australian Nationalism': 168-76 (quotation 173).
18. Hudson and Sharp, *Australian Independence*: 25-8; Long to Munro Ferguson, 13 Dec. 1918, Novar Papers, ANL MS 696/1534. Joseph Chamberlain had Reid introduce an amendment to the Federal Convention to grant the same right to the governor-general to act without the advice of his ministers as was held by the colonial governors. The Colonial Office was thus satisfied that the governor-general's position, 'as an imperial officer . . . is no longer in question'. M. Dunn, *Australia and Empire*: 60. For the colonial governors, Hudson and Sharp, *Australian Independence*: 11-12.

19. Cunneen, *War Letters*: 105; Spartalis thesis, 'Anglo-Australian Relations': 5. Northcote Papers, PRO 30/56, e.g. 26 May 1906 for the need for a strong federal government.
20. Cunneen, *King's Men*: 97.
21. Hudson and Sharp, *Australian Independence*: 41; McMinn, *George Reid*: 251, 256; Thompson thesis, 'The Australian High Commission': *passim*, but esp. pp.132–71.
22. Hudson, *Hughes in Paris*: xii; Penny, 'Australia's Reaction to the Boer War': 126.
23. Hudson and Sharp, *Australian Independence*: 15.
24. Keith, *Selected Speeches*: 213, 221–3; Meaney, *Under New Heavens*: 402.
25. Meaney, ibid.: 402, 404; Grimshaw, 'Australian Nationalism': 166; Robson, *Australian Commentaries*: v–vi, 25; Hall, *Australia and England*: 128, 130–5; Foster, *High Hopes*: viii, 10–11, 74. See also Blackton, 'Australian Nationalism and Nationality': 1–16. For Tennyson, Cunneen, *Kings' Men*: 46; for New Zealand, Sinclair, *A Destiny Apart*: 99–101.
26. Shields, 'Australian Opinion'; Meaney, *Search for Security*: 9.
27. Kendle, *Colonial and Imperial Conferences*: 10–11. For the difference of viewpoint between Australia and Britain, see also Hayes, 'British Foreign Policy': 102–13.
28. Heydon, *Quiet Decision*: 40. For the colonial background, Inglis, *The Rehearsal*: 22–3; Kendle, *Colonial and Imperial Conferences*: 10–11. For the Anglo-Japanese alliance, Nish, 'Australia and the Anglo-Japanese Alliance': 202–3. For the Canadians, Morton, *Canada and War*: 29–30.
29. Cunneen, *Kings' Men*: 77–9; Spartalis, *Diplomatic Battles of Billy Hughes*: 4.
30. Souter, *Lion and Kangaroo*: 129.
31. Tunstall, 'Imperial Defence': 569. Gordon, *Dominion Partnership*: 147. For a bitterly critical account of the Australians, see Hall, *Australia and England*: 248–52.
32. Dawson, *Development of Dominion Status*: 9.
33. Gordon, *Dominion Partnership*: 98–109.
34. Mahan had produced his book, *The Influence of Sea Power Upon History*, in 1890. See Earle, *Makers*: 415–45. Admiralty memorandum on imperial defence, Keith, *Selected Speeches*: 230–7. Gordon, *Dominion Partnership*: xii, 53–71.
35. *Commonwealth Parliamentary Debates (CPD)*, 24 Aug. 1906, vol. 33: 3358.
36. Mordike, 'Story of Anzac': 5–8; Booker, *Great Professional*: 99; Robertson, *Anzac and Empire*: 11. Some Australians did in fact volunteer to join the Japanese against the Russians in 1904. Sissons, 'Attitudes to Japan and Defence': 46; Robson, *First A.I.F.*: 15; Cunneen, *Kings' Men*: 46.
37. For the imperial viewpoint, Marder, *Dreadnought to Scapa Flow*: 40–3. Tunstall 'Imperial Defence': 569; Robson, *First A.I.F.*: 10; Gordon, *Dominion Partnership*: 147, 190–2, 195–6, 205, 208–9. See Souter, *Lion and Kangaroo*: 135–6, for an amusing account of the state of Australia's naval forces. For the outcry against the agreement in Australia, Merritt thesis, 'Pearce': 317–19.
38. Kendle, *Colonial and Imperial Conferences*: 186–8; Tunstall, 'Imperial Defence': 573–4; Gordon, *Dominion Partnership*: 270–1; Mackintosh, 'Committee of Imperial Defence': 490–503.
39. Robertson *Anzac and Empire*: 11; Coulthard-Clark, *No Australian Need Apply*: 42–3, 48; Souter, *Lion and Kangaroo*: 149. For an account of Hutton's clash with the Australian government, Mordike paper, 'Control by Committee'. Bean, *Two Men I Knew*.
40. Tunstall, 'Imperial Defence': 574; Williamson, *Politics of Grand Strategy*: 90–1.
41. Dawson, *Development of Dominion Status*: 15; Foster, *High Hopes*: 74, 76.
42. Kendle, *Colonial and Imperial Conferences*: 91–109; Hudson and Sharp, *Australian Independence*: 35–6, 47–8.
43. McGibbon, *Path to Gallipoli*: 132–5; Mordike, 'The Story of Anzac': 9; for Haldane, Lucas, *The Empire at War*: 186–8.
44. Gordon, *Dominion Partnership*: 210; Booker, *The Great Professional*: 123–7; Souter *Lion and Kangaroo*: 132–3, 140–44.
45. Briggs, 'A navy for the taking'.
46. Merritt thesis, 'Pearce': 304, 306–8, 311, 320–1, 324–6, 328.

47. Sissons thesis, 'Attitudes to Japan': 27–74 (quotation, 71); Meaney, *Under New Heavens*: 404; Spartalis, *Diplomatic Battles*: 2–3, 28. Cunneen, *Kings' Men*: 79. See Pearce's speech when he met the first ships of the RAN in November 1910, Heydon, *Quiet Decision*: 40–1, 54–60; Fitzhardinge, *That Fiery Particle*: 137, 143, 145; Booker, *Great Professional*: 111, 116; Mordike, 'Dreadnought to Gallipoli': 3–4; Souter, *Lion and Kangaroo*: 139.
48. Meaney, 'Proposition': 192–4.
49. Gammage, 'The crucible': 157.
50. Pugsley, *The Fringe of Hell*: 11.
51. Mordike paper, 'Dreadnought to Gallipoli': 5–9. See also Tunstall, 'Imperial Defence': 588–9; Robertson, *Anzac and Empire*: 12; Souter, *Lion and Kangaroo*: 151–2; Scott, *Australia During the War*: 194–5; Hill, *Chauvel*: 39–40.
52. Souter, *Lion and Kangaroo*: 163–5; Morton, *Canada and War*: 29; Merritt thesis, 'Pearce': 436–7, 549–52; Heydon, *Quiet Decision*: 40–3.
53. Foster, *High Hopes*: 162. For edited minutes of the debate, see Keith, *Selected Speeches*: 247–303, and an account of the conference is given in Hancock, '1911 Imperial Conference': 356–72.
54. Greenlee, *Education and Imperial Unity*: 100–6; Cross, 'The Colonial Office': 145.
55. Cross, 'The Colonial Office': 142–4; Hancock, '1911 Imperial Conference': 361–3.
56. The very interesting debate can be followed in 'Precis of Proceedings of the Imperial Conference of 1911', Cmd 5741, in Pearce Papers, ANL MS 1827/16. See also Kendle, *Colonial and Imperial Conferences*: 172–4, 184; Hudson and Sharp, *Australian Independence*: 45–7. Deakin had been concerned by decisions at the Hague Conference of 1907; Keith, *Dominions as Sovereign States*: 13 and *Selected Speeches*: 182–9 (quotation); Booker, *The Great Professional*: 129–31; Tunstall, 'Imperial Defence': 595.
57. Nish, 'Anglo-Japanese Alliance': 209; Booker, *Great Professional*: 132; Souter, *Lion and Kangaroo*: 162–3. For a survey of Britain and Japan, and the manipulation of Dominion opinion at the 1911 conference, see Nish, *Alliance in Decline*: 45–64. Fisher's biographer believes that 'Britain had conceded nothing to the Dominions': Murphy, 'Fisher'; and Hancock, '1911 Imperial Conference': 366 remarks that the Dominion leaders were unaware of the content of the Anglo-French conversations of 1906. For British worries before the conference, and the deliberate false impression that was given to the Dominions, see McGibbon, *Path to Gallipoli*: 210–12.
58. Foster, *High Hopes*: 163–4; Taylor, *English History*: 418.
59. Meaney, *Search*: 143.
60. Dawson, *Development*: 12–13; Gordon, *Dominion Partnership*: 271; Tunstall, 'Imperial Defence': 601.
61. Kendle, *Colonial and Imperial Conferences*: 219–20, 226–8; Dawson, *Development of Dominion Status*: 8.
62. Cross, 'Colonial Office': 146–7.
63. Cunneen, *Kings' Men*: 94–5; Gordon, *Dominion Partnership*: xii, 79, 285–8 (quotation on last page).
64. Primrose thesis, 'Australia's Naval Policy': 20–1, 23.
65. McGibbon, *Path to Gallipoli*: 215–21.
66. Quinault, 'Churchill and Australia'.
67. For Churchill's speech, see Keith, *Selected Speeches*: 343–56. Comments by Gordon, *Dominion Partnership*: 282, 289–96; Lucas, *Empire at War, III*: 225–6; Booker, *Great Professional*: 135–7.
68. Mordike, 'Story of Anzac': 5–17.
69. McGibbon, *Path to Gallipoli*: 238.
70. And most of the staff were British. Coulthard-Clark paper, 'Duntroon': 7–8.
71. For the secret conference at the War Office, PRO WO 106/43, cited in Mordike, 'Story of Anzac': 10–15, from which this account is drawn, together with his 'Dreadnought to Gallipoli': 10. For the change in Pearce's ideas, Merritt thesis, 'Pearce': 443, 445–7. For Bridges, Clark, 'Bridges': 32–3. For White, see Grey, *Military History*: 461. For New Zealand, Pugsley, *Gallipoli*: 41–4; McGibbon, *Path to Gallipoli*: 240–3.

72. Semmel, *Imperialism and Social Reform*: 31; Robson, *First A.I.F.*: 18; Cole ' "Nationalism" and "Imperialism" ': 176-7 and 'Crimson Thread': 514-5; interview with Fitzhardinge, cited; Nichols, *Bluejackets and Boxers*: 60.

73. Gammage, *Broken Years*: 3.

74. Fitzhardinge, *That Fiery Particle*: 224 (quotation). Coulthard-Clark, 'Bridges': 17-18 and *No Australian Need Apply*: 2; Kempe, 'Anzac': 7.

75. Ellis thesis, 'Bean': 98-101, 127-8, 134; quotation from Souter, *Lion and Kangaroo*: 113. Bean's colleagues during the war, the war artist Will Dyson, and his assistant F. M. Cutlack, both had English parents.

76. MacKenzie, *Propaganda and Empire*: 4; Cunneen, *Kings' Men*: 1, 17-18, 101; Clark, *History of Australia*: 322-3.

77. Sinclair, *Destiny Apart*: 96; Souter, *Lion and Kangaroo*: 155-7; Fisher Papers, ANL MS 2919/9/37.

78. McKernan, *Australian People*: 43; Firth thesis, 'Schooling in NSW': 68, 71, 79-85.

79. McKernan, *Australian People*: 43-4, 46. Firth, 'Social values': 124-43; see also his thesis, 'Schooling in NSW': 35, 41, 101-9, 116, 123, 138-9, 144, 152-9. Connell, 'British Influence': 170. *Round Table*, Aug. 1911, reprinted in Robson, *Australian Commentaries*: 24.

80. Gibb, 'Australian Nationalism': 23; Connell, 'British Influence': 165-6, 169.

81. McKernan, *Australian People*: 25, 27; Krause thesis, 'Attitudes': 2-3.

82. Meaney, *Under New Heavens*: 392. See also Greenlee, *Education and Imperial Unity* and also 'Imperial Studies': 321-35.

83. Firth thesis, 'Schooling in NSW': 138.

84. Grimshaw, 'Australian Nationalism': 163-4. Cf. Meaney, *Search for Security*: 4.

85. French, 'One People': 246; Souter, *Lion and Kangaroo*: 113-16.

86. Evans, *Loyalty and Disloyalty*: 8-9; Booker, *Great Professional*: 88-9, 93, 95, 97.

87. Connolly, 'Class, Birthplace, Loyalty': 210-32; and 'Manufacturing "Spontaneity" ': 106-17; Sinclair, *Destiny Apart*: 173.

88. *Round Table*, Aug. 1911, I, reprinted in Robson, *Australian Commentaries*: 25.

89. Firth thesis, 'Schooling in NSW': 46, 110, 113, 237.

90. For example, 63 per cent of those holding 'positions of influence' in Queensland in 1900 were British-born. Cited by Evans, *Loyalty and Disloyalty*: 7; see also Hudson and Sharp, *Australian Independence*: 18.

91. Inglis, *Rehearsal*: 83. Australian-born were 82.9 per cent of the population in 1911. *Yearbook of the Commonwealth of Australia*, No. 12, 1901-18: 107.

92. Meaney, *Search for Security*: 5-6; Cole, 'Crimson Thread of Kinship': 518, 522-3.

93. Alomes, 'Island, Nation and Empire'.

94. Springhall, 'Lord Meath': 105; French, 'One People': 236-248.

95. Leader in *The Argus*, 29 Oct. 1915; Evans, *Loyalty and Disloyalty*: 7, 19; Grimshaw, 'Australian Nationalism': 167.

## CHAPTER TWO    THE BUGLES OF ENGLAND

1. McKernan, *Australian People*: 59.

2. Haste, *Keep*: 5-7; Beckett and Simpson, *Nation in Arms*: 7-10; Parker, *The Old Lie*: 31-2, 240-1; Emeley, *European Armies*: 74-7.

3. Taylor, *English History*: 2-3.

4. Hudson and Sharp, *Australian Independence*: 48-50; Souter, *Lion and Kangaroo*: 210-11.

5. Scott, *Australia in the War*: 6-11, 13, 24, 204; Twomey thesis, 'Australian Relationship': 18. Offer of troops, AWM 48, 2044/14. Balfour wanted to mix the Canadians, Australians and British together, Munro Ferguson to Bonar Law, 7 Feb. 1916, Novar Papers, ANL 696/800.

6. Fitzhardinge, *The Little Digger*: 3-8; McKernan, *Australian People*: 2, 15; Evans, *Loyalty and Disloyalty*: 22-3. Welborn, *Lords of Death*: 43; Horne, *Search*: 58 (quotation).

7. Crowley, *Modern Australia*: 216. Cf. *Sydney Morning Herald*, 12 Aug. 1914.

8. Crowley, *Modern Australia*: 218-20; Hunt and Thomas, *God, King and Country*. St Andrew's Cathedral, *Sydney Morning Herald*, 8 Aug. 1914. Robson, *First A.I.F.*: 23-5; McKernan, *Australian People*: 17, 25. *Freeman's Journal*, Charleton, *Pozières*: 270.

9. McKernan, *The Australian People*: 46-51 (quotations); Stephens, 'Three Schools': 77-85; Coward thesis, 'Impact of war': 63-4.

10. Gammage, 'Monash': 4-7; Robson, *First A.I.F.*: 23, 28.

11. ibid.: 16, and McInnes, *Road to Gundagai*: 306. New Zealand reactions, Baker, *King and Country*: 15 and Pugsley, *Gallipoli*: 30-2. For Canada, Morton, *Canadian Military Experience*: 79.

12. Dawes and Robson, *Citizen to Soldier*: 61-2; Evans, *Loyalty and Disloyalty*: 27; Lake, *Divided Society*: 18-23.

13. Firth thesis, 'Schooling in N.S.W.' and 'Social Values': 123-59.

14. Horne, *Search*: 59.

15. Gerster, *Big Noting*: 75; Welborn, *Lords of Death*: 45, 53-4; papers of H. Paull and Captain R. H. Gill, Imperial War Museum, London; Robson, 'Origin and character': 744-5; cf. Fuller, *Troop Morale*: 171. Approximately 60 per cent of the first Canadian contingent was British-born: Brown and Loveridge, 'Unrequited Faith': 57; Pearce to Hughes, 24 Apr. 1919, Australian Archives (AA) CP 316/8, Bundle 1, pt 4 (cf. AWM 48 2096 and AA CP 78/23, File 89/328). For Waterloo, Cooper, 'Andrew Douglas White'.

16. See White, 'Motives', and 'Soldier as Tourist'.

17. Lake, *Divided Society*: 31; Evans, *Loyalty and Disloyalty*: 4, 24, 26-9; Horne, *Search*: 59; Coward thesis, 'Impact of war': 45-7; White, 'Motives': 3-15. A good analysis of the mixed motives of many volunteers can be found in Dawes and Robson, *Citizen to Soldier*: 52-5, 66-8, 86, 91-5, 98, 100-6, 114-15. See also Ross, *Myth of the Digger*: 16-18. For the proportions of British-born in the AIF, compare ibid.: 16 with Gammage, *Broken Years*: 281. For the 28th Battalion, Collett, *The 28th*: 16. For New Zealand, Baker, *King and Country*: 15-17; Canada, Brown and Loveridge, 'Unrequited Faith'; ex-soldiers, Gough, 'First Australian': 42.

18. The idea that these were unnecessarily high has recently been challenged. See Pilger, 'The other "Lost Generation"'.

19. Inglis, 'Remembering': 27. Evans, *Loyalty and Disloyalty*: 23. New Zealand, Boyack, *Behind the Lines*: 6.

20. *Loyalty and Disloyalty*: 26.

21. Coward thesis, 'Impact of war': synopsis, 43, 63 and 70.

22. ibid.: 75-7.

23. Evans, *Loyalty and Disloyalty*: 22; Quinlan thesis, 'N.S.W. Press': chs 2 and 3; Souter, *Lion and Kangaroo*: 212-14; Walker, *Newspaper Press*: 250-1. *Sydney Morning Herald*, Cunneen, *Kings' Men*: 117 and Souter, *Company*: 114-15; Robson, *First A.I.F.*: 24-8. For the pacifists, Morice, *Six Bob*: 45-7, and outright opposition, the *International Socialist*, 8 August 1914.

24. Heyes Papers, AWM 45, box 23, bundle 31; Hill, *Chauvel*: 45.

25. Fitzhardinge, *Little Digger*: 10. Cf. Colonial Secretary to Munro Ferguson, 6 Aug. 1914, AWM 3DRL 8042/94.

26. Hill, *Chauvel*: 53.

27. Hamilton to Munro Ferguson, 6 October 1915, Novar Papers, ANL 696/3658-63.

28. Hill, *Chauvel*: 43; Birdwood to Hamilton and reply, AWM 48 1640/14, file 2, pt 2. For Legge, Coulthard-Clark, *No Australian*. Elliott, *Australian Dictionary of Biography*, vol. 8: 428-31.

29. Liddle, *Men of Gallipoli*: 77-8, 82.

30. Robertson, *Anzac and Empire*: 32, 36-7; Robson, 'Images': 1-2.

31. Robson, ibid.: 1; New Zealand faith in the Empire, Boyack, *Behind the Lines*: 21; reactions to British troops, Sinclair, *Destiny Apart*: 159.

32. Robertson, *Anzac and Empire*: 268.

33. ibid.: 37; Robson, 'Images': 7.

34. Fewster, 'Wazza Riots'.
35. Wahlert thesis, 'Provost'. For relations with the Egyptians, Brugger, *Australians and Egypt*.
36. Robertson, *Anzac and Empire*: 60, 112. War Office, *Field Service Pocket Book 1914*, London: 220-3. General Godley, commander of the New Zealanders, and discipline, Pugsley, *Fringe of Hell*: 12-14, 68-9, 75-8, 81; Sinclair, *Destiny Apart*: 156-7.
37. Casey Diary, 7 June 1915, Bean Papers, AWM 3DRL 6673/170; also Laffin, *Digger*: 79.
38. 362 officers and 7779 other ranks, or a total of 8141 Australians, died on Gallipoli. In France 2368 officers and 46,249 other ranks died. (i.e. 48,617 in all) HMSO, *Statistics*: 238-9, 325. Cf. Robertson, *Anzac and Empire*: 7; Gough, 'First Australian': 45; Knightley, 'Murdoch's': 36.
39. Dawnay, Heyes Papers, AWM 45, box 23, bundle 31. Even Bean noted officer bickering, Fewster, *Gallipoli Correspondent*: 142; Murdoch, Liddle, *Men of Gallipoli*: 189-90.
40. James, *Gallipoli*: 168-9; cf. excerpts of Malone's diary in Phillip *et al.*, *Great Adventure*: 34-7, 44. Cf. Pugsley, *Gallipoli*: 169-70 for a defence of Braund. For the aftermath of the landing, see Aspinall-Oglander, *Gallipoli*: 197, 199; Thomson, 'History'.
41. Maxwell to Munro Ferguson 31 October 1915, Novar Papers, ANL 696/3523. Hill, *Chauvel*: 54; Robertson, *Anzac and Empire*: 58-63, 75-7, 97-8, 106, 116, 137-8, 150-1, and his own comment, 259. Bonar Law to Munro Ferguson, 24 Aug. 1915, quotes Hamilton's praise for the Australians, Davidson Papers 11, ANL AJCP mf M.1123. Monro's report, Fisher Papers, ANL MS 2919/7/6. Changed attitude of New Zealand troops, Boyack, *Behind the Lines*: 34-5, 46-7.
42. Birdwood to Rintoul, 12 September 1915, Birdwood Papers, Imperial War Museum (IWM) WRB/1; report in *Sunday Times*, 26 Sept. 1915, in Northcliffe Papers, British Library (BL) Add. MS 26332; Hankey to wife, 28 July 1915, Hankey Papers, Churchill College Archives, HNKY 3/20; Roskill, *Hankey*: 194-5.
43. Robertson, *Anzac and Empire*: 105-6; Fewster, *Gallipoli Correspondent*: 82-3, 149-50. Cf. Pugsley, *Gallipoli*: 170.
44. All accounts agree on the medical chaos, some being more explicit than others. Laffin, *Damn the Dardanelles*: 152, 166-7; McCarthy, *Gallipoli*: 185; Ashmead-Bartlett, *Uncensored Dardanelles*: 48; Bean's diary in Fewster, *Gallipoli Correspondent*: 99-100; North, *Gallipoli*: 73-5; Robertson, *Anzac and Empire*: 200-11. CO 616/31 (590-628) and Keyes Papers, British Library 5/33, have details. For Fetherston, Hill, 'Howse': 384-6. A recent account is Tyquin, 'Medical Evacuation'.
45. Dawnay, Robertson, *Anzac and Empire*: 2; Monash and Howse, ibid.: 210.
46. G. J. Johnston, for the information of Sir James Allen, Defence Minister, New Zealand, Jan. 1916: PRO CAB 45/233.
47. Hudson, *Casey*: 35, 41. Casey Diary, 29 May 1915, AWM 3DRL 6673/170. For Walker and the expedition, 'Historical Notes' in Bean Papers, AWM 3DRL 8042/36.
48. Laffin, *Damn the Dardanelles*: 79, 135-6.
49. Sinclair, *Destiny Apart*: 160; Pugsley, *Gallipoli*: 252.
50. 'Goose about God', letter, 3 Sept. 1915 in Collins Papers, IWM. Gammage, *Broken Years*: 85-7, 127; Robertson, *Anzac and Empire*: 135-6; Bean, *Anzac Book*: 31-2.
51. Legge to Novar, 5 Oct. 1915, Novar Papers, ANL 696/3606.
52. Bean, 'Sidelights': 221. Liddle, *Men of Gallipoli*: 189-92; Prior, 'Suvla Bay': 25-33. James, *Gallipoli*: 170.
53. McCarthy, *Gallipoli*: 210-11.
54. Sinclair, *Destiny Apart*: 159-61, Boyack, *Behind the Lines*: 39, 46; Fewster, *Gallipoli Correspondent*: 84.
55. Unless otherwise noted, the following passage is based on the minutes in PRO CAB 22/1, CAB 22/2, CID Minutes G-25 in CAB 42/3 and paper in CAB 24/1. The key dates were 12 June and 6, 11 and 14 October 1915. The best secondary account is Fewster, 'Bartlett', though Moorehead, *Gallipoli*: 304-13 is a good brief version.
56. Knightley, 'Murdoch's': 36.
57. Robertson, *Anzac and Empire*: 165, 170, 180-1.

58. *Sydney Morning Herald*, 25 Jan. 1969.
59. Fewster, 'Bartlett': 17-30; Knightley, 'Murdoch's: 36; Gerster, *Big Noting*: 25; Serle, 'Monash': 622-6; Robertson, *Anzac and Empire*: 152-8, 225. James, *Gallipoli*: 312-15. Bartlett's own account can be found in Ashmead-Bartlett, *Uncensored Dardanelles*: 239-43, 252. Pearce Papers, AWM 3DRL 2222, bundle 7, no. 23. For Asquith's comments, letter 20 Oct. 1915, Dawnay Papers, IWM 69/21/1. For Bean, AWM 3DRL 6673/472. Lloyd George Papers, HLRO, D17/2/1, 17/3/2, 17/8/8, 20/2/30. Bonar Law Papers, 25 Sept. 1915, box 51, folder 3, sheet 21, 51/3/21. See also CO 616/53, 59 and 63.
60. Osmond, *Eggleston*: 75.
61. Robertson, *Anzac and Empire*: 77-8, 82, 87-8, 108-9 (quotation). Novar Papers, ANL MS 696/42-3, 398, 730, 786. For the call for debate in parliament by J. H. Catts, see p. 192, above.
62. Munro Ferguson to Bonar Law, 8 Nov. 1915, Novar Papers, ANL 696/767. For the media, Gough, 'First AIF': 43.
63. Sorel, *Reflections*.
64. Murdoch letter, Jennings, *Australia*; reprinted in *Sydney Morning Herald*, 18-20 Nov. 1968.
65. AWM 48 1640/14, pts 1 and 2, file 2; McCarthy, *Gallipoli*: 76, 163-4; Compare Bean's criticism of Monash, ibid.: 142-3, 155, with Crumlin, '4th Brigade': 39-44.
66. Kent, '*Anzac Book* and Anzac Legend': 380; Fewster, *Gallipoli Correspondent*: 12-20, 44-5; Inglis, 'C. E. W. Bean'. Cf. his *Australian Historian*.
67. *Daily Mail* (overseas edn), 24 July 1915.
68. Robson, 'Origin and character': 739; A.Thompson, review in *Historical Studies*, 21, 1984: 147-8.
69. Gerster, *Big Noting*: 27-30; Kent, '*Anzac Book* and Anzac Legend': 376-90.
70. Eric Cupit, interviewed by the author on 7 April 1986, still cringed when recalling the artillery bombardment at Pozières—seventy years later.
71. Kent, '*Anzac Book* and Anzac Legend': 388-90; Robson, *Australian Commentaries*: 4.
72. Dawnay Papers, IWM; see also Papers of Brig. L. P. Collins, IWM. Bonar Law to Munro Ferguson, Novar Papers, ANL 696/1351-2 and AA 78 23/1 14/18/349.
73. Birdwood to Clive Wigram, 15, 20 Dec. 1915, 9 Jan. 1916, AWM 3DRL 8042/27. AWM 48 1640/14, file 2, pt 2; Birdwood Papers AWM 3DRL 3376, items 40, 46 and 47. Dardanelles Commission, Bean Papers, AWM 3DRL 8042/46.

## CHAPTER THREE   THE WAR OF THE POLITICIANS

1. Evans, *Loyalty and Disloyalty*: 30-1; Dawes and Robson, *Citizen to Soldier*: 56; quotation, Gilbert thesis, 'The Churches': 26.
2. The offer: Robertson, *Anzac and Empire*: 17; Bean I: 28-9, 33. Finance, Scott, *Australia in the War*: 495-6. (For more detailed figures, although slightly different, see Copland, 'Australia': 590-2.) Transport, letter in Bean files, 4 Apr. 1934, AWM 3DRL 8042, item 115.
3. General economics, Copland, 'Australia': 585; unemployment, Gilbert thesis, 'The Churches': 27. Evans, *Loyalty and Disloyalty*: 23-4; Lake, *Divided Society*: 17; Twomey thesis, 'Australian Relationship': 25; prices, Fitzhardinge, *Little Digger*: 60.
4. Scott, *Australia in the War*: 485-95. Quotation, Twomey thesis, 'Australian Relationship': 54. Attard thesis, 'Australian High Commissioners': 10-20. For Munro Ferguson, Novar Papers, ANL MS 696/1774-5.
5. Harcourt MS, Bodleian Library, Dep.463, ff.48-58 (cf. Dep. 49, ff. 40, 59, 60-1). Fisher Papers, ANL MS 2919/6/73-4; Novar Papers, ANL 696/3856, 3859, 3889; AA A2 1915/1722.
6. Reid to Minister for External Affairs, 20 Jan. 1915, Australian High Commission (London) Files, AWM 1313/27/14, cited Attard thesis, 'Australian High Commissioners': 7.

7. D. J. Murphy in the *Australian Dictionary of Biography (ADB)*, vol. 8: 507.

8. Fischer, *Enemy Aliens*: 138-40, 151-2; cf. his 'Botany Bay revisited'.

9. Scott, *Australia in the War*: 19-20, 168-9; Fitzhardinge, *Little Digger*: 46; Cunneen, *Kings' Men*: 110-11, 117; Edwards, *Prime Ministers and Diplomats*: 36-7.

10. Hudson and Sharp, *Australian Independence*: 39-41; McMinn, *Reid*: 264. High Commission, Thompson thesis, 'Australian High Commission'. G. C. T. Steward, Cunneen, *Kings' Men*: 140-1; *ADB*, vol. 12: 81-2. The High Commission was also limited by the continuing existence of six States agents-general in London: Attard, 'Australian High Commissioners': 6.

11. Novar Papers, ANL 696/9583-5, 9675, 9702, also 12, 70, 74, 263-4, 297, 428-9; Twomey thesis, 'Australian Relationship': 76; Spartalis thesis, 'Anglo-Australian Relations': 7-9: Dunn, *Australia and Empire*: 89.

12. Munro Ferguson to Fisher, 30 Nov. 1914, ANL MS 696/3850-1.

13. Cunneen, *Kings' Men*: 122 (quotation); Edwards, *Prime Ministers and Diplomats*: 38.

14. Twomey thesis, 'Australian Relationship': 166.

15. Cunneen, *Kings' Men*: 122, 130 (quotation). Cf. Pearce papers, ANL MS 213/5/15, 18-19, 289. For later discussion, Munro Ferguson to Colonial Secretary, 17 Mar. 1916, ANL MS 696/1692-4; Scott, *Australia in the War*: 182-3.

16. ANL 696/242, 5135-5344 (Hughes' opinion can be found at 5144-5). PRO CO 616/69: 503-5 (see also CO 616/2, 20 Aug. 1914).

17. ANL MS 696/185, 208-9, 259, 768-9, 1756. A.L. Stanley to Steel Maitland, 1 June 1915, Bonar Law Papers, box 50, folder 1, item 3.

18. ANL MS 696/3328-3482; Pearce Papers, AWM 3DRL 2222, bundle 1, folder 1. Legge, Monash and White, Coulthard-Clark, *No Australian*: 101, 187, 214. Cunneen, *Kings' Men*: 124-6, 130; Robson, *First A.I.F.*: 115-17; ANL MS 696/248.

19. Cunneen, *Kings' Men*: 128.

20. Fitzhardinge, *Little Digger*: 39-40. Horne, *Search*: 60-1 gives a sympathetic portrait of Fisher as prime minister. Munro Ferguson to Bonar Law, 8 Nov. 1915, ANL MS 696/768-9.

21. Interview with Fitzhardinge, cited. Bean V: 7 comments in his usual delphic style on 'the sad, gradual collapse of Andrew Fisher's mental powers'. Munro Ferguson to Harcourt, 13 Apr. 1915, Harcourt Papers, Bodleian Library, Dep. 479.

22. Fisher to Pearce, 11 Aug., 5 Sept. 1916, Pearce Papers, AWM 3DRL 2222, folder 3. Attard thesis, 'Australian High Commissioners': 26-7.

23. Munro Ferguson to Bonar Law, 8 Nov. 1915, ANL MS 696/768-9; Fitzhardinge, *Little Digger*: 47.

24. A phrase used by W. J. Hudson in a talk in Canberra.

25. Munro Ferguson also thought that Australian public opinion was flattered by the honours to Hughes and the idea that Britain was being galvanised to action by an Australian. Cable to Bonar Law, 27 Mar. 1916, ANL MS 696/1696-7.

26. Fitzhardinge, *Little Digger*: 51. Booker, *Great Professional*: 244-8. Cablegram by Hughes, 3 May 1916, and letter Hughes to Pearce, 21 Apr. 1916, Pearce Papers, AWM 3 DRL 2222, folder 3. Hughes to Munro Ferguson, 11 Nov. 1915, ANL MS 696/3845.

27. Fitzhardinge, *Fiery Particle*: 186-96; Booker, *Great Professional*: 128-9.

28. Twomey thesis, 'Australian Relationship': 25-8; Novar Papers, 28 Mar., 19 Apr. 1916, ANL MS 696/1708, 1935-63. British regulations, PRO CO 616/3. Australian copper, PRO CO 616/49: 36.

29. Horne, *Search*: 60; Fischer, *Enemy Aliens*: 47-8; assault on German firms, Dunn, *Australia and Empire*: 90-3, Booker, *Great Professional*: 182-4, Twomey thesis, 'Australian Relationship': 61-7, Fitzhardinge, *Little Digger*: 18-26; Munro Ferguson to Bonar Law, 22 Nov. 1915, Novar Papers, ANL MS 696/766. Hughes' biographer Douglas Sladen wrote that to promote his book, *From Boundary Rider to Prime Minister*, would be to 'add votes to his movement against one-sided Free Trade for which the *Daily Mail* has been fighting for years.' Letter, 2 July 1916, Sladen Collection, SLA 70, Richmond Public Library. Spartalis thesis, 'Anglo-Australian Relations': 91-4.

30. Tsokhas, *Pastoral Lobby*: 2.
31. Twomey thesis, 'Australian Relationship': 32-3; Copland, 'Australia': 595.
32. Tsokhas, *Pastoral Lobby*: 1-20.
33. Twomey thesis, 'Australian Relationship': 29-31.
34. ibid.: 35, 67-73. Board of Agriculture, Barnett, *British Food Policy*: 60-1.
35. For New Zealand, Pfeiffer, 'Exercises': 181, 183.
36. Scott, *Australia*: 533-4. Also Copland, 'Australia': 594; Fitzhardinge, *Little Digger*: 27. Admiralty, Hughes to Balfour, 1 May 1916, Balfour Papers, British Library Add.MS 49697.
37. Scott, *Australia*: 614-18; Hughes, *Policies and Potentates*: 181-91.
38. Koss, 'Destruction': 257-77. For Kitchener's failings, Hazelhurst, *Politicians at War*: 152-5.
39. McEwen, 'Fall of Asquith': 863-83.
40. Shepherd Memoirs, AA A1632: 313.
41. Fitzhardinge, *Little Digger*: 91.
42. ibid.: 95-6, 98. Cf. Hughes to Pearce, 21 Apr. 1916, Pearce Papers, AWM 3DRL 2222, folder 3. Hughes's conversation with Lloyd George is reported in the Riddell Papers, British Library, Add.MS 62977, 10 Mar. 1916. Booker, *Great Professional*: 243.
43. Fitzhardinge, *Fiery Particle*: 187-8; interview with author, 17 Dec. 1986. He added that Megan Lloyd George had told him that Hughes and her father were not really close, because they were 'a bit too much alike'. For Hughes and Lloyd George together on a speaking tour, Lloyd George Papers, House of Lords Record Office (HLRO), D/27/2/23 and 25.
44. Fitzhardinge, *Little Digger*: 96-8, 100-2, 275-7. Cf. Bean's first draft on Hughes in England, AWM 3 DRL 6673/219. Riddell Diary, 10 Mar. 1916; Riddell, *War Diary*: 162.
45. Edwards, *Prime Ministers and Diplomats*: 33.
46. Scott, *Australia*: 329-31. Fitzhardinge, *Little Digger*: 122-6. For George V, see Stamfordham to Novar, 20 May 1916, ANL MS 696/407-8. Bonar Law Papers 50/2/3; 53/1/8 and 53/6/72. Hughes, *Policies and Potentates*: 197-8.
47. Hudson, *Billy Hughes*: 2; Fitzhardinge, *Little Digger*: 93-4. Cf. Scott, Australia: 322.
48. Fitzhardinge, *Little Digger*: 76; Spartalis, *Diplomatic Battles*: 19.
49. Fitzhardinge, *Little Digger*: 79-81. A hint of the attitudes of business in April 1916 can be seen in the Northcliffe papers, BL Add.MS 62334. For Northcliffe himself, see *Daily Mail* (overseas edn) 15 Jan., 15 Apr., 24 June 1916.
50. Walker, *Powers of the Press*: 42; Wilson, *Myriad Faces*: 401-2; Clarke, *Northcliffe Diary*: 94. McEwen, 'Fall of Asquith': 881-2; Riddell Diary, 20 Apr., 5 June 1915, Riddell Papers, BL; Pound and Harmsworth, *Northcliffe*: 487-9.
51. Wilson to Milner, 22 May 1916, quoted in Fitzhardinge, *Little Digger*: 77.
52. Hankey Diary, 25 Mar. 1916, Churchill College Archives, Cambridge, HNKY 1/1-5.
53. Semmel, *Imperialism and Social reform*: 180-5; Spartalis thesis, 'Anglo-Australian Relations': 88; Stubbs, 'Lord Milner': 717-54 (quotation 730). Also Lockwood, 'Lord Milner's entry': 120-34 (esp. 120-4). For labour attitudes, see Jauncey, *Conscription in Australia*: 132-3. Notes on the meeting of 10 May 1916, by D. Sladen, Sladen Collection, Richmond Local History Library, London (unfortunately, it is not clear whether this was a quotation from Hughes or not).
54. Stubbs, 'Lord Milner': 730.
55. *Daily Mail* (overseas edn), 29 Apr. 1916; Fitzhardinge, *Little Digger*: 79; Lockwood, 'Lord Milner's entry': 125-6; Milner to Murdoch, 29 December 1915, Murdoch Papers, ANL MS 2823, folder 1; Milner Diary, 16 Mar. 1916, Bodleian Library, Milner Papers, Dep. 87.
56. *Carnarvon Herald* and the *Western Daily Mail*, Lloyd George Papers, HLRO D27/2/23 and 25.
57. Horne, *Search*: 67; Bonar Law to Munro Ferguson, 3 June 1916, Novar Papers, ANL MS 696/1376-7; Novar papers, 696/401, 813, 1376-7, 1381.
58. Fyfe, *Northcliffe*: 200-1, implies that Northcliffe was the one who pushed the idea of Hughes as a replacement for Asquith, but adds that he could not get support for it.

59. Clarke, *Northcliffe Diary*: 94. Interview with Fitzhardinge, Aug. 1986. McEwen, 'National Press': 462–3; Spartalis thesis, 'Anglo-Australian Relations': 95–6. Fisher to Hughes, 12 June 1916, Hughes Papers, ANL MS 1538/22/10. Booker, *Great Professional*: 243.

60. Fischer, *Enemy Aliens*: 54.

61. Hughes to J. N. H. Hume Cook, quoted Fitzhardinge, *Little Digger*: 144.

62. Murdoch's support, Murdoch to Pearce, 6 Apr. 1916, Pearce Papers, AWM 3DRL 2222/7/23. Third position, Fisher to Hughes, 12 June 1916, Hughes Papers 1538/22/20. See also Fisher Papers, Churchill College Archives, Cambridge, FISR 3/12 (2682, 2684, 2716 & 2736). Hughes report, Munro Ferguson to Long, 4 Jan. 1917, Novar Papers, 696/868.

63. Fitzhardinge, *Little Digger*: 93–4; Roskill, *Hankey*: 220. For CO, PRO CO 616/69: 65–7; Bean V: 8. For self-advertisement, Murdoch to Pearce, 6 Apr. 1916, Pearce Papers, AWM 3DRL 2222/7/23.

64. Shepherd Memoirs, AA A1632, folio 321.

65. *Daily Mail* (overseas edn), 24 June, 1 July 1916. F. Faithfull to D. Sladen, 3 June 1916; Hutchinson to Sladen, 30 June 1916. Sladen Collection, Richmond Local History Library, SLA 70; Lockwood, 'Lord Milner's entry': 127; Riddell Diary, 21 May 1916, British Library; McEwen, 'Fall of Asquith'; McGill, 'Asquith's Predicament'.

66. Blake, *Unknown*: 281–2, 288–9; Horne, Search: 67; Fitzhardinge, *Little Digger*: 94.

67. Bonar Law to Buxton, 17 Aug. 1916, Davidson Papers, HLRO, 12/105/17.

68. Hughes to Peace, 24 Feb. 1916, Pearce Papers, AWM 3 DRL 2222/3/91.

69. Interview with Fitzhardinge, cited; Fitzhardinge, *Little Digger*: 103–4. *Daily Mail* (overseas edn), 21 Oct, 1916. Robertson, *Anzac and Empire*: 52.

70. Spartalis thesis, 'Anglo-Australian Relations': 98.

71. Twomey thesis, 'Australian Relationship': 110–12.

72. Fitzhardinge, *Fiery Particle*: 206–8 and *Little Digger*: 3–6; Fischer, *Enemy Aliens*: 53.

73. Horne, *Search*: 68; Sladen, *Boundary Rider* and *My Long Life*: ch. 3 (in 'Book 3'). Sladen to Murdoch, 3 May 1916, Richmond Local History Library, London, SLA 70.

74. G. Riddell, R. Donald, G. Dawson, H. A. Gwynne and Northcliffe himself. Fitzhardinge, *Little Digger*: 86.

75. Spartalis thesis, 'Anglo-Australian Relations': 90.

76. Edwards, *Prime Ministers and Diplomats*: 32.

77. Dardanelles Commission, Murdoch Papers, ANL MS 2823, folder 17. Assurance to Birdwood, 8 Apr. 1917, AWM 3DRL 3376, item 27.

78. Murdoch Papers, ANL MS 2823, folder 21.

79. Munro Ferguson to Birdwood, 12 Sept. 1918, AWM 3DRL 3376, item 30, and reply, ibid., item 34.

80. Fischer, *Enemy Aliens*: 54; Fitzhardinge, *Little Digger*: 75; Murdoch to Birdwood, 12 Feb. 1917, AWM 3DRL 3376, item 27 (see other letters on 8 Apr. and 3 July 1917).

81. McEwen, 'Fall of Asquith': 864–5. Koss, 'Destruction': 264–6; Taylor, *Beaverbrook*: 87; Stamfordham to Munro Ferguson, 1 Dec. 1916, Novar Papers 696/429.

82. Ely, 'First Anzac Day': 56; *Age*, 3 Feb. 1916: 7.

83. Buitenhuis, *Great War of Words*: xvii.

84. Kent, *'Anzac Book* and Anzac Legend': 377, 389; Masefield, *Gallipoli*. Cf. Ely, 'First Anzac Day'.

85. *Illustrated London News*, 29 Apr. 1916: 547.

86. Fisher Papers, ANL MS 2919/1; AA A 6661/1/379–80; Novar Papers, ANL MS 696/394 and 3169–72. Spartalis thesis, 'Anglo-Australian Relations': 91–4. For the Anzac Day speech, Fitzhardinge, *Little Digger*: 90 and *The Times*, 26 Apr. 1916: 2. McKernan, *The Australian People*: 120.

87. Prefect, *Hornchurch*: 171–84.

88. For Milner Papers, Bodleian Library, Dep. 42, f. 108, cf. his diary for 25 Apr. 1916, Dep. 87. Charlton, *Pozières*: 66. Cf. Horne, *Search*: 65.

89. Robertson, *Anzac and Empire*: 246; Ely, 'First Anzac Day': 56–8. *Round Table*, Mar. 1916, in Robson, *Australian Commentaries*: 47–50.

90. Fisher Papers, ANL MS 2919, series 1, folio 202.
91. Pearce to Novar, 13 May 1916, ANL MS 696/3169-72; Ely, 'First Anzac Day': 57; AA A 2601/1, item 379; Munro Ferguson to Colonial Secretary, 17 Apr. 1916, AA A6661/1/379.
92. Fisher Papers, ANL MS 2919, series 1, folio 202B; AA A6661/1/379.
93. The large number of letters from Munro Ferguson to various correspondents can be found in AA A6661/1/379 and 380; AA A2606/1, item 379; and the Novar Papers, ANL MS 696/208-9, 213–14,242, 308, 379, 3169-72.
94. Novar Papers, ANL 696/1451-2. PRO CO 616/56.
95. Bonar Law to Munro Ferguson, 20 Sept. 1916, PRO CO 616/56: 122.
96. McKernan, *The Australian People*: 120.
97. Ibid.: 120-1.
98. *Daily Telegraph* and *Daily Mail*, 26 Apr. 1916; Welborn, *Lords of Death*: 107.
99. Robertson, *Anzac and Empire*: 247.
100. AA CP 78/23 14/89/275. Munro Ferguson to Stamfordham, 1 May 1917, ANL MS 696/281.
101. Evans, *Loyalty and Disloyalty*: 39.
102. Rest, interview with Anzac veteran Harold Todd, 17 Nov. 1986; machine guns, Fitzhardinge, *Little Digger*: 114; Haig, Charlton, *Pozières*: 272.
103. Fitzhardinge, *Little Digger*: 113–20; Twomey thesis, 'Australian Relationship': 100–2. E.g. Anderson to Robertson, 28 Apr. 1917, Robertson Papers, I/37/5. Hughes, Haig and the Australian divisions, ibid., I/35/51a-b; I/35/52/1-2, 53a-b; I/22/49a-d; Kiggell Papers, V/21-22.

## CHAPTER FOUR   THE CRUCIBLE OF WAR

1. Dawnay to his wife, 6 Feb. 1916, Dawnay Papers, IWM. Robertson, *Anzac and Empire*: 105.
2. Robertson Papers, King's College, London, Feb. and Mar. 1916 and AWM 45, box 23, bundle 31.
3. Pedersen, *Monash*: 130-1.
4. White, 'Six Bob-a-Day': 122–39. The CO of the British base at Marseilles wrote to McCay on 1 July 1916 in glowing terms about the Australian 5th Division, PRO WO 95/3527.
5. Bean III: 201; AWM 45, box 23, bundle 31.
6. For the weaknesses of British public school education, Barnett, *Collapse of British Power*: 36, 43, 60. Divisional commanders in 1916 averaged fifty-two years of age. Born around 1864, their formative years were 1882-6, before the internal combustion engine. Divisional weaknesses, Graham, 'Sans Doctrine': 75-6; artillery, Bidwell and Graham, *Fire Power*.
7. AWM 41 2/6.21 (typescript of Elliott's lecture to the Canberra RSL in 1920).
8. Bean's satiric account of the different plans, Bean III: 350; loss of confidence in British reports, ibid.: 446-7. Pedersen, 'AIF': 171-2. PRO WO 95/3527 and 3623. Charlton, *Pozières*: 112, 116, 2 63; McCarthy, *Gallipoli*: 232-3. Quotation from Horne, *Search*: 70. Elliott's account is in *Duckboard*, 1 Sept. 1930. For Australian staff work and command changes, Pedersen, 'AIF': 172, 177.
9. Author's interview with Eric Cupit, 7 Apr. 1986.
10. Farrar-Hockley, *Goughie*: 188. Pedersen, 'AIF': 173-4. Author's interview with Eric Cupit, cited. Haig Diary, 28 July 1916, National Library of Scotland, 3155, No. 107. Bean, *Anzac to Amiens*: 264.
11. Charlton, *Pozières*: 292-3.
12. Bean III: 872.
13. Bean Papers, 18 Apr. 1934, 3DRL 3953/30.
14. Apart from a few additional references given in the text, the material on the two battles of Bullecourt is taken from Andrews, 'Second Bullecourt' and 'Bean and Bullecourt'.

15. Artillery weaknesses at Pozières, Charlton, *Pozières*: 72, 80, 166–8, 177–8, 185–7, 200–1.
16. 3 May 1930, AWM 3DRL 7953/34.
17. Hurley Diary, 12 Oct. 1917.
18. Hurley, quoted Souter, *Lion and Kangaroo*: 240; Liddell Hart, quoting the *English Review*, Liddell Hart Papers, I/323/20.
19. Bitter reports against the tanks, Col. D. J. C. K. Bernard to Bean, 23 Oct. 1930, AWM 3DRL 7953, item 34: also PRO WO 95/3514, 3488 and 982. Canadians and Gough, Dancocks, *Legacy of Valour*: 68, 116, 140–1. Winding the battle down, PRO WO 158/248, 30 Apr. 1917. Haig was so inaccurate in assessing the results of engagements that it strongly suggests poor intelligence work in the British GHQ.
20. Birdwood to Gough, 16 Feb. 1916, AWM 51/52: 66.
21. Gough sacked Sir George Burrow, Liddell Hart Papers, 11/1934/36. Currie, Travers, *Killing Ground*: 97.
22. Andrews, 'C. E. W. Bean' and 'Bean and Bullecourt': 32. Birdwood to Northcliffe, 17 Apr., 3 June 1917. His cheerful dismissal of losses, claim to prescience, boyish description of killing Germans and comment that 'Personally, I do not feel in the least war weary . . .' can only be described as disgusting to anyone who has studied the battles. Northcliffe Papers, BL Add.MS 62159.
23. Fitzhardinge, *Little Digger*: 268; Pedersen, 'AIF': 176; Charlton, *Pozières*: 239.
24. Robertson, *Anzac and Empire*: 34–5; Bean I: 455–61; Ashmead-Bartlett, *Uncensored Dardanelles*: 50. General Cunliffe-Owen's War Diary, PRO CAB 45/246. For Howe's opinion, letter 1/2/72 in Papers of Capt. E. W. Bush, RN, IWM 75/56/2. North, *Gallipoli*: 229–31; Keyes, 14 Dec. 1915, Keyes Papers, British Library 2/18.
25. Pedersen, 'AIF': 185; Charlton, *Pozières*: 125, 132, 177, 191, 194, 198–9, 248–9, 254.
26. Edmonds to Bean, 7 Feb. 1928, Bean Papers, AWM 3DRL 7953/34. 'Extracts from Notes on Lord Kitchener's Correspondence' 11 Jan. 1915, AWM 51, item 1A. Boyack, *Behind the Lines*: 193–4.
27. Haig Diary, 6 May 1916, NLS 3155, No. 97.
28. Roskill, *Hankey*: 257. Haig's dislike of Birdwood, Charlton, *Pozières*: 188. Cf. Haig's comment when Birdwood criticised the Light Railways and the 3rd Australian Division that this was doubtless because neither was under his orders. Haig Diary, vol. 21, 23 Oct. 1917, NLS 3155, no. 118. Birdwood's failure as an operational commander, ibid., no. 108, 2 Sept. 1916.
29. Haig Diary, NLS 3155, no. 107, 15, 22–30 July, 1 Aug. 1916 and no. 108, 2 Sept. 1916.
30. Haig Diary, NLS 3155, 30 Mar. 1917, original diary, no. 97; Charlton, *Pozières*: 266.
31. Rawlinson Diary, 2 Feb., National Army Museum, item 27; handwritten diary, 11 Dec. 1916, 13 Feb. 1917 in Churchill College, Cambridge, RWLN 1/7.
32. General Staff, War Office, *Field Service Pocket Book*, London, 1914: 224–5; Gill and Dallas, *Unknown Army*: 38; Babington, *Example*: 190–2. Cf. Crossland, 'Pity of War': 9–11. Rupprecht, Bean V: 25n; 'more rigid', Lawrence, *Mutiny*: 84–5.
33. Glenister thesis, 'Desertion': 14–19.
34. Pugsley, *Fringe of Hell*: 206–13; 'civil jurisdiction', comment by Jeffrey Grey.
35. Beddie, 'Australian Navy': 75–6. The RAN was formally placed under control of the Admiralty in August 1914. Keith, *Responsible Government*: 1011.
36. In Australia, Munro Ferguson to Birdwood, 1 Apr., 5 Sept. 1916, AWM 3DRL 3376, item 30. On voyage out, Letters and Diary of Francis Anderson, transcript: 4, and Letter 4; Gammage, *Broken Years*: 34. There were riots and destruction at Freetown, Sierra Leone, in 1916, War Memoirs of Cmdr F. Poole, IWM DS/MISC/98: 161–4. McCarthy, *Gallipoli*: 95.
37. Gill and Dallas, *Unknown Army*: 124, fn 13; Papers of E. Perriman, IWM, and W. George Meade, IWM PP/MCR/7.
38. For a balanced assessment of the Australians in attack and defence, S. Rogerson, *Reveille*, 1 Apr. 1937.
39. Thomson, 'Steadfast': 470–2; Wahlert thesis, 'Provost': 63–5; Charlton, *Pozières*: 263–5.

40. Gammage, *Broken Years*: opp. 143, 236; Pugsley, *Fringe of Hell*: 14, 25, 50, 204; Glenister thesis, 'Desertion': 25-8; Dunn, *Infantry*: 573; Fuller, *Troop Morale*: 168-9 (cf. graph in the NLS Acc 3155/122); PRO WO 93/43 is confused, but appears to mention approx. 12,500 Canadian courts martial, as compared with PRO 93/42 which mentions approx. 22,500 Australian.

41. Gill and Dallas, *Unknown Army*: 66-7, 74, 78, 80, 104. Cf. Allison and Fairly, *Monocled Mutineer*: 66-7.

42. The 1916 plan for wounded Anzacs, Birdwood to Munro Ferguson, 3 May 1916, AWM 3DRL 3376, item 32. Canadians at Shoreham, War Cabinet 231, 12 Sept. 1917, PRO CAB 23/4. Quotation, Lawrence, *Mutiny*: 86. Haig to Lady Haig, 28 Feb. 1918, Blake, *Private Papers*: 290; cf. 24 Feb. 1918, Haig Diary, vol. 25, no. 123, NLS 3155. Childs, *Episodes*: 143-4, 170.

43. Gammage, *Broken Years*: 231.

44. Pugsley, *Fringe of Hell*: 101-2.

45. Birdwood to Munro Ferguson, 4 Apr. 1917, AWM 3DRL 3376, item 33, and to Second Army, 22 May 1916, CO 616/63: Birdwood to HQ Fourth Army, 11 Dec. 1916, AA MP 367, file 403-8-354. Babington, *Example*: 191.

46. PRO CO 616/73 (170-174) and (208-213); CAB 23/1 Cab 51; cf. AWM 51/113. Birdwood to Colonial Secretary, 31 Aug. 1917, Pearce Papers, AWM 3DRL 2222, folder 3. See note on cable from Colonial Secretary, 3 Feb. 1917, AA MP 367, 403-8-354. Pugsley, *Fringe of Hell*: 132.

47. PRO CO 616/64; Hobbs to Birdwood, 19 May 1917, Pearce Papers, AWM 3DRL 2222, bundle 3, folder 6.

48. Birdwood to Dept of Defence, 18 July 1917, AWM 51/113.

49. Glenister thesis, 'Desertion': 51-2.

50. Munro Ferguson to Colonial Office, 31 Aug. 1917, AA CP 78/31; Pearce to Birdwood, Munro Ferguson Papers, 20 Sept. 1917, AWM 3DRL 606/237.

51. Charlton, *Pozières*: 266; Birdwood to Pearce, 5 Nov. 1917, AWM 3DRL 606/237; Munro Ferguson to Long, 29 Aug. 1917, ANL MS 696/956.

52. McCarthy, *Gallipoli*: 157.

53. Coulthard-Clark, 'Bridges' and *No Australian*: 98-9; Robertson, *Anzac and Empire*: 37-8.

54. Robertson Papers, I/32/15a-b, Liddell Hart Collection, King's College, London.

55. Birdwood to Fisher, 31 July, 5 Aug., 1, 9 Sept. 1916, Fisher Papers, ANL MS 2919 1/218-28, 234-5, 246, 254, 354. Hill, 'Birdwood'.

56. Kitchener Papers, PRO 30/57, 11 Apr., 29 Sept. 1915. Birdwood Papers, AWM 3DRL 3376, items 32, 46, 55. For letters to Munro Ferguson and Hughes, 15 June, 15 Aug. 1918, Walter Long Papers, PRO 947/534 (AJCP Microfilm M1114-1119 and BL Add.MS 62422). Fisher Papers, ANL MS 2919. Hankey Papers, HNKY 1/1 & 4/18, Churchill College Archives. See also letter to Pearce, 1920, over his ambition to be commander-in-chief: Pearce Papers, AWM 3DRL 2222, bundle 1, folder 1. For the governor-generalship, interview with Fitzhardinge.

57. AWM 48 2194/12, 1 June 1916.

58. Hill, *Chauvel*: 67, 72-3, 110; Hughes and Birdwood, June and July 1916, Fisher Papers, ANL MS 2919 1/205-210. Munro Ferguson to Colonial Secretary, 25 Aug. 1917, Birdwood to Defence Melbourne, 27 Aug. 1917, Birdwood Papers, India Office Library. Bean III: 145-87. See also AWM 45, box 24, bundle 132. Bean, *Two Men*: 126-30; quotation from Perry, *Commonwealth*: 154. Anderson, Charlton, *Pozières*: 275-8. The New Zealanders in London, Pugsley, *Fringe of Hell*: 148. The Canadians, Morton, 'Canadian Military Experience': 84.

59. Hill, *Chauvel*: 96-8.

60. Pedersen, *Monash*: 123-4.

61. Ibid.: 131. Pearce to Birdwood, Heydon, *Quiet Decision*: 233.

62. Hill, *Chauvel*: 157; Haig Diary, 1 Sept. 1917, vol. 20, NLS 3155, No. 117. For Perley, Bonar Law to Kitchener, 30 Dec. 1915, Robertson Papers, I/22/5/4a-b.

63. Long to Munro Ferguson, 11 Aug. 1917, AWM 45, box 23, bundle 31.

64. McCay to Munro Ferguson, 1 Dec. 1915, Davidson Papers, HLRO, 17. Pearce to Munro Ferguson, 18 Dec. 1915, Novar Papers, ANL MS 696/3415-6.
65. Birdwood to Col. Fitzgerald, 7 Feb. 1916, Kitchener Papers, PRO 30/57; Robertson to Murray, 24 Feb. 1916, Robertson Papers, King's College, I/32/7a; Birdwood to Munro Ferguson, 24 Mar. 1916, 6 Aug. 1918, AWM 3DRL 3376, items 26A & 32; Birdwood to Murdoch, 26 Aug. 1916, 15 July 1917, Murdoch Papers, ANL MS 2823.
66. Birdwood to Hughes, 15 Aug. 1918, Pearce Papers, AWM 3 DRL 2222, folder 10.
67. Bean V: 6-8.
68. Bean Diary, AWM 3DRL 606/47: 38-9, Bean V: 8. Bean to Lloyd George, 15 July 1917, AWM 3DRL 606/82. Fisher to Hughes, 13 July 1917, Murdoch to Hughes, 7, 26 and 30 Aug., Murdoch Papers, ANL MS 2823, folder 34. Hughes to Haig, 16 June 1916, AWM 45, box 23, bundle 31. The Wigram–Murdoch approach to Kiggell can be found in the Robertson Papers, V/117-8, 121, 123.
69. Nos. 1-4 AFC were known as nos. 67, 68, 69 and 71 (Australian) squadrons, Coulthard-Clark thesis, 'Australia's Air Defence': 6. The navy, perhaps not unexpectedly, was the most 'imperial' of all the services. Australians in the navy were regarded as Englishmen and if they stayed, were as liable to settle in England as return to Australia. See papers of Capt. E. W. Bush, IWM 75/65/1.
70. Hill, Chauvel: 110-11, 118-19.
71. Bean Diary, 5 Nov. 1917, AWM 606/93; Long to Munro Ferguson, 12 Sept. 1917, Birdwood Papers, India Office Library, MS Eur.D 686/57.
72. Birdwood to Munro Ferguson, 9 Sept. 1917, AWM 3DRL 2574, item 13; Pearce to Hughes, 24 Sept. 1917, Pearce Papers, AWM 3DRL 2222, bundle 6, item 16. Munro Ferguson to Colonial Secretary, 26 Sept. 1917, Birdwood Papers, India Office Library, MS Eur.D 686/57. See also cables May to September 1917, and Birdwood Papers, AWL 3DRL 3376, items 25, 26A and 32. Bean V: 11.
73. Long to Munro Ferguson, 5 Oct. 1917; Haig to War Office, 19 Oct. 1917. AWM 45, box 23, bundle 31.
74. Hughes to Lloyd George, PRO Cab 261(a) CAB 23/4; Bean V: 8-13; PRO: Cab 261(a), 262(2) and 269(a), Cab 271 (9 and App.I) CAB 23/4.
75. Lord Derby to Haig, 9 Nov. 1917, Haig Diary, vol. 22, no. 119, NLS 3155.
76. War Office to Haig, 2 Dec. 1917, AWM 45, box 23, bundle 31; CO 616/74 and 77.

## CHAPTER FIVE   THE END OF EUPHORIA

1. PRO CO 616/55: 215 and 255. Pearce to Fisher, 26 July 1916, Fisher Papers, ANL MS 2919, MS 2919/1/216-7. Robertson, Anzac and Empire: 228; Australian Archives (AA), CP78 23/1 14/18/349 dated 26 and 30 July 1916. White to Murdoch, 7 Aug. 1916, Murdoch Papers, ANL MS 2823, folder 17. Age and Argus, 31 July 1916.
2. Robertson, Anzac and Empire: 227, 231.
3. ibid.: 230-41, 244; Pugsley, Gallipoli: 349; Murdoch Papers, 5 Feb. 1917, ANL MS 2823, folder 17.
4. Pfeiffer, 'Exercises': 180.
5. Charlton, Pozières: 271; Evans, Loyalty and Disloyalty: 40-1; Horne, Search: 74. See Sir John Madden's threat of conscription in a recruiting speech, Age, 3 Feb. 1916: 7.
6. Price controls, Horne, Billy Hughes: 64; duchessing, Gilbert thesis, 'The Churches': 27-8; Fischer, Enemy Aliens: 56 (quotation); Anstey, Fitzhardinge, Little Digger: 32-3; quotation, Glenister thesis, 'Desertion': 42.
7. Cunneen, Kings' Men: 131; Santamaria, Mannix: 77, fns 6-8.
8. For Britain, Blake, Unknown: 282-5; CAB 42/1/7,13, 20-2, PRO CO 616/49: 605. For Hughes and Australia, Shepherd Memoirs, AA A1632, folio 318; Hughes to Pearce, 11 May, and Pearce to Hughes, 11 July 1916, Pearce Papers, AWM 3DRL 2222, folder 3.
9. Fitzhardinge, Little Digger: 193.

10. Charlton, *Pozières*: 279-80; Spartalis thesis, 'Anglo-Australian Relations': 128-30. The most convincing account is that of Fitzhardinge, *Little Digger*: 182, 184-5, 198; Bean III: 866. Hughes' cables, 19 Aug., 4, 12, 19 Sept. 1916, AA CP 78/31.

11. Robertson to Murdoch, 26 Aug., 23 Oct. 1916, Murdoch Papers, ANL MS 2823, file 52.

12. Messages 2, 7, 8 Sept., Kiggell Papers V/37-8; Haig Diary, 16 Oct. 1916, vol II, NLS 3155, no. 108; Murdoch to Hughes, 24 Oct. 1916, Murdoch Papers, ANL MS 2823, file 52. For Birdwood and the reaction to speeches, Charlton, *Pozières*: 283-5. He is mistaken in writing that Birdwood had no authority to postpone the referendum among the troops; he was requested to do so by Hughes. See 16 Oct. 1916, Birdwood Papers, IWM WRB/1, and a fuller collection in AWM 3DRL 3376 items 27, 30, 74.

13. Murdoch to Lloyd George, 23 Oct. 1916, Lloyd George Papers, E/4/2/12; to Bonar Law, 20 Nov. 1916, ibid., E/2/17/3b-c; and to Hughes, Charlton, *Pozières*: 286. Charlton writes that 'Hughes lied' about the suppression being the result of a request by the British, but it is more likely to have been Murdoch's doing than Hughes'. British suspicion of Murdoch, see Lloyd George Papers, HLRO E/2/17/3 & 3a. George V, Stamfordham to Davidson, 30 Oct. 1916, Davidson Papers, HLRO.

14. Lloyd George supports Hughes, Fitzhardinge, *Little Digger*: 207. Murdoch to Hughes, Birdwood to Murdoch, 3, 8 Nov. 1916, Murdoch Papers, ANL MS 2823, file 23; For the governor-general, Cunneen, *Kings' Men*: 131-40; Novar Papers, ANL MS 696/9764-9847.

15. Murdoch had even had the British approach the French for a suitable message in an interview with himself. Hardinge to Lloyd George, 17 Oct. 1916, Lloyd George Papers, HLRO E/2/13/9.

16. Gilbert thesis, 'The Churches': 41. Hughes to Bonar Law, 6 Nov. 1916, Bonar Law Papers, box 53, folder 4, item 15.

17. Colonial Secretary and Hughes, 10, 11 Nov, 1916, AA CP 78/31; Robson, *Australian Commentaries*: 75.

18. Canada, Brown and Loveridge, 'Unrequited Faith': 60. Australia, PRO CO 616/70/224. Haig hoped Australian reinforcements would be maintained, Haig Diary, 17 Mar. 1917, (TS) NLS 3155, No. 111, while the British Cabinet got Lloyd George to send an appeal to Hughes for more troops, PRO Cab 378(5) CAB 23/5. Hughes and the peace conference, 10 Aug. 1917, AA CP 78/31.

19. Cab 172 (1 & App.I) and 187 (18) CAB 23/3.

20. PRO CO 616/70/381.

21. Pearce to Birdwood and reply, 9 Nov. 1917, Pearce Papers, AWM 3DRL 2222, bundle 1, folder 3.

22. Scott, *Australia in the War*: 579 for the figures; Gilbert thesis, 'The Churches': 42.

23. Murdoch to Birdwood, 27 Dec. 1917, Murdoch Papers, ANL MS 2823, folder 21; and analysis, end 1917, AWM 3DRL 3376, item 27.

24. Stamfordham to Munro Ferguson, 1 Dec. 1916; Munro Ferguson to Long, 2 Mar. 1917, Novar Papers, ANL MS 696/426-7, 886-7.

25. The comparison between Lloyd George and Hughes was made often by Stamfordham: see letter to Munro Ferguson, 21 Mar. 1917, Novar Papers, ANL MS 696/438-9.

26. Cunneen, *Kings' Men*: 133; for a bitter cable from the governor-general, Munro Ferguson to Stamfordham, 10 Nov. 1916, Novar Papers, ANL MS 696/252-3. Quotation, Fitzhardinge, *Little Digger*: 230.

27. Evans, *Loyalty and Disloyalty*: 141.

28. Gilbert thesis, 'The Churches': 46.

29. Ibid.: 48-58, 127, and 'Protestants': 20-5; Robson, *Australian Commentaries*: 5, 61.

30. Fitzhardinge, *Little Digger*: 262; Evans, *Loyalty and Disloyalty*: 100-1, 140, 149-50, 172-3.

31. Welfield, 'Labour Party'.

32. Gilbert, 'Conscription Referenda': 56; McKernan, *Australian People*: 19, 32, 44; Gilbert thesis, 'The Churches': 137; Santamaria, *Mannix*: 82-3.

33. Hunt and Thomas, *God, King and Country*: 15-16: Evans, *Loyalty and Disloyalty*: 89-90; Gilbert, 'Conscription Referenda': 66, 168-71; 'Protestants': 16-17, and thesis, 'The Churches': 140-55.

34. McKernan, *Australian People*: 32; Gilbert, 'Protestants': 19, and thesis 'The Churches': 157-61; Santamaria, Mannix: 79-81.

35. Munro Ferguson to Colonial Secretary, 12, 19 Sept. 1916, AA CP 78/31; Robson, *First A.I.F.*: 91-3.

36. See letters 7, 17 May, Lloyd George Papers, HLRO D/14/1/1-2. Pearce to Hughes, 30 June 1916, Pearce Papers, AWM 3DRL 2222, folder 3.

37. Fitzhardinge, *Little Digger*: 217.

38. Hughes to Lloyd George, 29 Dec. 1916, Novar Papers, ANL MS 696/1389-91; Lloyd George to Hughes, 18 Jan. 1917, Lloyd George Papers, HLRO F/32/4/22; cf. Kerr to Lloyd George 13 Jan. 1917, ibid., F/89/1/1. For impracticability, see Stamfordham to Munro Ferguson, 23 Jan. 1917, Novar Papers, ANL MS 696/431-3.

39. 8 Mar. 1917, Lloyd George Papers, HLRO F/32/4/48.

40. Hughes to Murdoch, 12 Mar. 1917, Murdoch Papers, ANL MS 2823, folder 33, HLRO F/28/2/1. J. H. Davies, Lloyd George's secretary, and others, thought Hughes would be helpful: see Spartalis thesis, 'Anglo-Australian Relations': 160, and 'WS' to Lloyd George, 19 Feb. 1917, Lloyd George Papers, HLRO F/93/2/1.

41. Santamaria, *Mannix*: 97-100. Tortuous negotiations went on between the Vatican, the British government, and Hughes, over the right of Mannix to have a personal cypher. Gilchrist, *Danniel Mannix*: 71.

42. Murdoch to Lloyd George, 29 Apr. 1917, Lloyd George Papers, HLRO F/94/1/87.

43. Scott, *Australia in the War*: 493; Twomey thesis, 'Australian Relationship': 136-7.

44. Cable, 8 Jan. 1917, AA CP78/31; correspondence 13, 16, 18, 19 Jan., 1, 2, & 10 Mar. 1917, in Walter Long Papers, 497/507, 17, 21 September 1917, ibid., 563. Stamfordham to Munro Ferguson, 23 Jan. 1917, Hughes to Munro Ferguson, 19 Feb. 1918, Novar Papers, ANL MS 696/431-3, 2697.

45. Memorandum by Sir Robert Garran at the peace conference, AA CP 351/1, bundle 1/16. For Watt's speech, Crowley, *Modern Australia*: 306-7.

46. Cables 22, 26 Jan. 1918, PRO CO 616/77; ammunition, Bean Diary, 26 June 1918, AWM 3DRL 606/116.

47. Twomey thesis, 'Australian Relationship': 138-41.

48. Scott, *Australia in the War*: 535-9, 588-92, 622-4, cf. PRO Cab 62, CAB 23/1 and Cab 283, CAB 23/4; Cab 355 CAB 23/5. Twomey thesis, 'Australian Relationship': 123, 141-4, 161-7, 187-9.

49. Attard thesis, 'Australian High Commissioners': 4-5.

50. Fitzhardinge, *Little Digger*: 155, 162-70, and 'Australia, Japan and Great Britain': *passim*. Spartalis, *Diplomatic Battles*: 7, 9, 11-15 (Montagu quotation: 12) and thesis 'Anglo-Australian Relations': 47-64, 148, 150-3, 156-8. See also Nish, *Alliance in Decline*: 143-7; Robertson, *Anzac and Empire*: 24-6; Scott, *Australia in the War*: 574-5, 766-7; Twomey thesis, 'Australian Relationship': 23, 44-7, 79-83, 103-5, 145-8, 181-3.

51. In Canada, Borden wrote that he could not 'willingly accept the position of ... receiving no more consideration than if we were toy automata'—though on second thoughts he cancelled the letter: Morton, *Military History*: 145. See also Bonar Law welcoming Andrew Fisher as new Australian High Commissioner, *Daily Mail* (overseas edn), 5 Feb. 1916. *The Times*, 14 Sept. 1915; Bonar Law, *Daily Mail* (overseas edn), 18 Mar. 1916; Guinn, *British Strategy*: 192-3, 197.

52. Cabinet meetings, 19, 22 Dec. 1916, PRO CAB 23/1; Morton, *Canada and War*: 70. Confused terminology and motives, Amery Diary, 26 Dec. 1918; Barnes and Nicholson, *Leo Amery Diaries*: 135-9, 141. *Round Table*, 27, June 1917: 605, 608; Keith, *Responsible Government*: 1193-4, 1196; Fitzhardinge, *Little Digger*: 250; Lloyd George, *Memoirs*: 1024-6; *Daily Mail* (overseas edn), 3 Feb. 1917.

53. Fitzhardinge, *Little Digger*: 250-5, 260-2; AA CP 78/31; Twomey thesis, 'Australian Relationship': 134; Hughes to Lloyd George, 29 Dec. 1916, Novar Papers, ANL MS

696/1389-91. Distrust of Fisher, Hughes and Murdoch, 3 Sept., 22 Nov. 1917, Murdoch Papers, ANL MS 2823, folder 33.

54. 16 Mar., 22 May 1917, Cabs 98 and 142, CAB 23/2; Minutes of 1st meeting, 20 Mar. 1916, CAB 23/40. Amery Diary, 2, 16 Mar. 1917. Barnes and Nicholson, *Amery Diaries*, vol. 1: 157. Stamfordham to Munro Ferguson 5 Apr. 1917, Novar Papers, ANL MS 696/444.

55. Cook, 'Borden': 379.

56. Brown, *Borden*: 80; Lloyd George, *Memoirs*: 1036, 1045. Smuts, Keith, *Responsible Government*: 1197-8; Imperial War Cabinets 30 Mar., 5, 26 Apr., PO CAB 23/40.

57. PRO CAB 21/77. Massey, 2 May 1916, PRO CAB 23/40. Hughes' frantic cable to Britain, 10 Dec. 1917, demanding firm adherence to Lloyd George's win-the-war policy, when Trotsky produced peace proposals, PRO CO 616/70: 431.

58. War Cabinet 227, 3 Sept. 1917, CAB 23/4; Amery to Hughes, 12 Oct. 1917, Barnes and Nicholson, *Amery Diaries*: 173-4; Walter Long Papers, 597/555.

59. AA A2911/1 1640/14C.

60. Robertson, *Anzac and Empire*: 177; PRO CO 616/3 & 77, CO 537/1140.

61. Cain, *Origins*: 106-7; Fischer, *Enemy Aliens*: 46. The *War Precautions Act*, Scott, *Australia in the War*: 570-3. Evans, *Loyalty and Disloyalty*: 32.

62. Ibid.: 39.

63. Robertson, *Anzac and Empire*: 131-3, 165-9, 171, 175, 187-9. Complaints about the censorship, Souter, *Company*: 116-17.

64. Bonar Law to Hughes, 9 Oct. 1915, AA CP 78/31; Scott, *Australia in the War*: 92; Evans, *Loyalty and Disloyalty*: 39.

65. *Round Table*, 27, June 1917: 611.

66. Evans, *Loyalty and Disloyalty*: 59. Postcards, Laffin, *World War I*; 'corpse factory', PRO CO 616/69: 213-4. Film propaganda, Reeves, *Propaganda*. Unfortunately it is not clear how many of the films were shown in Australia, and to what audiences. See photograph in Bassett, *Home Front*. Censorship of films, Evans, *Loyalty and Disloyalty*: 33.

67. Evans, *Loyalty and Disloyalty*: 32-3; Taylor, 'Smug-faced Crowds': 90-1; Marwick, *The Deluge*: 44-5, 47, 51, 212. Cavell, Robertson, *Anzac and Empire*: 163.

68. Buitenhuis, *Great War of Words*: xvi, 90-2, Grieves, 'Early Historical Responses'.

69. *Anzac Book*, Winter, '*Anzac Book* and Anzac Legend': 58-60; Bonar Law, PRO CO 616/67: 520-36.

70. Moses, 'Academic Garrison': 368. Cf. his 'Ideological Conflict', 'Ideas of 1914', and *Prussian German Militarism*. To the present author Moses seems to accept the Fischer thesis a little too completely, and his emotive language ('Kultur' etc.) and the comparison of Wilhelmine Germany with 'life under a communist dictatorship' (*Prussian German Militarism*: 23) is not dispassionate enough. He seems to have mistaken the anti-German propaganda of 1914-18 for absolute truth. Crawford, *Bit of a Rebel*. For Scott, Evans, *Loyalty and Disloyalty*: 2; for Strong, ibid., and Moses, 'Academic Garrison': 367; Robson, *Australian Commentaries*: 45; C. R. Bald in *Australian Quarterly*, 15 Dec. 1930.

71. Dawes and Robson, *Citizen to Soldier*: 55.

72. Murdoch confidential notes, end 1917, AWM 3DRL 3376, item 27.

73. Walker, *Newspaper Press*: 250. For difficulties in getting the newspapers to brave the censorship and criticise the government, Ashmead-Bartlett, *Uncensored Dardanelles*: 256.

74. Munro Ferguson to Birdwood 12 Sept. 1918, AWM 3DRL 3376, item 30.

75. 15 Nov, 1915, PRO CO 616/32: 156.

76. *Daily Mail* (overseas edn), 13 Feb. 1915, 15 Jan. 1916. 'Heroic' language, see Northcliffe's account of a visit to the Australians, ibid., 9 Sept. 1916; Novar Papers, ANL MS 696/80-81.

77. Riddell Diary, 23 May 1917, BL Add.MS 62979: 90. *Daily Mail* (overseas edn), 26 May, 6 Oct. 1917; Murdoch letters, 22 Aug., 11 Sept., 25 Oct., 19 Dec. 1917, Murdoch Papers, ANL MS 2823.

## CHAPTER SIX    ANZACS AND BRASSHATS

1. Pedersen, 'AIF': 181–2. Pugsley, *Fringe of Hell*: 190. Haig, Kiggell to Plumer, 17 June 1917, GHQ Correspondence, AWM 51, item 53.
2. Birdwood to Second Army, 8 Oct. 1917, ibid., folio 289; Pedersen, 'AIF': 179–83.
3. Birdwood to Haig, 23 Dec. 1917 and Birdwood to Wigram, 5 Jan. 1918, AWM 45, box 23, bundle 31. For the move to disband the battalions, Bean VI: 935–40.
4. Morton, 'Sovereign Allies': 61–5.
5. Bean V: 18.
6. Moore, *See How They Ran*. Panic in London, Hankey Diary, 25 Mar. 1918, Churchill College Archives, HNKY 1/4. The French complained about the collapse of morale in the Fifth Army: Joynt, *Channel Ports*: 3. For Haig's pessimism, Travers, *How the War Was Won*: 67–70. See Gough's statistics on length of front and German divisions against him, in letter to Long, 1918, Walter Long Papers, BL Add.MS 62423.
7. Bean Diary, 30 May 1918, AWM 3DRL 606/113.
8. Note (n.d.) between 11 June and 12 July 1918, Murdoch Papers, ANL MS 2823, folder 34. Lt Stanforth Smith to Pearce, 6 Feb. 1918, Pearce Papers, AWM 3DRL 2222, folder 10.
9. Andrews, 'The Media'. See also Hughes Papers, ANL MS 1538/23, folios 77, 80–2 and 103–13. For Monash, Godley to Pearce, 11 Dec. 1916 and 12 June 1917, Pearce Papers, AWM 3DRL 2222, bundle 6, no. 51. Murdoch's disillusionment with White, Murdoch to Bean, 12 July 1918, Murdoch Papers, ANL MS 2823, folder 34. For a gross underestimation of Monash, see Murdoch to Hughes, 23 Dec. 1917, ibid., folder 33. Fisher, Attard thesis, 'Australian High Commissioner's': 27. Birdwood to Batterby, 10 June 1918, Walter Long Papers 947/534(A). Watt to Hughes, 24 May 1918, AA CP 360/8 Bundle 1/1.
10. Souter, *Lion and Kangaroo*: 267; Cutlack, *War Letters*: 245–8. Monash to his wife, 30 Sept. 1916, Monash Papers, AWM MS 1884, folder 95, box 128; Pedersen, 'AIF': 186.
11. Hughes to Australian Cabinet, 1 Aug. 1918, AA A6006 1918/8/7.
12. Long to Munro Ferguson, 26 Aug. 1918, Novar Papers, ANL 696/1510; various correspondence in the Walter Long Papers, June–Aug. 1918, PRO 947/534.
13. Morton, 'Canadian Military Experience': 87, 89 and 'Exerting Control'; Dancocks, *Legacy of Valour*: 156, 223. Haig Diary, (TS) NLS 3155, 18 Apr. 1918, vol. 28. no. 126; 5 May 1918, vol. 29, no. 127; 6 May, 19 July 1918, vol. 30, no. 128. Blake, *Private Papers*: 303–4.
14. Quotation, Liddell Hart's review of Bean V in *Daily Telegraph* (London), 23 Sept. 1937, Liddell Hart Papers 10/1937/105. Dour orders and 'Tails up', Diary of Capt. A. M. McGrigor (ADC to Birdwood), 14, 27 Mar., 7 Apr. 1918, IWM. For assurance, see arrival of Monash at the Chateau of Montigny, Moore, *See How They Ran*: 168.
15. Ibid.: 235–6.
16. Montgomery-Massingberd, *Fourth Army*: 5–6.
17. Andrews, 'Hamel'; PRO Cab 441 (1) CAB 23/7, and IWC 24 (3) CAB 23/41: Pedersen, 'AIF': 188–90, cf. Blaxland, *Amiens*: 181; Montgomery-Massingberd, *Fourth Army*: 20–65; Terraine, *To Win a War*: 129, 150; Essame, quoted in Wilson, *Myriad Faces*: 599. For the losses of the German army, Travers, *How the War Was Won*: 154.
18. Souter, *Lion and Kangaroo*: 240; Bean VI: 1078; Ashmead-Bartlett, *Australians in Action*: 8; Cutlack, *War Letters*: 242.
19. Gammage, *Broken Years*: 200, 204, 226–8.
20. Knightley, 'Murdoch's'; Gerster, *Big Noting*: 74; Thomson, 'Steadfast': 464, 466, 471–2, 474, 477; and Gough, 'First Australian'. Ellis thesis, 'C.E.W. Bean': 135–43 analyses Bean's claim for country influences, and decides that Bean himself realised its weakness, but remained confused in his argument. Alistair Thomson's review of Fewster's *Gallipoli Correspondent* in *Historical Studies*, 21, 1984: 147–8 and Kent, 'Anzac Book and Anzac Legend': 377.
21. Morton, 'Canadian Military Experience' and Travers 'Comment' in it: 132. The year however is significant—the Australians were to come into their own later, in 1918.

22. Hurley Diary, 27 Oct. 1917, ANL 833/5.
23. 13 June, 30 Aug. 1917, AWM 45, box 24, bundle 32, box 23, bundle 30. For Bullecourt, Bean IV: 483, 487–8, 501.
24. Nicholson, *Behind the Lines*: 223; cf. Allenson Diary, 16–17 Feb. 1917, IWM.
25. For eagerness to learn, see Bean, 'Sidelights': 218–20. For the easier time in the Middle East, see Hurley, who was in both theatres of war, Diary, 31 Dec. 1917: 129.
26. Bean, letter to *The Times*, 19 Aug. 1918: 9.
27. See Casey Diary ANL MS 6150, series 4, Mar. 1917, for unrealistic training in Egypt. Cf. Monash to wife, 27 July 1917, ANL MS 1884, box 128, folder 945.
28. Edmonds to Bean, 7 Feb., 8 Aug. 1928, Bean Papers, AWM 3DRL 7953/34.
29. Bean Diary, 29 Sept. 1918, quoted Winter, *Making the Legend*: 221; Bean, 'Sidelights': 211; Bean and Edmonds, 17 Sept., 2 Oct. 1935, AWM 3DRL 7953/30.
30. Spears, *Prelude*: 480.
31. Quotation, F. C. Penny Papers, 1916, IWM; artillery officer, Bean Diary, 28 Apr. 1917, AWM 3DRL 606/77.
32. Travers, 'Could the Tanks': 398, cf. 124–5, 401–2. 'Finest fighters', ibid,: 126.
33. Pedersen, 'AIF': 192; Terraine, *To Win a War*: 186. For Rawlinson, Letters and circulars, Aug. 1918, e.g. letter to Clive Wigram, 20 Sept., Rawlinson Papers, National Army Museum 5201-33, items 20, 77; letter to the Australian Corps, 14 Oct. 1918, Rawlinson Papers, Churchill College RWLN 1/12.
34. Blaxland, *Amiens*: 243. Cf. Rawlinson to GHQ, 19 Sept. 1918, AWM 51, item 56. For prisoners, on 11 July four Australians on patrol near Merris captured 30–40 Germans: Boraston, *Despatches*: 251.
35. There are gaps in the surviving records for the Bullecourt period, which are shoddily kept. The contrast with those in 1918 is extreme. AWM 4/13/4. But Australian staff work still needs to be analysed.
36. See Maj.-Gen. G. H. N. Jackson, 4 Oct. 1935, Liddell Hart Papers, I/516; Pedersen, 'AIF': 180; Callinan, *Monash*: 12–13; Serle, *John Monash* and 'Monash'; Pedersen, *Monash*.
37. Dancocks, *Legacy of Valour*: 99–100.
38. Pedersen, 'AIF': *passim*.
39. Nicholson, *Behind the Lines*: 21–2, 163; Moore, *See How They Ran*: 194.
40. Stamfordham to Novar, 11 Dec. 1917, Novar Papers, ANL 696/467. For the Highland Division, Autobiography of Major-General Douglas Wimberley, Churchill College Archives, WIMB vol.I.
41. At Amiens, Morton, *Canada and War*: 79.
42. Quoted from Dancocks, *Legacy of Valour*: 102–3.
43. Morton, *Canada and War*: 64–6, and 'Canadian Military Experience': 88–9, 92.
44. E.g. Autobiography of Major-General Douglas Wimberley, 24 July 1916, Churchill College Archives, WIMB vol.I: 50.
45. For the weeding out of the unfit, see Pilger, 'The other "Lost Generation" '.
46. Barrett, *Falling In*: 159, 258–9.
47. White, 'Soldier as Tourist': *passim*; Prior, 'Suvla Bay': 33; Gough, 'First Australian': 44.
48. Papers of O. S. Blows, IWM; Denton, *Gallipoli*: 29; *Stand To*, quoted in Giles, *Flanders*: 179; Bean V: 16–18; Cupit MS: 9.
49. Denton, *Gallipoli*: 30.
50. *Daily Mail* (overseas edn), 24 July 1915, refers to Scots, north countrymen and miners.
51. Fuller, *Troop Morale*: 124–5, 133–4, 140–2; Bean, 'Sidelights': 221–3.
52. Fuller, *Troop Morale*: 45, 149–50, 161; Gough, 'First Australian': 46–8; Nicholson, *Behind the Lines*: 294; Woodward, *Great Britain*: xviii; Richards, *Old Soldiers*: 42; A. E. Perriman, TS: 8, IWM; Gough, 'First Australian': 46–7.
53. Adam-Smith, *Anzacs*: 319–21. Cf. Bean VI: 932–4, 940.
54. *CPD*, 85, 26 Sept. 1918: 6425–40.
55. PRO CO 616/77 and 79.
56. One of them had murdered another Australian. See Milner to Hughes, 14 Dec. 1918, Bodleian Library, Milner Adds C696, folio 161; cf. CO 616/79.

57. AWM 51/113.

58. Glenister thesis, 'Desertion': 28.

59. Haig Diary, 7 Sept. 1918, vol. 32, NLS Acc 3155, no. 131.

60. Roskill, *Hankey*: 257.

61. Hamilton to Kitchener, 3 June 1915, PRO 30/57 62/WL48; Butler, 'Memoirs', IWM PP MCR 107; Keyes to his wife, 3 May, 26 June, 29 July 1915, Keyes Papers, BL 2/11, 12 and 13 (though he bitterly criticised them for leaving stores behind for the Turks, ibid. 2/18); Memoirs of Maj.-Gen Lord Burnham, 1 Aug., 8, 19 Sept. 1915, IWM; Esher Diary, 27 July 1916, Churchill Archives ESHR 2/16.

62. Monash quoted in Terraine, *Douglas Haig*: 217; Liddell Hart in a review of Bean V, London *Daily Telegraph*, 23 Sept. 1937.

63. Egypt: Birdwood and Hamilton to Kitchener, Kitchener Papers, PRO 30/57, 61–WL17, 63–WL94 and 63–WL102. For Birdwood, Haig to Lady Haig, 28 Feb. 1918, Blake, *Private Papers*: 290.

64. Birdwood's attitude to discipline, Birdwood to Bridges, 27 Dec. 1914, Pearce Papers, 3DRL 2222, bundle 3, folder 6; Birdwood to Pearce, 9 Nov. 1917, AWM 3DRL 606/237; and circular to all divisional generals 21 May 1918, urging them to watch for battle trauma, Fisher Papers, ANL MS 2919, 1/458. Current attitudes, Ross, *Myth of the Digger*: 55.

65. E.g. Monash's flat refusal to allow a search of his troops' property to see if they had been looting, Monash to DA and QMG, 11 May 1918, AWM 3DRL 2316/27. Bean Diary, 4 June 1918, AWM 3DRL 606/116. Improvement in Anzac discipline, Diary of Capt. A. M. McGrigor, 26 Aug. 1917, IWM.

66. Monash, *Australian Victories*: 300; Bean to Street, 3 Nov. 1939, AA A5954, box 260.

67. Richards, *Old Soldiers*: 315; Sheffield, 'Effect': 88–9.

68. Fuller, *Troop Morale*: 51, 150; Canadian nurse, Lawrence, *Mutiny*: 88. Maj.-Gen. S. S. Butler, 'Memoirs', IWM PP MCR 107—emphasis in original.

69. Haig Diary, vol. 19, 2 and 29 Aug. 1917, NLS 3155, no. 116.

70. Morton, *Canada and War*: 133.

71. Rawlinson's shrewd assessment of GHQ, Diary, 13 Jan., 14 Feb. 1918, Churchill Archives, RWLN 1/9; concern about the use of tanks, 21–28 June RWLN 1/11. For his noting the increased firepower available to the infantry, and its effect on tactics, 17 June 1918, Rawlinson papers, National Army Museum, 5201–22–77. The brilliant maps that Fourth Army brought out under Rawlinson can be seen in the Montgomery-Massingberd Papers, King's College, London.

72. Haig Diary, 1 July 1918, Blake, *Private Papers*: 316; Terraine, *Haig*: 215. Fourth Army no. 45/26 (G) 17/7/18, 'Operations by the Australian Corps against Hamel, Bois de Hamel and Bois de Vaire, July 4th 1918', Rawlinson Papers, 529–33, item 77. Haig on air power at Hamel, PRO WO 158/252. Rawlinson and Mont St Quentin, Liddell Hart, obituary on Monash, *Daily Telegraph* (London) 9 Oct. 1931.

73. Letter to the *Listener*, 10 July 1939, Liddell Hart Papers 6/1939/1. Liddell Hart, 8 Apr. 1943, Lloyd George Papers, HLRO G/9/3/85.

74. Rawlinson Diary, Churchill College, Cambridge, RWLN 1/9 (esp. 14, 25 Apr. 1918), RWLN 1/11 (24 May, 8 Aug.), and RWLN 1/12. See also the Rawlinson diary kept in the National Army Museum 5201–33, esp. 5, 15 April. For Haig and Rawlinson's valedictory order to the Australians, RWLN 1/11, 31 Oct. 1918.

75. Haig Diary, NLS 3155, 17 May 1918 (vol. 29, no. 127), 31 July 1918 (vol. 31, no. 129). Monash to BGGS, 8 July 1918, AWM 26, box 361, item 3. Quotation, Haig Diary, 12 July 1918 (no. 129). This has a style and quality that suggests it originated in the Fourth Army.

76. Montgomery-Massingberd, *Fourth Army*: 28, 334–5, map 19.

77. Terraine, *First World War*: 151, 177; *White Heat*: 137. Keith *Responsible Government*: 990, gives the proportion of casualties to men sent overseas as Britain 43 per cent, Canada 44.88 per cent, New Zealand 50.7 per cent and Australia 63.36 per cent.

78. Haldane, 5 Aug. 1914, PRO CAB 22/1/1. Comparison of enlistments: in the British Isles the percentage of the male population which had enlisted was 16.08;

Canada 9.6; Australia 10.7; New Zealand 11.9 and South Africa 1.7. (Cabinet 41, 23 January 1917, PRO CAB 23/1). Cf. Twomey thesis, 'Australian Relationship': 150. Praise for Gallipoli, Kitchener in the House of Lords, 15 Sept. 1915, Pearce Papers, AWM 3DRL 2222, bundle 6, no. 51.

79. Graham, 'Sans Doctrine': 89.
80. Charteris, *At G.H.Q.*: 245.
81. Bean Papers, AWM 3DRL 8042/67. Birdwood argued that the Anzacs did not need publicity, AWM 3DRL 3376, item 34.
82. The correspondence with Bean can be found in AWM 3DRL 6673/195. For the press see Rawlinson Papers, n.d. but probably August, Churchill College RWLN 1/10.
83. For Gallipoli, *Daily Mail* (overseas edn), 5 Jan., 14 Sept. 1918. Cf. Murdoch letters, 23 Apr., 8 May, 10 July 1918, Murdoch Papers, ANL MS 2823.
84. Bean VI: 876-7; for Monash's role, see letter to his wife, Cutlack, *War Letters*: 267-8; McMullin, *Will Dyson*: 175.
85. Long to Birdwood, 23 Oct.; Birdwood to Long, 26 Oct. 1918, Walter Long Papers, AJCP Mf M1114-1119. Cabinet discussion, 24 Oct. 1918, PRO Cab 460(6) CAB 23/8.
86. Haig Diary, 25 Oct. 1918, MS copy, NLS 3155.
87. C. H. Harrington to Edmonds, 15 Dec. 1932, AWM 3DRL 7953/34.
88. Haig Diary (orig.), 20 Apr. 1917, NLS 3155, no. 97; cf. plan of divisional usage at the end of 1917, Haig Diary, vol. 24A, NLS 3155, no. 122.
89. Frontages in May, Rawlinson Papers, Churchill College Archives, RWLN 1/12. For 11 Aug., see AWM 45, box 21, bundle 27. Haig's map, Terraine, *To Win a War*: opp. 149.
90. Fourth Army statistics, Rawlinson Papers, IWM, vol. 52 (a detailed breakdown can be found in vol. 26, no. 14). Bean's casualty figures are quoted in Ross, *Myth of the Digger*: 30.
91. Bean, first draft of Volume VI, AWM 3DRL 6673/42.
92. Interview with Eric Cupit, linesman, 7 Apr. 1986.
93. Bean Diary, June 1916, AWM 3DRL 607, item 47: 4; Keyes to his wife, 14 Dec. 1915, Keyes Papers, 2/18.
94. Bean, *Two Men*: 184, 191. Cf. Grey, 'White'.
95. Bean, *Anzac Book*: 10.
96. Kent, '*Anzac Book* and the Anzac Legend'.
97. Coulthard-Clark, *No Australian*: 125, 147, 150, and Appendix 2; review by David Horner in *Sydney Morning Herald*, 23 Apr. 1988; Charlton, *Pozières*: 189, 194.
98. Elliott to OC War Records, AIF HQ, 25 May 1918, AWM Elliott Papers, 2DRL 513, Item 46a.
99. For example, the remark, 'instead of providing [a smokescreen, they] sent the tanks forward when the ground was white with snow, so that every tank stood out like a nigger on a whitewashed fence' and his contrast between them and Monash: 28 Apr. 1921, *CPD*, 95: 7825.
100. Gellibrand, Bean IV: 897n, cf. letter, AWM 3DRL 188/1.
101. Hurley Diary, 14 Jan. 1918. Horner, talk in Canberra, 14 May 1986.
102. Rule, *Jacka's Mob*: 250; Charlton, *Pozières*: 239.
103. James, *Gallipoli*: 181.
104. Monash to Birdwood, 3 Jan. 1918, Monash Papers, ANL MS 1884, box 73, folder 497. H. V. Howe to Capt. E. W. Bush, 1 Feb. 1972, Bush Papers, IWM.

## CHAPTER SEVEN    OF BRITAIN AND THE BRITISH

1. Hurley Diary, 14 Jan. 1918.
2. Hill, *Chauvel*: 140.
3. Brugger, *Australians and Egypt*: 77-9, 82-3; Hill, *Chauvel*: 192. For recognition of Arab forces, ibid.: 193.
4. Hobbs, Welborne, *Lords of Death*: 139-41; Monash, Bean Papers, AWM 3DRL 6673/57; Monash to his wife, 4 Apr. 1918, Monash Papers.

5. Pugsley, *Fringe of Hell*: 281.
6. Bean Diary, 18 Apr. 1915, AWM 3DRL 606/3.
7. Bean to Lloyd George, 15 July 1917, AWM 3DRL 606/82.
8. McCarthy, *Gallipoli*: 341. Criticism of Haig and Gough at Pozières, Bean, *Two Men*: 135-6, 137, 140.
9. Bean's draft of the last chapter for Volume VI, AWM 3DRL 6673, item 42.
10. Bean on Haig, Diary, 20 June 1916, 22 Aug. 1917, AWM 3DRL 606/47 and 132. Edmonds' view, Liddell Hart Papers, 11/1928/16; 11/1930/15; 11/1935/107. For the Somme and Gough, Bean Papers, 14 May 1931, and letter to Gough, 28 Apr. 1928, AWM 3DRL 7953, item 34.
11. Bean I: 80.
12. Bean on Monash, Bean Papers, 3DRL 606/277; Gellibrand, Gerster, *Big Noting*: 71-2, and Bean Diary, vol. 47: 15, 17; quotation, AWM 3DRL 8042 111-111J.
13. Cunliffe Owen Diary 7 May 1915: 21-2, PRO CAB 45/246; Elliott Diary, vol. 3, 11 Apr. 1917, AWM 2DRL 513 1A1.11.
14. Ross, *Myth of the Digger*: 97.
15. Harassment and no man's land, Cupit, interview with author; lack of consideration, E. C. Powell Papers, IWM, MCR 37: 78; petty disputes, Rule, *Jacka's Mob*: 205.
16. Joynt, *Channel Ports*: 2-3; Phillip, *Great Adventure*: 147-50, 242-3.
17. Gammage, *Broken Years*: 241-3.
18. 'Roughish', R. Storm to 'Fitz', 5 Dec. 1914, PRO 30/57/45 (00/69); quotation, Robson, 'Images': 6; hygiene, C. J. L. Allanson to 'Harry', 23 Sept. 1915, Allanson Papers, IWM DS/MISC/69; 'much to learn', e.g. ignorance of artillery problems, Cunliffe Owen Diary, 7 May 1915, PRO CAB 45/246.
19. Diary of Capt. E. J. Rule, AWM 51, item 55, 'Ploegstreet': 3. For others, Capt. W. Holland to Bean, 18 Nov. 1917, AWM 3DRL 8042/81, and the Diaries of Capt. A. M. McGrigor, IWM (a Hussar officer who became Birdwood's ADC).
20. Joynt, *Channel Ports*: 9-10.
21. Monash, *Australian Victories*: 32; for Smithers, Gammage, 'Monash': 114.
22. Hill, *Chauvel*: 67.
23. Richards, *Old Soldiers*: 226; Dunn, *Infantry*: 401.
24. Gill and Dallas, *Unknown Army*: 83.
25. Edmonds and Bean, Sept. 1932, AWM 3DRL 3953/34; Graham, 'Sans Doctrine': 89 thinks that the colonials were treated 'more considerately'.
26. 26 June 1917, Papers of G. O. Hawkins, IWM 78/41/1.
27. Fuller, *Troop Morale*: 76 One soldier commented on a dull stay in a French village in 1917, 'the highly paid Australians had just gone, so the price of everything ... was appalling.' Dunn, *Infantry*: 288.
28. Collett, *The 28th*: 40-1.
29. CID Paper 114-C CAB 5/3; Cabinet meetings, 5, 20 Sept., CAB 22/47 and 22/50.
30. *House of Commons Debates*, 21 Mar. 1917 (XCI): 1961. For pay scales, see Derby's memorandum on army pay, PRO CAB 24/21 GT 1562.
31. War Cabinet 231, 12 Sept. 1917, PRO CAB 23/4.
32. Gibbs, *Battles*: 16-17 and *Realities of War*: 11, 14-15.
33. Riddell, *War Diary*: 24. See Buxton's complaint, Dec. 1918, that the papers always mentioned the Anzacs, but never the Sussex Yeomanry: Howell Papers, King's College, London, V/C/4/16.
34. Bean, first draft of Volume VI, AWM 3DRL 6673/42.
35. Fuller, *Troop Morale*: 160.
36. McCarthy, *Gallipoli*: 342; cf. Bean, 'Sidelights': 220.
37. Quotation, Fuller, *Troop Morale*: 167. Lawrence, *Mutiny*: 88.
38. Bean Diary, 29 Apr. 1915, AWM 3DRL 606/6; Elliott Diary, vol. 2, 18 Nov. 1915, AWM 2DRL 513 1A1.11; Elliott and the British, E. W. Pinder to Bean, 4 Apr. 1960, AWM 3DRL 6673/46. For 1918, Hill, 'Elliott': 430.
39. Charlton, *Pozières*: 128.
40. Elliott, 'Fleurbaix'; Bean IV: 353-4.

41. Gammage, *Broken Years*: 208.
42. Poor officers, interview with George Todd, a Lieutenant of the 1st Australian Division, 30 Jan. 1987. Polygon Wood, Bean to Edmonds, 26 Oct. 1932, AWM 3DRL 7953/34. British loss of ground, interview with Harold Todd, Jan. 1987; Rule Diary, AWM 51-55: 49.
43. Fuller, Troop Morale: 165.
44. Gerster, *Big Noting*: 73: Pilger, 'The other "Lost Generation" ': 13.
45. Munro Ferguson to Colonial Secretary, 22 Nov. 1916, Lloyd George Papers, E2/17/3 (A); 'cruise', PRO CO 616/57: 270–1; Birdwood to Gough, 9 May 1917, PRO WO 158/248; Falls, *Military Operations*: 475.
46. Lewis, *Our War*: 291–3.
47. Twomey thesis, 'Australian Relationship': 180.
48. Letter to an aunt, Rule Diary, 26 Sept. 1918, 'Offensive 18–19 September 1918', AWM 51/55; Cutlack, *War Letters*: 268; Robson, 'Images': 2–3; Bean Diary, 19 Apr. 1918, AWM 3DRL 606/107.
49. Moore, *See How They Ran*: 158–9 (see also 187–8); Dunn, *Infantry*: 468, 476.
50. Bean V: 540.
51. E.g. the 9th Brigade before Villers-Bretonneux, 4 Apr. 1918, Moore, *See How They Ran*: 168, 170.
52. Travers, *How the War Was Won*: 50–65.
53. A linesman 68 years later still remembered the British collapse: interview with Cupit, 7 Apr. 1986. Elliott once ordered his men to shoot any British troops who refused to rally: Elliott Papers, AWM 3DRL 3856, box 38, item 4, and letters to his cousin, folder 1. Also Diary 2DRL 513 1A1.11, vol. 4, 25 Mar., 4 Apr. 1918.
54. Dancocks, *Legacy of Valour*: 222–3.
55. Gammage, *Broken Years*: 209.
56. 30 Apr., 1 May 1918, PRO Cabs 401 & 402, CAB 23/6; CO 616/80.
57. Haig Diary (TS and docs), July 1918, vol. 31, NLS Acc 3155, No. 129.
58. Bean VI: 933. Cf. the complaint of G. V. Rose, July 1918, about having to retake trenches the Queen's Regiment had lost. Rose Papers, IWM.
59. See the bitter letter by an unknown person, in Hughes Papers, ANL 1538/23/185. Cf. Bean's complaint in 1917, Bean Diary, AWM 3DRL 606/78. Monash quoted in Lewis, *Our War*: 294.
60. Barclay, *Empire is Marching*: 78.
61. Bean to G. A. Street, 3 Nov. 1939, AA A5954, box 260 (Sheddon Papers).
62. Cabinets, 4, 5 July, PRO CAB 23/7 and Imperial War Cabinet, 12 July, IWC 24(3) CAB 23/41; Charteris, *At G.H.Q.*: 245, 248.
63. Birdwood to Heads of all Divisions, 11 Apr., AWM 26, box 360, item 3; ditto 30 Apr., Monash Papers, AWM 3DRL 2316/27.
64. Twomey thesis, 'Australian Relationship': 119. Fisher to Pearce, 11 Aug. 1916, Pearce Papers, AWM 3DRL 2222, folder 3; Stamfordham to Munro Ferguson, 22 Aug., 11 Sept., 11 Dec. 1917, Novar Papers, ANL MS 696/450–1, 460 and 467; Haig Diary, 26 Aug. 1917, TS and Papers, vol. 19, NLS 3155, no. 116.
65. Fuller, *Troop Morale*: 16.
66. Long to Birdwood, 23 Oct. 1918, Walter Long Papers, AJCP M1114–1119; 'let them win it', Bean VI: 876.
67. Cutlack, *War Letters*: 268, cf. Monash's article in *Smith's Weekly*, 19 Apr. 1930, in Bean Papers, AWM 3DRL 606/277. Interview with Cupit, 7 Apr. 1986.
68. AWM 3DRL 8042, item 65.
69. Wigram to Kiggell, 18 Nov. 1916, AWM 45, box 23, bundle 31; White, 'Motives' and 'Six-Bob-a-Day'.
70. White, 'Bluebells and Fogtown': 49.
71. McKernan, *Australian People*: 120.
72. British-born, ibid.: 116; visiting relatives, Rule Diary; tourism, White, 'Soldier as Tourist': 70–1. Cf. Gammage, *Broken Years*: 205.
73. Hurley Diary, 3 Aug. 1918.

74. McKernan, *Australian People*: 118, 126, 128; Diary of Charles H. Capel, IWM, and Cupit MS: 26; Manning, letter, 11 Feb. 1917.

75. Souter, *Lion and Kangaroo*: 242; McKernan, *Australian People*: 127–9. Formalism and red tape, Brown, *On the London Front*: 10–16; air raids, Anderson, letter, 14 Dec. 1917 and diary, Feb. 1918; cf. Bean, *Anzac Book*: 145 for a slightly flippant account of it.

76. Cupit MS: 25, 48; McKernan, *Australian People*: 131; Welborn, *Lords of Death*: 129–30; Souter, *Lion and Kangaroo*: 242–3; A. Bryant to friend, 17 Nov. 1918, IWM.

77. Bean VI: 1061; McKernan, *Australian People*: 135–6, 137–9, 144; Anderson, letter to his mother, 14 Dec. 1917. For Eggleston's criticism of the unconventional behaviour of Englishwomen, see Osmond, *Eggleston*: 80.

78. McKernan, *Australian People*: 132–3; Manning Letters, 11 Feb., 3 Mar. 1917.

79. Birdwood to Long, 17 Apr. 1917, Fisher Papers, ANL MS 2919 1/330–3, and Pearce Papers, 3DRL 2222, bundle 1, folder 1. See also 3DRL 3376, item 33; and Buckley, 'Problem of Venereal Disease'. McKernan, *Australian People*: 133–4.

80. Beckett and Simpson, *Nation in Arms*: 19; Long to Lloyd George, 5 Mar. 1918, Lloyd George Papers, HLRO, F32/5/11 and 12. July debate, AA A2939, file SC 76.

81. McKernan, *Australian People*: 140–3.

82. O'Keefe paper, 'Butler'.

83. McKernan, *Australian People*: 144; Boyack, *Behind the Lines*: 99–103; Osmond, *Eggleston*: 81.

84. McKernan, *Australian People*: 148; for soldiers and idealisation of their homeland, Lindstrom thesis, 'Stress and Identity': 194–5. Cf. Lt Gaby's longing for the Ord River, trailing a mob of bullocks, Welborn, *Lords of Death*: 141. Osmond, *Eggleston*: 81–2.

85. Charlton, *Pozières*: 67–9; McKernan, *Australian People*: 123–5. Brown, *On the London Front* is an extended thanks for the entertainment given to Australian troops in the houses of the English well-to-do.

86. Charlton, *Pozières*: 66–9; McKernan, *Australian People*: 122–3; cf. Bean Diary, June 1917, AWM 3DRL 606/82.

87. McKernan, *Australian People*: 125–6, 131, 135, 137 (quotation), 138–9, 145.

88. Wahlert thesis, 'Provost': 71–5.

89. McKernan, *Australian People*: 144–8. For the march past, Brown, *On the London Front*: 16. Amery thought the Canadians looked best, praised the New Zealanders and the Newfoundlanders, but pointedly omitted the Australians: Diary, 3 May 1919.

90. McNicol, *Thirty-Seventh*: 167; Longmore, 'Eggs-A-Cook': 126; Rose Memoirs, Aug., Sept. 1917. Food parcels, interview with Harold Jelbart, 1990. Farewells, *Daily Mail* (overseas edn), 4, 25 Jan. 1919.

91. 'Remarkable friendship', Bean III: 754 and 'Sidelights': 220. Cf. Fuller, *Troop Morale*: 161–2; respect as soldiers, Bean IV: 513, 521, 524; Redcaps, interview with Harold Todd, 17 Nov. 1986; Rose Memoirs, 27 Aug. 1918; Etaples, Gill and Dallas, *Unknown Army*: 100–1.

92. McNicol, *Thirty-Seventh*: 167.

93. Cupit MS: 39, 48; Rule Diary: n.d..

94. Dancocks, *Legacy of Valour*: 117–18, 135; Montgomery-Massingberd, *Fourth Army*: 36; McCarthy, *Gallipoli*: 305–6.

95. Phillip, *Great Adventure*: 254; Godley Papers, Old War Office, vol. 1, 26 Nov., 22 Dec. 1916, 3 Nov., 3 Dec. 1917; also Godley to Pearce, 11 Dec. 1916, 12 June, 3 Dec. 1917, Pearce Papers, AWM 3DRL 2222, bundle 6, no. 51.

## CHAPTER EIGHT    A PEACE OF SORTS

1. Barnes and Nicholson, *Amery Diaries*: 173–4.

2. Hankey Diary, 2, 4 July 1918, HNKY 1/4.

3. Spartalis, *Diplomatic Battles*: 55–6; Cutlack, *War Letters*: 202.

4. Hughes to Murdoch, 3 Sept. 1917, Murdoch Papers, ANL MS 2383. Meetings 11, 13, 14 June 1918, PRO CAB 23/41 and 43. Dancocks, *Legacy of Valour*: 223-4; Borden, *Letters*: vi; Brown, *Borden*: 36-7.

5. 29 Oct. 1915, *CPD* 79: 7022.

6. Cook, *Borden*: 380.

7. Imperial War Cabinet (IWC) 19b, 24 June 1918, CAB 23/44 R1. Hankey Diary, same date, 1/4. Hughes to Lloyd George, 4 Apr. 1918, PRO CO 616/77.

8. The use of Currie and Monash is mentioned in Dancocks, *Legacy of Valour*: 225 (quoting H. M. Urquhart, *Arthur Currie: the Biography of a Great Canadian*, Toronto, 1950: 226-7) but no dates are given. Cook, 'Borden': 385-7. Bean and Hughes, 1926, AWM 3DRL 6673/130; Brown, *Borden*: 137-8, 141; Scott, *Australia in the War*: 741-2. IWC 26A, 23 July 1918, PRO CAB 23/44; Amery Diary, 20 June 1918; Fitzhardinge, *Little Digger*: 320-3.

9. IWC 22, 28 June, and IWC 24, 12 July 1918, PRO CAB 23/43. Hughes to Bean, 28 June 1918, AWM 3DRL 606/116. Hughes and air power, Booker, *Great Professional*: 253-4, cf. 24 June, IWC 19b, PRO CAB 23/44 R1.

10. Technology, IWC, 31 July, 1 Aug. 1918, PRO CAB 23/44; Bolsheviks, Fitzhardinge, *Little Digger*: 323; cf. debate, 26 June 1918, CAB 23/44.

11. 'Waiting', CAB 23/44; Hughes and German morale, 31 July, CAB 23/44; Fitzhardinge, *Little Digger*: 326.

12. Letters to Munro Ferguson, 10 July, 1 Sept. 1918, Novar Papers, ANL MS 696/2722-3, 2729.

13. Return of Anzacs to Australia, Scott, *Australia in the War*: 745: anger in August, Bean VI: 878. Hughes and Wilson, Jeffery, *Military Correspondence*: 44-5, 58-61. Horne, *Search*: 101-2. No permanent occupation force, IWC 42, 12 Dec. 1918, PRO CAB 23/42. Hughes and the generals, Booker, *Great Professional*: 250.

14. Canadians, Brown, *Borden*: 134; Australia House, AA CP 360/8, bundle 1/1; the press, Horne, *Search*: 102.

15. Anzac Day march, Robertson, *Anzac and Empire*: 248; PRO CO 616/82: 555-8. Cf. *Daily Mail* (overseas edn), 3 May 1919.

16. PRO Cab 502 (1) CAB 23/8.

17. Shipping Controller, AA CP 360/8, bundle 1, pts 3 & 4; War Office Committee, AA A6006, 9 Jan. 1919.

18. PRO CO 616/71: 330-6; 73, 77, 80-82; *The Times*, 8 Dec. 1918; Scott, *Australia in the War*: 239-47, 264-76.

19. Spartalis thesis, 'Anglo-Australian Relations': 182-4: Long to Hughes, 18 Aug. 1918, Hughes Papers, ANL MS 1538/23/178. Cf. ibid., 2818; *Westminster Gazette*, ibid., 481. Fitzhardinge, *Little Digger*: 330-4. Clash with Lloyd George on raw materials, 11 June 1919, AA CP 316/8, bundle 1, pt 4.

20. Hughes to Bonar Law, 21 Nov. 1918, Hughes Papers, ANL MS 1538/23/257-68, 271. To Munro Ferguson, 1, 28 Sept. 1918, Novar Papers, ANL MS 696/2729. Wool, Hughes Papers, ANL MS 1538/23/227, 275-6a, 293-9; wheat, 1538/23, sub-series 5, folder 35, and 1538/24/177, 180-1. Fitzhardinge, *Little Digger*: 335-6. Hughes to Lloyd George, Lloyd George Papers, F28/3/7-16, F28/3/23, 28, 31, 33.

21. Hughes to Lloyd George, 14 Aug. 1917, Lloyd George Papers F/32/4/95.

22. 22 Nov. 1917, PRO Cab 280(10) CAB 23/4.

23. Minutes of the Imperial War Conference, 12 June 1918, AA A2939 C76.

24. Cf. above pp. 115-16. PRO CO 616/74 (cf. ibid., 77 and 79, for other instances of delays and confusion). Amery Diary, 22 Oct., 13 Nov. 1917.

25. Scott, *Australia in the War*: 204.

26. Munro Ferguson to Long, 13 May, 4 June and a reply, 1 Nov. 1917, ANL MS 696/1975, 922 & 1458; Fitzhardinge, *Little Digger*: 270. For the raid on Hughes' home, Twomey thesis, 'Australian Relationship': 174-5.

27. Amery to Lloyd George, 9 July 1918, Lloyd George Papers F/2/1/26, 8 June 1918, F/2/1/24. Amery Diary, 20 June 1918.

28. Long to Munro Ferguson 17 June, 3 July 1918, Novar Papers, 696/1488-95.

29. Crawford, *Bit of a Rebel*: 306-8. For Massey, Pfeiffer, 'Exercises': 183. The minutes of the meetings can be found in PRO IWC 26 and 27, CAB 23/41. (See also Hughes Papers, ANL MS 1538/23, series 4, folder 8.) Barnes and Nicholson, *Amery Diaries*: 228-30. For a summary, see Fitzhardinge, *Little Digger*: 327-8, or Hudson and Sharp, *Australian Independence*: 52-3. The text of the resolution can be found in Keith, *Selected Speeches*: 7.

30. Cunneen, *Kings' Men*: 143-4; Novar Papers, 696/1896-1900, 1908-13; Spartalis, *Diplomatic Battles*: 67-8.

31. Munro Ferguson correspondence 23, 25 July, Novar Papers, 696/2016-2020, 5161, 5170, 5187, 5218. Munro Ferguson to Long, 28 Oct. 1918, ibid., 2072-8. Long and Lloyd George, Lloyd George Papers, F/32/5/57, F/33/1/5-12, 16 and 36. Long's resignation, Long to Munro Ferguson, 1 Aug. 1918, Novar Papers, 696/1498-1504. General comments, Spartalis, *Diplomatic Battles*: 70-2; Scott, *Australia in the War*: 184-7. Arrogance of the Colonial Office, see minute from H. L. Lambert to Sir G. Fiddes, 25 May 1918, PRO CO 687/47/24539; while Curzon regarded them as 'the ignorant backswoodsmen from the Dominions', Amery Diary, 16 May 1918. For a sympathetic analysis of Munro Ferguson's arguments, Cunneen, *Kings' Men*: 144-7.

32. IWC 29, PRO CAB 23/41.

33. Cabinet, 4 Nov. 1918, Cab 496(9) CAB 23/8.

34. Cable to Fisher, 7 Jan. 1915, Fisher Papers, ANL 2919/6/79-81.

35. Hankey Diary, 17, 19 Oct., Roskill, *Hankey*: 615-18; Cabinet meeting, 18 Oct. 1918, Lloyd George Papers, F/23/3/17. Spartalis thesis, 'Anglo-Australian Relations': 205-10; *Diplomatic Battles*: 79-80; Fitzhardinge, *Little Digger*: 345-6.

36. IWC 36a, 6 Nov. 1918, PRO CAB 23/44. Twomey thesis, 'Australian Relationship': 213; 'palpable evasion', Hughes to Watt, 13 Nov. 1918, AA A6006 1918/12/4.

37. *The Times*, 8, 9 Nov. 1918. Latham to Kerr, 9 Nov., Bean Diary: 269; Amery Diary, 8, 12 Nov.; Amery Memorandum, 14 Nov., Balfour Papers, BL Add.MS 49775: 191-4. Lloyd George's letter can still be found in the Hughes Papers, 1538/23/245-8. For general story, Spartalis, *Diplomatic Battles*: 84-6; Hudson and Sharp, *Australian Independence*: 5-6.

38. IWC 47, 30 Dec. 1918, PRO CAB 23/42.

39. Spartalis, *Diplomatic Battles*: 83, 114 (for Hankey); IWC 43, 18 Dec. 1918, PRO CAB 23/42. The Australian Cabinet and the Fourteen Points, AA A6006 1918/12/4; Scott, *Australia in the War*: 748-9.

40. Hughes and Watt, 14, 19 Nov. 1918, AA A6006 1918/11/18.

41. Hankey Diary, 4 Dec. 1918, HNKY 1/5.

42. Hudson, *Billy Hughes*: 3, 9. Borden to Lloyd George, 29 Oct. 1918, and reply 3 Nov., Lloyd George Papers F/39/1/39. Brown, 'Sir Robert Borden'; Fitzhardinge, 'Dominion Representation' and *Little Digger*: 363-9; Spartalis, *Diplomatic Battles*: 116-18.

43. Spartalis, ibid.: 96, 104-14, 155-67; Scott, *Australia in the War*: 804-5. IWC 38, 26 Nov., PRO CAB 23/43, and 23/40, 23/46, 3, 24 Dec. 1918, PRO CAB 23/42; Smuts to Lloyd George, 4 Dec. 1918, Hughes to Lloyd George, 17 March 1919, Lloyd George Papers, F/45/9/25 and F/213/2/1, and Hughes' draft letter to Lloyd George, 11 Apr. 1919, Hughes Papers, 1538/24/92-3. Fitzhardinge, *Little Digger*: 379-87; Booker, *Great Professional*: 258; Hudson, *Billy Hughes*: 35-41. Riddell Diary, 26 Apr. 1919.

44. Fitzhardinge, *Little Digger*: 168-70; Spartalis, *Diplomatic Battles*: 50.

45. Fitzhardinge, 'Triangular Diplomacy': 257; Thornton, 'Invaluable Ally': 8-11, 16-18; PRO CAB 21/77.

46. I am indebted for this phrase to W. J. Hudson, in a talk in Canberra, May 1990.

47. Twomey thesis, 'Australian Relationship': 196; Booker, *Great Professional*: 252; Barnes and Nicholson, *Amery Diaries*: 225. Hughes' Monroe Doctrine speech, *Daily Mail* (overseas edn), 20 July 1918.

48. 19 Dec. 1918, Lloyd George Papers, F/23/3/30.

49. Spartalis, *Diplomatic Battles*: 193-217; IWC 30 and 31, 13-14 Aug. 1918, PRO CAB 23/42.

50. Spartalis, *Diplomatic Battles*: 58, 82. Hughes and Lloyd George, 4 Nov., 31 Dec. 1918, Lloyd George Papers, F/33/1/44b.

51. Thornton, 'Invaluable Ally': 15; Scott, *Australia in the War*: 764–5; Spartalis thesis, 'Anglo-Australian Relations': 41–52.

52. Barnes and Nicholson, *Amery Diaries*: 229; Spartalis, *Diplomatic Battles*: 80, 99; 'Anglo-Australian Relations': 163–4; Scott, *Australia in the War*: 770. Australian Cabinet, cable to Hughes, 26 Nov. 1918, AA A6006 1918/11/26; 31 Jan. 1919, AA CP 360/8 bundle 1, pt 3; 13 Feb. A6006 18 Feb. 1919. White Australia policy, 31 Mar., AA CP360/8 bundle 1, pt 3.

53. IWC 31, 14 Aug. and 38, 26 Nov. PRO CAB 23/42; Hudson, *Billy Hughes*: 14.

54. Fitzhardinge, *Little Digger*: 387–92; Spartalis, *Diplomatic Battles*: 122–50. Cf. Scott, *Australia in the War*: 774–87.

55. Riddell Diary, 30 Jan. 1919; Amery Diary, 2 Feb. 1919, Barnes and Nicholson, *Amery Diaries*: 255; Amery to Hughes, same date, Hughes Papers, ANL MS 1538/24/32; Hankey to Lloyd George, 21 Feb. 1919, Lloyd George Papers, F/23/4/18.

56. Montagu to Balfour, 20 Dec. 1918, Balfour Papers, BL Add.MS 49748; Montagu to Lloyd George, 28 Jan. 1919, Lloyd George Papers, F/40/2/34; Fitzhardinge, *Little Digger*: 394–6, 414.

57. Spartalis, *Diplomatic Battles*: 178–88; Fitzhardinge, *Little Digger*: 401–6; Pfeiffer, 'Exercises': 188–9.

58. IWC, 5, 6, 26 Nov. 1918, CAB 23/42.

59. Hughes Papers, 1538/24/456.

60. Keith, *War Governments*: 155. Hudson and Sharp, *Australian Independence*: 57–8; Scott, *Australia in the War*: 813–15. For the legal and constitutional complexities of the issue, see Wheare, 'The Empire': 662–6.

61. Pfeiffer, 'Exercises': 187.

62. Edwards, *Prime Ministers and Diplomats*: 45, 51–2; AA CP 360/8 bundle 1, pt 3; Riddell Diary, 5 May 1919.

63. Jan. 1935, Simon Papers, PRO FO 800/290.

64. Edwards, *Prime Ministers and Diplomats*: 45.

65. Wilson's 'doctrinaire proposals', Booker, *Great Professional*: 259; Lloyd George on tactics, IWC 48, 31 Dec. 1918, PRO CAB 23/42; 'dissatisfaction', Riddell Diary, 1 Apr. 1919; Hughes pleased, Amery Diary, 6 July 1919.

66. Hudson and Sharp, *Australian Independence*: 54–5.

67. In a cable to Pearce and in Paris in 1918: text forwarded by Australia House to Bean, Oct. 1918, Bean Papers, AWM 3DRL 605.

68. Hudson, *Billy Hughes*: 74.

69. Hughes to Pearce, 26 November 1918, AWM 3DRL 2222, bundle 3, item 69.

70. Souter, *Lion and Kangaroo*: 273.

71. Wheare, 'The Empire': 650–2.

72. Fitzhardinge, *Little Digger*: 320.

73. Stamfordham to Munro Ferguson, 18 Aug. 1918, Novar Papers, 696/477–8.

74. Quoted Spartalis, *Diplomatic Battles*: 57.

75. Booker, *Great Professional*: 239.

## CONCLUSIONS

1. Kent, '*Anzac Book* and the Anzac Legend'; Gough, 'First Australian'; Bean, 'The Writing': 91.

2. Pearce Papers, AWM 3DRL 2222 bundle 1, folder 2.

3. Australian privates drew six shillings a day, or £109 10s a year. In 1917 Maj.-Gen. Sinclair MacLagen had his salary made up to the British level of £1773 15s p.a., or 16 times the private's pay: AA CP 78/23 1918/89/342.

4. Bean to Edmonds, 17 Sept. 1935, AWM 3DRL 7953/30.

5. Thomson, 'Digger memories': 10; cf. Andrews, *Isolationism*: 17, 22, 57.

6. Grey, *Australian Brass*: 7, 21, 36–7.
7. Maier, *Unmasterable Past*: 12.
8. For British denigration of Australian soldiers in World War II, see David Day, 'Anzacs on the Run'.
9. Populations in round figures were Britain 42,082,000; Canada 7,206,000; Australia 4,900,000; and New Zealand 1,100,000. Britain sent overseas or trained 4,970,902 men; Canada 458,218; Australia 331,814; New Zealand 112,223. This represented for Britain 27.28 per cent of the adult males in the population; New Zealand 19.35 per cent; Canada 13.48 per cent; and Australia 13.43 per cent. Lloyd George, *Memoirs*, vol. 2: 2006 cites the *Statistics of the Military Effort of the British Empire*. Cf. the table in Adam-Smith, *Anzacs*: Appendix II; Keith, *Responsible Government*: 988–90.
10. Tsokhas, ' "A Pound of Flesh" '. See also his book, *Markets*.
11. Evans, *Loyalty and Disloyalty*: 20–1.
12. Hughes' speaking tour in 1916 is not discussed, and he is only briefly described later— 'the pugnacious little Welshman', etc. Lloyd George, *Memoirs*: 1034.
13. E.g. W. A. McClaughey, born in Adelaide, became Air Vice Marshal in World War II. McClaughey Papers, IWM.
14. E. L. Patten, editorial, in *RMC Journal*, Dec. 1919: 5. He concluded that 'the Australian spirit must be a British spirit, that is to say, an Imperial spirit.'
15. Horne, *Search*: 110.
16. Diary of E. J. Rule, AWM 51, item 55; Bean to Edmonds, 11 Oct. 1932, AWM 3DRL 7953/34.
17. White, 'Six-Bob-a-Day': 139.
18. Morton, 'Sovereign Allies': 56.
19. Jeffery, *British Army*: 9, 31–2. Morton, in 'Canadian Military Experience': 79, thinks that 'Four years of war had left nothing in Canada untouched.'.
20. Watt to Hughes, 17 Apr. 1919, AA CP 316/8 bundle 1, pt 4.
21. Souter, *Lion and Kangaroo*: 281.
22. Lindstrom thesis, 'Stress': 144–6, 194–9, 227–31.
23. Fisher, Gammage, *Broken Years*: 269; Munro Ferguson to Stamfordham, 28 Aug. 1918, Novar Papers, 696/321–2.
24. Gerster, *Big Noting*: 169.
25. Munro Ferguson to Colonial Secretary, 14 Mar. 1919, Novar Papers, 696/2160. Author's interview with Harold Todd, 29 Jan. 1987.
26. Osmond, *Eggleston*: 81–2. Bean to Edmonds, 17 Sept. 1935, AWM 3DRL 7953/30; Bean Diary, 28 Apr. 1917, AWM 3DRL 606/77; Barrett, 'No Straw Man': 113; Eggleston Papers, 432/6/14.
27. Spartalis, *Diplomatic Battles*: 191–2.
28. Borrie, 'British': 106; Dunn, *Australia and Empire*: 110–11; Fedorowich, ' "Society Pets" '.
29. Dunn, *Australia and Empire*: 97–8, 106; Novar Papers, 1 May 1919, 696/2194–2022.
30. Hudson, *Billy Hughes*: 69–76.
31. Toll thesis, 'Australia': 6.
32. Hughes in the 1921 conference, Booker, *Great Professional*: 268–75. Edwards, *Prime Ministers and Diplomats*: 63–5.
33. Cunneen, *Kings' Men*: 145. For the inter-war period, Andrews, *Writing*: 1–6. For Bruce, Hudson and Sharp, *Australian Independence*: 72, 86–7.
34. Amery to Lloyd George, 27 Dec. 1918, Barnes and Nicholson, *Amery Diaries*: 247–8; Hankey to Esher, 10 Feb. 1919, Hankey Papers, HNKY 4/9; Amery Diary, 6, 10, 14 Feb. 1919; Hudson, *Billy Hughes*: 74–5.
35. Fitzhardinge, *Little Digger*: 329; AA A2939 file SC76.
36. Cunneen, *Kings' Men*: 150–2.
37. Single navy, Keith, *Responsible Government*: 1012–13; Lloyd George Papers, F18/2/1. Spartalis, *Diplomatic Battles*: 74; Toll thesis, 'Australia': 73–5.
38. Hughes to Lloyd George, 7 Oct. 1919, Lloyd George Papers, F/33/2/75 (a & b); Meaney, *Search*: 12; Spartalis, *Diplomatic Battles*: 75–6.

39. Robertson, *Anzac and Empire*: 242–4, (quotation) 261.
40. Gordon, *Dominion Partnership*: 203–4; Lucas, *Empire at War*: 184.
41. Fitzhardinge, 'Triangular Diplomacy': 258–9.
42. Minutes of the Defence Committee, 11 Apr. 1930, AA A2031, vol. I.
43. Andrews, 'Broken Promise': 109–11.
44. Coulthard-Clark, 'Australia's Air Defence'. As for the effect of British education, one soldier in the Vietnam War recounts how the 'ripping yarns' he read in the *Boys' Own Annual* influenced him—for example tethering a goat to a post as bait for a tiger! Barry Petersen, *Tiger Men: An Australian Soldier's Secret War in Vietnam*, Melbourne, 1988, cited G. Lockhart, review in the *Journal of the Australian War Memorial*, 13, 1988: 57.
45. Review by Philip Knightley in *Sunday Times*, 17 July 1988.
46. Hudson and Sharp, *Australian Independence*: 6.

# Bibliography

## ARCHIVAL COLLECTIONS

**Australian Archives, Canberra**

Assorted minor files in A1, A2, A487, A494, A1606.

A1632, Memoirs of M. L. Shepherd.

A1973/362, Miscellaneous Correspondence of the High Commissioner.

A2911, Cables from High Commission, London.

A5954, Shedden Papers.

A6006, Reconstituted Cabinet Minutes.

A6661, Ceremonial matters:
    1/379 Anzac Day 1916 sprung on Australian authorities.
    380 Anzac Day message 1916.

CP78/23, Governor-Generals' Papers.

CP151, Pearce Papers.

CP359, Hughes Correspondence.

CP360/8, Prime Minister's Department.

**Australian National Library, Canberra**

Casey Papers, MS 6150.
Fisher Papers, MS 2919.
Hughes Papers, MS 1538.
Hurley Diary, MS 833.
Latham Papers, MS 1009.
Monash Papers, MS 1884.
Murdoch Papers, MS 2823.
Novar Papers, MS 696.
Pearce Papers, MS 213, 1827 & 1927.
Piesse Papers, MS 882.

**Menzies Library, Australian National University**

Eggleston Papers.

**Australian War Memorial, Canberra**

AWM4, War Diaries.
AWM26, Operations Files.
AWM41, Elliott Papers.
AWM44, *Official History* MS.
AWM45, Heyes Papers.
AWM48, High Commissioner's Office, London.

AWM51, Ex-confidential documents.
3DRL606, Diaries and notebooks of C. E. W. Bean.
3DRL1438, Birdwood Papers.
3DRL1722, Bean Notebooks.
3DRL1731, Birdwood Papers.
3DRL2222, Pearce Papers.
3DRL2316, Monash Papers.
3DRL2574, Birdwood Papers.
3DRL3297, Elliott Papers.
3DRL3376, Birdwood Papers.
3DRL6673, Bean Collection—War Service Papers.
3DRL7953, Bean—correspondence re *Official History.*
3DRL8042, Records used for *Official History.*
3DRL8050, Gellibrand Papers (previously 1473).
PR83, White Papers.
PR88, Rosenthal Papers.

**Bodleian Library, Oxford**

Asquith Papers.
Gwynne Papers.
Harcourt Papers.
Milner Papers.
Violet Milner Papers.

**British Library, London**

Balfour Papers.
Keyes Papers.
Northcliffe Papers.
Riddell Diary.
Walter Long Papers.

**Churchill College Archives, Cambridge**

Esher Papers.
Fisher Papers.
Hankey Papers.
Harper Papers.
Knatchbull-Hugessen Papers.
Primrose Papers.

Rawlinson Diary and Papers.
Woodward Papers.

**House of Lords Record Office, London**

Balfour Papers.
Bonar Law Papers.
Davidson Papers.
Keyes Papers.
Lloyd George Papers.
Riddell Papers.

**Imperial War Museum, London**

Twenty-one assorted sets of private papers,
  together with:
Birdwood Papers.
Bush Papers.
Dawnay Papers.
Maxse Papers.
Rawlinson Papers.
Wedgewood Papers.
Wilson Papers.

**India Office Library, London**

Birdwood Collection.

**King's College, London University**

Edmonds Papers.
Howell Papers.
Kiggell Papers.

Liddell Hart Papers.
Montgomery-Massingberd Papers.
Robertson Papers.

**National Army Museum, London**

Rawlinson Papers.

**National Library of Scotland, Edinburgh**

Haig Papers.

**Public Record Office, London**

CAB 23/1–9, 40–44 Cabinet Minutes.
CAB 2, 4–5, 21–2, 24, 41–2, 45, 63.
CO 418, 532, 537, 616, 701, 706–7, 714, 752–3,
  881.
CID CAB 2.
PRO 30/57 Kitchener Papers.
WO 79, 93, 95, 106, 158.

**Old War Office Library, London**

Godley Papers.

**Richmond Borough Library, London**

D. Sladen Papers.

**Wiltshire County Record Office,
Trowbridge**

Walter Long Papers.

PRIVATE PAPERS

Amery, Leo. Diary held by Mr Julian Amery, Eaton Square, London (referred to in notes
  as 'Amery Diary').
Anderson, F. G. Letters and Diary, in possession of family.
Cupit, E. MS of recollections, in possession of family.
Manning, C. Letters to his wife (1894–1971) held by his son.
Rose, G. V. Memoirs, IWM.
Rule, J. Diary of Captain E. J. Rule, AWM 51, item 55.

UNPUBLISHED THESES AND PAPERS

Andrews, E. M. 'C. E. W. Bean and Bullecourt: Walking the battlefield and new findings',
  paper presented to the Australian War Memorial Conference, November 1991.
Attard, B. 'The Australian High Commissioner's Office: Politics and Anglo-Australian
  Relations, 1901–1939, D.Phil. thesis, Cambridge University, 1991.
Briggs, M. 'A navy for the taking: the Admiralty and Australia at the 1909 Conference
  on the Naval and Military Defence of the Empire', paper presented to the Australian
  War Memorial History Conference, July 1987.
Coulthard-Clark, C. D. 'Duntroon and the First World War', paper presented to the
  Australian War Memorial Conference, February 1982.

——. 'Australia's Air Defence between the World Wars: The development of Australian air power and its contribution to defence 1918-40', Ph.D. thesis, University of NSW, ADFA 1991.

Coward, D. H. 'The Impact of War on N.S.W: Some Aspects of the Social and Political History, 1914-1917', Ph.D. thesis, ANU, 1974.

Ellis, S. C. 'C. E. W. Bean: a study of his life and work', MA thesis, University of New England, 1969.

Fewster, K. J. 'Expression and Suppression: Aspects of Military Censorship in Australia during the Great War.' Ph.D. thesis, University of NSW, 1980.

Firth, S. G. 'Schooling in NSW, 1880-1914', MA thesis, ANU, 1968.

Gilbert, A. 'The Churches and the Conscription Referendum 1916-17', MA thesis, ANU, 1967.

Glenister, R. ' "Desertion without Execution": Decisions that saved Australian Imperial Force deserters from the firing squad in World War I', BA Honours thesis, La Trobe University, 1984.

Krause, G. 'Attitudes to Peace and War: the Protestant Churches and sects of New South Wales 1910-14; 1930-39', BA Honours thesis, University of Newcastle, 1986.

Lindstrom, R. G. 'Stress and Identity: Australian Soldiers during the First World War', MA thesis, University of Melbourne, 1985.

Merritt, J. 'George Foster Pearce: Labour Leader', MA thesis, University of Western Australia, 1963.

Mordike, J. 'Control by Committee: the first Military Board, 1905', paper presented to the Australian War Memorial Conference, 1987.

——. 'From Dreadnought to Gallipoli', paper presented to the Australian War Memorial Conference, July 1990.

O'Keefe, B. 'Colonel Arthur Graham Butler and the Writing of *The Official History of the Australian Army Medical Services in the War of 1914-18*', paper presented to the Australian War Memorial Conference, 1987.

Primrose, N. 'Australia's Naval Policy, 1919-1942: a Case Study in Empire Relations', Ph.D. thesis, ANU, 1974 .

Quinlan, G. F. 'The N.S.W. Press and the Growing European Crisis, June 28 to August 6 1914', BA Honours thesis, University of Newcastle, 1972.

Sissons, D. C. S. 'Attitudes to Japan and Defence 1890-1923', MA thesis, University of Melbourne, 1956.

Spartalis, P. J. 'Anglo-Australian Relations: A Critique of the Foreign Policy of William Morris Hughes, Prime Minister of Australia, 1915-23', Ph.D. thesis, University of Alberta, 1977.

Toll, M. J. 'Australia in the Evolution of the British Commonwealth, 1919-1939: The Impact of the International Environment', Ph.D. thesis, Johns Hopkins University, 1972.

Thompson, J. R. 'The Australian High Commission in London, Its Origins and Early History, 1901-1916', MA thesis, ANU, 1972.

Twomey, P. 'The Australian Relationship with Great Britain, 1914-1918', BA Honours thesis, University of Queensland, 1982.

Wahlert, G. 'Provost: Friend or Foe? The Development of an Australian Provost Service, 1914-1918', BA Honours thesis, Deakin University, 1990.

## BOOKS, CHAPTERS AND ARTICLES

Adam-Smith, P. *The Anzacs*, Melbourne, 1978.

Adams, R. J. Q. *The Great War, 1914–18: Essays on the Military, Political and Social History of the First World War*, London, 1990.

Allison, W., and Fairly, J. *The Monocled Mutineer*, London, 1978.

Alomes, S. G. 'Island, Nation and Empire; Collective Identifications in Hobart during the Boer War', *Tasmanian Historical Research Association: Papers and Proceedings*, 21, 1, 1976: 9-20.

Andrews, E. M. *Isolationism and Appeasement in Australia: Reactions to the European Crises, 1935-1939*, Canberra, 1970.

———. 'The Broken Promise—Britain's Failure to Consult its Commonwealth on Defence in 1934 and its Implications for Australian Foreign and Defence Policy', *Australian Journal of Defence Studies*, November 1978, pp. 2-113.

———. *The Writing on the Wall*, Sydney, 1987.

———. 'Second Bullecourt Revisited: the Australians in France, 3 May 1917', *Journal of the Australian War Memorial*, October 1989: 34-44.

———. 'Bean and Bullecourt: weaknesses and strengths of the official history of Australia in the First World War', *Revue Internationale d'Histoire Militaire*, August 1990: 25-47.

———. 'The Media and the Military: Australian war correspondents and the appointment of a Corps Commander, 1918—A Case Study', *War and Society*, October 1990: 83-103.

———. 'The Battle of Hamel—a re-assessment', *Journal of the Australian War Memorial*, April 1991: 5-12.

Ashmead-Bartlett, E. *Australians in Action: The Story of Gallipoli*, Sydney, 1915.

———. *The Uncensored Dardanelles*, London, 1928.

Aspinall-Oglander, C. F. *Military Operations: Gallipoli*, I, London, 1929.

Attard, B. *The Australian High Commissioners*, Working Papers in Australian Studies No. 68, Sir Robert Menzies Centre for Australian Studies, London, 1991.

Baker, P. *King and Country Call: New Zealanders, Conscription and the Great War*, Auckland, 1988.

Babington, A. *For the Sake of Example: Capital Courts-Martial, 1914-1920*, London, 1985.

Barclay, G. *The Empire is Marching: A study of the military effort of the British Empire, 1800-1945*, London, 1976.

Barnes, J., and Nicholson, D. *The Leo Amery Diaries, I: 1896-1929*, London, 1980.

Barnett, C. *The Swordbearers: Studies of Command in the First World War*, Penguin edn, London, 1963.

———. *The Collapse of British Power*, London, 1972.

Barnett, L. M. *British Food Policy During the First World War*, London, 1985.

Barrett, J. *Falling In: Australians and Boy Conscription, 1911-1915*, Sydney, 1979.

———. 'No Straw Man: C. E. W. Bean and some critics', *Australian Historical Studies*, 23, 1988: 102-14.

Bassett, J. *The Home Front, 1914-1918*, Melbourne, 1983.

Bean, C. E. W. *The Anzac Book*, London, 1916.

———. 'Sidelights of the War on Australian Character', *Journal of the Royal Australian Historical Society*, 13, 4, 1927: 211-21.

———. *Official History of Australia in the War of 1914-18*, 11 vols, Sydney, 1921-42.

———. 'The Writing of the Australian Official History of the Great War: Sources, Methods and Some Conclusions', *Royal Australian Historical Society, Journal and Proceedings*, XXIV, 1938, part 2: 85-112.

———. 'The Technique of a Contemporary War Historian', *Historical Studies of Australia and New Zealand*, November 1942: 65-79.

———. *Two Men I Knew: William Bridges and Brudenell White*, Sydney, 1957.

Beckett, I., and Simpson, K. (eds). *A Nation in Arms: A social study of the British army in the First World War*, Manchester, 1985.

Beddie, B. D. 'The Australian Navy and Imperial Legislation', *War and Society*, September 1987: 73-88.

Best, G. 'Militarism and the Victorian Public School', in Simon and Bradley, *Victorian Public School*: 129-146.

Blainey, G. *The Tyranny of Distance*, Melbourne, 1966.

Bidwell, S., and Graham, D. *Fire Power: British Army Weapons and Theories of War, 1904-1945*, Boston, 1985.

Blackton, C. S. 'Australian Nationalism and Nationality: the Imperial Federationist Interlude, 1885-1901', *Historical Studies, Australia and New Zealand*, VII, 1955: 1-16.

Blake, R. *The Private Papers of Douglas Haig, 1914-1919*, London, 1952.

———. *The Unknown Prime Minister*, London, 1955.

Blaxland, G. *Amiens: 1918*, London, 1968.

Bond, B. *The First World War and British Military History*, Oxford, 1991.

Bond, B., and Roy, I. (eds). *War and Society: a year book of military history*, vol. 2, 1977.

Booker, M. *The Great Professional: A Study of W. M. Hughes*, Sydney, 1980.

Boraston, J. M. (ed.). *Sir Douglas Haig's Despatches*, London, 1979.

Borden, H. (ed.). *Letters to Limbo*, Toronto, 1971.

Borrie, W. D. ' "British" Immigration to Australia', in Madden and Morris-Jones, *Australia and Britain*: 101–16.

Boyack, N. *Behind the Lines: The Lives of New Zealand Soldiers in the First World War*, Wellington, 1989.

Brown, L. *On the London Front, 1915–19*, Parramatta, 1921.

Brown, R. C. 'Sir Robert Borden and Canada's War Aims', in P. Hunt and A. Preston, *War Aims and Strategic Policy in the Great War, 1914–1918*, London, 1977: 55–65.

——. *Robert Laud Borden: A Biography*, II: *1914–37*, Toronto, 1980.

Brown, R. C., and Loveridge, D. 'Unrequited Faith: Recruiting the CEF, 1914–1918', *Revue Internationale d'Histoire Militaire*, 541, 1982: 53–79.

Brugger, S. *Australians and Egypt, 1914–1919*, Melbourne, 1980.

Buckley, Suzann. 'The Failure to Resolve the Problem of Venereal Disease amongst the troops in Britain during World War I', in Bond and Roy, *War and Society*: 65–85.

Buitenhuis, P. *The Great War of Words: British, American and Canadian Propaganda and Fiction, 1914–1933*, Vancouver, 1987.

Cain, F. *The Origins of Political Surveillance in Australia*, Sydney, 1983.

Callinan, B. *Sir John Monash*, Melbourne, 1981.

Cannon, M. *The Long Last Summer: Australia's Upper Class before the War*, Sydney, 1985.

Carroll, J. (ed.). *Intruders in the Bush: The Australian Quest for Identity*, Melbourne, 1982.

Charlton, P. *Pozières: Australians on the Somme*, Sydney, 1986.

Charteris, J. *At G.H.Q.*, London, 1931.

Childs, W. *Episodes and Reflections*, London, 1930.

Clark, C. D. 'General Bridges: The Reluctant Commandant', *RMC Historical Journal*, 2, 1973: 31–6.

Clark, C. M. H. *A History of Australia*, 5: *1888–1915*, Melbourne, 1981.

Clarke, T. *My Northcliffe Diary*, London, 1931.

Cole, D. 'The Problem of "Nationalism" and "Imperialism" in British Settlement Colonies', *Journal of British Studies*, 10, 2, 1971: 160–82.

——. 'The Crimson Thread of Kinship: Ethnic Ideas in Australia, 1870–1914', *Historical Studies*, 14, October 1969–April 1971: 511–25.

Collett, H. B. *The 28th*, Perth, 1922.

Connell, W. F. 'British Influence on Australian Education in the Twentieth Century', in Madden and Morris-Jones, *Australia and Britain*: 162–79.

Connolly, C. N. 'Manufacturing "Spontaneity": the Australian offers of troops for the Boer War', *Historical Studies* 18, 1978: 106–17.

——. 'Class, Birthplace, Loyalty: Australian Attitudes to the Boer War', *Historical Studies*, 18, 71, 1978: 210–32.

Cook, G. L. 'Sir Robert Borden, Lloyd George and British Military Policy, 1917–1918', *Historical Journal*, xiv, 2 (1971): 371–95.

Cooper, R. K. 'Andrew Douglas White, RE (1798–1837)', *Despatch: Journal of the New South Wales Military Historical Society*, September–October 1991.

Copland, D. B. 'Australia in the World War', *The Cambridge History of the British Empire*, VII, (part 1: Australia), Cambridge, 1933.

Coulthard-Clark, C. 'Major-General Sir William Bridges: Australia's First Field Commander', in Horner, *The Commanders*: 13–25.

——. *No Australian Need Apply: The Troubled Career of Lieutenant-General Gordon Legge*, Sydney, 1988.

Crawford, R. M. *'A Bit of a Rebel': the Life and Work of George Arnold Wood*, Sydney, 1975.

Cross, J. A. 'The Colonial Office and the Dominions before 1914', *Journal of Commonwealth Political Studies*, 4, 1966: 138–48.

Crossland, J. 'The Pity of War', *History Today*, 41, 1991: 9–11.

Crowley, F. K. 'The British Contribution to the Australian Population, 1860-1919', *University Studies in History and Economics*, II, 2, July 1954: 55–88.

——. *Modern Australia in Documents*, I: *1901-1939*, Melbourne, 1973.

Crumlin, J. 'In the steps of the 4th Brigade,' *Journal of the Australian War Memorial*, 16, April 1990: 39-44.

Cunneen, C. *Kings' Men*, Sydney, 1983.

Cutlack, F. M. (ed.). *War Letters of General Monash*, Sydney, 1934.

Dancocks, D. G. *Legacy of Valour: the Canadians at Passchendaele*, Edmonton, 1986.

Dawes, J. N. I. and Robson, L. L. *Citizen to Soldier: Australia before the Great War, Recollections of Members of the First A.I.F.*, Melbourne, 1977.

Dawson, R. M. (ed.). *The Development of Dominion Status*, London, 1937.

Day, D. 'Anzacs on the Run: The View from Whitehall, 1941-42', *Journal of Imperial and Commonwealth History*, XIV, 3, 1986: 187-202.

Denton, K. *Gallipoli: One Long Grave*, Sydney, 1986.

Dunn, J. C. *The War the Infantry Knew, 1914-1919*, London, 1987.

Dunn, M. *Australia and the Empire: from 1788 to the present*, Sydney, 1984.

Edwards, P. *Prime Ministers and Diplomats: The Making of Australian Foreign Policy, 1901-1945*, Melbourne, 1983.

Eggleston, F. W. 'Australia and the Empire, 1855-1921', *The Cambridge History of the British Empire*, VII, part I: Australia, Cambridge, 1933: 523-43.

Elliott, H. E. 'The Battle of Fleurbaix', *The Duckboard*, 1 September 1930: 4-14.

Ely, R. 'The First Anzac Day: Invented or Discovered?', *Journal of Australian Studies*, 17, November 1985: 41-58.

Emeley, C. 'European armies, governments and societies in 1914: the question of the reasons for men volunteering in Britain in 1914', in Marwick, *Europe on the Eve*: 69-79.

Enser, A. G. S. *A Subject Bibliography of the First World War (second edition): Books in English 1914-1987*, London, 1990.

Evans, R. *Loyalty and Disloyalty: Social Conflict on the Queensland Homefront, 1914-18*, Sydney, 1987.

Falls, C. *History of the Great War . . . Military Operations France and Belgium 1917*, London, 1940.

Farrar-Hockley, A. H. *Goughie*, London, 1975.

Fedorowich, K. ' '"Society Pets and Morning Coated Farmers": Australian Soldier Settlement and the Participation of British Ex-servicemen, 1915-1929', *War and Society*, October 1990: 38-56.

Fewster, K. 'Ellis Ashmead-Bartlett and the Making of the Anzac Legend', *Journal of Australian Studies*, 10, 1982: 17-30.

——. (ed). *Gallipoli Correspondent: The Frontline Diary of C. E. W. Bean*, Sydney, 1983.

——. 'The Wazza Riots, 1915', *Journal of the Australian War Memorial*, 4, April 1984: 47-53.

Fieldhouse, D. K. *The Theory of Capitalist Imperialism*, London, 1967.

Firth, S. G. 'Social Values in NSW Primary Schools 1880-1914: An Analysis of School Texts', *Melbourne Studies in Education*, 1970: 123-59.

Fischer, G. 'Botany Bay revisited: the transportation of prisoners of war and civilian internees to Australia during the first world war', *Journal of the Australian War Memorial*, 5, 1984: 36-43.

——. *Enemy Aliens: Internment and the Home Front Experience in Australia, 1914-1920*, St Lucia, 1989.

Fitzhardinge, L. F. *William Morris Hughes: A Political Biography*. I: *That Fiery Particle*, Sydney, 1964.

——. 'Hughes, Borden, and Dominion Representation at the Paris Peace Conference', *Canadian Historical Review*, XLIX, 2, June 1968: 160-9.

——. 'Australia, Japan and Great Britain, a Study in Triangular Diplomacy', *Historical Studies*, 14, 1970: 250-9.

——. *William Morris Hughes: A Political Biography*, II: *The Little Digger 1914-1953*, Sydney, 1979.

Foster, L. *High Hopes: The Men and Motives of the Australian Round Table*, Melbourne, 1986.

French, M. ' "One People, One Destiny"—A Question of Loyalty: The Origins of Empire Day in New South Wales, 1900-1905', *Journal of the Royal Australian Historical Society*, December 1975: 236-48.

Fuller, J. G. *Troop Morale and Popular Culture in the British and Dominion Armies, 1914-1919*, Oxford, 1990.

Fyfe, H. *Northcliffe: an intimate biography*, London, 1930.

Gammage, W. 'Sir John Monash: A Military Review', *Historical Studies*, 16, 62, 1974: 112-18.

——. *The Broken Years: Australian Soldiers in the Great War*, Penguin edn, Ringwood, Vic., 1975.

——. 'Anzac', ch. 4 in Carroll, *Intruders*: 54-66.

——. 'The crucible: the establishment of the Anzac tradition, 1899-1918', ch. 6 in McKernan and Browne, *Two Centuries*.

Gerster, R. *Big Noting: the heroic theme in Australian war writing*, Melbourne, 1987.

Geyl, Pieter. *Napoleon For and Against*, London, 1964.

Gibb, D. M. 'Australian Nationalism and the Background to the Great War', *Journal of History*, September 1971: 16-24.

Gibbs, P. *The Battles of the Somme*, London, 1917.

——. *Realities of War*, London, 1920.

Gilbert, A. 'The Conscription Referenda, 1916-17: The Impact of the Irish Crisis', *Historical Studies*, 14, 1969-71: 54-72.

——. 'Protestants, Catholics and loyalty: an aspect of the conscription controversies, 1916-17', *Politics*, VI, May 1971: 15-25.

Gilchrist, M. *Daniel Mannix: Priest and Patriot*, Blackburn, Vic., 1982.

Giles, J. *Flanders, then and now: the Ypres Salient and Passchendaele*, London, 1987.

Gill, D., and Dallas, G. *The Unknown Army*, London, 1985.

Gordon, D. *The Dominion Partnership in Imperial Defence, 1870-1914*, Maryland, 1965.

Gough, Tony. 'The First Australian Imperial Force: C. E. W. Bean's Coloured Authenticity', *World Review*, 16, 3, 1977: 40-9.

Graham, D. 'Sans Doctrine: British Army Tactics in the First World War', in Travers and Archer, *Men at War*: 69-92.

Greenlee, J. 'Imperial Studies and the Unity of the Empire', *Journal of Imperial and Commonwealth History*, VII, 1979: 321-35.

——. *Education and Imperial Unity, 1901-1926*, New York, 1987.

Grey, J. *A Military History of Australia*, Melbourne, 1990.

——. 'White', *Australian Dictionary of Biography*, 12, Melbourne, 1990: 460-3.

——. *Australian Brass: The Career of Lieutenant-General Sir Horace Robertson*, Melbourne, 1992.

Grieves, K. 'Early Historical Responses to the Great War: Fortesque, Conan Doyle, and Buchan', in Bond, *British Military History*: 15-39.

Grimshaw, C. 'Australian Nationalism and the Imperial Connection, 1900-1914', *Australian Journal of Politics and History*, 3, 1, 1957: 161-82.

Guinn, P. *British Strategy and Politics, 1914-1918*, Oxford, 1965.

Hall, H. *Australia and England: A Study in Imperial Relations*, London, 1934.

Hancock, I. R. 'The 1911 Imperial Conference', *Historical Studies*, October 1966: 356-72.

Harvie, C. *War and Society in the Nineteenth Century*, Open University, Bletchley, 1973.

Haste, C. *Keep the Home Fires Burning: Propaganda in the First World War*, London, 1977.

Hastings, A. P. 'Writing Military History in Australia', *Melbourne Historical Journal*, 13, 1981: 51-5.

Hayes, P. 'British Foreign Policy and the Influence of Empire, 1870-1920', *Journal of Imperial and Commonwealth History*, 12, 1984: 102-24.

Hazelhurst, C. *Politicians at War: July 1914-May 1915*, London, 1971.

Heydon, P. *Quiet Decision: A Study of George Foster Pearce*, Melbourne, 1965.

Hill, A. J. *Chauvel of the Light Horse*, Melbourne, 1978.

——. 'Birdwood', *Australian Dictionary of Biography*, 7, Melbourne, 1979: 293-6.

——. 'Elliott', *Australian Dictionary of Biography*, 8, Melbourne, 1983: 428–31.

——. 'Howse', *Australian Dictionary of Biography*, 9, Melbourne, 1986: 384–6.

HMSO. *Statistics of the Military Effort of the British Empire during the Great War, 1914–20*, London, 1922.

Hobson, J. A. *The Evolution of Modern Capitalism*, London, 1894.

——. *Imperialism: A Study*, London, 1902.

Horne, D. *The Search for Billy Hughes*, Melbourne, 1979.

Horner, D. (ed.). *The Commanders: Australian military leadership in the twentieth century*, Sydney, 1984.

Hudson, W. J. *Billy Hughes in Paris*, Melbourne, 1978.

——. *Casey*, Melbourne, 1986.

——. 'Strategy for survival', in McKernan and Browne, *Two Centuries*: 28–42.

Hudson, W. J., and Sharp, M. P. *Australian Independence: colony to reluctant kingdom*, Melbourne, 1988.

Hughes, W. M. *Policies and Potentates*, Sydney, 1950.

Hunt, A. D. and Thomas, R. P. *For God, King and Country: A study of the attitudes of the Methodist and Catholic Press in South Australia to the Great War 1914-l918*, South Australia, 1979.

Inglis, K. 'The Anzac Tradition', *Meanjin Quarterly*, 24, 1, 1965: 25–44.

——. 'Conscription in Peace and War, 1911–1945', *Teaching History*, October 1967: 5–41.

——. *C. E. W. Bean, Australian Historian*, St Lucia, Qld, 1970.

——. 'C. E. W. Bean' in *Australian Dictionary of Biography*, 7, Melbourne, 1979: 226–9.

——. 'The Imperial Connection: Telegraphic communication Between England and Australia, 1872-1902', in Madden and Morris-Jones, *Australia and Britain*.

——. 'The Rehearsal': *Australians at War in the Sudan, 1885*, Sydney, 1985.

——. 'Remembering Australians on the Somme, Anzac Day 1989', *Overland*, 115, August 1989: 20–8.

——. 'Anzac and the Australian Military Tradition', *Revue Internationale d'Histoire Militaire*, Canberra, 1990: 1–25.

James, R. R. *Gallipoli*, London, 1989.

Jauncey, L. C. *The Story of Conscription in Australia*, Melbourne, 1968 (orig. London, 1935).

Jeffery, K. *The British army and the crisis of empire, 1918–1922*, Manchester, 1984.

——. (ed.). *The military correspondence of Field Marshal Sir Henry Wilson, 1918–1922*, London, 1985.

Jennings, M. *Australia in the Great War*, Melbourne, 1969.

Joynt, W. *Saving the Channel Ports*, Melbourne, 1975.

Keith, A. B. *War Governments of the British Dominions*, London, 1921.

——. *Responsible Government in the Dominions*, I, Oxford, 1928.

——. *The Dominions as Sovereign States*, London, 1938.

——. *Selected Speeches and Documents on British Colonial Policy, 1763–1917*, London, 1953.

Kempe, J. 'Anzac: the substitute religion', *Nation*, 42, 23 April 1960.

Kendle, J. E. *The Colonial and Imperial Conferences, 1887–1914: A study in imperial organisation*, London, 1967.

Kent, D. A. 'The *Anzac Book* and the Anzac Legend: C. E. W. Bean as editor and image-maker', *Historical Studies*, 21, 84, 1985: 376–90.

——. 'The *Anzac Book*: A reply to Denis Winter', *Journal of the Australian War Memorial*, 17, October 1990: 54–5.

Knightley, P. 'Murdoch's Bloody Lies', *Sydney Morning Herald*, 14 April 1990: 36.

Koss, S. E. 'The Destruction of Britain's Last Liberal Government', *Journal of Modern History*, 40, 1968: 257–77.

Laffin, J. *Digger: the Legend of the Australian Soldier*, London, 1959.

——. *Damn the Dardanelles*, Sydney, 1980.

——. *World War I in Postcards*, Melbourne, 1990.

Lake, M. *A Divided Society: Tasmania during World War I*, Melbourne, 1975.

Lawrence, J. *Mutiny in the British and Commonwealth Forces, 1797–1956*, London, 1987.

Lewis, B. *Our War: Australia During World War I*, Melbourne, 1980.

Liddle, P. *Men of Gallipoli*, London, 1976.

Lloyd George, D. *War Memoirs of David Lloyd George*, 2 vols, London, 1933-6.

Lockwood, P. 'Lord Milner's entry into the War Cabinet, December 1916', *Historical Journal*, VII, I, 1964, 120-34.

Longmore, C. *'Eggs-A-Cook': The Story of the 44th*, Perth, 1921.

Lucas, C. (ed.). *The Empire at War*, I-III: *Australia; New Zealand; The Pacific Islands*, London, 1924-6.

MacKenzie, J. M. *Propaganda and Empire: The Manipulation of British Public Opinion, 1880-1960*, Manchester, 1984.

Mackintosh, J. P. 'The Role of the Committee of Imperial Defence Before 1914', *English Historical Review*, LXXVII, 1962: 490-503.

Madden, A. F. and Morris-Jones, W. H. (eds). *Australia and Britain: Studies in a Changing Relationship*, Sydney, 1980.

Mahan, A. T. *The Influence of Sea Power Upon History, 1660-1783*, London, 1890.

Maier, C. S. *The Unmasterable Past: History, Holocaust and German National Identity*, Cambridge, Mass., 1988.

Marder, A. J. *From the Dreadnought to Scapa Flow: the Royal Navy in the Fisher Era, 1904-1914*, I: *The Road to War 1904-1914*, London, 1961.

Marwick, A. *The Deluge: British Society and the First World War*, London, 1965.

Marwick, A., et. al. *Europe on the Eve of War, 1900-1914*, Buckingham, 1990.

Masefield, J. *Gallipoli*, London, 1916.

McCarthy, D. *Gallipoli to the Somme: The Story of C. E. W. Bean*, Sydney, 1983.

McEwen, J. M. 'The Press and the Fall of Asquith', *Historical Journal*, 21, 4, 1978: 863-83.

——. 'The National Press during the First World War: Ownership and Circulation', *Journal of Contemporary History*, 17, 3, 1982, 459-86.

McGibbon, I. C. *The Path to Gallipoli: Defending New Zealand, 1840-1915*, Wellington, 1991.

McGill, B. 'Asquith's Predicament, 1914-1918', *Journal of Modern History*, 39, September 1967, 283-303.

McInnes, G. *The Road to Gundagai*, London, 1965.

McKernan, M. *The Australian People in the Great War*, Melbourne, 1980.

McKernan, M., and Browne, M. (eds). *Australia: Two Centuries of War and Peace*, Sydney, 1988.

McInnes, C., and Sheffield, G. *Warfare in the Twentieth Century: Theory and Practice*, London, 1988.

McMinn, W. G. *George Reid: A Biography*, Melbourne, 1989.

McMullin, R. *Will Dyson: Cartoonist, etcher, and Australia's first war artist*, Sydney, 1984.

McNicol, W. G. *The Thirty-Seventh*, Melbourne, 1936.

Meaney, N. ' "A Proposition of the Highest International Importance"; Alfred Deakin's Pacific Agreement Proposal and its Significance for Australian-Imperial Relations', *Journal of Commonwealth Political Studies*, V, 1967: 200-14.

——. *A History of Australian Defence and Foreign Policy, 1901-1923*, 1: *The Search for Security in the Pacific, 1901-14*, Sydney, 1976.

Meaney, N. (ed.). *Under New Heavens*, Sydney, 1990.

Mearsheimer, J. J. *Liddell Hart and the Weight of History*, London, 1988.

Monash, Sir J. *Australian Victories in France*, London, 1920.

Montgomery-Massingberd, A. *The Story of Fourth Army in the Battles of the Hundred Days, August 8th to November 11th, 1918*, London, 1920.

Moore, W. *See How They Ran*, London, 1970.

Moorehead, A. *Gallipoli*, London, 1956.

Mordike, J. 'The Story of Anzac: A new approach', *Journal of the Australian War Memorial*, 16, April 1990: 5-17.

Morice, J. *Six Bob a Day Tourist*, Victoria, 1985.

Morris, J. *Farewell the Trumpets: An Imperial Retreat*, London, 1978.

Morton, D. ' "Junior but Sovereign Allies": The Transformation of the Canadian Expeditionary Force, 1914-1918', *Journal of Imperial and Commonwealth History*, October 1979: 56-67.

——. *Canada and War: A Military and Political History*, Toronto, 1981.

——. 'Exerting Control: The Development of Canadian Authority over the Canadian Expeditionary Force, 1914-1919', in Travers and Archer, *Men at War*: 7-19.

——. *A Military History of Canada*, Edmonton, 1985.

——. 'The Canadian Military Experience in the First World War, 1914-18', in Adams, *The Great War*: 79-98.

Moses, J. 'The Great War as Ideological Conflict: An Australian Perspective', *War and Society*, September 1989: 56-73.

——. 'Australia's Academic Garrison, 1914-1918', *Australian Journal of Politics and History* 36, 3, 1990: 361-76.

——. 'The "Ideas of 1914" in Germany and Australia: A Case of Conflicting Perceptions', *War and Society*, October 1991: 61-82.

——. *Prussian-German Militarism, 1914-18, in Australian Perspective: The Thought of George Arnold Wood*, Berne, 1991.

Murphy, D. J. 'Fisher', *Australian Dictionary of Biography*, 8, Melbourne, 1981: 502-7.

Nicholls, B. *Bluejackets and Boxers: Australia's Naval Expedition to the Boxer Uprising*, Sydney, 1986.

Nicholson, W. N. *Behind the Lines: An Account of Administrative Staffwork in the British Army, 1914-18*, Stevenage, 1989.

Nile, R. 'Peace, Unreliable Memory and the Necessities of Anzac Mythology', in Seymour and Nile, *Anzac*.

Nish, I. H. 'Australia and the Anglo-Japanese Alliance', *Australian Journal of Politics and History*, IX, November 1963: 200-12.

——. *Alliance in Decline: A Study in Anglo-Japanese Relations, 1908-23*, London, 1972.

North, J. *Gallipoli, the Fading Vision*, London, 1966.

Osmond, W. G. *Frederic Eggleston: An Intellectual in Australian Politics*, Sydney, 1985.

Parker, P. *The Old Lie: The Great War and the Public School Ethos*, London, 1987.

Parsons, M. C. 'Was Australia's contribution to World War I in her national interests?', *RMC Historical Journal*, 2, 1973: 37-41.

Pedersen, P. A. *Monash as Military Commander*, Melbourne, 1985.

——. 'The AIF on the western front: the role of training and command', in McKernan and Browne, *Two Centuries*: 167-93.

Penny, B. 'Australia's Reaction to the Boer War: A Study in Colonial Imperialism', *Journal of British Studies*, 7, 1, 1967: 97-130.

——. 'The Australian Debate on the Boer War', *Historical Studies*, 14, October 1969-April 1971: 526-45.

Perry, F. W. *The Commonwealth Armies: Manpower and Organisation in Two World Wars*, Manchester, 1988.

Pfeiffer, R. 'Exercises in Loyalty and Trouble-making: Anglo-New Zealand Friction at the Time of the Great War, 1914-1919', *Australian Journal of Politics and History*, 38, 2, 1992: 178-92.

Phillip, J., *et. al. The Great Adventure: New Zealand Soldiers Describe the First World War*, Wellington, 1988.

Pilger, A. 'The other "Lost Generation": rejected Australian volunteers, 1914-18', *Journal of the Australian War Memorial*, 21, 1992: 11-19.

Pound, R., and Harmsworth, G. *Northcliffe*, London, 1959.

Prefect, C. *Hornchurch During the Great War*, Colchester, 1920.

Preston, R. (ed.). *Contemporary Australia: Studies in History, Politics and Economics*, Duke, 1967.

Prior, R. 'The Suvla Bay tea-party: a re-assessment', *Journal of the Australian War Memorial*, 7, October 1985: 25-33.

Prior, R., and Wilson, T. 'What Manner of Victory? Reflections on the Termination of the First World War', *Revue Internationale d'Histoire Militaire*, 72, Canberra, 1990: 80-96.

——. *Command on the Western Front: The Military Career of Sir Henry Rawlinson, 1914-18*, Oxford, 1992.

Pugsley, C. *Gallipoli: The New Zealand Story*, Auckland, 1984.

——. *On the Fringe of Hell: New Zealanders and Military Discipline in the First World War*, Auckland, 1991.

Quinault, R. 'Churchill and Australia: the Military Relationship, 1899-1945', *War and Society*, 6, 1, 1988: 41-64.

Reader, W. J. *At Duty's Call: A Study in Obsolete Patriotism*, Manchester, 1988.

Reeves, N. *Official British Film Propaganda During the First World War*, London, 1986.

Richards, F. *Old Soldiers Never Die*, London, 1964.

Riddell, G. A. *Lord Riddell's War Diary, 1914-1918*, London, 1933.

Robertson, J. *Anzac and Empire: The Tragedy and Glory of Gallipoli*, Melbourne, 1990.

Robson, L. L. *The First A.I.F.: A Study of its Recruitment, 1914-1918*, Melbourne, 1970.

——. 'The origin and character of the first A.I.F., 1914-18', *Historical Studies of Australia and New Zealand*, 15, 1973: 737-49.

——. (ed.). *Australian Commentaries: Select Articles from 'The Round Table'*, Melbourne, 1975.

——. 'Images of the Warrior: Australian-British perceptions in the Great War', *Journal of the Australian War Memorial*, 1, October 1982: 1-7.

Roskill, S. *Hankey Man of Secrets*, I, London, 1970.

Ross, J. *The Myth of the Digger*, Sydney, 1985.

Rule, J. *Jacka's Mob*, Sydney, 1933.

Santamaria, B. A. *Daniel Mannix: The Quality of Leadership*, Melbourne, 1984.

Scott, E. *The Official History of Australia in the War*, XI: *Australia During the War*, Sydney, 1936.

Semmel, B. *Imperialism and Social Reform: English Social-Imperial Thought, 1895-1914*, London, 1960.

Serle, G. 'Australia and Britain', in Preston, *Contemporary Australia*.

——. *John Monash*, Melbourne, 1982.

——. 'Sir John Monash' in *Australian Dictionary of Biography*, 10, Melbourne, 1986: 543-9.

——. 'Murdoch', ibid.: 622-6.

Seymour, A., and Nile, R. (eds). *Anzac: Meaning, Memory and Myth*, London, 1991.

Sheffield, G. D. 'The Effect of the Great War on Class Relations in Britain: The Career of Major Christopher Stone DSO MC', *War and Society*, 7, 1, May 1989: 87-105.

Shields, R. A. 'Australian Opinion and Defence of the Empire: A Study in Imperial Relations, 1880-1890', *Australian Journal of Politics and History*, X, 1964: 41-53.

Simon, B., and Bradley, I. (eds). *The Victorian Public School: Studies in the Development of an Educational Institution*, London, 1973.

Sinclair, K. *A Destiny Apart: New Zealand's Search for National Identity*, Wellington, 1986.

Sladen, D. *From Boundary Rider to Prime Minister: Hughes of Australia*, London, 1916.

——. *My Long Life: Anecdotes and Adventures*, London, 1939.

Souter, G. *Lion and Kangaroo*, Sydney, 1976.

——. *Company of Heralds*, Melbourne, 1981.

Sorel, G. *Reflections on Violence*, London, 1915.

Spartalis, P. J. *The Diplomatic Battles of Billy Hughes*, Sydney, 1983.

Spears, E. *Prelude to Victory*, London, 1939.

Springhall, J. O. 'Lord Meath, Youth and Empire', *Journal of Contemporary History*, 5, 4, 1970: 97-111.

Stephens, G. 'Three Schools and the Great War', *Tasmanian Historical Research Association*, September 1976: 77-85.

Stubbs, J. O. 'Lord Milner and Patriotic Labour', *English Historical Review*, 87, October 1972: 717-54.

Summers, A. 'Militarism in Britain before the Great War', *History Workshop*, 2, 1976: 104-23.

Taylor, A. J. P. *English History, 1914-1945*, Oxford, 1965.

——. *Beaverbrook*, London, 1972.

Taylor, M. ' "You Smug-Faced Crowds": Poetry and the Home Front in the First World War', *Imperial War Museum Review*, 3, 1988: 87-96.

Terraine, J. *Douglas Haig, the Educated Soldier*, London, 1963.

——. (ed.). *General Jack's Diary*, London, 1964.

——. *To Win a War: 1918, The Year of Victory*, London, 1978.

——. *White Heat: The New Warfare 1914-1918*, London, 1982.

——. *The First World War*, London, 1983.

Thomson, A. 'Steadfast until death?: C. E. W. Bean and the representation of Australian military manhood', *Australian Historical Studies*, 23, 93, 1989: 462-78.

——. 'A past you can live with: digger memories and the Anzac legend', *Journal of the Australian War Memorial*, 20, April 1992: 5-10.

——. 'History and "Betrayal": The Anzac Controversy', *History Today*, 43, Jan. 1993: 8-11.

Thornton, R. 'Invaluable Ally or Imminent Aggressor? Australia and Japanese Naval Assistance, 1914-18', *Journal of Australian Studies*, 12, 1983: 5-21.

Travers, T. H. E. *The Killing Ground*, London 1987.

——. *How the War Was Won: Command and Technology in the British Army on the Western Front, 1917-1918*, London and New York, 1992.

——. 'Could the Tanks of 1918 Have Been War-Winners for the British Expeditionary Force?', *Journal of Contemporary History*, 27, 1992: 389-406.

Travers, T., and Archer, C. (eds). *Men at War: Politics, Technology and Innovation in the Twentieth Century*, Chicago, 1982.

Tsokhas, K. *W. M. Hughes, the Imperial Wool Purchase and the Pastoral Lobby 1914-1920*, Working Papers in Economic History No.106, Canberra, 1988.

——. *Markets, Money and Empire*, Melbourne, 1990.

——. '"A Pound of Flesh": War Debts and Anglo-Australian Relations, 1919-1932', *Australian Journal of Politics and History*, 38, 1, 1992: 12-26.

Tunstall, M. A. 'Imperial Defence, 1897-1914', in *The Cambridge History of the British Empire*, III: *The Empire-Commonwealth, 1870-1919*, Cambridge, 1967.

Tyquin, M. B. 'Medical Evacuation During the Gallipoli Campaign—an Australian Perspective', *War and Society*, October 1992: 57-72.

Walker, M. *Powers of the Press: Twelve of the World's Influential Newspapers*, London, 1927.

Walker, R. B. *The Newspaper Press in NSW, 1803-1920*, Sydney, 1976.

Welborn, S. *Lords of Death: a people, a place, a legend*, Perth, 1982.

Welfield, J. B. 'The Labour Party and the War, 1914-1915', *Armidale and District Historical Society Journal*, 9, November 1966: 30-43.

Wheare, M. A. 'The Empire and the Peace Treaties, 1918-21', *The Cambridge History of the British Empire*, III: *The Empire-Commonwealth, 1870-1919*, Cambridge, 1967: 650-2.

White, R. 'Motives for Joining up: Self Sacrifice, Self Interest and Social Class, 1914-1918', *Journal of the Australian War Memorial*, 9, 1986: 3-15.

——. 'Bluebells and Fogtown: Australians' First Impression of England, 1860-1940', *Australian Cultural History*, 5, 1986: 46-50.

——. 'The Soldier as Tourist: The Australian Experience of the Great War', *War and Society*, 5, 1, 1987: 63-77.

——. 'Europe and the Six-Bob-a-Day Tourist: The Great War as a Grand Tour, or Getting Civilised', *Australian Studies*, 5, April 1991: 122-39.

Williamson, S. R. *The Politics of Grand Strategy: Britain and France Prepare for War, 1904-1914* (paperback edn), London, 1990.

Wilson, T. *The Myriad Faces of War*, Cambridge, 1986.

——. 'The Significance of the First World War in Modern History', in Adams, *The Great War*: 7-27.

Winter, D. 'The Anzac landing—the great gamble?', *Journal of the Australian War Memorial*, 4, April 1984: 13-21.

——. '*The Anzac Book*: A re-appraisal', *Journal of the Australian War Memorial*, 16, April 1990: 58-61.

——. *Making the Legend: The War Writings of C. E. W. Bean*, St Lucia, 1992.

Woodward, Sir L. *Great Britain and the War of 1914-1918*, London, 1967.

# Index